Mistresses

Mistresses

True Stories of Seduction, Power and Ambition

LEIGH EDUARDO

Michael O'Mara Books Ltd

First published in 2005 by
Michael O'Mara Books Limited
9 Lion Yard
Tremadoc Road
London SW4 7NQ

A CIP catalogue record for this book is available from the British Library.

ISBN 1-84317-141-4

1 3 5 7 9 10 8 6 4 2

Designed and typeset by E-Type

Cover and plate section by Button Design

Printed and bound in England by Clays Ltd, St Ives plc

www.mombooks.com

Contents

This book is for
John Carmichael and Peter Eversden

'Think where man's glory most begins and ends,
And say my glory was I had such friends.'

W. B. Yeats

Acknowledgements

I am deeply grateful to many generous people, without whose help, suggestions and guidance this book might never have been completed.

In particular I thank Mme Barbara Casassus, for assistance with research and generous hospitality in Paris; Peter Eversden for the thousands of miles' driving to appropriate sites, museums, records offices and libraries in England, Europe and Australia; John Carmichael for constructive criticism, helpful translation, and many useful suggestions on the text. A massive debt of gratitude to the wonderful, unselfish staff of the British Library and their colleagues at Colindale Newspaper Library; Frau Ingrid Baederstadt of the German Embassy in Munich for unstinted hospitality and help in researching Lola Montez, Ludwig I, Ludwig II and Eva Braun; Peter Thornton for hospitality in Burgundy whilst researching at Besançon; Peter Roulands for encouraging support and a constant supply of research material; Ms Hazel Colinson, whose single discussion with me about the mistress situation in Hollywood was inspirational; the staff at the Charterhouse at Valldemossa, Mallorca for help with George Sand. In Australia, I was particularly grateful to the staff of the Mechanics' Institute Library, Ballarat, Victoria for information on Lola Montez; Ms Jan Croggin for use of archival material concerning Lola Montez at the gold-mining settlement at Sovereign City, Ballarat; the archives staffs of the State Libraries at Sydney and Melbourne; and many thanks to John Polla Mounter and Peter Norris for extended hospitality during this research. Heartfelt thanks, too, to Gerald Polley who devoted much time and effort in travelling to San Francisco to research the Hearst/Davies archives and contemporary newspaper files.

I am deeply grateful to my agent, Kate Hordern, whose faith in the book never once wavered. Finally, a special thanks to Michael O'Mara Books, in particular to editors Lindsay Davies and Kate Gribble, whose many suggestions, discussions, and (occasional) insistence did much to hone and present the manuscript.

I am most grateful to the following publishers for granting permission to quote from the named books:

Curtis Brown: *Love Letters, An Anthology*, chosen by Antonia Fraser. (Acknowledgement by Curtis Brown on behalf of Antonia Fraser.) © Antonia Fraser, 1976.
Secker and Warburg: *My Apprenticeships*, by Colette. Translation by Helen Beauclerk, ©1967.
Librairie Plon: *Mes Cahiers Bleus (My Blue Notebooks)*, by Liane de Pougy. Translation by Diana Athill, ©1979.
Thames and Hudson: *Cartier*, by Hans Nadelhoffer, ©1984.
Cassell: *Private Lives: Curious Facts about the Famous and Infamous*, by Mark Bryant, ©1996.

Every effort has been made to honour ownership and copyright. In some cases and after reasonable effort, the author has been unable to trace a publisher, or a source of copyright. For this he tenders sincere apologies to those concerned. Michael O'Mara Books will be pleased to rectify any omission in future editions of the work, if contacted.

Leigh Eduardo
London, 2005

Picture Acknowledgements

The Art Archive: 3, Château de Maintenon, France / Dagli Orti; 4 (top), Bibliothèque des Arts Décoratifs, Paris / Dagli Orti; 7, Musée Carnavalet, Paris / JFB; 8 (top left), Musée Carnavalet, Paris / Dagli Orti.

The Bridgeman Art Library (www.bridgeman.co.uk): 5 (below right), portrait of Sir William Hamilton (1730-1803) after a portrait by Charles Grignion, *c.* 1802 (enamel on copper), Craft, William Hopkins (fl. 1774-1805) / Ashmolean Museum, University of Oxford, UK; 15, poster advertising 'La Belle Otero' at the Folies-Bergères, 1894 (colour litho), Bataille, G. (nineteenth century) / Private Collection.

Corbis: 2 (top) © Corbis; 8 (top right) © Leonard de Selva / Corbis; 12 (top), 14 (below right) © Bettman / Corbis; 13 (below) © John Springer Collection / Corbis.

Getty Images: 10 (top), 11, 14 (below left), 9, 14 (top), Time Life Pictures / Getty Images.

Mary Evans Picture Library: 5 (top & below left), 6, 8 (below), 16 (right).

© **popperfoto.com**: 10 (below), 13 (top).

TopFoto.co.uk: 1, 2 (below left & right), 12 (below), 16 (left), 4 (below), TopFoto / Charles Walker.

Introduction

'Given my time again, I would never marry;
being a mistress is much more fun.'

English wife of a Hollywood director, 1996

The dictionary describes a mistress variously as 'a kept woman; a female favourite; a paramour; a woman (other than his wife) with whom a married man has a (usually prolonged) sexual relationship; a woman who has a continuing extramarital relationship with a man.' While all these qualifications aptly describe a mistress, the same terms were equally applicable to a courtesan, with a few marked variations.

The principal difference between a courtesan and a mistress was one of monetary gain. Many women of the upper echelons became mistresses for almost any reason other than financial benefit. Often they were married, socially well-placed and with a certain degree of independence. Once started, tact and discretion were essential to the smooth running of the affair, especially in retaining a domestic status quo. And no one would deny that intrigue added glamour – and the thrill of danger – to the liaison. These were women with little on their minds other than their own sexual pleasure and fulfilment, and their appeal to the opposite sex.

But there were other motivations. Many women were genuinely love-starved and lonely. Some sought an emotional outlet as a result of an 'arranged', often loveless marriage. Some, married to much older men, longed for the excitement of a young and virile lover; others took lovers in revenge against a philandering spouse. Then there were those who welcomed the marital state for the smokescreen it provided in disguising deception. These ladies would be open to occasional gifts and other discreet signs of respect or desire. They avoided the degrading status of prostitution simply by not accepting (or needing) hard cash.

There was (and is) the kind of mistress who was 'set up' with an establishment – a house or apartment – and was allotted a steady

I

allowance; her relationship in many respects was akin to that of a wife, but without the legal bond. The ties involved varying degrees of mutual attraction, respect, love and companionship. This mistress enjoyed her personal independence; although an infrequent occurrence, she was capable of leaving her lover at a moment's notice, regardless of security and income – especially when the desertion involved another, more affluent protector. Similarly, the lover could (and often did) desert both mistress and wife for another, usually younger, mistress; the man's way of holding on to his own youth. Despite the legal responsibilities involving wife and children, history shows that desertion has always been more a male prerogative.

While a courtesan was often (and correctly) referred to as a mistress, very few mistresses were courtesans. A mistress might find her lover in any strata of society; a courtesan's lovers were always from the upper classes – or, at the very least, they were rich, powerful and influential.

Until 1914, the courtesan's world was one of wealth, acquisition and privilege. Without these three factors she could not have existed. A courtesan accepted money and stipend and truly fabulous gifts as a right; in one sense she was bought – paid for her services – but those services were light years beyond those of the prostitute who sold only sex, and that indiscriminately.

The essential prerequisites of a leading courtesan included elegance, a sense of *soignée*, humour, a ready wit, intelligence, education, sophisticated companionship and sex – although in some cases sex, surprisingly, was not the most important factor in the package she offered. Some courtesans (but more mistresses) had a paucity of these qualities but still managed to survive all competition. Eva Braun, Adolf Hitler's mistress (never a courtesan), is a case in point.

A courtesan may not always respond to the highest bidder. Some, powerful in their own right, were enough in demand to be able to pick and choose. One need look no further than seventeenth-century Anne 'Ninon' de Lenclos, whose amatory career was indeed busy (she was still much sought after in her seventies). In her fortieth year Ninon opened a 'School of Gallantry' with the full approval and backing of many aristocratic mothers, who wanted their sons to know the ropes when it came to love, scheming mistresses and intrigues. Closer to our own times, La Belle Otero would enjoy a similar popularity, with a clientele that was worldwide.

Mistresses shunned promiscuity; on the other hand, it was understood that a courtesan's ongoing relationship with a protector did not preclude other lovers; not unless an agreement was reached. The courtesan was, after all, in business; the mistress was not.

The liaisons of a mistress, then, had little or nothing to do with sexually-earned income; their relationships were usually monogamous and independent of any financial consideration. This is particularly the case today in a world where many women earn as much as, or more than, their partners.

By removing the monetary consideration that divides courtesan from mistress, the two become loosely synonymous. For convenience, I have classed all eight ladies who appear in this book as mistresses. The period covered spans the three hundred and twenty-four years between 1641 and 1965.

Five of the mistresses under observation were involved at some time with royalty; three of the five had more than one royal lover.

Barbara Villiers was ruthlessly ambitious, sexually rapacious and blatantly deceitful. Her beauty was dazzling; even her enemies (and they were plenteous) could not deny this. The combination proved irresistible to Charles II; for years he was as putty in Barbara's hands. She was the monarch's favourite of his many mistresses, and only relinquished her power after twelve years' supremacy. During this time, she established a vast fortune and gained, via the royal bed, a clutch of titles which included Countess of Castlemaine and Duchess of Cleveland. A royal protector in no way curtailed Barbara Villiers from taking other lovers. Her turnover was awesome and varied, from a king to a rope-dancer, from an archbishop to a highwayman, taking in along the way the King's illegitimate son by a previous mistress, her coach-runner (whose brawny thighs were irresistible!) and even the mummified body of a three-hundred-year-old ecclesiastic.

She matched in beauty, ambition and acquisitiveness, but never in style, the magnificent **Athénaïs, Marquise de Montespan**, whose domination of the alarmingly promiscuous French king, Louis XIV, lasted for twelve years (with a little help from the Devil, and a few dabblings in the black arts). The marquise was at the core of what became known as the Affair of the Poisons, one of the most sensational police investigations in French history. During one period both the marquise and the Duchess of Cleveland resided simultaneously at the royal palace at Versailles. Understandably, their relations were guarded, never exceeding the bounds of polite acquaintanceship, each being wary of the other's notoriety.

Lady Emma Hamilton's early life in England was very lively; indeed, when she met the Honourable Charles Greville she was no stranger to the casual pick-up, or chance encounter; for a short time, she resided in Mother Kelly's friendly little brothel. But from her first encounter with the aforementioned Charles, it is curious and somehow touching to observe how, once she had embarked on a serious liaison, she was unswervingly faithful despite numerous opportunities to be otherwise. Her flaunted grand passion for Horatio, Lord Nelson, was a shocking, scandalous, selfish, sometimes pathetic affair; at the same time, it has proved one of history's most enduring, passionate love affairs.

Lola Montez is one of the brightest, most audacious jewels in this collection. This irresistible Irish adventuress slept her way around Europe, creating enough colourful havoc for the authorities to ban her in several countries. What she couldn't achieve with her looks she achieved with her constant companion: her whip. Known in America as the 'Mid-Victorian Bad Girl', Lola caressed a vast fortune out of King Ludwig I of Bavaria, and brought his realm to near bankruptcy and the brink of civil war before she made her escape to create mischief anew elsewhere. Her stormy showpieces on stage, coupled with her equally tempestuous liaisons, ensured that Lola was always excellent copy for the press.

Lola managed to inveigle an entrée into the august salon of the French pioneer feminist-writer, **George Sand**. Where sexual rapacity was concerned, the detractors of the nineteenth century's most famous female writer considered her, in a word, destructive. Commenting on George Sand's sexual voracity, a French writer I met recently said: 'She had her hands in just about every man's trousers!' Possibly; but reading her voluminous autobiography and equally enormous correspondence, she seems never to have had them in the right trousers at the right time. Variously named 'nympho', 'vampire', 'slut' and 'mother', George Sand was a mistress in the true sense; she was never a courtesan. A powerful intellectual force in the salon, in the privacy of her bedroom she was known to have preferred the rough hands of a carter, or the sweaty promise of a farm labourer – which makes her affairs with the composer Frederick Chopin and the poet Alfred de Musset, and other *saloniers*, something of an enigma.

The Musset and Chopin liaisons are two of the most controversial love stories of the nineteenth century – not because they were rampantly sexual, and certainly not because they were idyllic. Far from it; they were, in many ways, disastrous. This was especially the case during George's nightmarish Venetian affair with Musset, the complications of which led Sand into a clumsy *faux ménage* involving her poet-lover and a handsome Italian doctor. As a mistress, she was her own worst enemy: she longed desperately to be a seductive enigma, but inevitably ended up as a *femme provinçale*. The philanderer Prosper Mérimée was scathing about her boudoir prowess. Poor Musset, bordering on schizophrenia at the best of times, would later admit his feeling of increasing incestuousness during their affair, describing George simultaneously as his 'mistress' and his 'mother'. Chopin described her frustrated appetites as 'a real disease … to be understood and forgiven.'

Caroline Otero – better known as **La Belle Otero** – was the last of the great courtesans/mistresses. If prizes were given for notching up royal sexual encounters, La Belle Otero would win hands down. Over thirty years, she was the mistress of many of the crowned heads of Europe, the Middle East and Russia. In between (and not infrequently, concurrently) she made time for many of the lesser, but wealthier, luminaries, such as William Kissam Vanderbilt and any number of multimillionaires. Her price was high; she obviously delivered the goods, for many of her lovers paid court over years. And, as if her amatory life wasn't busy enough, she found time for a fast-moving, very successful, international career as a Spanish dancer. She was the principal attraction for a decade at the world-famous Folies-Bergère in Paris.

Although no one realized it at the time, the First World War became the funeral cortège of the opulent, secure world which many privileged late Victorians and Edwardians had enjoyed. By 1918, it was starkly apparent that the previous four years had left devastation, not only of countries and governments, but also of an era. It presaged the twilight years of the great courtesan.

At the commencement of hostilities between Germany and Great Britain in 1914, Otero had already entered into the autumn of her boudoir career. By 1918, when the flags of freedom were once again unfurled, she had all but retired from the active bedroom scene – an amatory living ghost who did not belong in the harsh, brave new world now being boisterously ushered in to the triumphant fanfare of negro jazz trumpets and large-scale organized crime. La Belle Otero tried to adapt but she eventually retreated to the safety of grand reminiscence. When she died, aged ninety-seven, she had outlived all her lovers and contemporaries and had gambled away all of the $25 million she had earned on the world's stages – and in many of the world's most lucrative beds.

Eva Braun's story is a far cry from the flamboyant careers of La Belle Otero. The passion for life that made the extrovert Otero so much in demand was entirely lacking in Eva's personality. Apart from her own enigmatic role in the Nazi pantheon, what makes Eva's story so fascinating are the people who crossed her life and times. Whatever Eva Braun lacked in dazzle, intellect or personality, in the end she was the only one of Hitler's mistresses who survived his murderous eccentricities, until the bizarre bunker suicide-pact with her husband of one day. Researching her, there were many times when I felt a certain pity; sometimes, she seemed not to exist – a woman confined to the shadows, overwhelmed by Hitler's 'Court' and by the escalating ghastly events she preferred to ignore which would lead to the downfall of Nazi Germany.

The **Marion Davies**/William Randolph Hearst liaison lasted a contented thirty-two years. The little dancer from Brooklyn who enthralled the most powerful publishing magnate of his time was arguably the wealthiest mistress in history. To Marion's credit, much of her wealth was the result of her own enterprise and acute business sense. Hearst spent millions of dollars in his ambition to make his mistress the most famous dramatic actress in Hollywood. He failed, not because his protégée lacked talent, but because he didn't recognize the area, or the scope of that talent. It is no exaggeration to say that Marion Davies was loved by everybody. Her generosity – she gave away millions – became legendary. She donated enormous sums towards improving public health; at the same time, she helped many private individuals who were in need. Under Hearst's protection, she gained an enviable fame as Hollywood's most lavish party-thrower; indeed, the Davies/Hearst parties were unquestionably the most lavish in the history of Hollywood. A short and snappy cocktail party could set her back $30,000; an 'intimate' little dinner at her 110-roomed beach-house, or at Hearst's world-famous castle at San Simeon, might be for forty or fifty guests; while the Davies/Hearst guest list for costume-parties could run into hundreds. Everybody, from Winston Churchill to the acerbic gossip columnist Hedda Hopper, from Einstein to Cecil Beaton, from George Bernard Shaw to the studio prop man, loved Marion Davies.

When Orson Welles parodied the lovers and their lifestyle in *Citizen Kane*, he not only brought the wrath of the mighty Hearst press down on his head, he also made many enemies in the movie business. Much of Marion's film output may have been misguided and at times mediocre, but Hollywood adored Marion and respected Hearst; most of the film colony at some time had been recipients of their incredible generosity.

Through these eight ladies, a certain 'mistress pattern' emerges: the poor girl making good; the nonentity with fierce ambition; the women who used the stage as a means to better things (a common mistress practice across history); those who, in later life, found religion; and then there are those whose biggest enemy is also their only true, if invariably treacherous, lover: the gambling casino. Whether or not the individual condemns these fascinating beauties on moral grounds, one cannot deny that they have all enlivened the pages of our history books.

Barbara Villiers

Miss of State

'Great wits and great braves
Have always a punk to their mother.'

William Wycherley (c.1640–1716), Love in a Wood

Barbara, Lady Castlemaine, Duchess of Cleveland certainly was a punk [whore], but her five children by King Charles II were anything but brave or witty; indeed, they were known at Court as 'the blockheads'. The duchess spent her last years living at Walpole House in Chiswick, an embittered, despotic, avaricious, despairing creature whose sexual appetite had been gargantuan. Nothing remained of her former beauty which had established her as the monarch's favourite mistress. Contemporary historian John Oldmixon described her as the 'lewdest as well as the fairest of all the king's concubines', while the playwright William Wycherley eulogized: 'You have that perfection of beauty (without thinking it so) which others of your sex but think they have.'

Barbara loved life and responded fully to it, according to whim and impulse. Her remarkably good health and boundless energy undoubtedly contributed to her unalloyed enjoyment of her countless bedroom adventures. While her maternal instincts were decidedly shaky, in her own careless way she did all she could to safeguard the futures of her royal brood. Reviled, envied, admired, hated as she was, her turbulent reign as 'Miss of State' (as she was known) has ensured her fascination down the centuries.

★

Barbara Villiers was born in 1641, to one of the oldest and most illustrious families in England; she is an ancestor of the late Diana,

Princess of Wales. Her father, the staunch royalist Lord Grandison, had fought and died under the flag of Charles I during the futile Civil War of 1642-5. An unconcerned mother contributed to an upbringing which was far from strict resulting in Barbara, at fifteen, being already sexually precocious. The diarist Samuel Pepys wrote, on 21 October 1666, that Sir Harry Cholmly told him

> how young Harry Killigrew is banished from Court lately for saying that my Lady Castlemayne was a little lecherous girl when she was young, and used to rub her thing with her fingers or against the end of forms, and that she must be rubbed with something else.

Barbara responded in particular to the ever-roving eye of Lord Chesterfield, a twenty-three-year-old, self-confessed libertine, who had been a widower for three years. In 1656 he wooed the all too willing girl with missives like the following:

> Is it not a strange magic in love which gives so powerful a charm to the least of your cruel words, that they endanger to kill a man at a hundred miles distance?

However, since Chesterfield was not contemplating holy matrimony, Barbara married the royalist Roger Palmer in 1659. He was kind and faithful but – compared with the lusty Chesterfield – very dull. Despite knowing that the libidinous Earl was concurrently dallying with three other high-born ladies, Barbara had begged him to elope with her prior to her marriage – alas, in vain.

Villiers' first encounter with the future King Charles II of England materialized when Barbara accompanied her husband to Holland; Palmer was delivering a large present of much-needed money from the English Royalists to the imminent monarch.

The diarist John Evelyn describes Charles as 'a tall, dark man above two yard high', whose swarthy good looks made him popular with most women. Barbara, at nineteen, was immediately attracted to this athletic prince, who kept his body healthy and supple by swimming, hunting and playing a great deal of early-morning tennis. Although she surrendered to the admiring Charles almost overnight, she did not become his mistress until the monarch's triumphant return to his homeland on 29 May 1660 – by coincidence his thirtieth birthday. Thus began the tempestuous, twelve-year reign of one of the most infamous, rapacious royal mistresses of that or any age. The historian Osmund Airy, writing at the beginning of the twentieth century, describes how she

> established from that moment, an unquestioned despotism over the debauchee of southern blood for whom she was indeed a fitting mate; a despotism which suffered no weakening as every day she increasingly betrayed a coarseness of tongue, a vulgarity of hate, an insatiable rapacity and a promiscuity of vice …

Charles's initial fascination with Barbara was easy to understand. The girl was simply ravishing. 'I never tire of painting her,' Sir Peter Lely enthused, 'she is wondrously beautiful.' Samuel Pepys raved, 'I glutted myself with looking on her.' Four years later, the fascination was still there, when Pepys bought not one but three prints of Lady Castlemaine's head sketched by Lely. Her flaming red hair and vivid blue eyes were only two of her assets.

Apart from matching Charles's insatiable libido, Barbara was enormous fun, with a zest for life that defied all authority. Unlike his French cousin King Louis XIV (an emotional miser with his many mistresses), Charles combined lust with genuine affection. The same day he arrived in London to reclaim the throne, in the aftermath of the day's glorious pomp and ceremony – when fireworks lit up a river Thames so tightly packed with celebratory boats and barges that, noted John Evelyn, 'you could have walked across it' – the exhausted but happy new ruler escaped into Barbara's bed. The poet Andrew Marvell succinctly summed up the situation:

> In a slashed doublet then he came to shore,
> And dubbed poor Palmer's wife his Royal Whore.

With the consummate ease of the natural liar, Barbara told the king he was the only man she had ever truly loved. Charles smirked, preferring not to mention what he knew of the Chesterfield liaison. Palmer, she said, was tiresome; her life was frustrated. Barbara's woes were soon overcome as she firmly established herself as Miss of State (referred to in Court circles simply as 'The Miss'). Regardless of marital status, at this time respectable ladies at Court were referred to as 'Mrs', 'Miss' being reserved for ladies of decidedly relaxed virtue.

Eight months after reclaiming his kingdom, Charles had the grim satisfaction of approving the exhumation of Oliver Cromwell's body and ramming his decapitated head on to a pole, to be displayed prominently over Westminster Hall, where it remained as a warning to would-be usurpers for the next twenty-five years. It was thanks to Cromwell's audacity in selling off the regalia necessary for Charles's coronation ceremony that the occasion was delayed for almost a year. However, on 23 April 1661, Samuel Pepys arose at four in the morning and waited in Westminster Abbey until eleven, in order to be part of that memorable day. He recalls, among the many spectacles, 'the clergy in cloth-of-gold copes ... the nobility in their parliamentary robes ... fiddlers in red vests ... silver medals flung among the spectators ...'

In an age still smarting from the austerities of Puritanism, the new freedom was warmly welcomed. Censorship of the written word was relaxed considerably, giving way to a coarser expression and a relish for the lewd. Pleasure ruled freely; it quickly became apparent that hedonism and libertinism were at the very heart of Court life. How could it be otherwise, when the king and his mistress, despite their insatiable passion for each other, were both notoriously promiscuous, showing little concern for any form of decorum?

On 25 February 1661, 'My Lady Barbary' – a favourite of the many scurrilous soubriquets Barbara's sexual rapacity provoked – was delivered of her first child by the king. It was thought to have been conceived on the day of Charles's triumphant return to London. Christened Anne, she would become the Countess of Sussex at thirteen. Lord Dartmouth and many others, however, firmly believed the father to be the Earl of Chesterfield. 'The child resembleth Chesterfield so, in both face and person, it is hard to believe otherwise,' Dartmouth persisted. Charles, in love, never questioned the parentage. Choosing the name Fitzroy for progeny on his mistress, the king would acknowledge five royal bastards between 1661 and 1665.

In 1661 The Miss was granted permanent apartments at Whitehall Palace. The king had elevated Roger Palmer as Earl of Castlemaine and declared Barbara his *maîtresse en titre* around the same time. Palmer accepted his earldom with stoicism; he knew he had 'earned' the honour simply by turning a blind eye to his wife's royal liaison. The marriage was over in all but name when Barbara left her husband in July 1662. Ruthlessly commandeering all their plate and jewellery, she went to live with her uncle, Colonel Edward Villiers, who resided at Richmond Palace.

Regardless of his feelings for Barbara, Charles was aware that he had to marry to ensure a legitimate heir to the throne. The narrow choice was finally reduced to the Portuguese princess, Catherine of Braganza, daughter of John IV of Portugal. Succumbing to inevitable Court gossip, Charles was far from happy. Catherine looked plain, he thought, judging by her portrait – and he knew that prenuptial portraits had a habit of flattering the sitter in excess. John Evelyn was blunt: 'Her teeth wrong her mouth by sticking too far out.' Nevertheless, Catherine of Braganza brought £300,000 to the much-depleted English coffers, paid in instalments over eighteen years – the largest settlement ever bestowed on an English king – as well as Tangier and the island and city of Bombay.

When Charles first saw Catherine in person, his face lit up in agreeable surprise. The princess was no beauty, but neither was she as plain as he had been led to believe. Lord Chesterfield, that connoisseur of feminine pulchritude, said of her:

> You may credit her being a very extraordinary woman ... As to her person, she is exactly shaped, and has lovely hands, excellent eyes, a good countenance, a pleasing voice, fine hair, and in a word, is what an understanding man would wish a wife.

Two marriage ceremonies – one Roman Catholic and secret, the other Protestant – took place at Portsmouth on 21 May 1662. Time and Charles's affectionate nature brought about not a grand passion but a genuine fondness for his consort. On this day, he wrote to Clarendon that 'she must be as good a woman as ever was born'.

At Whitehall, the queen's out-dated and massively farthingaled clothes caused rude amusement; Catherine was quick to adapt to more flowing, revealing gowns. Her neckline was seen to plunge lower, even as her skirts were shortened. She remained, however, an essentially good person, a quality which won her royal spouse's further esteem. Catherine's Portuguese ladies-in-waiting however were appalled to see their mistress adopt the ways of the sinful English Court. John Evelyn noted how their complexions were 'olive and sufficiently unagreeable', and even Charles's chief adviser, Edward Hyde, Earl of Clarendon, called them 'for the most part old and ugly and proud'. Earl Chesterfield, Chamberlain to the queen, commented wryly:

> You may judge how hard it is to please the Portuguese ladies by their refusing to lie in any bed wherein any man has ever lain before, and yesterday they complained that they cannot stir abroad without seeing in every corner great beastly English pricks battering against every wall.

Evidently these ladies were unused to this overt English custom of responding to Nature's demands!

Barbara expressed her disapproval of the royal marriage in a series of petty insults. She was alone, for instance, in not lighting a bonfire to welcome the future queen of England. Even more insulting was the enthusiasm with which she lured the betrothed husband to her bed on the princess's first evening at Whitehall, during which, noted Pepys, 'they sent for a pair of scales so that they could weigh each other.' Barbara was the heavier, being well advanced with her second royal bastard. Newly arrived in the country and therefore ignorant of Barbara's identity, the young princess had permitted Lady Castlemaine to kiss her hand. On being informed who she was, Catherine had promptly fainted.

As the engagement continued, Barbara had yet more tricks up her sleeve. On the day of the royal union, the 'beautiful meadow laid out like a garden' (the centrepiece of Whitehall Palace) was ostentatiously utilized to dry a great pile of The Miss's freshly-laundered 'finest smocks and linen petticoats', which were draped indecorously across bush and branch. She insisted that she should face confinement on royal premises, preferably at Hampton Court Palace; this was dismissed by Charles as vulgar and provocative; he was, after all, to pass his honeymoon there. Barbara ranted and screamed – for once, to no avail. Catherine never forgot nor forgave Lady Castlemaine's behaviour at this time.

Barbara's second royal child, Charles, was born at her house at Westminster in June 1662. Later she would refer to him as 'a very kokish, idle boy'. From the beginning the Court openly commented on The Miss's cruelty to her own son, '... thus impairing an intellect which never promised very well', commented the diarist John Aubrey. But whatever her maternal skills, the king was putty in Barbara's hands, as Pepys comments in his diary entry of 15 October 1663:

> My Lady Castlemayne rules him, who hath all the tricks of Aretin [Aretino, an earlier erotic writer] that are to be practised to give pleasure – in which he is too able, having a large prick; but that which is the unhappiness is that, as the Italian proverb says, *Cazzo dritto non vuolt consiglio* [He with an erection needs no advice].

Ironically, although Charles fathered at least thirteen bastards by various mistresses, by the time he died he had produced no legitimate heir. Despite conceiving on several occasions, the queen remained fruitless and was pronounced barren. (There were rumours in 1664 that first-minister Clarendon had known of the Catholic princess's sterility before she became queen of England.) Charles never blamed his consort, nor would he consider divorce. The following anonymous lines from 'Satyr on the King and Duke' (1680) were not so kind:

> Dukes thou creat'st, yet want an heir,
> Thy Portuguese is barren;
> Marry again and ne're despair.
> In this lewd age, we are in:
> Some Harry Jermin[1] may be found
> To get an heir fit to be crown'd.

Catherine knew from the start that she could never compete with 'th' Imperial Whore', as Alexander Pope dubbed Lady Castlemaine in his *Sober Advice From Horace*. This was made very clear to her in the 'Affair of the Ladies of the Bedchamber'. Catherine was expected to select from a chosen list, those she favoured for duties in the royal bedchamber. The king was particularly anxious that his mistress should be among those chosen. Having the queen select Barbara was tantamount to informing the Court that Catherine accepted her husband's mistress. The queen had been warned by the Earl of Clarendon, who strongly advised her to resist pressure in this affair. Knowing what was expected of her, the queen defied the issue even when Charles unwisely extolled Lady Castlemaine's suitability for fulfilling the position. Temporarily defeated, the furious monarch now cruelly ostracized his consort. He wrote an impassioned, unequivocal letter to Clarendon, which left no doubt as to his passion for Barbara:

> [I] desire you give Brodericke [Sir Allen] good councell not to meddle any more with what concernes my Lady Castlemaine and to let him have a care how he is the author of any scandalous reports; for if I find him guilty of any such thing, I will make him repent it, to the last moment of his life … I wish I may be unhappy in this world and the world to come if I fail in the least degree of what I have resolved, which is of making my Lady Castlemaine of my wife's bedchamber. And whosoever I find use any endeavour to hinder this resolution of mine (except it be only myself) I will be his enemy to the last moment of my life.

---

[1] Harry Jermin (Jermyn): one of Barbara's many lovers (*see page 26*).

Pepys noted:

the Queen is much grieved of late at the king's neglecting her, he having not supped once with her this quarter of a year, and almost every night with my Lady Castlemayne, who hath been with him this St George's feast at Windsor and come home with him last night; and which is more, they say is removed, as to her bed, from her house to a chamber in Whitehall next to the king's own.

Lonely and deeply unhappy, Catherine finally capitulated to her royal spouse's demands; she began by showing her rival a marked respect and, gradually, even friendliness, going so far as to dine at Lady Castlemaine's apartments. The Miss had won the first round. But the queen was gaining confidence. Dr Pierce, Pepys' surgeon friend, told him on 4 June 1663 that 'the Queen begins to be brisk, and play like other ladies, and is quite another woman from what she was.' Five weeks later, the diarist observed 'the king [riding] hand in hand with her'.

When occasion permitted, Catherine was quick to put her rival down. One morning, having been 'under her dresser's hands' longer than usual, a bored Barbara commented: 'I wonder your Majesty can have the patience to sit so long a-dressing.' The queen replied lightly: 'I have so much reason to use patience, madam, that I can very well bear with it.'

Charles's sexual indifference to his queen did not blind him as to her royal status, as Lady Castlemaine quickly discovered. When Catherine mildly complained, in the presence of her Ladies, that she was afraid the king had caught cold staying so late at Lady Castlemaine's apartments, The Miss was quick to explain that his Majesty did not stay so late with her, and therefore must stay 'somewhere else'. (This was true; the king was a frequent *habitué* at the brothels on the banks of the Thames.) According to Pepys, 'the King then coming in, and overhearing, did whisper in the eare aside, and told [Barbara] she was a bold, impertinent woman and bid her to be gone out of the Court' at his pleasure.

On 20 September 1663, Barbara gave birth to Henry, her third royal bastard. At first, the king refused to acknowledge the child. He had not been intimate with The Miss for some time, therefore he knew the child could not be his. Barbara stormed and raged until, worn out by her vitriolic attacks, Charles capitulated. By Christmas all was serene again to the point where, noted Pepys:

my Lady Castlemayne hath all the King's Christmas presents [mostly silver] made him by the peers, given to her, which is a most abominable thing; and that at the great ball she was much richer in jewells than the Queene and Duchesse put together.

Some time before Henry's birth (wrote John Aubrey), Barbara had the two front teeth of her first son, Charles, removed because they resembled those of the queen. The king was furious, condemning her for defying Nature's law. However, that same year, when The Miss converted to Catholicism, Charles immediately supplied her with a private oratory.

Barbara's religious conversion did not go unnoticed by the Court. A lady of the bedchamber is alleged to have said in conversation with Sir Edward Stillingfleet, the king's chaplain, that The Miss was known to like the pomp and ceremony of the service regardless of the reason for it. While Barbara's religious scruples may well have been genuine, she was also fully aware of Charles's papal tendencies and must have realized that a sudden conversion could only strengthen her position in the royal bed. Also, the conversion would inevitably show The Miss in a better light to the pious Queen Catherine. Sir Edward's comment in response was pithy.

'One thing is certain, madam, the Protestant loss is not a Catholic gain!'

On 5 September 1664 Barbara delighted her royal lover when she gave birth to their fourth child, Charlotte. Charles's delight quickly turned to fury when The Miss, walking in St James's Park, was first insulted and then dubbed 'a Jane Shore' by three masked courtiers. They were never traced. (Jane Shore had been the mistress of Edward IV. She died in abject poverty in 1527, aged eighty-two. Barbara's life resembled hers in many ways.)

The Earl of Clarendon had always disapproved of Barbara; but disapproval turned to loathing from the time of her elevation as *maîtresse en titre*. Lord Chancellor since 1658, he had opposed The Miss in every conceivable manner, acknowledging her scathingly as a 'lady of youth and beauty, with whom the king had lived in great and notorious familiarity from the time of his coming into England.' Hoping to smooth matters, Lady Clarendon suggested that she should invite Lady Castlemaine to visit one afternoon. Her husband reacted vehemently, insisting that there could be no question of receiving 'the lady', since he had declared himself her implacable enemy.

Clarendon refused to accept Barbara's name on any document and froze all monies made payable to her by the king. Indeed, he could not bring himself actually to speak her name, always coldly referring to her as 'the lady'. Barbara recognized a mortal enemy in the minister. Survival instincts to the fore, she became part of an anti-Clarendon cabal bent on destroying the earl. Her hatred reached its zenith when Clarendon successfully quashed the appointment of her friend, Sir Harry Bennet, Keeper of the King's Privy Purse, to the lucrative appointment as Postmaster General. It was the last straw; the cabal were now determined on Clarendon's downfall.

Success came sooner than expected. In August 1667, disagreements over government policy between the king and his ministers caused the frustrated Chancellor to overreach his authority. His comments were hardly subtle when he hinted at Lady Castlemaine's involvement in state decisions. In a combination of embarrassment (because it was true) and anger, Charles stormed out of the council chamber. Clarendon had provided the double insult of belittling the king's intelligence and of indirectly affronting Lady Castlemaine. The monarch would never tolerate the implication that he was a mere puppet, subject to any political string Lady Castlemaine cared to manipulate.

For Clarendon, it was the end of his long service to the Crown. In 1667 the king requested the return of the Chancellor's Seal of Office. With open ribaldry the Castlemaine cabal, headed by The Miss herself ('who,' commented Pepys, 'was still in bed at noon, but appeared at the window in her shift'), witnessed the crushed old man walk into exile. The Miss led the jeering of both courtiers and crowd. Clarendon's humiliation was made the more painful by the recent death of his wife. Later, Clarendon, in his *Life*, recalled his humiliation vividly: 'The lady, the Lord Babington and Mr May looked together out of her open window with great gaiety and triumph, which all people observed.' It was, to say the least, a shoddy victory – proof, no doubt, of the 'enormously vicious and ravenous creature' that Barbara was in the eyes of the contemporary historian, Gabriel Burnet.

Although the king issued angry denials, it was common knowledge that The Miss had influenced government decisions on several occasions, usually to bring pressure concerning her own advancement, or regarding the selling of offices, or the elevation of beneficiaries who would end up in her debt.

Despite the intriguing sexual imbroglio they had created, both the king and Barbara continued to pursue separate, less personal intrigues. Charles's sexual stamina was such that he could easily pass the evening with Barbara and then, disguised, quietly slip away to one of the many bawdy houses across the river. And should the king desire a more personal arrangement, he had only to turn to Will Chiffinch, his private messenger, who was also his pimp, confidant and procurer. Chiffinch's ear was constantly to the ground, picking up whatever gossip or scandal would serve his master. On one occasion he had been drinking with his friend, the lawyer and chronicler Roger North, who informed him about Lady Castlemaine's secret liaisons with Sir Charles Berkeley and Colonel James Hamilton. When Chiffinch related what he had learned about the favourite, the king's reply surprised him.

'Do not concern yourself unduly on my account, William. I know it all. Sadly, I care not whom she may love.'

But the king did care when it became apparent that the Duke of Monmouth – his natural, acknowledged son by Lucy Walter, an earlier mistress – was becoming far too attentive to The Miss. Thus, he hurried on the young man's marriage, 'in order to withdraw him from my Lady Castlemaine's attractions,' Pepys gossiped to his diary. The marriage took place on 20 April 1663, when Charles wrote to his adored sister Henriette Anne (known as Minette and unhappily married to Philippe, Duc d'Orléans, Louis XIV's homosexual brother), that 'we intend to dance and see them a-bed together, but the ceremony shall stop there, for they are both too young to lie all night together.' Monmouth was fourteen years old and his bride, Lady Ann Scott, heiress to the House of Buccleuch, was twelve.

Meanwhile, the Merry Monarch's subjects were increasingly disenchanted with the reported licentiousness of the Court. In October 1663, only three years into the reign, Pepys' friend Dr Pierce 'told me also how loose the Court is, nobody looking after business, but every man his lust and gain', while John Lacy's satyr asks:

> Was ever Prince's soul so meanly poor,
> To be a slave to every little whore?
> The seaman's needle nobly points the Pole,
> But thine still points to every craving hole.

It was rare for a broadsheet or a pamphlet to appear that did not have its share of salty, sexual titillation to enhance its comments condemning His Majesty and his harem. They attacked the king for ennobling these women, as much as for ignoring his duties to the realm. As Lacy further points out:

> Every day they do the monster see,
> They let ten thousand curses fly at thee.
> Aloud, in public streets, they use thee thus
> And none dare quell 'em, they're so numerous.

Determined to quash inflammatory comment, Charles threatened to close all coffee houses, knowing these popular meeting-places were the cauldrons where unrest was brewed. Ministers stressed the inadvisability of such action, which could only antagonize and increase the anger of the people. Discretion, and a policy of laissez-faire would surely tire the pamphleteers.

In 1662, the fifteen-year-old Frances Stewart arrived from the French Court, 'the prettiest girl in the world and one of the best fitted of any I know to adorn a Court' – thus Charles was informed by his adored sister. Minette had kindly sent this delicious young beauty to be part of Queen Catherine's entourage. Unfortunately, lacking in wit and conversation, Frances was happiest building houses out of cards and playing blind man's buff. Gramont's comment was accurate when he wrote 'it was hardly possible for a woman to have less wit or more beauty.' Acutely aware that the lovely newcomer was eight years her junior, a seething Lady Castlemaine watched as Charles openly lusted after her; the fact that she was genuinely virtuous, an exceptional quality in the pleasure-hungry environs of the Carolean Court, made her all the more desirable.

The more Charles pursued, the more Frances was adamant. She was that most unusual creature: a woman who was indifferent to royal patronage and the rich pickings a dalliance with the king could provide.

In October, the queen became desperately ill with 'the spotted fever', wrote Pepys. 'She is as full of the spots as a Leopard.' The king let it be known that, should anything untoward happen to his lady, he would seriously consider making Frances Stewart his queen. To do him justice, the king rarely left Catherine's bedside during the crucial days when her life hung in the balance. 'But for all that, that he hath not missed one night since she was sick, of supping with my Lady Castlemayne,' condemned Pepys. Expecting to die, Catherine had begged her husband to remarry immediately, urging him to choose someone prettier and capable of providing him with an heir. The king wept openly. Now, he heartily, genuinely welcomed Catherine's return to good health – and promptly resumed his pursuit of Frances Stewart extramaritally. In January 1664, Pepys noted:

He values not who sees him or stands by him while he dallies with her openly – and then privately in her chamber below, where the very sentries observe his going in and out – and that so commonly that the Duke or any of the nobles, when they would ask where the King is, they will ordinarily say, 'Is the King above or below?' meaning Mrs Stewart.

Despite these observations, however, it is generally thought that Frances resisted Charles's physical advances, and remained true to her virtue. According to the National Biography, Charles was prepared 'to rearrange his seraglio' – while Burnet tells us that in 1667 the monarch asked Archbishop Sheldon if the Church of England would allow a divorce where both parties were consenting and one lay under a natural incapacity for having children.

Lady Castlemaine, acutely aware of her threatened position, now set about procuring the newcomer Stewart for the king's bed. With a challenged mistress's intuition, she recognized Frances to be no Circe – no temptress. Better to help her lover achieve his desire than allow a more ambitious, more pliant beauty to succeed. Left to The Miss, little Frances would be a bawd soon enough!

So, the Castlemaine befriended her rival and passed much of her time with the girl, sometimes inviting her to share her bed. (Innocent bed-sharing was not uncommon at this time.) 'The King,' noted the emigré Comte de Gramont, 'who rarely failed to visit the Castlemaine before she got up, also rare failed to find Mrs Stewart in bed with her.' In this way, Barbara slyly increased the king's desire by allowing him, in silence, to gaze on the sleeping girl. His frustration was great, knowing that his mistress spent each night where he so passionately wanted to be!

Although Lord Sandwich considered her a cunning slut, it is widely believed that Frances Stewart succeeded in remaining *virgo intacta* against the untiring assaults, conniving and strategies of the king to deflower her. Even the honour of having her image as 'Britannia' perpetuated on the country's coinage did nothing to woo Frances into submission. In fact, La Belle Stewart seems to have been infuriatingly impregnable.

It seems that the little Stewart wanted only an honourable marriage, which she finally attained by eloping with the Duke of Richmond. At first, Charles was flabbergasted; then he was hurt. Finally, realizing that he had been thwarted, he was furious. On 26 August 1667 he wrote to Minette, 'if you consider how hard a thing 'tis to swallow an injury done by a person I had so much tenderness for, you will in some degree excuse the resentment I use towards her.' Barbara purred with satisfaction and even more so later, when she heard that the young beauty had contracted smallpox. No stranger to the disease herself, Barbara had miraculously recovered from a severe bout of it in 1659 which had left her unmarked. It took time, but Frances Stewart also made a complete recovery. Meanwhile, Lady Castlemaine's power increased.

★

The king's failure to seduce Frances Stewart drove him into a vortex of indiscriminate sexual activity with many varied partners, including the blatantly vulgar Jane Roberts (the daughter of a clergyman, who was reputed to be singularly stimulating in bed), as well as the actress/dancer Moll Davis, 'a most homely jade', who belonged to the Duke's Theatre and was known for 'singing several wild and mad songs', wrote Gramont. 'On one occasion she danced a wild jig with such abandon that the Queen took to her heels and Charles scooped [Moll] up and took her to bed!' Pepys called her 'the most impertinent slut in the world'. In October 1673, Moll gave birth to Charles's daughter, Mary Tudor. Barbara loathed her rival. In retaliation to Charles's affairs, The Miss dallied indifferently with an actor called Charles Hart.

The historian Airy is corrosive about the bestial Court at this time, it being

> in an uproar with their loose amours; [Sir Charles] Sedley and [Lord] Buckhurst running naked through the streets, beaten by the watch, and locked up all night […] the King taking their parts; Charles too drunk to give audience to Arlington on his way to Newmarket, and making the fiddlers at Thetford sing all the obscene songs they could think of […] Charles robbed and kidnapped in a disreputable house at Newmarket, and obliged to disclose his identity before he was set free …

Meanwhile, John Lacy expressed similar disillusionment:

> How poorly squander'st thou thy seed away,
> Which should get kings for nations to obey!

Lady Castlemaine now seems to have been energized by Charles's rampancy in her own search for lustier, cruder lovers. Her steady progress down the ladder of immorality and increased hedonism was next enhanced by excessive gambling. Pepys recalled on 14 February 1668, 'I was told tonight that my Lady Castlemaine is so great a gamester as to have won £15,000 in one night, and lost £25,000 on another night, at play, and hath played £1,000 and £1,500 at a cast.' (This, in an age when a housemaid earned around £3 a year; when five shillings – 25p – would buy dinner for four at a good inn; when £50 would buy a stylish coach.)

Barbara would always refuse to stop play, even if her luck was against her. 'If Dame Chance has deserted me, the king will pay,' she would snap.

In this, she was correct. In 1673 an account came before the House of Commons showing that £400,000 of war reserve funds had been monopolized by the Privy Purse since the last session. Much of the money found its way into the coffers of Lady Castlemaine; the residue was claimed by Louise de Kéroualle, a feisty beauty who arrived at Court from Paris in 1671.

★

Louise de Kéroualle, born in Brittany, had reluctantly found herself being carefully groomed at the French Court, charged with influencing the English monarch, through her considerable charms, into a more favourable alliance with France. The year before, her mistress, Henriette d'Angleterre (Charles's beloved sister Minette), had successfully negotiated for King Louis the secret Treaty of Dover (1670), guaranteeing English support to France against the Netherlands. When the French Ambassador Colbert de Croisy failed to gain secret information from Lady Castlemaine, Louis realised that new tactics were called for. Louise de Kéroualle, already admired by Charles when she came to England as part of Henriette's entourage, was thus brought into service as a spy. She understood the seductress's art to perfection, inflaming the English monarch with subtle flirtation, only to deny him at her bedroom door. Charles pleaded; he begged – but Louise held out. At length Lady Arlington, a French supporter, was deputed by minister Colbert to speak openly to the girl: she must 'lay aside her scruples without delay, or retire to a convent'. Not inclined to monastic life, Louise became Charles's acknowledged mistress on 9 October 1671. She proved politically astute and adept – so much so that in 1674 King Louis awarded her the fiefdom of Aubigny in recognition of her efforts in keeping the English monarch dependent on France. The year before, Charles had ennobled her as Duchess of Portsmouth, thus consolidating her success as an amoureuse in the monarch's harem. Politically – and even more so than Barbara – she made her influence felt, resulting in those politicians she aided not forgetting her love of money and jewels. However, the great British public detested her, the combination of French haughtiness and Catholic persuasion being overwhelming. The following verse – a poem in its own right and taken from *Poems On Affairs Of State* – makes this abundantly clear:

The Downfall of the French Bitch,
England's Metropolitan Strumpet,
The Three Nations' Grievance,
The pickle pocky Whore,
Rowley's Dalilah;
All in a word,
The damn'd dirty duchess.

The populace truly hated this mistress, but they were also thoroughly disgusted with Charles's mismanagement of the 1665–7 war with Holland. Pepys noted that on 2 June 1665:

> while the Dutch burned and pillaged the English ships off Lowestoft, the King was with Lady Castlemaine [...] spending 'mad time in hunting a moth' while the Dutch guns could be heard roaring in the Thames.

Four months later on 16 October 1665, while in conversation with Mr Povy, the Court Treasurer, Pepys learned of his friend's decision to leave office,

> for the King doth spend most of his time in feeling and kissing them naked all over their bodies in bed – and contents himself without doing the other thing but as he finds himself inclined; but this lechery will never leave him.

In the early months of 1665, the great plague which had swept and devastated Europe at last reached England. Disease swept through London; on 29 June Pepys recorded 'the Mortality Bill is come to 267'; on this same day, the king and his courtiers escaped from London to Hampton Court. Things grew increasingly worse until, during the month of September, more than 30,000 Londoners died. Normal burial procedure was abandoned in favour of 'plague pits'. By this time the Court had settled at Oxford, where new standards in hedonism and moral laxity were introduced.

'Oxford may be free of the plague,' wryly commented one observer, 'but it is undergoing the infection of Love!'

The Court was accused of cowardice for deserting the capital, and of sapping the population of what little moral stamina its presence would afford.

'Where is the king?' was the cry.

'Where he is free of the plague, and able to service Castlemaine!' came the angry response.

But the accusations fell on deaf ears; Oxford was being treated to the Court's latest fashion, when Queen Catherine introduced the wearing of men's apparel. Charles approved, although he was of the opinion that an English leg was the finest to be seen, and the finest of all was Frances Stewart's.

Christmas drew closer. Physically uncomfortable, an irate Barbara was delivered of George, her fifth child by the King. She hated her lodgings, the humble rooms of a fellow at Merton College, where her somewhat bizarre method of relieving herself at the hearth filled that gentleman with amazement and disgust. She, above all others, symbolized what the undergraduates saw as a completely decadent Court. They made their feelings known by blatantly pasting on Lady Castlemaine's door the following:

> The reason why she is not duck'd?
> Because she is by Caesar fuck'd.

Charles was furious, promising a reward of £1,000 for delivery of the author's name. Lady Castlemaine may have been insulted, but he was the laughing stock! Not even the handsome reward could unearth the poet, although rumour had it that it was the work of the Earl of Rochester, Barbara's libertine cousin.

By 1 February 1666, it was deemed safe for the Court to move back to London. Barbara, celebrating, went on a spending spree which was outrageous even by her standards. She gambled for even higher stakes, thus causing further outrage at the frivolous misuse of the country's rapidly dwindling revenue. One woman presented a petition to the king which openly stated: 'Give the King his Castlemayne and he cares not what the nation suffers.'

In April 1666, the Court went into mourning for the death of Queen Catherine's mother. It was during this short period that Pepys reassessed The Miss, considering her 'to be a much more ordinary woman than ever I durst have thought she was.' But Barbara's power continued unabated. At this point Charles never queried her expenses, as he would later on. He paid off her latest debts of over £30,000 with the taxpayers' money.

On 2 September 1666 a small fire got out of hand in a bakery in Pudding Lane in east London; it was to spread across 400 acres, in the process destroying eighty-seven churches including St Paul's Cathedral and over 13,000 homes. The Great Fire of London rang the death knell for Old London. What remained of the plague was destroyed in a blaze that many believed had been a deliberate attempt to cleanse the capital; some even suspected the fire to be by order of the king. In fact, both Charles and his brother James won enormous popularity when they fought the flames side by side with the populace.

Among the monumental damage caused was the dislodgement of the tomb of a fourteenth-century bishop at St Paul's cathedral. His perfectly mummified body became a popular curiosity for all to see. Lady Castlemaine was no exception. Her bizarre visit was still being remarked upon a decade later, by Lord Coleraine, who relates the tale as it was told to him by Thomas Boys, Keeper of the Chapter House:

> … the Duchess of Cleveland attended there by a gentleman and two or three gentlewomen, desired to see this body and to be left alone by it for a while, whereupon her train together with Thomas Boys withdrew out of sight and as they retired, perceived her Ladyship addressing herself towards the carcass with many crossings and great token of superstition, afterwards coming away to her company with much satisfaction she told them she had done, and went away having gratified the Keeper of this curiosity Thomas Boys – he returned to shut up the carcass, but unexpectedly found it served like a Turkish eunuch and dismembered of as much of the privity as the Lady could get into her mouth to bite (for want of a circumcizing penknife to cut) … She had, though a very tough bit, yet bit a very small morsel (*vix major uncia singula vel tribus longior*[1]) and though some ladys of late have got Bishopricks for others, yet I have not heard of any but this that got one for herself. This odd piece of devotion shall I call it, or curiosity (if not worse) was so notorious that he still avers, that Bishop Braybrook was thus more despoiled by a kind lady in a quarter of an hour, than by the teeth of time for almost three centuries of years.

On 13 June 1667, the Dutch not only savagely attacked the naval base at Chatham, they also towed away the *Royal Charles*, the warship that had conveyed the king back to his realm. As the battle raged the king and Lady Castlemaine, naked again, were running around her boudoir, this time chasing butterflies (how did Pepys forage such intimacies?). On 17 July of that year, on a visit to London from Leigh, Pepys' brother-in-law's wife,

---

[1] No bigger than an inch, nor made longer by rubbing.

Esther St Michel ('my sister Michell', as the diarist called her), talked so much of the Dutch wars that the diarist was weary of it. 'Yet it is worthy remembering what she says: that she hath heard both seamen and soldiers swear they would rather serve the Dutch than the king, for they should be better used.' Dissent was increasing; people were restless and embittered. St Michel adds:

'Of all places, if there's a hell, it is here; no faith, no truth, no love, nor any agreement between man and wife, or friends.'

On 25 March 1668, one of the most scathing anonymous attacks against The Miss appeared in the form of 'A Petition of the Poor Whores to the Most Splendid, Illustrious, Serene, and Eminent Lady of Pleasure, the Countess of Castlemaine'. Known famously as the Whore's Petition, and obviously written by one of the Court wits, Lady Castlemaine was 'horribly vexed' by it. Over the Easter period, and encouraged by religious zeal, the London prentices had attacked some of the brothels, bagnios and 'disorderly houses', causing considerable damage. It was an annual religious hazard; on this occasion a number of the houses were destroyed, despite militia intervention. Blood was spilt and eight of the ringleaders were condemned to die. Gramont wrote:

> The soldiers were in arms throughout the 24th and 25th […] The brothels were the great grievances of the nation, according to these lads, who thought they had only done ill in not pulling down, in place of the little ones, the great one at Whitehall.

The 'victims' of these attacks (in actuality a Court wit) decided to petition Lady Castlemaine, 'an expert in the profession', for help and protection, in the form of a 'response'. On 24 April there appeared in print an equally brilliant 'Reply To The Whore's Petition', couched as though written by Barbara herself. Obviously penned by a sophisticate, anonymity denied a seething Lady Castlemaine the revenge she so feverishly sought. She had, after all, had nothing whatsoever to do with either document!

★

Meanwhile, the hedonism at Court continued unabated. John Fenn, Paymaster to the Navy Treasurer and a friend of Pepys, was no stranger to the Court's practices. Despondently, he informed Pepys that 'the King and Court were never in the world so bad as they are now for gaming, swearing, whoring, and drinking, and the most abominable vices that ever were in the world … so that all must come to naught.'

Jealousies and petty rivalries were rife as the Merry Monarch and The Miss's halcyon first years now dwindled into mere lustful promiscuity. Respect for royal status was at an ebb. For his part, Charles was particularly scathing about one of Barbara's lovers, Henry Jermyn (mentioned earlier in an anonymous scurrilous poem), a weak politician, a supposed 'wit' (supposed, because all his wit consisted of expressions he had learned by rote) and an incurable rake who was supported by his uncle's vast fortune. Jermyn was small, with a large head and short legs. 'This was the whole foundation of the merit of a man so formidable in amours,' commented Gramont, witheringly. Barbara's curiously intense infatuation with Jermyn baffled Charles, who could not understand the attraction. He was consequently spectacularly jealous. Gramont observed:

> Charles did not think it consistent with his dignity that a mistress, whom he had honoured with public distinction, and who still received a considerable support from him, should appear chained to the car of the most ridiculous conqueror that ever existed […] advising her rather to bestow her favours upon Jacob Hall, the rope-dancer, who was able to return them.

The Miss instantly took umbrage at the monarch's interference, screeching ripostes about the king's own infidelities. Charles registered his disgust and intolerance of such a shrew. But The Miss still knew how to cajole and flatter her lover's vanity, resulting in him apologizing, literally and humiliatingly on his knees, and before witnesses – vindicating himself with a gift of 5,600 ounces of plate from the jewel-house.

Barbara's lovers now became legion, ranging from handsome but penniless aristos, to actors and even her own servants. She was once excited by the athletic legs of one of her coach-runners. She immediately commanded the man to join her – in her bath!

The same male muscularity magnetized her when she next visited Bartholomew Fair. The king had surmised correctly; after watching the rope-dancer Jacob Hall (whom Pepys described as 'a mighty strong man'), she longed to know what he was like beneath his clothes. She found out by taking him home to bed, and must have been well-satisfied, for she patronized him with a steady wage from then on. Meantime, The Miss still continued to stamp, fume or blaze to get her own way, as Comte de Gramont frequently witnessed:

Floods of tears, from rage, generally attended these storms; after which, resuming the part of Medea, the scene closed with menaces of tearing her children in pieces and setting his palace on fire ... beautiful as she was [she] resembled Medea less than her dragons, when she was thus enraged!

Through Gramont's intercession, an agreement was reached between The Miss and the monarch, whereby Barbara would give up Jermyn and rail no more against Charles's indiscretions, in particular his infatuation with Frances Stewart (the king had forgiven her for marrying Richmond and, as Pepys put it, 'He was again mighty hot upon the Duchess of Richmond'), and a current dalliance, Winifred Wells (one of the queen's maids of honour). In consideration of these condescensions, his Majesty should immediately give Barbara the title of Duchess [of Cleveland], with all the honours and privileges thereupon belonging, and an addition to her pension, in order to enable her to support the dignity. The Miss was also elevated to Countess of Southampton 'by reason of her own virtue': a reason which caused not a few sniggers. Incidentally, apropos of Winifred Wells: Pepys recorded in July 1663 that she was alleged to have 'dropped' a baby (thought to be the king's) during a ball at Court. No one was certain, because the lady went on dancing,

> it [the baby] being taken up by somebody in their handkerchief. The next morning all the Ladies of Honour appeared early at Court for their vindication, so that nobody could tell whose this mischance should be. But it seems Mrs Wells fell sick that afternoon and hath disappeared ever since, so that it is concluded it was her.

★

A saucy little actress had recently caught the king's eye. Nell Gwynne, unlike Barbara, was refreshingly devoid of ostentation; she gazed upon the antics of the courtiers and their devious methods in achieving royal favour with cheerful mockery. Although Nellie was the least frowned-upon of the mistresses, even she was unable to quell the people's resentment:

> Look back and see the people mad with rage,
> To see the bitch in so high equipage.

Another Court wit commented bitterly:

Then next turn Nelly out of door,
That hare-brain'd, wrinkl'd stopp'd-up whore,
Daily struck, stabb'd by half the pricks in Town,
Yet still her stubborn courses come not down.
But lie and nourish old diseases there
Which thou, and many of thy poor subjects share.

At this time, Nellie, Moll Davis and Barbara were all neighbours in the Pall Mall area of London. As the 1660s drew to a close, Barbara recognized her approaching dismissal from favour; after eight years, the king had finally tired of her insatiable acquisitiveness and ungoverned promiscuity. Her temper had become ferocious, her ostentation an embarrassment. On 4 February 1667, John Starkey wrote to Sir Willoughby Aston at Stone, Staffordshire:

This night there is a play acted at Court by the Duchess of Monmouth, Countess of Castlemaine and others. The Countess is adorned with jewels to the value of £200,000, the Crown jewels being taken from the Tower for her. There are none but the nobility admitted to see it. The play is Madam Phillips' translation of Corneille's *Horace*.

During his early days with Nell, the king would enjoy her, leave her – 'another lady of pleasure and curse of our nation', commented John Evelyn bitterly – and then proceed to Barbara. However, the king's increasing interest in Nell (not to mention Louise de Kéroualle) finally pushed him towards a momentous decision. He confided in William Chiffinch, as he did all amatory matters: Lady Castlemaine must be pensioned off. Barbara had suspected Charles's intention when she was quietly supplanted in the queen's bedchamber by the recently-arrived Kéroualle. Decision made, Charles showered The Miss with jewels and pensions; she was further ennobled as the Baroness Nonsuch with which honour went the great Tudor palace of Nonsuch. This she immediately had demolished, disposing of the great house's valuable contents – probably the most philistine single act that the Castlemaine ever committed. Charles also gave her Berkshire House, a particularly personal, if hollow, triumph, since the house had once belonged to her erstwhile enemy, Lord Clarendon. In presenting her with Phoenix Park in Dublin, Charles fanned the flames of an already explosive situation in Ireland. The Duke of Ormonde, Lord Lieutenant of Ireland, found it intolerable. Lady

Castlemaine had obtained a warrant from the king for the grant of both the Park and the house. Ormonde refused to accept the warrant, stopped the grant and begged his Majesty to fit up the house to make it an acceptable official abode instead.

Barbara, of course, loathed Ormonde. She met the duke one day in the corridors of Whitehall and gave full vent to her fury in language which made the servants blush. She ended her tirade by hoping to live long enough to see him hanged. But Ormonde had the last word. 'And I, Madam, hope I live long enough to see you old.'

Equally determined for her royal brood, Barbara secured the Garter for Charles, Duke of Southampton; Henry, Duke of Grafton was made Duke of Euston (at the age of nine he also became betrothed to the Earl of Arlington's five-year-old daughter); her third son became Lord George Fitzroy; and her daughters Anne and Charlotte were granted royal arms, their heraldic design a lozenge with a baton sinister ermine (a truncheon within a shield, which was usually a sign of bastardy). Such wholesale elevation and ennoblement among the mistresses led to the king writing the following ditty:

> This making of bastards great,
> And duchessing every whore,
> The surplus and Treasury cheat
> Hath made me damnably poor.

Once removed from the immediacy of Whitehall Palace, Barbara had no influence. Though many newcomers passed through the royal bedchamber, only Louise de Kéroualle, the lately-arrived Hortensia Mazarin (a beautiful Italian adventuress) and Nell Gwynne became long-term members of Charles's punk establishment. In an earlier, generous moment, Barbara had given her patronage to the talented Nellie – an ironic investment which badly misfired when the actress supplanted her in the royal bed. Nell treated Barbara as a friendly rival, without envy and always with good humour. For Barbara, being a royal mistress had been a profession; for Nell, it was another facet of her life.

Nellie had little time for 'Squintabella' (her nickname for Louise de Kéroualle, who suffered from a slight squint) and had no compunction at showing her disdain. On one occasion they had a quarrel, ending in a scuffle on the floor, with Nell the successful aggressor. As contemporary writer Alexander Smith recalled in his *School of Venus*, she promptly took up Louise's coats, then she burnt with a candle all the hair off those parts which modesty obliges us to conceal. This indignity made the Duchess presently complain thereof to the King who was very angry at Nell's rudeness. He fell in a great passion with Nell, who was entering the Presence-Chamber just as the complainant had ended her story. She soon appeased him by saying: 'May it please Your Majesty, that as there is an Act of Parliament for burning all French commodities that are prohibited, [she] hopes [he] could not be angry at [her] care in putting the Act in force.'

Charles always fell an easy victim to Nellie's quick wit and sense of humour. She had dubbed her royal lover 'Charles The Third', having had two previous Charlies as lovers. Unlike Lady Castlemaine's occasional dalliance into advantageous political fray, Nellie had no interest at all in swaying the king's authority, nor in intrigues involving Court advancement. An anonymous poet wrote:

> Hard by Pall Mall lives a wench call'd Nell,
> King Charles the Second he kept her.
> She hath got a trick to handle his prick
> But never lays hands on his sceptre.

Once, after the now erstwhile Miss had cajoled a magnificent coach-and-six from the king, Nell, her tongue firmly in her cheek, retaliated by hiring a dilapidated country cart with six oxen. She rode through the streets, at intervals cracking an oversized whip, until she reached Barbara's new house, where she slowed down the team to yell: 'Whores, to market, ho!'

On another occasion, knowing the hatred between Barbara and Moll Davis, and Nell herself disliking her fellow thespian, she invited both Moll and Barbara to 'a collation of sweetmeats' before Moll's assignation with the monarch. Poor Moll had no idea (but Barbara had!) that Nellie had laced the food with 'physical ingredients' – in other words, a powerful purgative. Alexander Smith wrote that

> the effect thereof had such an operation upon the harlot, when the King was caressing her in bed with the amorous sport of Venus, that a violent and sudden looseness obliging her ladyship to discharge her artillery, she made the King, as well as her self, in the most lamentable pickle; which caused her Royal Master to turn her off, with a small

pension of a £1,000 per annum, in consideration for her former services in the affairs of love ...

As early as 1667, the ever-observant Pepys commented that, although Barbara no longer had the power of a royal mistress, she continued to treat the king as an underling, verbally abusing and insulting him. Like a hen-pecked husband, Charles accepted it all without comment, before escaping to less turbulent environs.

Remarkably, instead of diminishing, Barbara's sexual appetite increased with age. She had no compunction whatsoever about paying for her pleasures (many believed she even took a perverse enjoyment from the transaction), leading to outright condemnation by Charles, Earl of Dorset:

> Ah, Barbary! thy execrable name
> Is sure embalmed with everlasting shame.

The debauched Rochester grudgingly admired his cousin. She was bizarrely pretentious, unfailingly vulgar and her avariciousness was almost legendary – but she was also abidingly generous with her lovers. He knew, for example, that she had hired in swift succession the Duke of Monmouth, the Earl of Cavendish, Sir Carr Scrope, her cousin Villiers, Lord Newport, Will Henningham and Henry Savile, all at an average cost of £5,000.

For a short period the duchess took John Ellis, a civil servant, as her lover. He was notoriously lewd, at one point crudely boasting about his intimacy with the king's 'Imperial Whore'. This was an unwise piece of bragging, for a furious Barbara had the man waylaid by a gang, who then proceeded to castrate him. The incident was recorded by Alexander Pope, in his *Sober Advice From Horace* (Second Sermon); Wycherley, Pope's close friend, supplied the information. Pope asks (and then answers himself):

> What push'd poor Ellis on th'Imperial Whore?
> 'Twas but to be where Charles had been before.

He then continues on poor Ellis's fate:

> The fatal Steel unjustly was apply'd,
> When not his Lust offended, but his Pride:
> Too hard a penance for defeated sin,
> Himself shut out, and Jacob Hall let in.

Ellis never married, but the drastic butchery performed on him did not interfere with a long life. He died at ninety-five.

In adversity, and with her income no longer stable, Barbara's largesse with her lovers perversely increased. Many of them were ruthless extortioners. John Churchill (the future first Duke of Marlborough, ancestor of Sir Winston Churchill) was perhaps her favourite. Charming of manner, he was exceptionally handsome, his military uniform enhancing his good looks. Even the acerbic poet John Dryden admitted his boudoir potential:

> Broad-back'd, and brawny, built for love's delight;
> A prophet formed to make a female proselyte.

Unfortunately, his charming, easy-going manner belied the ruthless egoism that served his ambition well. Philalethes, in his *Remarks Upon Bishop Burnet's Posthumous History*, comments: 'it was hard to find one with limbs more brawny, conscience more supple, or principles more loose.'

Churchill bled Barbara mercilessly at every opportunity, showing very little gratitude over the years that he was intimate with her. He was the father of her daughter, Barbara, but showed not the slightest interest in the child. In 1668 the king, in a sudden burst of unreasonable jealousy, interrupted a coital assignation between the erstwhile favourite and young Churchill. In his *History*, Gabriel Burnet tells us that the soldier 'leapt out of the window but not to have escaped recognition by Charles,' which led to Charles's oft-quoted comment: 'Nay, hasten not. I forgive you, for you do it for your bread!'

Churchill was far from circumspect about his liaison with Barbara. Indiscretion in such matters seemed natural to him, especially since Lady Castlemaine made no attempt to curtail his disclosures. Her infatuation led her to deprive Jacob Hall of his salary and Sir Harry Jermyn of his pension 'because the merits and qualifications of both were united in his person.'

As a balance against his ruthless ego and selfish amorality, John Churchill turned out to be one of the finest military leaders England has ever produced. He won brilliant victories at, among others, Ramillies, Blenheim, Oudenarde and Malplaquet. Away from the battlefield, however, he continued in the role of practised opportunist. On one occasion when his finances were seriously depleted, he demanded £5,000 from Barbara. She had no intention of financially inconveniencing herself, but so besotted was The Miss that she determined to raise the money. She cashed in on Sir Edward Hungerford, a dreadful, seventy-year-old rake and spendthrift, who had long wanted 'to be where the King had been'. She told him she was at last willing, for £10,000. But Sir Edward was made to conduct the transaction in a darkened room, thus allowing Barbara the opportunity to substitute another in her place. Adding insult to injury, she brazenly admitted to the hoax, impudently suggesting that a return visit for the real thing was possible – for a similar fee! The incident was the talk of the Court (and yet was curiously never fully catalogued). This money, for which Barbara sank lower than ever before, combined with the prize-money Churchill collected from his military successes, would be the basis of John Churchill's future vast fortune. Pope makes reference to the incident in *Sober Advice From Horace* (Second Sermon):

> ... who of ten thousand gulled her knight,
> Then asked ten thousand for a second night;
> The gallant too, to whom she paid it down,
> Lived to refuse that mistress half a crown.

The last couplet refers to an incident when (according to Mrs Manley, who had lived as companion to the Duchess of Cleveland) 'the Duke, who had received thousands from the Duchess, refused the common civility of lending her twenty guineas at basset.' In fact, by the time they parted the duchess had funded Churchill with more than £100,000.

An outright condemnation of the Duchess of Cleveland appeared in an anonymous poem called 'The Lady of Pleasure'. In it, the Duke of Buckingham, who detested his cousin (and may even have penned the verse himself) berates the king:

> I wonder you should dote so like a fop
> On Cleaveland's cunt, which all her footmen grope
> D'you think you don't your Parliament offend
> That all they give, you on a baggage spend?
> Permit me, Sir, to help you to a whore;
> Fuck her but once, you'll ne're fuck Cleaveland more.

For several years Barbara supported Churchill 'by the season' (as a soldier he was frequently abroad), dismissing all others in his favour whenever he was available. She even exiled 'brawny William Wycherley' for him, who was at the time considered the most handsome, virile man in town.

'Wycherley is the best-endowed man I've known – after Old Rowley!' Barbara admitted salaciously, using the Court's licentious soubriquet for the king (apparently, after a highly-sexed, well-hung royal stallion).

Wycherley had first met Barbara at the same time as his playwriting talent was manifesting itself. Their first meeting has become legendary. In the early spring of 1671 he was enjoying his first dramatic success with his play *Love in a Wood*. The ribald nature of the piece was greatly to Barbara's taste. The day after she had attended a performance, the duchess was out in her carriage when she saw Wycherley, whom she had never met, passing by. Barbara leaned out of her carriage window and yelled, 'Wycherley, you are the son of a whore!' Only when he heard the duchess laugh loudly did he realize that she was quoting a line from one of the songs in his play, which railed against marriage and delighted in free and easy sexual encounter. Amused, and taking up the proffered gauntlet, the playwright turned his carriage round and presently drew up alongside Barbara's. John Dennis, a minor playwright and a close friend of Wycherley, describes that meeting in his *Familiar Letters*, allegedly as told to him by Wycherley himself:

> 'Madam, you have been pleased to bestow a title on me which generally belongs to the fortunate. Will your Ladyship be at the play tonight?'
>
> 'Well,' she reply'd, 'what if I am there?'
>
> 'Why, then I will be there to wait upon your Ladyship, tho' I disappoint a very fine woman who has made me an assignation.'
>
> 'So,' said she, 'you are sure to disappoint a woman who had favoured for one who had not.'
>
> 'Yes,' reply'd he, 'if she who has not favoured me is the finer woman of the two. But he who will be constant to your Ladyship till he can find a finer woman is sure to die your captive.'

That evening Barbara was in the front row of the king's box at Drury Lane. When the play was published, Wycherley prefaced it with a dedication to 'Her Grace, the Duchess of Cleveland'. Some time later, in 1682, these lines from 'Mrs Nelly's Complaint' (1682) expressed Barbara's physical ecstasy with the playwright:

> But when his charming limbs the first time pressed
> My hectic body, ne'er was bawd so blest.

For the next few months, Wycherley was in regular attendance at Barbara's house, his passion for the quondam royal mistress inspiring *The*

Country Wife, one of the best comedies of the Restoration. Although she was now in her early thirties (considered middle age at the time), Barbara was still remarkably lovely, causing Wycherley to say, 'You have that perfection of beauty (without thinking it so) which others of your sex but think they have.' Burnet, too, in his *History*, considered Lady Castlemaine's beauty to be 'very extraordinary and has been now of long continuance.'

According to Pepys, Charles only considered troilism with Barbara and her sometime lover Jermyn to boost flagging passions, but Barbara allegedly indulged in actuality. It may have been the malicious-tongued Rochester who informed the sovereign that Wycherley was servicing both Barbara and Mary Knight (who had had a previous short liaison with Charles), Barbara's singer friend and companion-in-lust, at the latter's house. In his *Court Satires of the Restoration*, the historian J. H. Wilson tells the anecdote of the king arriving unexpectedly at the house 'and found [Wycherley] muffled in his cloak upon the stair head'. The monarch entered and challenged his ex-mistress about Rochester's rumours.

'Nay, think what you will, Sire,' an unruffled Barbara riposted, 'I am, as you see, staying with my friend. We utilize the time in preparation for Easter duties.'

'And I suppose that was your confessor who just left!'

Expert in love, Charles was equally adept with *un bon mot*. Unfortunately, he had by now earned for himself a permanent reputation:

> Silly and sauntering he goes,
> From French whore to Italian, [Kéroualle; Mazarin]
> Unlucky in whate'er he does,
> An old ill-favoured Stallion.

Though all the royal mistresses were mocked in the contemporary literature, none was lampooned and ridiculed more than Barbara. Not only her own sexual rapacity, but also her choice of lovers (ranging from the weak and penniless, to low-bred or criminal), made her an obvious victim for the Court wits. The following anonymous lampoon is a perfect example. In a few deft quatrains, my Lady Castlemaine's sexual avarice is epitomized:

> [...] lechery so oversway'd her,
> She had no discretion at all;
> The cunt that first had rais'd her
> Was now the cause of her fall.

Churchill's delicate shape
Her dazzling eyes had struck,
But her wider cunt did gape
For a more substantial fuck.

Which made her in pattins,they say, [clogs to avoid mud]
To the Temple so often to trudge,
Where brawny Wycherley lay,
Who performed the part of a drudge. [hard worker; slave]

'Twas bad in such as did know it
To go about to betray her.
Why might she not fuck with a poet,
When his Majesty fucks with a player?

Jermyn shou'd not be forgott,
Who us'd to fuck her before;
'Tis hard to say who did not –
There's Brymwych and thousands more. [sometime lover]

The number can never be reckon'd;
She's fucked with great and small,
From good King Charles the Second
To honest Jacob Hall.

But now she must travell abroad
And be forc'd to frigg with the nunns.
For giving our sovereign lord
So many good butter'd bunns. [overworked prostitutes]

The reference to 'nuns' was no unlikely invention. In 1676, when the duchess thought she might be in danger of having her incomes seriously decreased by outraged ministers, she left for Paris, 'and saith she intends to put herself into a monastery.' She sailed from Dover on 13 March, accompanied by her sons, forty servants and a retinue of horses and carriages.

Anticipating this voluntary exile, the year before she had placed her son Charles at Oxford University. Humphrey Prideaux, at that time tutor of Christ Church College, was not pleased. In a letter dated February 1677, he informed his friend John Ellis (the same who was so brutally castrated), 'it is the general desire among us that he come not.' After only one year with the young Charles, Prideaux was able to confirm his suspicions that his charge would 'ever be very simple, and scarce, I believe, ever attain to the reputation of not being a fool.'

Despite her threat to 'retire from the world and live in a monastery', Barbara was happy abroad, spontaneously combining lascivious pursuits with close association with the Church. One of her most fervent admirers was François de Harlay de Champvallon, the morally-corrupt Archbishop of Paris. Their liaison was sufficiently unguarded to be reported to Humphrey Prideaux, who promptly informed John Ellis that

> the Duchess driveth a cunning trade and followeth her old employment very hard there, especially with the Arch Bishop of Paris, who is her principal gallant.

Even the increasingly austere Louis XIV fell victim to Barbara's charm, granting her, 'on the spur of the moment', says the French diarist Saint-Simon in his memoirs, 'the rare honour of a tabouret at Court'. (At Versailles, only the king and queen reclined in chairs with armrests; tabourets, or low stools, were permitted only to those aspiring to the rank of duchess and higher.)

There were many other lovers from this period in France, including the English Ambassador, Ralph Montagu, for whom Barbara felt a genuine love and with whom she lived – until he rewarded her trust by seducing her daughter during her absence on a visit to London. Perhaps Montagu was seeking revenge for the secret liaison Barbara was also conducting with the young, handsome and penniless Alexis, Marquis de Châtillon, who was First Gentleman of the Bedchamber to Louis XIV. The treacherous Montagu had in some way gained possession of several compromising letters from the duchess to her young aristocratic buck. Fearing that exposure of their salacious contents could influence drastic cuts in her pensions, The Miss wrote several enormously long letters to Charles in an effort to exonerate herself:

> Now all I have to say for myself is, that you know, as to love, one is not mistress of one's self, and that you ought not to be offended with me, since all things of this nature is at an end with you and I; so that I could do you no prejudice.

The Carolean Court had a love/hate attitude towards the rapacious Castlemaine. With Montagu, however, his reprehensible behaviour with

Barbara's (and the king's) daughter made him an outlaw at Whitehall, where he found himself disgraced and ostracized. In 1678 he was dismissed and given no further posting during Charles's lifetime.

Surprisingly, King Charles was extremely jealous of Barbara's amours in Paris. On the several occasions when she had cause to return to England, she always managed to extract large sums from the monarch, much against ministerial advice. Distance, it seemed, counted for nothing whenever the ex-Miss of State exerted her powers. John Lacy made the situation clear:

> To pay the debts, what sums can'st thou advance
> Now thy exchequer is gone into France
> To enrich a harlot, all made up of French,
> Not worthy to be call'd a whore, but wench?
> Cleaveland indeed deserv'd that noble name;
> Whose minutes lechery exceeds all fame.
> The empress Messalina tir'd in lust at least
> Thou ne're could'st have to satisfy this beast.
> Cleveland, I say, was much to be admired,
> For she was never satisfied or tired.
> Full forty men a day have swived the whore,
> Yet like a bitch she wags her tail for more.

Barbara finally returned to London for good in 1684, no doubt bored by the new austerity at the French Court since her friend, King Louis, had morganatically married the pious and devout Madame de Maintenon. She resided at Cleveland House, which she had built in the grounds of her former residence, Berkshire House. Here, she seems to have reached into the very dregs of her lust. The Earl of Dorset wrote:

> Now Churchill, Dover, see how they are sunk
> Into her loathsome, sapless, aged trunk.
> And yet remains her cunt's insatiate itch,
> And there's a devil that can hug the witch.

The 'devil' was Cardonell Goodman, referred to by many simply as 'Scum'. The son of a clergyman, sent down from Cambridge for insubordination, Scum spent five years as a backstairs page to Charles II until he was dismissed for negligence. In 1677 he had appeared at Drury Lane theatre to much acclaim, especially as Alexander the Great and Julius

Caesar. He was even more successful pursuing a lucrative second career as a highway robber, until he was captured and condemned to death. This punishment was fortuitously avoided, however, as the eighteenth-century writer Theophilus Lucas reveals:

> being condemn'd for his life, a petition was deliver'd to King Charles the Second in [Scum's] favour, praying that before he died, he might act the part of Alexander; which being granted, and His Majesty there present, he perform'd it so much to admiration that his life was granted him.

This occasion would appear to be the time when Barbara first encountered her future lover, for Lucas continues

> and afterwards the Duchess of Cleveland taking a fancy to him, he was withdrawn from the stage, and at her Grace's sole cost and charges maintain'd without acting for the future.

Scum was very greedy, and although Barbara openly admitted that he treated her appallingly, it seems that she was more distressed by his steady reluctance to wash.

Before taking up with Barbara, Scum had been so poor that he had been forced to share 'the same bed [as his friend, Captain Griffin] and the same shirt and that a duel was fought on [Scum's] appropriating the common clothing out of his turn,' according to the actor and dramatist, Colley Cibber. Ten years older than her new *amour*, Barbara adored his good looks and his larger-than-life personality. When he was found guilty of trying to poison two of her sons, Scum was ordered to pay £1,000, which he obtained on the highway. Although the relationship was a constant clash of ecstatic passion and thoughtless hatred, and allowing for his often crude and selfish manner, Scum truly cared about Barbara. On several evenings, when he was still performing, he flatly refused to allow the curtain to rise until his mistress had taken her place in the audience. One evening,

> [when] some of the actors [were] telling him that it was the Queen's express orders they should draw up the curtain, he swore several great oaths, [saying] that if the pit and boxes too were lin'd with Queens, he would not act till his Duchess was come.

Their affair continued for six more years, ending abruptly when Barbara discovered that Scum was involved in a Jacobite plot. She had had no knowledge of his political change of heart nor, consequently, of the arms and ammunition that were found at her home. They parted quickly, he escaping to France, as she fled to Tunbridge Wells.

In 1685, Charles, ailing for some time, was now nearing the end of his reign. He remained hedonistic to the finish, as John Evelyn noted on 25 January, only twelve days before the royal passing:

> I saw this evening such a sceane of profuse gaming, and luxurious dallying and profanesse, the King in the midst of his 3 concubines [Portsmouth, Cleveland and Mazarin] as I had never before.

On 6 February 1685, King Charles II died of uremia (a most unpleasant malfunctioning of the kidneys) combined with a stroke. His last words were, 'Let not poor Nellie starve.' Charles's devoted brother, the future James II, honoured this request.

The Merry Monarch was buried at Westminster Abbey. Curiously, for a man who so delighted in *éclat*, he was buried at night, 'without any manner of pomp', recorded Evelyn. His queen, never totally happy at the English Court, remained in Britain seven more years until 1692, when she returned to Portugal. As for the ex-Miss of State, her grief was genuine but short-lived; the monarch's death barely affected her lifestyle.

Barbara was sixty-four when she had news of the death of her husband, Roger Palmer, in 1705. She was unmoved. Married for forty-six years, most of that time spent in separation, they were all but strangers. But Anne, the king's eldest child by Barbara, wept. Palmer had always shown her a deep attachment even though he had spent much of his life abroad. He bequeathed to her his entire estate – all his property in the Savoy, his leaseholds in Monmouthshire, as well as jewels and plate – a natural bequest, perhaps, since there was some doubt concerning the true paternity of the girl. Was she actually the child of the Earl of Castlemaine, or was the king, or even Chesterfield, her natural father?

Four months later, and in her twilight years, the indomitable Barbara married her latest conquest. 'Beau' Fielding, a former major-general, was considered to be one of the most handsome men in town. Theophilus Lucas, however, wrote scathingly about him,

> whose vain imaginings roving after the fair sex, he distinguish'd himself always by his extraordinary dress ... to signalize himself for the greatest fop which ever appear'd in England. [He is] a volume of methodical errata, bound up in a gilt cover [whose] draper was afraid

of losing him in a labyrinth of his own cloth, it was so cover'd with the finery of the laceman.

It was the Merry Monarch himself who acknowledged Fielding as 'Handsome Beau'. Lucas explains, 'This royal notice ... made him in great vogue among several of the female sex, by whom [...] he was maintained as a stallion.' Never in possession of enough money, Beau had no compunction in 'bribing jockeys to ride foul matches'. Nor was he averse to betting on a savage cockfight, or demanding high stakes in chess and backgammon.

Fielding's greed matched Barbara's, but she was unaware of this when they met. That same avarice had energized him into an outrageous plot, involving deceit and bigamy. Unafraid of the branding of the hand, the usual punishment inflicted on exposed bigamists, he coolly laid plans to ensnare two wealthy women, intending to extract a fortune from each of them. Unfortunately for him, the deceiver became the deceived when Charlotte Villars, his accomplice-in-crime, introduced him not to the young heiress Anne Delaune ('a gentlewoman of about £20,000 portion'), whom she did not know, but to an imposter, 'a jilt of the town called Mary Wadsworth who was only recently out of prison'.

The plot had a bizarre conclusion. Fielding married Mary Wadsworth, believing her to be Anne Delaune. Playing for time, to avoid exposure Wadsworth requested that the ceremony remain a secret for a few weeks. Fielding agreed, despite his impatience.

The con man then married Barbara bigamously, demanding £500 from her immediately – to pay off his accomplice! The two weddings were separated by sixteen days.

From the day of their union, Barbara's life became a misery. Fielding extorted most of her money and then began to sell off her furniture. In desperation, she challenged him; his reply was to beat her, then lock her up and starve her. He threatened her life when he realized that she had told her family about the situation. Only when he was committed to Newgate prison did she become aware of the bigamy. (Fielding had discovered how his accomplice had tricked him and had beaten both her and the impersonating 'heiress'. They, in turn, had taken their revenge by informing the duchess of the truth.) If these events by themselves were insufficient to condemn the bigamous Fielding, a batch of his letters came into Barbara's hands, showing his cool treachery to both women, and which proved beyond doubt that he was well and truly married to Mary Wadsworth:

14 November 1705

I have not lain in my lodgings since I saw my dearest wife, and this night we shall leave them altogether to lie at her Grace's; however, I shall always keep the conveniency to meet you there when I will, and will (God willing) lie there tomorrow night, being Wednesday night, where I hope Nanette [Mary Wadsworth] will come lie with me, which she may do by coming at 10 or 11 clock to my lodgings, and lie till next morning. Pray fail not, for I long to have my dearest Nanette in my arms. Adieu, I am always yours, and loving husband ...

Fielding was convicted of bigamy, 'but escap'd burning in the hand by Her Majesty's [Queen Anne's] gracious pardon'. His marriage to Barbara was annulled in 1707; curiously, he settled into a happy and lasting relationship with Mary Wadsworth.

Barbara now left the town for the tranquillity of Chiswick, a small village on the western outskirts of the capital. There, on the bank of the river Thames, she resided at Walpole House for the last two years of her life.

My Lady Castlemaine died peacefully on 9 October 1709. The greatest beauty of her age had become of monstrous size by the end, due to the dropsy which had destroyed the remains of her beauty. Buried in St Nicholas Parish Church, Chiswick, her grave lies unmarked and forgotten in the crypt. The duchess made her final journey escorted by two dukes and four peers as pall-bearers. Once one of the richest women in England, as a result of profligacy, living well beyond her means, and her pathetic generosity to her many worthless lovers, she died lonely and penniless.

Yet memories of her remarkable beauty lived on, and do to this day. Contemporary historian Abel Boyer remembered her as 'by far the handsomest of all King Charles's mistresses, and, taking her person every way, perhaps the finest woman in England in her time.' The duchess loved life, with a sense of humour that was vulgar and bawdy even as her generosity to lovers was foolishly bountiful. She lived fully, if selfishly. Of course, there are countless reasons to condemn Barbara's turbulent rule as Miss of State but, in the end, her personality, excesses, audacity and verve ensure that she will certainly never be forgotten.

Madame de Montespan

An Affair with the Devil

'That whore will be the death of me!'

Marie Thérèse, Queen of France (1660–83)

A large chest, locked and sealed, stood near the enormous marble fireplace in the Council Chamber of the Royal Palace at Versailles. Nearby sat King Louis XIV, who, at seventy-one, was more fiercely protective than ever of his illustrious name and of the glory in which he had spent a lifetime draping it. He had earned his flattering soubriquets: Louis Dieudonné (the God-Given), Louis the Great, the Sun King, Jupiter …

Thirty-one years ago, almost to the day, the most sensational criminal inquiry of seventeenth-century France had been launched. Some of the noblest names in the country were found guilty of sinister, frequently horrific deeds that had shaken the whole of Europe. The crimes that were exposed were so heinous that a special secret court was created to conduct the trials. Poison was afoot … and many of the guilty were among the king's closest friends.

'Justice,' the king had declared at the time, 'without distinction of person, rank or sex'; yet all the while he was aiding and abetting the escape of several high-ranking ladies, whose guilt was unquestioned, but who had graced the royal bed.

Justice would run even more awry when the king's favourite, Madame de Montespan, was accused of involvement in murder, sexual perversion, blood rites, witchcraft and Satanism. One thing was certain: history could not be seen to link King Louis with the scandal. The contents of the trunk, with its all too damning evidence, must be destroyed. At a sign, Chancellor Pontchartrain broke the seals on the chest and respectfully stepped back. Europe's greatest ruling monarch now resolutely gathered up each document and dropped it carefully into the fire. It was a lengthy business. Staring at the charred final page, the king sighed deeply. Now, his *gloire* would remain untarnished; nothing remained that could trace his name to the dark, unspeakable deeds of Madame de Montespan. Fortunately for history, in this His Majesty was mistaken.

★

King Louis XIV of France was born on 5 September 1638, at the Château-Neuf Saint-Germain-en-Laye. Five years later, he succeeded his father, Louis XIII, to the throne and was crowned king the following year. His mother, Anne of Austria, had had conferred upon her 'the free, absolute and complete administration of the kingdom's affairs during the minority' of her son. With considerable support and advice from chief minister Cardinal Mazarin (who was certainly her lover, possibly her morganatic husband), she proved to be an excellent regent until her son, aged thirteen in 1651, reached his royal majority.

As a child, Louis survived the anti-Royalist *Fronde*, the violent civil war which pitted rebel aristocrats against the Crown. He learned quickly about fear and deprivation, at the same time never losing sight of his great destiny. With his mother's unflinching support and Mazarin's cunning connivances, he subdued his enemies and gradually converted them from near-feudal ruffians into civilized courtiers. Their eventual polish and sophistication, acquired in the artificial hothouse atmosphere at the Courts of Saint-Germain and Versailles, became the envy of every royal house in Europe. During his seventy-two-year sovereignty – the longest in European history – Louis was the supreme absolutist whose political acumen and wily, far-seeing stratagems led to France's continually increasing prosperity during the first half of those years. The king's policy was to keep the aristocrats under one roof, allowing them absolutely no involvement in state affairs. They may have needed to supervise their estates, but it soon became evident that absence from Court was anathema to favour and advancement. After the death of Cardinal Mazarin, Louis relied totally upon his own judgement, his ego reaching an early zenith when, on 13 April 1655, he informed the Parlement de Paris: '*L'État? C'est moi.*' ('The State? I am the State!') Parlement was resentful; at seventeen Louis didn't care a jot.

Intelligent and good-looking, he had penetrating, blue-grey eyes, luxuriant dark hair, and a sensual mouth, emphasized by a cleft chin. At 5 feet 5 inches, he was not tall – one of the reasons he eventually set the fashion for high heels and tall wigs. King Louis' sexual appetite was gargantuan. He was initiated in his early teens by Madame de Beauvais, one of his mother's ladies-in-waiting, who was twenty years his senior and 'somewhat wanton and alluring'. The lady must have been an excellent tutor, for Louis remained sexually active throughout his long life. At fifteen, he took full advantage of the royal prerogative whenever opportunity presented itself. Not surprisingly, at seventeen he contracted gonorrhoea.

In his seventies, his morganatic wife, the pious and scheming Mme de Maintenon, sought advice from the Vatican about putting a restraint on her rampant husband, who still expected her to fulfil her marital duties at least twice a day. The Vatican tutted in sympathy, advising that she grin and bear the royal ardour since in so doing she would be effectively stopping him from falling into the darker sins of adultery and fornication.

Louis' first grand infatuation was with Marie Mancini, niece of Cardinal Mazarin – early nipped in the bud by a watchful Queen Mother, who was not impressed by the serious prospect of an imminent wedding with a minor Italian aristocrat. Louis' attentions turned next to the spirited Henrietta of England (always addressed as *Madame*), wife of Philippe, Duc d'Orléans, his homosexual brother – until he fell violently in love with Louise-Françoise de la Baume le Blanc, an impoverished minor aristocrat who had reached Court by the kindness of the Orléans household, where she became a maid of honour to *Madame*.

Mlle le Blanc was sweetness itself, with a country-fresh complexion, china-blue eyes, silver-blonde hair and a delicious body, hardly impeded by a slight limp. She was also somewhat vapid, sentimental, a trifle stupid and certainly no conversationalist. The novelist Mme de la Fayette thought her 'very sweet, very pretty, and very naïve'. Mme de Sévigné, famed letter-writing gossip, wrote to her daughter that the girl 'is as modest as a violet, shrinking into the grass to hide'. (Mme de Sévigné might be forgiven her sniffy disdain: at one time her daughter had had reason to entertain hopes of becoming the king's mistress.) Mlle le Blanc would have much preferred to have enjoyed her royal lover's company in private, rather than be a target for the veiled jibes and whispered satires of a malicious Court. Touched by her simplicity, Louis promptly raised her to Duchesse de la Vallière.

By 1661, it was common knowledge that La Vallière was the king's mistress. No one believed that the new duchesse had the personality to hold the king's attention for long – but they were wrong. Anne of Austria reluctantly tolerated the liaison, recognizing the natural urges of her over-sexed son. However, she drew the line at his officially installing La Vallière as *maîtresse déclarée*.

Thus, the lovers' more intimate moments were conducted in secret places at peculiar times. This was a curious subjugation, given Louis' god-related opinion of himself and his destiny. Asserting himself, two years later in 1663 (just in time for the delivery of her first child), the king installed La Vallière in an apartment of her own. His mother threatened to enter a convent, a convenient escape at that time for high-born ladies with unsolvable problems. When she realized her son's adamance, she thought better of it. As soon as it was born, the baby was whisked away into obscurity. La Vallière would bear her royal lover three more children, of which only two survived infancy.

In 1666, Anne of Austria died. After the weeping and wailing ceased, the monarch took a firm hold of the royal reins, declared La Vallière his official mistress and legitimized their daughter, Marie-Anne de Bourbon, as Mademoiselle de Blois. In 1667, La Vallière was created Duchesse de Vaujours. She was delighted. She had no idea that the elevation was a final pay-off to salve the conscience of a grateful but increasingly bored monarch. A translated street-song put it cheekily:

> La Vallière, so we've been told,
> Is losing favour fast;
> In bed with her the King is cold
> With *ennui* unsurpassed.

At twenty-nine years of age, God's representative on earth had suddenly become infatuated with another, far more tantalizing love goddess. Her name was Athénaïs, Marquise de Montespan.

★

Françoise-Athénaïs de Mortemart-Rochechouart – the future Madame de Montespan – was born on 5 October 1641, at Tonnay-Charente in south-west France. Her mother reared her five children as she herself had lived, surrounded by the arts and with a healthy respect for God. She encouraged their marked individuality and hauled them off to prayer several times a week. Religion became a deciding influence on her two youngest daughters, who took the veil shortly after completing the convent education bestowed on most young girls of their station.

Françoise first encountered the king in 1661 when, in her late teens, she was formally presented at Court. She performed the required three *révérences* with elegance and natural grace; the king barely noticed her.

Both her parents were already in the service of the royal family: her father as First Gentleman of the Bedchamber, and her mother a lady-in-waiting to the Queen Mother. Her only brother, Louis-Victor, Duc de Vivonne, was very popular at Court. At eight years he was chosen as a *menin*, a gentleman-in-waiting to the boy-king, two years his junior. His good nature and happy disposition made him the young king's favourite childhood playmate and, later, his trusted adult companion.

Françoise immediately took up her duties as a maid of honour to *Madame*. Her remarkable appearance and superb deportment made an instant impression in the Court's extravagant ballets; she was rewarded with illustrious partners in Philippe, the king's brother (known as *Monsieur*) and King Louis, himself an accomplished dancer. In 1652, he had appeared as the Rising Sun in the thirteen-hour *Ballet de la Nuit*. Handsome, young, radiating health and energy, the allegory was immediate. Since that performance, Louis *was* the 'Sun King', a soubriquet by which he is remembered to this day.

Françoise was exceptionally beautiful, with flawless skin, suspiciously fair hair (Louis preferred blondes) and a shapely body. Primi Visconti, sometime Venetian Ambassador to Paris, wrote 'Her face is sheer perfection.' All the Mortemarts were vibrant and intelligent. *Monsieur* regarded Françoise and her older sister Gabrielle as *femmes d'esprits* whose barbed wit and scandalous stories made them the most popular ladies at Court. Of the two, Gabrielle was the more outrageous. *Monsieur* and the king adored her, *Monsieur* for her undiluted bitchery, which matched his own; the king, for her directness. She was a terrible snob. One day, she informed an amused, tolerant Louis that she thought little of his Bourbon ancestry.

'May one enquire why, *madame*?'

'Because, Sire, only La Rochefoucauld is worthy of comparison with the Mortemarts.'

At seventeen, Gabrielle married the Marquis de Thianges. Residing at Court some time before her sister's arrival, she had willingly fallen prey to the king's insatiable sexual appetite, a practice she would repeat from time to time.

As for Françoise, she was in her element at Court. She responded wholeheartedly to the elaborate sophistication and intricate etiquette, never questioning for a moment its shallowness, or its ostentatious pomp and ceremony. She was not long established at Saint-Germain when she began using her preferred second name, Athénaïs.

It was also not long before she became implicated in her mistress's complicated marriage. *Madame* was embarrassed by her husband's effeminacy, a persuasion early encouraged by his mother in order to protect Louis' throne from sibling rivalry. She despised her husband's male lovers, especially the Chevaliers Remecourt and Lorraine, the latter his preferred favourite. Lorraine, an extremely handsome bisexual, made no bones about using his good looks to further his advancement. ('Baneful vampires', Athénaïs called them both.) Despising *Madame*, Lorraine was unconcerned by the mounting friction he caused in the Orléans household. Athénaïs became caught up in one of these ongoing quarrels; blatantly ignoring her official role, she took *Monsieur*'s part. There had been rumours that Athénaïs, having temporarily weaned *Monsieur* away from the boys, had had a brief affair with him herself. Mme de la Fayette emphatically thought otherwise … but such an affair would account for the Chevaliers' detestation of the marquise.

Madame was infuriated by Athénaïs' treachery; Athénaïs herself was little concerned, having other things on her mind. She had fallen deeply in love with the Marquis de Noirmontier, a handsome, eligible young man whom her father turned away in favour of Henri, Marquis d'Antin. *His* ancient family name – Pardaillan de Gondrin – was as old as Mortemart. Unfortunately, Henri was killed in a duel. By a strange irony, Noirmontier acted as one of his seconds and was forced to flee the country to escape the death penalty, which was demanded by the king for this most condemned manner of gratifying honour.

Antin's younger brother, Louis Henri, Marquis de Montespan, made a special journey to Paris to console the desolate young woman. Athénaïs quickly perked up: their mutual attraction was instant. Eighteen months later, on 21 January 1663, they were married, their union being regarded as a love-match (as opposed to the pre-arranged union promulgated for gain or position, common at the time). Athénaïs' role as maid of honour was, of course, terminated *ipso facto*.

A year younger than his bride, Montespan possessed the dark good looks of the southerner. He was impetuous, brave, daring; he was also petulant and pig-headed, qualities which overbalanced the good and which Athénaïs would discover early on with increasing distaste. In a very short time, their initial love had soured, the couple barely managing a public show of devotion for appearances' sake. Monetary quarrels were frequent. Athénaïs' dowry was on loan to Montespan *père,* while his son, an inveterate gambler, had a penchant for losing. Soon, Athénaïs would be compelled to pawn her prized diamond earrings to help pay debts approaching a million *livres.* The solution would have been for the couple to return to the Montespan country seat, where temptation was nil and the monotonous landscape matched the social activity. On 15 May 1667, M. de Montespan wrote to his wife:

> The more magnificent the Court is, the more uneasy do I become. Wealth and opulence are needed there [...] I promise you that our stay in the Provinces shall last no longer than is necessary – three, four, five, let us say six years [...] By the time we come back we shall both of us still be young ...

But Athénaïs flatly refused to leave Paris, since her happiness and escape from marital frustration lay at Court. Increasingly, Athénaïs' problems fuelled an ambition to shed a worthless husband and replace La Vallière in the king's affections. But how? M. de Montespan was much nearer the truth than he realized when he wrote back:

> You are deceiving me, madame, and it is your intention to dishonour me.

On 17 November 1663, Athénaïs gave birth to a daughter, Marie-Christine. Her lack of motherly concern was blatantly apparent when, although weak, she immediately left her bed to appear in a Court ballet, *Amours déguisés,* partnered by *Monsieur.* But this delicious entertainment was a mere *soupçon* compared to the grand *fête* given by the king the following May in honour of La Vallière. *Plaisirs de l'Ile Enchantée,* based on *Orlando Furioso* by Ariosto, had more magnificent spectacle, innovative stage machinery and special effects than had so far been witnessed in the glorious new gardens of the château at Versailles. The celebration lasted for eight days – an orgy of music, theatre, banquets, games, masquerades, balls and opera, climaxing in a brilliant fireworks display. No *maîtresse en titre* could have asked for more; and no lady of the Court was more jealous than Mme de Montespan.

★

King Louis XIV married Marie Thérèse of Spain in 1660. It was common knowledge that the king's union with the Infanta, daughter of Philip IV of Spain and of Elizabeth (daughter of Henri IV of France), was a political necessity. Marie Thérèse was small and very plain and, due to repeated in-breeding, something of a dullard. While Louis was not in love with his wife, he did his marital duty by France ('twice a month', noted Primi Visconti) and invariably slept with her nightly, after enjoying the company and more sensual delights of the current mistress. The queen learned to hate every one of them in turn. She would bear Louis six children, the first, known as *Monseigneur*, being the only one to survive.

In 1664, Athénaïs was chosen as one of the queen's six *dames d'honneurs*. As well as admiring her social graces, the queen considered her to be that rare thing at Court: a model of virtue and sweet innocence. Everyone was well aware of Athénaïs' ambition and thought the situation amusing, particularly since it was common knowledge that the king was surprisingly indifferent to the marquise's undoubted charms. Louis detested being pursued; unfortunately, as he commented to his brother, the marquise tried too hard to secure his attentions.

The following year, Athénaïs crossly gave birth to her second child, the Marquis d'Antin. Both she and her sister, Gabrielle, were extremely irritated by La Vallière's sentimentality and her cow-like devotion to the king. From personal boudoir experience, Gabrielle knew that the king needed stimulating every bit as much above his navel as he did below, a fact the present *maîtresse en titre* seemed incapable of effecting. Silently agreeing with these shrewd observations, Athénaïs now set about using La Vallière's weaknesses to her own advantage. With the ruthless manoeuvring of a true vanquisher, she initiated a closer friendship with the unsuspecting mistress, stimulated by an obvious logic: 'Closer to the favourite, closer to the king.'

La Vallière was enchanted to have the enormously popular Athénaïs seeking her out. Within a short time, she had invited her new friend to share her apartments. Never did the cat have an easier *entrée* into the birdcage! La Vallière noticed with gratification that the king seemed more relaxed; he laughed much more since Athénaïs had moved in; he also seemed more predisposed to extend his daily visits. No conversationalist, and never comfortable with sex (she tolerated Louis' passion with a heavy sense of religious guilt), La Vallière nonetheless loved the king with all her heart, and was pleased to see him more settled. Louis, for his part, had never denied Athénaïs' glowing beauty; now, he was discovering the extent of her wit, intelligence and her bubbling sense of humour. Lacking those gifts himself, he valued them in others. During the king's visits, Athénaïs went out of her way to be accommodating and gay, and always attentive whenever Louis expressed an opinion.

But one swallow never made a summer; amicable conversation was no guarantee of La Montespan achieving her ultimate goal. The progress being slow along the pathway to the king's heart, the ambitious marquise decided it was time to seek help of a darker nature.

★

During the sixteenth and seventeenth centuries, while the belief in, and pursuit of, witchcraft and sorcery were punishable by law, there was nonetheless a widespread belief in the occult and supernatural powers. Through Gabrielle, her more experienced sister, Athénaïs was brought to the house of the well-known sorceress, Catherine Deshayes Monvoisin. La Voisin, as she was known, had been successful in creating for herself a profitable niche within aristocratic circles. Many a courtier had sought her advice in solving amatory or marital problems. She had charms, potions, charts, ointments and love philtres for every emotional situation. This was but a front to disguise a much more sinister practice, as those regularly seeking La Voisin's services knew. She was well-connected in the Paris underworld; for the right price, she would turn her hand to abortion or a black mass; and certainly, she knew a thing or two about hastening on an advantageous death!

Athénaïs was totally honest about her ambitions and her need for help; La Voisin supplied the goods. The marquise considered her money well spent when the king suddenly became noticeably more attentive, just at the time when M. de Montespan conveniently decided to embark alone on a six-month visit to his remote estates in the Pyrenees. The king's interest in La Montespan was confirmed when, in December, Louis gave a grand *fête, Le Ballet des Muses*, in her honour. The situation was complex; although Louis lusted for La Montespan, he was reluctant to make the final break with La Vallière, the pregnant mother of three of his children.

In 1667, the king suddenly left Paris. War was in the air with the 'cheese merchants', as Louis derogatorily referred to the Dutch. Since Philip IV of Spain had been somewhat remiss about paying his daughter's dowry of 500,000 gold *écus*, Louis decided to take his due in territories; in particular, the Spanish Netherlands. This War of Devolution, as it became known, was a glorious plume and lace affair, with the invading army parading ostentatiously in a myriad of peacock uniforms. The king had made it known that he expected every man 'to dress magnificently', as befitted a member of the military marching under the flag of Europe's greatest monarch.

Louis sent for the ladies to come and watch the progress – a common practice at the time – while he preened himself in all his *gloire*. Mme de Montespan was among them; conveniently pregnant, La Vallière had not been invited. Imagine the surprise when the swollen favourite suddenly appeared in her own coach in a desperate attempt to combat what she already knew to be a lost cause. The queen, usually outwardly docile where the mistresses were concerned, was enraged. She commanded La Vallière to return immediately. Yet not only did La Vallière remain, on Louis' intervention she rode in the same coach as Marie Thérèse. She was an embarrassed hanger-on in the presence of a tight-lipped, angry queen, whose entourage, following the royal lead, expressed collective disdain.

At Avesnes, dodging between the queen's wrath and La Vallière's suspicions, King Louis made Athénaïs his unofficial, secret mistress. She was twenty-seven. From the beginning, the liaison was more wild and passionate than sentimental and loving. Despite the attempt at secrecy everyone was aware of the affair when, for instance, Mme de Montespan's absence from the queen's card table – a coveted seat she would never vacate without good reason – coincided with the king's sudden need for privacy to deal with urgent documents and pressing affairs of state. On several occasions, he entered the queen's bedroom at dawn, again pleading the strain of serious decision and the pressure of correspondence. Amazingly, Marie Thérèse believed him, despite her knowledge of the monarch's inflexible daily routine. Courtiers even joked that you could look at a clock at any one time, and you would know exactly where His Majesty was and what he was doing.

On 4 October 1667, La Vallière gave birth to Louis, Comte de Vermandois, her fourth and last child by the king. Once again a royal bastard was whisked away from its mother; she would not be allowed to see her son for several years. Nor did La Vallière see much of the king after the delivery; Louis was by now desperately in love with the Marquise de Montespan.

★

The king officially recognized Mme de Montespan as his *maîtresse en titre* in 1668, although the declaration was closely guarded as a precaution against the irascible, unpredictable Marquis de Montespan. La Vallière wept bitterly, her short-lived outbursts against her treacherous 'friend' meeting with little sympathy at Court. The ex-favourite's wish to enter a Carmelite convent was denied her by the king, who required her to play a part in a humiliating cover-up to gull the Church, the Court, and Athénaïs' husband.

Montespan himself was in the south, subduing border marauders, when the leaked news of his wife's official recognition reached him. He seethed with anger; an unusual reaction, since most husbands accepted the inevitability of royal desire, knowing their compliance would be amply rewarded. Even Montespan's father rejoiced. No more worries about unpaid debts, he told his son; Athénaïs would see to those!

Unknown to La Montespan, her husband was in truth behaving no better than she, having broken his marital vows on numerous occasions. He had been particularly frolicsome with a lush, under-age, peasant girl, whom he had disguised as one of his soldiers and who rode aggressively with his men when she wasn't pleasuring the marquis.

Meanwhile, the country was celebrating the birth of the fifth child of France. Numerous miscarriages and stillbirths were blamed not on the queen, but on Louis the Magnificent, whose sperm (said the royal physicians) was always at the dregs after the monarch had been lusting with his various mistresses.

Back in Paris, when the marquis met his wife, he insulted her in language originating in a bawdy house. Not to be outdone, and because she was rather good at it, Athénaïs retaliated in kind. The Court loved the vulgar display, and even more so when Montespan, all eyes on Athénaïs, gave her face a resounding slap.

This was only the beginning. In his determination to humiliate and embarrass the sovereign, the marquis attired himself and his two children in mourning and had a requiem mass said for 'the loss of my children's mother, my own dearly-departed wife'. With his coach bearing the horns of cuckoldry at each corner, he drove to the royal residence, where he paraded himself in front of the palace wearing the same symbol of humiliation on his head. He became a laughing stock, a joke – but so did the king. Montespan let it be known that he intended to contract 'an unpleasant distemper', preferably syphilis, which would infect his Majesty through his 'whore'. He set out on an odyssey of brothel-cruising with this intention. 'He had only to look around the Court if he was really serious!' commented the diarist, Saint-Simon. He had a point; the Court was a hotbed of sexual disease. A furious Louis disbanded Montespan's company and banished the marquis to his southern estates.

Louis longed to have children by his new mistress. He was aware, however, that the unpredictable marquis would have the law on his side in claiming any offspring from Athénaïs as his own. Furthermore the church, always having turned a lowered, if not blind eye to a sovereign's extramarital affairs, commented little about a young, ambitious mistress: but a *folie d'amour* involving double adultery was intolerable. Thus the Archbishop of Sens, coincidentally Montespan's uncle, took his nephew's part in the scandal. He published an angry treatise against adultery and then publicly denounced a woman of his congregation for her adulterous liaison. His intention could not have been plainer. Athénaïs' furious complaints to the king resulted in the archbishop being confined to Sens. Nevertheless, the incident made Louis aware of the delicacy of the situation. As a safeguard, he installed La Vallière and Mme de Montespan – they had made an uneasy reconciliation – in adjoining apartments in the Palace of the Tuileries. The Court dubbed it *Chez les Dames*. There, with barely a nod to the ex-favourite, Louis would continue his grand progress through the apartments of the unhappy ci-devant, until he reached the delights which awaited him in the arms of La Montespan. The message to the Court was clever and clear: no one, including M. de Montespan, would really know which of the two mistresses Louis was enjoying.

In 1668, Athénaïs became pregnant with the first of seven children she would bear the king. She designed a peculiar, loose-fitting garment, a *robe battante*, falsely convincing herself that it hid her much-increased girth. She gave birth to a daughter in March 1669, the child being taken away immediately by Athénaïs' personal maid, Mlle d'Oeillets. Beyond these facts, little is known of the girl, who died in her third year. Exactly one year later, on 31 March 1670, the king was present when Athénaïs was brought to bed with her second baby, Louis-Auguste, the future Duc du Maine. The child was confided to the Comte de Lauzun, who kept him in Paris.

The lovers agreed that they needed someone absolutely trustworthy who had the tact, intelligence and patience to be tutor to their children. After some thought, a Madame Françoise Scarron was the final choice: a slightly older woman, intelligent, not unattractive, but certainly no beauty. She would be perfect.

Françoise d'Aubigné had escaped a dreary life by marrying Paul Scarron, a burlesque poet of some talent. The marriage had proved a happy one, although sexual activity disgusted her, being conducted orally due to Scarron's partial paralysis. His death in 1660 had left his wife near-destitute. Thus, when eventually the post of royal tutor was offered to her, she accepted with delight; it was exactly the sort of niche the widow had longed for. Mme de Montespan liked and trusted the new tutor immediately. Athénaïs could not know then that the woman she had befriended would one day ruin her life.

★

For a time, power sat well on the shapely shoulders of the favourite. Mme de Sévigné wrote to her daughter that 'her success, at first conducted in secret, became thunderous and triumphant.' Everyone commented on her sparkling contribution to Court life. Meanwhile, the king insisted that Athénaïs apply for an immediate marital separation. It turned out to be a tedious, drawn-out, four-year struggle. One day, Princess de Soubise, briefly the king's mistress, remarked to Athénaïs on the king's widely recognized love for her.

'Not love, *madame*,' La Montespan replied reflectively. 'Louis is a King and, as such, he must own the most beautiful woman at Court.'

La Soubise flushed. An acknowledged great beauty herself, the unintended insult was a mark of Athénaïs' increasing arrogance. Queen Marie Thérèse grew to detest her. 'That whore will be the death of me!' she shrieked repeatedly.

Meanwhile, despite the earlier prediction of Montespan's father, his daughter-in-law did nothing to replenish the family coffers. When the old man died suddenly, he bequeathed to his eldest son a load of debts to add to his own. Powerless without money, the marquis was thus compelled to seek the king's pardon, which was duly given; Louis knew the danger of providing his mistress's husband with the opportunity to cross the nearby Spanish border, free to spread unpleasant (but true) stories about him.

Conversely, Athénaïs made sure her own family benefited from her position. Her brother Vivonne became Commander of the Galleys; her father was made Mayor of Paris and her youngest sister, Marie-Madeleine, despite enormous opposition from Rome on account of her extreme youth, became the Abbess of Fontevrault; she was twenty-four. Marie-Madeleine remained at Fontevrault for the next thirty-four years, until her death. It was one of life's ironies that, while 'the pearl of all Abbesses' was writing well-received treatises on morality, her older sister was nightly committing double-adultery in the king's bed.

★

On 29 June 1670, the whole Court was aghast to learn of the unexpected death of *Madame*; she had suddenly crumpled and died in great pain nine hours after drinking a glass of chicory water.

'[But] the glass of water could not have been poisoned,' commented Voltaire, 'since Mme de la Fayette and another person drank the remainder without experiencing the slightest discomfort.'

Yet the morbid rumour persisted; poison was suspected, even after an autopsy produced no sign of any. Lord Montagu, the English Ambassador, was convinced of foul play. Athénaïs, too, embraced the poison theory. She was appalled at what she saw as a clumsy cover-up, although she knew it was meant to pacify *Madame*'s loving brother, Charles II of England. She wrote in her memoirs:

> According to the written statement, which was also published in the newspapers, *Madame* had been carried off by an attack of bilious colic. Five or six bribed physicians certified to that effect, and a lying set of depositions, made for mere form's sake, bore out their statements in due course.

In truth, at twenty-six and without knowing it, *Madame* was a very sick woman. A dried-out liver was the least of her ailments. Some short time before her death, she had delivered a stillborn child, which, according to the doctors, had been rotting inside her for more than ten days. Notwithstanding all this, the Court suspected *Monsieur* of killing his wife, aided and abetted by his lover, the Chevalier de Lorraine. The death deeply affected the king. He told Athénaïs: 'If this crime is my brother's handiwork, his head shall fall on the scaffold.' This, of course, would never happen; the Abbé Bossuet saw to that when, according to Athénaïs, he

> was apparently as desirous of being obliging as the doctors. His homily led off with such fulsome praise of *Monsieur* that, from that day forward, he lost all his credit, and sensible people thereafter only looked upon him as a vile sycophant.

While the scandal faded, it was never forgotten. Within a few years, people would have good cause to remember *Madame*'s ghastly end.

★

An astrologer had once warned *Monsieur* that he would marry more than once; Philippe had thought this very amusing until, in 1671, he found himself wed to Elizabeth-Charlotte, Princess-Palatine of Bavaria. Heavy-boned, solidly built, she was the antithesis of the attractive, lively first *Madame*. Athénaïs, in the assurance of her own devastating beauty, commented that 'surely it is not allowable to come into the world with such a face and form, such a voice [...] as this singular princess displayed.' Fortunately, Liselotte (as Elizabeth-Charlotte was known) had the king's full support, their mutual enjoyment of long walks and riding providing an instant bond.

Blunt, often eccentric, Liselotte was also observant. She soon had the measure of Court intrigue surrounding the favourite, who, for some reason, she immediately detested. Whatever the occasion, she attempted to humiliate Athénaïs by mocking her at every opportunity. She reached the apogee of her insults by wearing in public ridiculous wigs in the style Athénaïs wore her hair; she also referred to her as 'that Montespan woman'. Unfortunately, Liselotte had not been warned of the famous Mortemart devastating repartee, or that, while the Montespan's beauty was for the king, her sarcasm was reserved for her enemies. After a particularly unpleasant encounter one day, Athénaïs blazed:

'Madame, you managed to give up your religion in order to marry a French prince; you might just as well have left behind your gross Palatine vulgarity also.'

Monsieur, embarrassed, apologized for his wife's behaviour.

'Allow me to quote to you the speech of Mlle de Montpensier [first cousin to the king],' responded Athénaïs icily. 'You had a charming and accomplished wife; you ought to have prevented her from being poisoned, and then we should not have to have had this hag at Court!'

Liselotte spoke the truth, though, when she said that 'the Montespan woman derides La Vallière in public, treats her abominably, and obliges the king to follow suit.' The whole Court knew that the ci-devant mistress was deeply unhappy. The truth was, Athénaïs felt threatened by La Vallière; after nearly three years of secrecy and subterfuge, she wanted her position publicly acknowledged. Athénaïs harangued the king with frequent outbursts of ill-temper and salty language; Louis took it all in his stride.

In 1671, the king set out for Flanders. There were no important battles to win and, therefore, no need for the journey, other than to descend like Zeus and make his godlike presence felt. He would have liked nothing better than to leave the ladies behind, except for La Montespan. Louis was too wise to do this, knowing the scandal such a slight to the queen would cause. So, Marie Thérèse went along, together with an entourage which included a reluctant La Vallière. The monarch's wife was fêted, but it was Athénaïs who received the real homage. Marie Thérèse, never over-bright, was fortunately unaware of this.

In 1672, King Louis paid a much more aggressive visit to Flanders, intending to attack Holland from the north-east. With over 100,000 men, he was determined to bring the 'cheese merchants' to heel. Even stronger than his political motive, the Sun King needed to teach the Dutch a lesson for the manner in which they lampooned and caricatured his sex life. However, on 12 June 1672, he abandoned the siege of Amsterdam on the eve of the city's surrender, to return to Versailles and Mme de Montespan for the delivery of their third child. Meanwhile, the Dutch put paid to a return attack by bravely opening up their dykes and flooding vast areas. The Comte de Vexin was born one week later. Louis was delighted and encouraging.

'Be of good courage, madame; present princes to the Crown, and let those be scandalized who will!'

One year later, the siege of Maastricht was in progress. Heavily pregnant – she was nothing if not fecund – Athénaïs left the entourage at Tournai. There, on 1 June 1673, she gave birth to her and Louis' fourth child, who would be known as Mlle de Nantes. Mme Scarron was with Athénaïs at the delivery and hastened back to Paris with the tiny bundle. Athénaïs happily tossed her *robe battante* to one side for another year and, more confident than ever, rejoined the queen and La Vallière near the front. The wayside crowds were fascinated by the spectacle of the 'Three Queens' sitting side by side.

At this time, Athénaïs' ambition reached new heights when she began to imagine her future as the king's morganatic wife, should the queen die. Loved and hated as she was, there were many who would have welcomed this. La Montespan had the breeding, panache, glamour, personality and sense of occasion to fill the sovereign role admirably. Primi Visconti wrote: 'She is Queen in all but name.' The King of Arda (Africa) sent an embassy to Versailles, bearing gifts of exotic animals for the king and queen. For the 'loved one', Athénaïs recalled:

> They presented me with a necklace of large pearls and two bracelets of priceless value, splendid Oriental sapphires, the finest in the world.

There were other signs of the marquise's high favour. Her apartment was twice the size of the queen's, for instance, and in public Louis often chose to ride beside his mistress while the queen followed in her own coach. Enchanted by the novelty of a mistress actually refusing jewellery ('it seems extraordinary, but she will not listen to reason when it comes to presents'), Louis insisted that Colbert, Minister of Finance, prepare a collection of rare esteem. He also tossed in another expensive bauble, the estate at Clagny on which he would build 'a palace to rival Versailles, only smaller'. Too small for Athénaïs, she dismissed it as only worthy of a dancer. Fresh designs were drawn up and executed by the royal architect, François Mansard. For ten years, 1,200 men worked day and night to complete the palace at a cost of nearly three million *livres*. Mme de Montespan was satisfied. The Court dubbed it the *Hôtel de Vénus*.

The king finally gave his consent for La Vallière to enter a Carmelite convent. She left Court for the last time in 1674; ironically, having taken her last meal with the outside world at Athénaïs' table. Louis told her he could never forgive her for preferring God to himself.

Athénaïs was most solicitous when the king had a sudden return of the gnawing headaches he had known over the last few years. Sometimes they were so fierce that he felt giddy; occasionally his sight was temporarily affected and he had been known to faint. The Court physicians were unable to diagnose. Louis would not discover the cause until the beginning of the next decade.

Two years later, in 1676, the Court was electrified when the Marquise de Brinvilliers was arrested and found guilty of poisoning several of her family, including her father, sisters, two brothers and an attempt on her husband. Tried and found guilty, she was executed on 16 July 1676 in the Place de Grève. Mme de Sévigné told her daughter:

> At length it is all over. La Brinvilliers is in the air; after her execution, her poor little body was flung into a great fire, and her ashes dispersed by the wind, so that whenever we breathe, we shall draw in some particles of her, and by the communication of the minute spirits, we may be all infected with an itch for poisoning …

How right she was! The Brinvilliers affair opened a tiny can of worms, which was about to expose the biggest scandal of seventeenth-century France.

★

Although the king considered Mme Scarron a pious bore, both he and Mme de Montespan were delighted at the progress and discipline she had instilled into the royal brood. In gratitude, Louis gave her money enough to buy a marquisate at Maintenon, a title she lived by ever after. Mme de Maintenon's perseverance with the little Duc du Maine's leg infirmity was steadily gaining a more positive prognosis. He was a delightful, well-loved child and Louis' favourite offspring. La Fontaine, writer of fables, lived up to his reputation for sycophancy, calling the boy 'the son of Jupiter'. Considering the child's short, half-paralysed leg, this was a somewhat hyperbolic dislocation. Being one of Athénaïs' *protégés*, however, La Fontaine had discovered the benefits resulting from a well-placed, if superficial, *bon mot*.

As the autumn of 1672 slipped into winter, the king was agreeably surprised to find that for some time now he had been increasingly drawn to the pious governess. He didn't know, of course, that Mme de Maintenon, with the aid of Bishop Bossuet, was quite determined to bring Louis to God and make him repent the error of his libidinous ways. Athénaïs observed the growing bond:

> I distinguished on the part of the King a gradual and increasing attachment for the governess, and at the same time a negligence in regard to me, a coldness, a cooling down …

In 1674 and 1677 respectively, Athénaïs bore the king two more daughters: Mlle de Tours and Mlle de Blois (this latter title bestowed upon La Montespan's daughter once La Vallière's child, the first Mlle de Blois, renounced the name on the day she married the Prince de Conti). Athénaïs was also granted a legal separation from the Marquis de Montespan, who had been found guilty of profligacy, lack of financial stability and physical cruelty. Ironically, Athénaïs now had no doubts about the distinct change in Louis' attitude towards her. She recognized, not without panic, that the early ecstasies had dwindled to predictability; she no longer held any surprises for her lover. Worse, the dawn of middle age seemed only to have increased the king's libido and his need for casual encounters, while the once-ravishing marquise had surrendered to gross embonpoint – the result of good living and annual childbearing. Climbing into her coach, Comte de Rébenac had observed that 'each leg was thicker than a thin man!' The young Marquis de Feuquières, son of the Ambassador to Sweden and close to Athénaïs, noted her unhappiness: 'She drowns herself in perfume, hoping to win back the king. Is she so unhappy that she's forgotten he detests excess?'

Louis took advantage of his waning feelings for Athénaïs by occasionally bedding her maid, Mme d'Oeillets. Visconti wrote:

> She [d'Oeillets] seemed to be very sure that she had had several children by him! She is not beautiful, but the King was often with her when her mistress was not around, or was ill.

Louis' many dalliances usually lasted no more than a few days. The exquisite Princess de Soubise was one, accepting her ultimate sacrifice stoically, correctly surmising that time spent in the royal bed could make her adored, much older (by forty years) husband rich and favoured. The situation was much more serious in the case of Mme de Ludres, a maid of honour to the second *Madame*. She was an experienced adventuress and a would-be blackmailer, who had long since deserted the cloisters in favour of a profligate life as mistress to several men, including Athénaïs' brother, the Duc de Vivonne. She then set out to ensnare the king. Three years older than La Montespan, she was, physically, still all that the marquise had been in her youth. Loathing her, Athénaïs called her 'rag-bag'. The scene seemed set for 'La Belle de Ludres' to dethrone the favourite. But the affair ended as suddenly as it had begun when Mme de Ludres boasted of a success she had not yet achieved. Louis' brief entanglement cost the taxpayer a 200,000 francs honorarium. A triumphant Athénaïs sailed back into power as though for the first time – renewed, invigorated and determined. Mme de Sévigné wrote of her as being considerably slimmer, ablaze in diamonds, '… her back is perfectly straight and her looks are amazing'. The indefatigable Sun King was in love all over again!

The governess, now addressed as Mme de Maintenon, was irritated; this phoenix-like revival interfered with her struggle for the king's spirituality. A clever and unscrupulous schemer, she invoked the concerted aid of some of her more intimate connections in the Church. At Easter, when His Majesty paid special attention to his devotions, she plotted with Bishop Bossuet, tutor to the Dauphin and an inspired preacher; she consulted with the Jesuit theologian, Louis Bourdaloue, whose sermons were brilliant and frequently disturbing. (And they were lengthy – so lengthy that ladies discreetly fitted special receptacles known as *bourdalous* under their dresses for convenient relief during each three-hour ordeal.) This coordinated attack wore down the king. Just before Easter 1675, he dismissed La Montespan, and headed straight for holy communion.

But anyone who believed that Athénaïs had finally been demoted hadn't reckoned with the marquise's flirtation with the black arts. An interesting conversation with La Voisin and a couple of her cronies resulted in a few spells being cast, a clutch of love philtres being purchased, and a lot of money exchanging hands.

After a short time, and with more inexplicable headaches and dizziness, Louis reclaimed his mistress. Although they met in a room filled with plain old granddames, they soon escaped and gave vent to the built-up passions of several weeks. This was to be the peak of Athénaïs' reign; like an Indian summer, it was regrettably short-lived. To welcome the favourite's return to Versailles, Madame de Sévigné recalls that M. de Langlée, an authority on sartorial elegance, presented Athénaïs with 'a dress of gold on gold, all edged with gold [...] which makes up the most divinest of stuffs ever invented by man.'

In June 1678, Athénaïs presented Louis with their seventh child, the Comte de Toulouse, probably the outcome of that impassioned reunion some months before. Mme de Maintenon was voluble; the birth was further salt in the wound of a woman who had felt uncharitable since Mlle de Blois' birth the year before.

'Neither of the children are pleasing to the eye,' she complained peevishly to Athénaïs, 'and that probably means that both infants are weakly and prone to illness ... perhaps even worse. They are all blighted. The first mercifully died, with a head so enormous that its neck could not support it. Du Maine has a deformed leg; Mme d'Orléans is deformed and Mme la Duchesse de Bourbon limps! Only Toulouse is whole!'

In an effort to soothe the irate governess, and to ensure that in her distress she did not contemplate leaving the Court, a diplomatic Louis now arranged for Mme de Louvois, the minister's wife, to administer to his children's future needs.

Even for God's temporal representative, Louis was playing a complex emotional game. Tiring of La Montespan, he was reluctant to announce her *congé*; he had also fallen madly in love with an exquisite newcomer to Court, even as he increasingly sought the novel solace that Madame de Maintenon brought to him.

The newcomer, Marie-Angélique de Scorailles de Rouissille, was *Madame*'s newest lady-in-waiting – a younger version of the blonde, blue-eyed La Vallière, and even less bright.

Marie-Angélique had had a great deal of time and money spent on her by her family, who saw her as an investment. Seducing the king was much easier than she had expected; probably the reason for her incredible arrogance. She totally ignored the queen, even to the point of neglecting the *de rigueur* curtsey; Louis she treated like a child.

Knowing Athénaïs' violent rages, the king had conducted the affair in strict secrecy. No one had the vaguest idea where he had lodged this beauty. The wily newcomer and the toppling favourite were seen at church together, smiling, charming – each of them ready to cut the other's throat. Mercifully, Athénaïs' rages were short. 'Were it lasting, 'twould be impossible to bear it,' commented Mme de Maintenon in 1677.

Only when Louis created the newcomer Duchesse de Fontanges did Athénaïs explode at last. The creature a duchess, and she was still only a miserable marquise! She was so furious that she released two tame bears to do their worst in the new favourite's freshly-decorated apartments. Adding to her misery, Athénaïs wrongly suspected Mme de Maintenon of having carnal relations with the king. In 1679 Mme de Maintenon explained to a friend:

> He relates his faults to me; I am his confidante and Mme de Montespan is positive that I am his mistress. 'But, Madam,' said I to her, 'he must then have three.' 'Yes,' answered she smartly. 'I am but a nominal one, that girl [La Fontanges] is so in fact, and you are mistress of his heart.' I calmly represented to her that she listened too much to her resentments. She answered me that she was no stranger to my artifices.

Athénaïs recognized that the newcomer's elevation signalled her own approaching fall from grace. Medea-like, she decided to end the affair by poisoning both La Fontanges and the king. Decision made, she sought out La Voisin again. Now, more than ever before, Athénaïs needed her help. Over a cosy chat she gained some useful, if unhealthy, advice. It will never be known whether her threats against the king and his new mistress were serious; but later she was openly accused of poisoning La Fontanges. More ominously, when La Voisin was arrested as she left Notre-Dame-de-Bonne-Nouvelle, her parish church, on 13 March 1679, she was carrying a poisoned petition intended for the king – instigated, it was said, by Mme de Montespan.

★

In 1678, a dinner was in progress at a house in the Rue Courtauvilain. Madame Vigoureux, a *devineresse* (fortune teller) and wife of a lady's tailor, was the hostess. Another *devineresse* called Marie Bosse drank a little too much wine, resulting in her regaling her fellow diners with some fascinating revelations about her work for the nation's best lords and ladies. Made indiscreet by alcohol and general bonhomie, she made mention of several poisonings that she had undertaken in the course of her 'duties'.

Maître Perrin, a lawyer in a suburban practice, was a newcomer to La Vigoureux's table. Had he heard correctly? Was someone joking? Or was there more truth behind the woman's babblings than any of the other guests had realized? He decided to report the conversation to his friend, Desgrez, an ambitious detective who had distinguished himself in the Brinvilliers affair. Desgrez was impressed. Immediately, he contacted his superior officer, Nicholas de la Reynie, newly appointed Chief-Lieutenant of the Paris Police. La Reynie arranged an immediate assignment for a female police spy to visit Mme Bosse as a client with a need to dispose of a troublesome husband. The fortune teller was only too happy to oblige when she saw the generous purse. With proof of Mme Bosse's dubious occupation, a raid on the house quickly uncovered a virtual arsenal of poisons.

In January 1679, Madame Bosse, her two sons, her daughter and La Vigoureux (all of whom were asleep in the same bed – an unhealthy but traditional inbreeding custom common among sorcerers), were arrested and closely questioned. As a result, La Reynie collected the names of an astonishing number of implicated courtiers, some of them belonging to the noblest families in France. The majority of the poisoners were female, their reason for such drastic measures involving either love or inheritance, mostly the former. Husbands were poisoned to make way for lustier lovers, or to claim an inheritance which would tempt the younger lover. It seemed that where love was concerned, poison was the name of the game.

Poisoning was often reinforced with a black mass. 'The description of a service [back] in 1668,' writes historian Rossell Hope Robbins, 'was simply a regular service said with amatory intent, a written request for success in *amour* being kept on the altar. By 1680, however, the mass became replete with slashed babies and nude bellies.'

Further questioning of La Bosse and La Vigoureux revealed tales of murder so horrific that La Reynie reported:

> Death is almost the only remedy employed in family embarrassments; impieties, sacrileges, abominations are common practices in Paris, in the surrounding country, in the provinces.

King Louis was alarmed. On 10 April 1679, he set up a special court of inquiry known as the *Chambre ardente,* so named because of the lighted candles in the black-draped room.

One of the first to be questioned, as La Reynie's purge continued, was La Montespan's favourite La Voisin, who angrily pleaded that she dealt only in chiromancy and physiognomy; she did, but largely as a front for darker activities. She had, for instance, a private chapel in her garden where the worship of the Old Gods was common among many aristocrats. Further investigation uncovered a well-organized witch's coven. And more names … lists of clients so long that both the Bastille and the prison at Vincennes were soon overflowing with suspects awaiting interrogation.

Friends and colleagues out to save their skins further accused La Voisin of aiding in 2,000 abortions and dispensing with more than 2,500 unwanted babies, all with the aid of another notorious witch, La Lepère. Worse, they asserted that on her instigation young innocents were kidnapped from the slums of Paris and sacrificed in Satanic blood-ceremonies. Many of these babies were buried in and around La Voisin's garden. An oven discovered there contained ashes and fragments of infants' charred bones.

With proof of guilt, La Bosse and La Vigoureux were sentenced on 6 May 1678 and publicly burned alive in the Place de Grève. La Voisin suffered the same death nine months later. Her suffering in prison was appalling; she endured weeks of excruciating agony, with her legs and feet being horribly mangled in *brodequins*, a kind of boot designed to hold the legs steady while the mallet descended heavily on them. Her shrieks chilled the onlookers. The scribe of the court recorded, 'At the second blow she shrieked: "Oh, My God! Holy Virgin! I have nothing to say".' The jury thought her treatment too soft; they threatened to cut out her tongue and chop off her hands. Instead, she was burned alive on 22 February 1680. Madame de Sévigné delighted in reporting the whole hideous ritual to her daughter:

> At five o'clock she was bound and set on the sledge, dressed in white, with a taper in her hand. She was extremely red in the face, and we could see her push away the confessor and the crucifix with great violence [...] When she came to the Church of Notre-Dame, she refused to pronounce the *amen de honorable*; and at the Grève, she struggled with all her might, to prevent their taking her out of the sledge. However, she was dragged out by main force, and made to sit down at the stake, to which she was bound in iron chains, and then covered over with straw; she swore prodigiously, and pushed away the straw five or six times; but at length the fire got the better, she sunk down out of sight, and her ashes are by this time floating in the air.

As the trials continued, a complicated network of sorcery and witchcraft was exposed. It is difficult today (and perhaps it was then for thinking people) to define the honesty of these confessions wrung out of the witnesses through torture. Some of the accused later retracted, having responded as required simply in order to stop the excruciating pain they were forced to endure. In other cases, however, confessions gained in this appalling manner were backed by other witnesses who were not tortured, and who had had no contact with any of the other witnesses. In truth, we will never know for certain how many of the accused were falsely condemned.

The ongoing investigation led to the discovery of numerous love philtres, which contained arsenic, sulphur, vitriol, cantharides, dried bats' wings, toads' eyes, semen and menstrual blood. Wax dolls daily proliferated, with black candles, nail-clippings and books on spell-casting. Nor were these findings restricted to Paris; La Reynie uncovered proof of poison rings and covens spread throughout France and across Europe, many of them sinisterly connected.

Although, at this stage, there had been no mention of Mme de Montespan, we can surmise that these were the philtres, or similar ones at least, which the marquise had surreptitiously slipped into the king's food. Louis' mysterious ailments had long been recorded: D'Arquin, First Physician to the King, states in the *Journal de la Sante du Roi Louis XIV* that his

> illustrious patient suffered from violent headaches [...] on 1 January 1674 he was attacked by dizziness of such a kind that his sight became clouded and he was unable to stand without support.

The reason for these inexplicable illnesses was about to be revealed.

On 5 June 1679, Madame de Poulaillon was the first noblewoman to be accused of multiple attempted poisonings of her husband. Others quickly followed: Comtesse de Soissons, accused of poisoning her husband; the Marquise d'Alluye, for poisoning her father-in-law; Mme de Polignac, for seeking charms, spells and poisons to get rid of La Vallière; the dramatist, Jean-Baptiste Racine, accused of poisoning his mistress; the Duchesse de Bouillon, accused of poisoning her valet rather than risk him exposing her lovers; and the Duc de Luxemburg, for casting spells on the guardian of his lover and also on his unwanted wife. Louis was adamant: rich or poor, whoever was guilty must pay the price – but he conveniently tipped off two ex-mistresses, La Soissons and La Polignac, giving them the chance to leave the country.

One Adam du Coeuret, known as Lesage, proved to be a particularly glib, slippery witness. A vicious magician and alchemist, he had already been sent to the galleys (1668) for committing impieties. Eventually freed, he showed no remorse and continued as before. Having been La Voisin's sometime lover had made it convenient for him to participate in the sinister activities that took place at her house. When accusations of Satanism were voiced, Lesage named two priests, Abbé Davot and Abbé Mariette, as being involved: both of whom had been called to Saint-Germain early in 1668 by Mme de Thianges (Athénaïs' sister, Gabrielle).

Both priests, Lesage added, conducted black masses over the naked bellies of young girls. A priest from Saint-Sauveur was accused of similar crimes and also of having debauched his female acolyte. Even the deceased Henrietta, the first *Madame*, had allegedly ordered a black mass said against *Monsieur*.

The Abbé Mariette was arrested, together with La Filastre, another *sage femme*, who freely admitted to sacrificing a baby to the Devil. (When she was burned alive, she screamed out that she had lied under torture.) One Father Davot admitted to performing a love-ritual mass, during which he had spent much of the ceremony kissing the female client's intimate parts.

There were stories, all with named participants from the Court, of atrocities in the woods near Fontainebleau. Mme de Lusignan was but one observed with her priest, obscenely utilizing a massive Easter candle. Father Touret climaxed his ceremony by publicly having sex with a girl whom he had used as an improvised altar. Tension reached fever pitch when the Abbé Mariette announced that several ladies of the Court had sought supernatural aid in disposing of La Vallière. These ladies included the Marquise de Soissons, the Duchesse de Vivonne – and the Marquise de Montespan.

This was the biggest shock since the trials had commenced. Lesage elaborated: a conjuration, specially written out for the marquise by Abbé Mariette, was chanted by her; it contained the names of the king, herself and that of the then favourite. The spell was to obtain the good graces of the king and to bring about the death of La Vallière. At Abbé Mariette's request, the marquise gave the priests the hearts of two pigeons. A mass was said over them at Saint-Severin, where they were passed under the chalice. Madame de Montespan assisted them.

The Abbé Guibourg, one of history's most evil creatures, confirmed that Mme de Montespan was a seasoned Satanist. He was supported by other witnesses, who confirmed, individually, the horrific testimony that he revealed. Rotten within, Guibourg was equally ugly without. To temper his unsightliness, the sixty-six-year-old hunchback, sacristan of the Church of Saint-Marcel, dressed in scarlet shoes and gold-trimmed, lace-lined vestments. He had a mistress, Chanfrain, by whom he had had several children – at least two of which they freely admitted to having killed.

When Guibourg was arrested, he told the *Chambre* that the marquise had been involved in black ceremonies before 1668; she had contacted him when the efforts of Fathers Mariette and Davot failed to achieve results. Guibourg confessed to officiating at a mass where he had mixed the menstrual blood of Mlle d'Oeillets with the collected semen of her male companion, a mysterious English milord, adding dried bat's blood and flour – a mixture supposedly guaranteed to allow them influence over the king. La Reynie reported to King Louis:

> I have perused many times all that might persuade me that these accusations were false, but such a conclusion is not possible.

Louis quickly realized the mass hysteria such revelations could awaken if made public; exposing the degeneracy at Court could only incense the populace.

The Abbé Guibourg, in the course of his testimonial, admitted to officiating at several black masses said for the benefit of Madame de Montespan. In court, he described the ceremonies as follows:

> The marquise stripped off her clothes, then lay naked across the altar, which I had covered in black material. Her legs hung down the front and her arms were stretched out, each hand holding a lighted black candle. I took my place, as the ritual demands, between her legs. The empty chalice was next placed on Madame la Marquise's exposed belly by Mlle Monvoisin, who assisted at the ceremony. Then I prayed to Ashtaroth and the Horned God [Asmodeus]. A naked child was raised high above Mme de Montespan and dedicated to Ashtaroth. Its throat was then cut and its blood allowed to drain into the chalice. This was mixed with flour, necessary to 'firm' the host. Throughout the ceremony, I kissed the marquise's body as I consecrated the host over her genitalia. Then I inserted it into the marquise's vagina, just before copulating with her. Afterwards, her intimate parts and mine were smeared with the blood from the chalice. Mme la Marquise was then given a small vial of the blood to take away to mix with the king's food and drink.

La Reynie, sickened, could not conceive of how to inform the king of these unspeakable deeds. Guibourg went on to report that this innocent's body was later burned in the furnace at La Voisin's, and also confessed to the murder of countless other young children. Of these, he said, some were committed to the furnace too, while others were taken away, in order to salvage the heart and entrails for subsequent masses. Sometimes, the rest of the corpse might be utilized in the preparation of love philtres.

The Abbé was questioned as to how often the marquise had participated in these despicable masses: the priest confirmed it was on several occasions.

La Voisin's daughter also confessed to having seen Mme de Montespan lying naked across a mattress, her legs hanging to one side, a cross placed over her stomach and the chalice on her belly. She described what she had observed:

> At Mme de Montespan's mass there was presented an infant. Guibourg cut its throat, poured the blood into the chalice and consecrated it with the wafer [...] my mother took the blood [...] to be distilled and Mme de Montespan carried it away in a glass phial.

The girl added that the marquise had 'wished to go to the full extremity', which she believed meant great harm to the king.

Amazingly, Guibourg suffered no punishment beyond imprisonment. In solitary confinement he lived into his mid-seventies, a chained prisoner in a filthy cell in Besançon Castle in Burgundy. La Reynie noted, 'It is no ordinary man who does not hesitate to sacrifice children by cutting their throats and saying mass on the bodies of naked women.'

In August 1680 the king suspended all activity of the *Chambre ardente*, but La Reynie was requested to carry on investigating, under the greatest possible secrecy. Louis was torn between duty to the State and the personal ridicule which would destroy his image. In his dilemma, he ultimately betrayed his own standards. But would he not be the laughing stock of Europe if it should ever be known that the mistress of the Sun King had fed him disgusting love-potions for over ten years, was involved in obscene, sacrilegious practices and had tried to poison both him and his new mistress? His reputation, his *gloire* and all that made him the greatest living monarch would crumple to nothing.

La Reynie spent two years uncovering proof beyond doubt that Mme de Montespan was the most important name involved in Satanic rituals celebrated under the guidance of La Voisin and her colleagues – but the authorities were powerless to dispense justice, thanks to an egoistic monarch who refused to allow her guilt to be exposed. As the historian M. Funck-Brentano summed up:

> The *Chambre Ardente* deliberated on the fate of 442 accused persons and ordered the arrest of 367 of them. Of the arrests, 218 were sustained. Thirty-six persons were condemned to the extreme penalty, torture ordinary and extraordinary and execution; two of them died a natural death in gaol; five were sent to the galleys; twenty-three were exiled; but the majority had accomplices in such high places that their cases were never carried to an end.

M. Ravaisson, author of *Archives de la Bastille* (1870), gave the following opinion of the Church's role in the scandal:

> The Church came very badly out of this affair. The clergy shared the general uneasiness in regard to the proceedings against the poisoners. They feared that the great number of priests compromised would not add to the consideration in which the Church was held.

With so many participants walking free, the resulting changes in the law seemed too little, too late. Fortune telling was banned; poisons were allowed to be sold only under special control; and, by the Edict of 1682, witchcraft was officially declared an illusion. La Reynie, believing in a single justice for all, begged the king to reconsider his decision of silence. Louis refused. After all, what was a slight bending of the rules compared to the national debacle which would undoubtedly result if silence did not prevail?

Louis issued a series of *lettres de cachet*, inviolate royal orders which could bring about arrest and detention without trial or formal accusation. The *lettres* worked both ways, affecting both the guilty and the innocent: while they saved the lives of well over a hundred guilty prisoners, by the same order, many innocents awaiting trial were automatically found guilty.

The *Chambre ardente* was terminated on 21 July 1682. All the prisoners – the guilty and the innocent-deemed-guilty by *lettre de cachet* – were chained up in dungeons and kept well apart. Anyone who even mentioned Madame de Montespan's name was brutally whipped. There was no question of Athénaïs' guilt; what will never be known fully is the extent of it.

★

Although the Poisons Affair dominated for many months, other things were happening at Court. King Louis' affair with La Fontanges lasted but a short year. Bearing his stillborn child left her with greatly deteriorated health. Louis placed her in a convent where, in 1681, she conveniently died of pneumonia. There were those, including the second *Madame*, who openly accused Athénaïs of poisoning the girl, but a post-mortem, insisted upon by La Fontanges' family, showed no trace. Few believed, or trusted, the findings.

To alleviate the tensions created by her now perilously insecure position, Mme de Montespan turned to her other love: gambling. Her game was basset. It became an obsession, a drug to obliterate, if only temporarily, the mounting consequences of the Poisons Affair. Regardless of Bourdaloue's savage sermon against gambling (he had condemned play without limit as 'a business ... a trade'), Athénaïs held frequent sessions in her own apartments, where it was common for her to lose 100,000 *écus* in an evening. On one occasion she lost four million *livres*, only to win it all back again before dawn.

With the demise of La Fontanges, Louis turned more and more for solace to Mme de Maintenon. The outcome of the poison trials was grist to this pious lady's hard-working mill as she sped a considerably chastened Louis to increased religious zeal. Politically, he realized that he dare not turn the Montespan out of Versailles without adding fuel to the fires of suspicion about her, resulting in his own ridicule. Thus, she was allowed to stay on in her apartments. However, the king shortened his daily visits, making them long enough only to quell gossip. There was nothing whatsoever left of the old love.

In January 1680, the first Mlle de Blois, the attractive daughter of La Vallière, was happily married to the Prince de Conti. It was a lavish occasion, the first in which the king proposed to marry off his illegitimate children to members of the royal family, thus mingling bastard blood with the blood royal. Some thought it outrageous; others, merely unhealthy. (Originally Louis had offered his eldest daughter as consort to William of Orange. The dour Dutchman turned the proposal down. 'I am not pious enough to marry the daughter of a Carmelite nun!' he explained.)

In 1683 Queen Marie Thérèse died. Louis' grief was short-lived but sincere. 'This is the first trouble she has ever caused me,' he commented, then immediately took himself off to Fontainebleau since, by tradition, the monarch must not be under the same roof as the deceased. Louis had noticed that Mme de Maintenon was wearing a ring the queen had taken from her own hand and had slipped on to the governess's finger just before her demise. He had no idea that it was a symbol of gratitude for the Maintenon's steadfastness during the dethronement of Mme de Montespan, and for her strength in resisting Louis' amorous advances.

At forty-five, the king had suddenly discovered himself in love with Mme de Maintenon. For some time he had wanted to make her his mistress but the Maintenon, playing for much higher stakes, had demurred. How could she lay claim to an upright life if she indulged in the very immorality she was combatting daily at Court? But, now, there was no reason why she should not become the morganatic wife of Europe's greatest monarch ...

They were married between September 1683 and January 1684. The actual date was lost when, after the king's demise, the Maintenon destroyed all the relevant documents ('I want to be an enigma to history,' she stated unctuously). Understandably, the Court was appalled. There were countless derogatory comments, but perhaps the most cuttingly understated was that of the memoirist, the Comte de Saint-Simon, who said with infinite simplification: 'The King of France and Navarre ... with the Widow Scarron?'

In fairness to Mme de Maintenon (she continued to be so addressed), her character went unquestioned. However, her genuine piety, acknowledged by the entire Court, presaged a very humdrum existence as Louis daily turned more and more to God. Eventually, he even insisted upon ladies being *non-décolleté;* even bare arms were banned. In a letter to her aunt Sophie dated 2 February 1691, *Madame* complains that:

> the King's Old Drab [Maintenon] has ordered all the ladies who use rouge not to do so any longer [...] This is what piety consists of here.

Louis' second marriage naturally created further estrangement between Athénaïs and Louis. She would reside at Versailles for another decade, after being relegated downstairs to the Appartement des Bains. Between 1686 and 1691 she still moved among the upper echelons of Court society, but she was totally without power. Only her constant display of wit, unflagging humour and amazing resilience gave the impression that all was well.

Meanwhile, the king continued his shrewd policy of marrying off his bastards into the aristocracy by uniting the twelve-year-old Mlle de Nantes and the seventeen-year-old Duc de Bourbon-Condé. Fearing an annulment, Athénaïs insisted that the marriage should be consummated immediately; fortunately for the child-bride, Louis insisted upon a delay of several years.

The marquise particularly felt her demotion through her exclusion from the many excursions and fêtes that made life so delightful at Court. These included visits with the king's party to Barèges to take the spa waters, and that privilege of privileges – an invitation to the king's private hideaway at Marly. While Athénaïs was now recognized as a powerless Court fixture, the Maintenon reigned supreme, quietly dominating her ailing, bigoted husband. Was this the same Great Louis who once said, 'It is enough, I am happy to have given to the French the taste for magnificence'?

In 1691, Athénaïs was suddenly faced with her son, the Duc du Maine, who had grown to despise his mother under the Maintenon's tutelage. He carried a blunt message from the king, commanding the ci-devant favourite to 'retire from the Court and from Versailles'. A visit from a subtly jubilant Bishop Bossuet confirmed the royal command. Only the Mortemart pride gave Athénaïs the strength to act without delay. She would leave for her house in Paris, but not before a final confrontation with her erstwhile royal lover.

The meeting was ugly, as Athénaïs reports in her memoirs. She tongue-lashed and insulted the king without mercy, until Louis coldly interrupted her diatribe.

'Madame, I have done everything to make you happy; you take pleasure in making me the most unhappy of men. For twelve years I have endured your complaints and your caprices of every kind.'

'And I, Monsieur, *your odour!*'

This was a cruel and unforgivable condemnation, cutting straight to the heart of a vanity nurtured on a lifetime of political success, amatory conquests and battlefield glory. However, it seems that Louis did emanate a slight, nauseous odour which, curiously, was said to be often associated with red-haired men. The king, aware of the problem, took to using a strong amber perfume. However, Louis was not the most regular of bathers; he is alleged to have taken only three baths in his entire life! His morning ablutions consisted of wetting his fingers and lips then dabbing himself dry.

So, in 1691, Mme de Montespan at last departed from Versailles, retiring on a handsome pension. Her reign was truly over. As if to emphasize the fact, the Duc du Maine tossed out everything his mother had left behind, including priceless furniture and *objets d'art*. He wanted her apartment: but he wanted nothing of his mother in it. Athénaïs spent her time wandering between Clagny and the Abbey at Fontevrault as her sister's guest, with snatched, painful visits to Versailles to see her daughters. She had no sense of permanency anywhere. Eventually she retired to the Convent of St Joseph, which she had built as a refuge for a hundred orphan girls. In gratitude for her many generous donations, she was elected a lay Mother Superior.

Now, however, Louis made it clear to Athénaïs that 'Clagny was uncomfortably close to Versailles'. Taking the hint, the marquise gave up her 'jewel of a palace' as a wedding gift to the disdainful Maine and his bride, Anne Louise, daughter of the Prince de Condé – another mixed-blood match that took place at Versailles in 1692. She also gave the pair a bed, on which gold embroidery was mixed with pearls; and for the bride, a casket of priceless jewels. Maine showed his gratitude by refusing to have his mother at the wedding.

Even the most blasé courtiers raised a discerning eyebrow when the king arranged the next family marriage: that of his daughter by Athénaïs, the second Mlle de Blois, to his own brother's son, the Duc de Chartres. Many thought they deserved each other: the king's nephew had a dreadful reputation as a corrupt libertine, and Athénaïs' daughter was probably the laziest woman at Court. Perhaps it is no wonder that *Madame*, taking a leaf out of the Marquis de Montespan's book, publicly slapped her son's face when she discovered how easily he had been manipulated into the union. Later, '[she] was marching about, handkerchief in hand, weeping unrestrainedly,' wrote Saint-Simon. As for Mlle de Blois, far from being honoured, this haughty girl regarded her husband as inferior; pointing out (with some accuracy), that he was only the king's nephew – she was his daughter! The wedding celebrations ranked with the grandest of Louis' reign. Athénaïs was not invited.

The years 1693 and 1694 found France facing unprecedented famine brought about by appalling, fluctuating weather and abysmal harvests; an estimated three million people died. Mme de Maintenon's influence over the king's national budget was thought to be at the root of the famines. She had become the most hated, most feared of all Louis' bed-partners.

The disputed succession to the Spanish throne, culminating in the War of the Spanish Succession (1701–14), only added to the rapid decline in the fortunes of France. Saint-Simon records that Louis, incredulous at the ever-widening chink in his armour of invincibility after losing the Battle of Blenheim to Lord Marlborough, cried, 'How could God do this to me after all I have done for Him?' Finance was so short that Louis gave up the greater part of his silver furniture for melting down, and urged others to do the same. In addition, he cut down all salaries and pensions; Mme de Montespan's was cut by two-thirds. She could afford to shrug off the loss.

In 1701, Athénaïs' indifference to the death of her husband was more than balanced by her enormous grief when *Monsieur* died. They had had many altercations and not a few outright quarrels, but they had remained close since her arrival at Court forty years before. He left debts of over seven and a half million francs, much of it spent on his male lovers. 'It appears that three young men alone drew 100,000 *thalers* apiece per annum,' wrote *Madame* on 7 July. Three years later, in 1704, Athénaïs was absolutely devastated by the death of her favourite sister, the Abbess de Fontevrault. Her grief precipitated a sudden physical deterioration. In a letter to her aunt Sophie, written on 29 December 1701, *Madame* wrote:

> Mme de Montespan's skin looks like paper which children have folded over and over, for her face is covered with minute lines so close together that it is astonishing.

The marquise now pursued the scriptures in her fear of the dark and of death. She even engaged women to sit up all night in her apartment so that should she waken, there would be someone there to comfort her. Particularly generous to her only legitimate son, the twenty-year-old Duc d'Antin, she gained for him the command of a regiment, and the position of Gentleman of the Bedchamber to the Dauphin. When d'Antin married Marie-Victoire de Noailles, Athénaïs bestowed over 100,000 francs' worth of jewels on the bride. Sadly, like his half-brother, d'Antin treated his mother with increasing disdain; perhaps he recalled her neglect of him during his early years.

Two years before she died, Mme de Montespan released herself totally from Versailles and the Court. She was overwhelmed by a feeling for God and was determined to make amends for her past. More than one biographer has stated that she wore rough-hair undergarments and slept between coarse sheets, and that she even wore a metal girdle with sharpened points on its inside. However, the preface to her memoirs (Grolier Society, 1904) states that

> her austerities went no further than almsgiving; as for hair shirts and discipline, she believed that she could obtain salvation without them.

Much of Athénaïs' enormous fortune was distributed among the many charities she patronized. For two years she lived the life of a penitent, hoping to achieve inner peace; instead, her mental distress seemed only to increase. She gave in to hypochondria, visiting health spas in search of a cure for an illness which was imaginary. Ironically, it was during a visit to the spa at Bourbon l'Archambault in May 1707 that she suddenly succumbed to a peculiar fainting spell. In panic, her ladies gave her an emetic ... the worst thing they could have done. Within hours, Athénaïs, Marquise de Montespan, was dead.

★

Her end was disgraceful. None of her family paid their last respects, but they showed enormous interest in her will. Her coffin was left to lie in a doorway while the officiating clergy argued over the correct precedence in the funeral procession. Only her daughters were distressed, but they were forbidden by their father to attend the funeral or to wear the customary black. Louis surlily declared that, since Athénaïs had never been their legal mother, she did not warrant that token of respect. Mme de Maintenon surprisingly and unaccountably sobbed genuine tears, and wrote that 'never did mistress reign more'.

And King Louis? He was entirely unmoved by Athénaïs' death. 'I cannot mourn for someone who, for me, has been dead for some years,' he remarked coldly to the Duchess de Bourgogne, 'indeed, since the Marquise retired from Versailles.'

★

The Sun King's heart was embalmed after his death in 1715. Eighty-four years later, during the French Revolution, it was stolen and sold to Lord Harcourt, who, in turn, sold it to William Buckland, geologist, Dean of Westminster from 1845, and a noted gourmand. It is said that he cooked and ate it.

Emma Hamilton

A Legacy to King and Country

'My soul is God's, my body Emma's.'

Horatio, Lord Nelson (1758–1805)

S arah Kidd lived in the tiny village of Hawarden in Flintshire, Wales, where she made a skimpy living selling produce in Chester market. Her daughter Mary had married Henry Lyon, a blacksmith, and had gone to live a few miles away in Ness. On 26 April 1765, Mary gave birth to a daughter. Two years later, the child was baptized and christened Amy Lyon, the illiterate parents making their sign in the parish register. In this inauspicious manner, the future Emma, Lady Hamilton – whose blatant, much publicized affair with the great naval commander Horatio, Lord Nelson, was destined to scandalize Europe and beyond – made her entry into the world.

Less than a month after the christening Mrs Lyon and her baby daughter returned to Mrs Kidd's house, after Henry Lyon died suddenly from unknown causes. Not much is known about those early years, except that the family was closely-knit. Before long, the child's name, Amy, was discarded in favour of the more refined Emily. Mrs Lyon remained with her little girl until she was twelve; then, having satisfactorily placed her as second nursemaid in a local family, she set out for London and what she hoped would be more lucrative opportunities for herself. Once established in the capital as a domestic, she sent for her daughter, having secured for her the position of housemaid with a Dr Richard Budd in Blackfriars. Emily was just thirteen, but even at so young an age her thick, red-gold hair and sparkling chameleon eyes, complementing her 'English-rose' complexion, foretold the great beauty she would become.

Emily was soon befriended by Jane Powell, another domestic at the house. Determined to become an actress, Jane announced one day that she was going to audition at Drury Lane Theatre for the famous playwright/manager Richard Brinsley Sheridan. She persuaded Emily to join her, insisting that with her lovely singing voice and good looks, she could not fail to impress.

Sheridan was impressed enough by the flamboyant talents of young Jane to offer her a try-out. Emily, unfortunately, failed her audition, but was offered instead the position of maid in the London home of Thomas Linley, Sheridan's father-in-law. Her new employer was a well-known composer whose three daughters, all operatic singers, were to achieve an even greater fame than their father; Elizabeth, in particular, was already a respected international *prima donna*. Emily was happy with the Linleys; later, with a natural, glorious voice of her own, she would acknowledge the influence that living and working in a continual atmosphere of music had had on her love of the art.

When the Linleys' second son, Samuel, was stricken with a recurring fever he had contracted as a midshipman on board HMS *Thunderer*, Emily never left his bedside; he and the young girl grew very fond of each other. Unfortunately, a further particularly virulent attack resulted in Samuel's death. Emily was inconsolable; haunted by memories, she left the Linleys early in 1779 and found employment first as a shop assistant, then as a barmaid – complementing her earnings with occasional prostitution. She must have lost, or given up, her 'legitimate' employment, for when the fencer/writer Henry Angelo picked her up one night, she was starving. 'She had not tasted food that day,' he recorded, 'the truth of which she proved by the voracious manner in which she devoured some biscuits I ordered to be placed before her.'

Emily's luck changed when she became a domestic maid to Mrs Kelly, a flamboyant, outgoing woman who ran an 'interesting' establishment for jaded gentlemen. Seeing more in Emily's physical potential than that of a menial, she suggested a more lucrative employment. Emily jumped at the chance. She liked the good-natured Mrs Kelly, whom she was encouraged to call 'Mother'.

Mrs Kelly – known by the delightful soubriquet 'the Abbess' – was a good-hearted, if shameless procuress of young flesh. She called her girls 'The Nuns' and was very much the Mother Superior to them. She invested money in attractive clothes for Emily and the two of them were frequently seen taking the air, or out on a shopping spree, ostensibly to show off the latest addition to The Nunnery.

By pure chance, Emily discovered that her cousin, Billy Masters, had been press-ganged into the navy. Knowing that he had a wife and family, she sought out the captain of Masters' proposed ship and pleaded for his release. Captain John Willet-Payne listened with amused tolerance. When Emily stopped he continued to stare at her, his eyes twinkling. Yes … it might just be possible to release Masters from his predicament – but there was a price. Emily fully comprehended the captain's meaning. The bargain was struck: Billy Masters was released and the wily captain became Emily's first serious lover. When he returned to sea, he left her pregnant. Desertion and a stillborn child by the captain was a high price to pay for a girl who was still only fifteen.

★

Emily's next employment was with the fashionable Scotsman Doctor James Graham. While many considered him a quack, there were those who thought he worked fertility miracles with his peculiar concoction of the new electrolysis, hot baths in milk, illustrated lectures and various questionable stimulants. His methods lured numerous men and women with fertility problems to spend a great deal of money in the hope of a cure. Graham's Temple of Aeschlapius, situated in the Adelphi, was established in 1779 and for the next three years was enormously popular. Ladies, escorted by their gentlemen, went 'incognito', with their faces masked, to stare at young girls – including Emily Lyon – posing as classical 'living statues'. Emily's alleged speciality was appearing as Hygeia, the Greek goddess of health, 'with no more clothing than Venus when she rose from the sea'; though the French portraitist, Madame Vigée-Lebrun, insisted that 'she was … covered with a veil.' The highlight of the Temple was the 'Celestial Bed'. John Jeaffreson wrote that for 20 guineas, Graham would provide a solution guaranteed to conquer sterility; however, Henry Angelo explained

> the doctor, whose studies were directed to indulge the passions rather than check disease, pretended to effect miracles … No less a personage than a noble duke paid his 500 guineas [*not* 20!] for an heir to a *charlatan* for drawing the curtains.

Inevitably, at the Temple of Health the *statues vivantes* found ample opportunity for being admired by wealthy bucks seeking feminine diversion. It was in this questionable environment that Emily first encountered Sir Harry Fetherstonhaugh. The young baronet took an immediate fancy to Emily, who could not deny Sir Harry's good looks and charm – to say nothing of his libido. In 1781, Fetherstonhaugh established his sixteen-year-old mistress in a neat little cottage, easily accessible on foot from Uppark, his large estate in Sussex.

A typical eighteenth-century country squire, Sir Harry's life revolved around such bucolic pleasures as hunting, fishing and riding, his social life limited not only by his rural isolation, but also by his unstretched intelligence. Life at Uppark was a revelation to Emily. She had never before seen anything so opulent as this beautiful mansion, furnished with the taste of the careful connoisseur that Sir Harry's father undoubtedly had been. The young baronet made sure that his mistress learned to sit a lively horse; he was proud of her spirit and natural elegance when following the hunt. Emily met other local landowners whose addiction to brandy and porter was equalled only by their passion for race meetings, serious gambling parties and libidinous pleasures. Approving of the girl's lack of pretension, they liked her even more when treated to an exuberant near-naked Emily dancing on Sir Harry's dining table.

One of the occasional guests at Uppark was the Honourable Charles Francis Greville. Fastidious, reserved, parsimonious, scholarly and an aesthete, this second son of the Earl of Warwick considered himself impecunious with only his father's allowance of £600 a year on which to live (around £30,000 a year in modern terms). It is difficult to imagine what bond of friendship could possibly have existed between the lusty, easy-going Fetherstonhaugh and the tight-fisted, censorious Greville. One night, while the other guests were playing for high stakes at the faro table, Emily caught Greville unawares. He was staring at her. He thought her common but ravishing, with her perfect figure, gleaming copper hair and dancing eyes. A surprising, easy intimacy quickly sprang up between the two. Emily felt a genuine liking, even attraction – a singular occurrence in Greville's life, for most women found him stodgy and pompous.

Within a few weeks, Sir Harry unceremoniously evicted Emily from her cottage and his life, without support, without regret – and pregnant. He had become aware of the bond between Greville and his mistress, and also of their secret assignations in London: knowledge which gave him cause to question the paternity of her unborn child. Emily made her way back to Hawarden, and her grandmother's stiff, but ultimately kind reception. Since she was now living as Emily Hart rather than Lyon, it is probable that she had invented a husband in order to retain respectability in her birthplace.

When, after several unanswered letters, Emily finally accepted that the breach with Sir Harry was permanent, she turned in desperation to Greville:

January, 1782

I am allmost distracktid I have never hard from Sir H … I have wrote 7 letters, and no answer O G what shall I dow? … O dear Grevell write to me … G adue and believe me yours for ever … Emily Hart.

Emily's alarming grammar was not unusual; even well-bred ladies of this period suffered the same orthographic limitations. It seems strange that a man of Greville's parsimonious, fussy nature should accept responsibility for the pregnant Emily, as well as her mother (who was now mysteriously known as Mrs Cadogan) – but that was exactly what he did, on condition that she should have absolutely no contact with any of her old acquaintances from Uppark. Emily readily agreed. With her change in fortune, she also changed her name again – this time, permanently, to Emma.

Emma became Greville's mistress on 10 January 1782; the attachment would last for nearly five years. With the need to economize, Greville moved his 'family' into a smaller house in the less fashionable but more salubrious Edgware Road, Paddington Green. Mrs Cadogan, asking no questions about the 'arrangement' but knowing everything, made Greville an excellent and willing housekeeper. In March 1782, Emma gave birth to a girl, always referred to as 'Little Emma'. At Greville's insistence, the child was immediately taken to Hawarden and placed in the care of Emma's grandmother.

Greville owned an enviable collection of mineral curios and antiques, of which he was very proud. In some ways he regarded his beautiful mistress as an addition to the collection: as yet, raw material, rough and unpolished. But the challenge to make her sparkle and gleam in keeping with his other virtu – now that would be a real achievement! Greville would give her something of his learning and patience and she would become his creation, a living Galatea to his Pygmalion – or, as he sometimes spoke of her, 'a modern piece of virtu'.

'My education began when I was seventeen,' Emma would say in future years. She received lessons in singing and drawing; she was introduced to edifying books; her writing and spelling improved as did her social refinement. That Greville enjoyed and was proud of her progress was a tribute to Emma's native intelligence. Physically, they were well-suited.

'Emma is so clean,' Greville would later boast to his uncle. 'I couldn't wish for a sweeter bed companion.'

In terms of personality, however, they were poles apart. Later in 1782, during a portrait-sitting for her friend, the fashionable painter George Romney, Emma confided that she had greatly upset Greville. Her lover had taken her to the Ranelagh Pleasure Gardens, which she had found delightful, with its gay crowds and beautiful music ... and since Emma knew the tune and she was so happy, she had mounted the table and had sung full out with the orchestra. Everyone applauded, including the Prince of Wales; but Greville had been mortified and had threatened never to take her to Ranelagh's again. Regrettably, this tension was a sign of things to come. (Years later, the Prince recalled that he had once before seen Emma, 'standing in clogs at a fruiterer's door', which must have been around the time she left the Linley household. Did 'Prinny' bring to mind these two episodes when in 1791 he commissioned two portraits of Emma?)

★

Greville's best friend was also his uncle. Sir William Hamilton had been the British ambassador at the Neapolitan Court of King Ferdinand and Queen Maria Carolina since 1764. The two men were genuinely fond of each other – enough for Greville to expect to be his uncle's heir one day. Sir William's passion was also virtu; in his case, a collection of antiquarian Greek and Roman vases, which at one time included the exquisite Portland Vase.

In February 1783, Sir William secured a period of extended leave, which he spent with his nephew in London. Emma had been Greville's mistress for over a year, during which time diligence, perseverance and a desire to please her protector in all things had turned Emma into a poised, sophisticated beauty, who had already turned down several advantageous proposals of marriage (and, it seems likely, an entirely different kind of proposal from the Prince of Wales) in favour of 'my belov'd Greville', whom she genuinely loved. Sir William made no attempt to disguise his admiration of his nephew's companion.

'She is enchanting, but – God knows why! – I fear she is a little in awe of me.'

It didn't take the fifty-three-year-old handsome aristocrat, who treated queens and concubines with equal ease, long to break Emma's reserve. It was the beginning of a sweet friendship, he calling her 'the fair Tea-Maker of Edgware Road', and she naming him 'Pliny', after the first-century Roman writer, who, like Sir William, had spent many scholarly hours in the precincts of Mount Vesuvius.

Sir William had been a widower for two years at this time. After a marriage based more on companionship than passion, Lady Catherine's demise had left an emptiness he had never envisaged during her lifetime, despite his many extramarital affairs. Now, suddenly, Emma's fresh exuberance stimulated emotions he had long sublimated, the friendship he professed disguising something much more disturbing. A philanderer at heart, Sir William confessed to his nephew that Emma's 'exquisite beauty had frequently its effects on me ... for I am sensible I am not a match for so much youth and beauty.'

Meanwhile, Greville had begun to realize that living openly with a young mistress was incompatible with his political aspirations. When his father, the Earl of Warwick, died, the young man found his income somewhat depleted – a problematic situation since financial stability was essential in order to support the political career to which he aspired. The solution, Greville realized, lay in a wealthy marriage. His present arrangement with Emma had suddenly become a hindrance and a social embarrassment; regretfully, he decided she would have to go.

Pompously, and influenced by the prize of a £25,000 dowry, he fully expected the Honourable Henrietta Willoughby to be delighted at the prospect of wedding him. But neither Henrietta, nor her astute father, Lord Middleton, were attracted by the proposal. Ironically, at about the same time that Greville was being rejected by Miss Willoughby, Emma was rejecting a marriage proposal from the lady's brother!

With a cold shrewdness that hinted at his suitability in his chosen career, Greville took matters into his own hands, callously pushing his all-too-willing uncle into an uneasy 'contract' involving the unsuspecting Emma. The plan was entirely of Greville's design – which is not to excuse Sir William for entering into a plot where, wrote his godson Henry Angelo, he 'all but purchased his future wife from his nephew, and this without her concurrence or knowledge'. Greville would clear the path for Sir William to take over as Emma's lover, in return for payment of his debts. There was another, darker reason for Greville's plotting: with a pretty mistress to occupy all his free time, Sir William would more likely remain a widower, thus ensuring Greville's inheritance. By the time Sir William returned to his ambassadorial duties in Naples, it was loosely arranged that Emma and Greville would visit him there at the first opportunity.

★

That opportunity arose when Emma, in a nostalgic moment, said how much she missed Sir William. Greville carefully reminded his mistress of his uncle's warm invitation to visit. Emma was delighted at the prospect – until she was told that she would have to go alone, since Greville was so busy. Emma was dubious, even when she was told that she would live well, and that Sir William was an honoured friend of King Ferdinand and

Queen Maria Carolina. What finally persuaded Emma was Greville's enthusiasm for the brilliance of the Neapolitan singing teachers. Once Emma had agreed to make the journey, Greville realized suddenly how much he would miss her, their love-making, and Mrs Cadogan's cooking; but these were necessary sacrifices for what he hoped would be better things to come.

Sir William confirmed his pleasure at receiving Emma and it was agreed that she would travel to Naples for a six-month visit, chaperoned by her mother. Emma's northern accent, about which she had been sensitive only since living with Greville, had been considerably reduced thanks to his patience. Now, she welcomed the chance to be with Sir William because she had always admired his diction.

★

The unsuspecting erstwhile mistress and her mother, who had largely recovered from a recent stroke, left England in March 1786, escorted by Gavin Hamilton, the charming and talented painter kinsman of Sir William. Emma had no idea as she embraced Greville on the morning of her departure that his kiss sealed the end of their liaison.

The little party arrived in Naples on 26 April, Emma's twenty-first birthday. She would have been inhuman not to have responded to the city's extravagant beauty, the startling blues of the sea and sky, the brightly coloured roofs of the Neapolitan houses and the grander architecture of the state buildings. Even the 60,000 *lazzaroni*, that unique colony filling the streets begging or filching, added to the sheer vividness of a city which would soon take Emma to its heart.

At this time, the tiny Kingdom of the Two Sicilies (comprising the island of Sicily and the southern Italian mainland) was high on the European itinerary, with its easy informality and agreeable economy. It made a pleasant substitute for Paris, which was no longer popular due to the growing threats of unrest and revolution. Seemingly isolated from the larger European political scene, the kingdom would only come under threat (from the French) after the French Revolution. In 1786, however, perhaps because of the excellence of Sir William's ambassadorial hospitality, the English contingent veered towards the Palazzo Sessa, the sumptuous, three-storeyed government residence. It dated back to the eleventh century and had once been a monastery. Emma's rooms were luxurious, her reception and treatment lavish; Sir William had even provided her with a maid. However, it soon became apparent that Emma's host was offering much more than simple hospitality. He rarely took his eyes off his guest, who was acutely embarrassed by his attentions. Sir William's service to his country, however, had taught him the value of biding one's time.

Meanwhile, he made certain that his guest was given every opportunity to indulge in the considerable pleasures of a city that had much to offer, and where life was much less formal than in most other European states. Thus, Emma enjoyed the opera, the theatre and island-hopping on Sir William's little boat. She indulged in long walks and passed charming interludes at Caserta, the royal country residence based on the Palace of Versailles. Emma's natural charm and beauty, and especially her vivacity, quickly established her as a favourite with the Neapolitans, not least with the Austrian Maria Carolina, Queen of the Two Sicilies (although protocol would not permit her to receive Emma officially at Court). Sir William also provided his guest with voice and instrument masters, a drawing teacher and a language tutor, from whom Emma learned to speak fluent Italian in a very short time. The sizeable English colony was pleasantly impressed with the vivacious Englishwoman, whom they erroneously assumed was Sir William's mistress. However, even as Sir William desired Emma, he was sorry for the girl who daily wrote passionate letters to a lover who had already forgotten her. Emma wrote to Greville on 30 April 1786:

> To live without you is impossible. I love you to that degree that at this time there is not a hardship upon earth [that I would not endure for you], either of poverty, hunger, cold death or even to walk barefoot to Scotland to see you …

There is a sense of desperation in Emma's urgent postscript:

> Pray, for God's sake, wright to me and come to me, for Sir William shall not be any thing to me but your friend.

Eleven weeks later, on 22 July, Emma seems almost resigned:

> I am now onely writing to beg of you, for God's sake, to send me one letter if it is only a farewell … you have written one letter to me … I have sent fourteen to you …

At last, Greville wrote and made it clear that he had no intention of travelling to Naples; nor, he insisted, could they resume their old relationship. It had gone forever. He advised her, in her own interests, to turn to Sir William. Emma responded bitterly on 1 August:

Oh, if you knew what pain I feel in reading those lines when you advise me to whore! Nothing can express my rage! I am all madness! Greville, to advise me! – you that used to envy my smiles! How, with cool indifference, to advise me to go [to] Sir William …

A final postscript suggested that Emma would not take desertion lightly:

Pray write, for nothing will make me so angry [as silence], and it is not to your interest to disoblige me, for you don't know the power I have hear [sic]. Only I never will be his mistress. If you affront me, I will make him marry me …

Sir William was very gentle. The shock of betrayal changed Emma from a guileless, fun-loving girl into a sobered woman, temporarily maimed by humiliation. She had been thoroughly duped. To add to her unhappiness, she realized that she was losing her shapely figure. In an attempt to escape her despondency, Emma threw herself wholeheartedly into performances of a *salon* entertainment that was unique to her, and which became *de rigueur* at the many social occasions held at the Palazzo Sessa. Described as 'Attitudes', they were to become the talk of the European *salons*. A solo presentation with a remarkably stylish quality, the *Attitudes* were based on various painted and sculpted representations of great or mythological figures. Emma's physical interpretations became so renowned that Romney painted her portrayals a number of times.

These evenings were largely honed and directed by Sir William. When the diplomat the Earl of Minto witnessed the *Attitudes* a few nights before Christmas Eve 1796, he was adulatory about Emma:

… by candlelight; they come up to my expectations fully, which is saying everything. They set [Emma] in a very different light from any I had seen her in before; nothing about her, neither her conversation, her manners, nor figure announce the very refined taste which she discovers in this performance, besides the extraordinary talent that is necessary for the execution; and besides all this, says Sir Willum (Emma's pronunciation), 'she makes my apple pies'.

The German poet Goethe had commented on the spectacle a few years earlier, on 16 March 1787 (the *Attitudes* were popular for many years). He, too, had been absolutely delighted by Emma's performance.

Whether she posed standing, kneeling, sitting or reclining, utilizing her abundant hair, a shawl, or a scarf, her *tableaux vivants* were brought startlingly to life – as though the painted image or chiselled sculpture had mysteriously gained a human soul. There was no pause, each image gliding gracefully, effortlessly from one to the next. However, Goethe's enchantment lasted but a short time, for on his return from Sicily in late May 1787, he commented cruelly:

> 27 May 1787 ... if I may be allowed to make a remark that a guest who has been treated as well as I have should never even consider voicing, I have to confess that our lovely entertainer is rather soulless – perhaps having a lovely face is its own recompense. Her speech and voice are most inexpressive. Her singing voice lacks fullness and the ability to charm.

It would be interesting to know just what changed Goethe's opinion during that interval of two months. In any case, he should not be taken seriously. Only two months after this curiously sour criticism, Emma wrote delightedly to Greville, 'It is a most extraordinary thing that my voice is totally altered. It is the finest soprano you ever heard, so that Sir William shuts his eyes and thinks one of the *Castratos* is singing.'

This was not Emma being hyperbolic about her own talents. Her recognized improvement was thanks to maestros Gallucci and Aprile, the two finest vocal teachers in Italy, both of whom respected Emma's musicality (as did the illustrious composer Giovanni Paisiello, who wrote music especially for her). She often sang duets or trios with the reigning opera stars, Casacelli and the coloratura, Brigida Banti. In 1791, Emma was invited to join the Italian opera in Madrid, the first foreign woman to be so honoured. Although offered a handsome £6,000 for three years' work, plus benefits, she prudently turned the offer down.

★

The pain of Greville's desertion was balanced in part by Sir William's genuine concern for Emma's happiness and mental peace. Such solicitation nurtured an increased fondness for her host; it was but a step to feelings of a more intense, intimate nature. Emma's metamorphosis evinced a willing vulnerability that Sir William was only too eager to develop. The thirty-four years' difference between their ages counted for nothing when she finally succumbed to the knight; Sir William's high libido was easily aroused and Emma's response was genuine. Or was it self-interest? Perhaps revenge on Greville? Certainly not the latter, as John Jeaffreson writes in *Lady Hamilton and Lord Nelson* (1897): 'To the last hour of her residence in Italy, she used her influence over Sir William Hamilton for his nephew's advantage.'

The fact was, over the next few weeks Emma rapidly fell in love with Sir William and impulsively decided she wanted to marry him. The ambassador was reluctant, not without reason. Apart from the considerable age difference, he was concerned about the effects marrying Emma might have on his career. He was undoubtedly very proud of her; as he had written to his friend Sir Joseph Banks on 20 October 1789, 'it is impossible that any one could improve more than she has done in the time in every respect.' However, if the broadminded King and Queen of Naples merely tolerated Emma rather than acknowledging her openly in Court, the English Court would most certainly ignore her. His career would be over.

At first, Emma was bemused by Sir William's reservations. When at last she realized that the situation was political and not personal, she set out to win the Neapolitan queen's support. In fact, the proposed match suited Maria Carolina. With the vivacious Emma as his wife, Sir William could only be more affable, a positive outcome for the queen, who hoped to improve the diplomatic relationship with the British Ambassador, a man she liked, but whom she currently considered stiff and full of English reserve. Through Emma, the queen hoped to cement stronger relations with the British government and, more importantly, the invincible British Navy. King Ferdinand may have fathered seventeen children on his wife, but it was Queen Maria Carolina who wore the trousers of state! She may also have had more personal reasons for wanting Emma married. Apart from attracting several proposals of marriage since her arrival in Naples, Emma had received many offers of a more dubious nature, one of them from King Ferdinand himself (even though he purported to be Sir William's friend). The queen, fully au fait with her husband's lechery, knew Emma to be innocent, and unresponsive to these propositions. Following a discreet word in Sir William's ear, the ambassador was now only too happy to revise his ideas on matrimony.

The couple embarked for England and were married at London's Marylebone Church on 6 September 1791. A few days later, Sir William received a shock: the straight-laced Queen Charlotte, wife of George III, refused to receive Emma at the English Court. All associated with the Court were, of course, expected to follow suit, a dilemma which created considerable embarrassment to those courtiers who had received lavish hospitality at Naples. Sir William was furious; he never forgave the queen.

In a lighter vein, the union created some amusing consequences: Emma was now Greville's aunt; rough and hearty Mrs Cadogan became mother-in-law to the suave Sir William, and 'Little Emma' was suddenly Sir William's stepdaughter. The knight was already paying £100 a year for the child's education, an expensive schooling at the time. Meanwhile, Greville must have spent some sleepless nights, worrying about his inheritance. He had schemed to block his uncle from remarrying, only to discover that the mistress he had carefully planted had become his uncle's wife!

One evening, Sir William took Emma to Drury Lane to see Richard Brinsley Sheridan's latest play, *Pizarro*, a dramatic failure still being presented for the wondrous special effects. The principal parts were played by the glorious Sarah Siddons and Charles Kemble – and Emma's old friend, Jane Powell, in the role of Elvira. A respected celebrity now, Jane had no wish to be reminded of her humble origins. It was the last time the two women met.

★

Just a few days after the marriage ceremony, the Hamiltons left England to return to Naples, travelling via Paris, where they were the guests of Sir William's old friend Lord Palmerston. He was quite taken with Emma, finding her 'very good-humoured, very happy and very attentive to him [Sir William]'. Palmerston proved an excellent guide around revolutionary Paris; Sir William was particularly fascinated and much disturbed by the effects of the great upheaval which had erupted two years before, and which had ripped France apart. Despite the general air of enthusiasm at this dawn of a new era, there was an omnipresent feeling of threat, confusion and uncertainty. The visitors well understood how the royal courts of Europe were observing developments with serious misgivings.

The couple were honoured to be received by the incarcerated French queen, Marie-Antoinette, who begged Emma to carry a letter to Maria Carolina, Queen of the Two Sicilies; it would be the last letter the condemned consort would write to her younger sister; she would be guillotined two years later on 16 October 1793.

Lord Minto and his wife dined with the newly-weds at Caserta two months after their visit to Paris, on 27 December 1791. The earl wrote kindly, if reservedly, of Emma:

She really behaves as well as possible, and quite wonderfully considering her origin and education. The Queen [Maria Carolina] has received her very kindly as Lady Hamilton, though not as the English Minister's wife.

Facially, Emma had never been more beautiful than at this present time. Good living and contentment had rounded her figure to a voluptuous degree, but it would be another five years before she gained the embonpoint that caused the increasingly censorious Lord Minto to describe her as

one of the marvels of Naples that could not be passed over in silence. She is the most extraordinary compound I ever beheld. Her person is nothing short of monstrous for its enormity, and is growing every day. She tries hard to think size advantageous to her beauty, but she is not easy about it. Her face is beautiful; she is all Nature, and yet all Art; that is to say, her manners are perfectly unpolished, of course very easy, though not with the ease of good breeding; but of a barmaid.

This description was confirmed in 1799 by the newly married, twenty-one-year-old Lady Elgin, who described Emma as 'a Whapper ... and I think her manner very vulgar'.

However, in March 1792, Emma was of a more standard size, and delighting in her new role as Sir William's wife. The Palmerstons, having been in Naples since the New Year, one day returned from an excursion into the country to tea and music at the ambassador's residence. Palmerston's comment on the entertainment was hardly flattering: 'I like Lady H too well not to wish that she had never learned to sing.' The criticism is curious considering that, while Emma and Sir William were in England just some months before, the London impresario Gallini had offered Emma £2,000 a year and two benefits if she would engage with him. (Sir William, answering for his wife, graciously informed Gallini that he had 'engaged' her for life.) All those involved in the performing arts will draw their supporters and detractors. Emma's great pride was in the knowledge that Europe's most respected impresarios, namely from England and Italy, had considered her talents worthy of high fees and international presentation.

When Emma delivered Marie-Antoinette's letter into the hands of her sister, she won the eternal gratitude of the Queen of Naples. It marked a turning point for the two women, their warm acquaintanceship slipping easily into a friendship of substance. Theirs was one of the most remarkable bonds of the late eighteenth century. Utilizing this connection in her desire for a stronger English alliance, Maria Carolina had no scruples in 'borrowing' important documents from her husband's postbag and allowing Emma to take relevant extracts to send back to London, via the diplomatic bag and other means. Such complicity is surely proof of the remarkable trust between two women of such polarized backgrounds. On 21 September 1796, Emma wrote to Greville (now Vice-Chamberlain to King George III, thanks to his elder brother's considerable influence at Court): 'They [the government] ought to be grateful to Sir William and myself in particular, as my situation at this Court is very extraordinary.'

The French Revolution should have been contained within the perimeters of that country, but it wasn't. The stink rising from the blood of the dead was far surpassed by the sweet smell of freedom and personal liberty that was rapidly drifting across Europe. Its pungency reached far and wide, increasingly unnerving other European Courts.

In April 1794, Naples felt the first tremors of civil unrest. A complicated, almost perfect plot to murder King Ferdinand and Queen Maria Carolina by poison was foiled at the eleventh hour. Meanwhile, the liberating effects of the French Revolution continued to sweep across Europe. In 1798, the news reached Naples that the Corsican, Napoleon Bonaparte, was planning a massive attack on their tiny kingdom. Revered as the liberator of France, Bonaparte had sky-rocketed to both military and political prominence in post-revolution France, posing an increasingly dangerous threat to monarchist Europe. Sir William warned the Admiralty: 'Naples wants the protection of a British fleet' – the same conclusion reached by King Ferdinand and Queen Maria Carolina. Sir John Acton, Commander-in-Chief of the Neapolitan navy (and the queen's lover), who had been resident in Naples since 1779, became even more powerful.

Emma, too, quickly recognized the gravity of the situation and took it upon herself to warn one of the British naval commanders-in-chief, Earl St Vincent. As a consequence, he immediately sent the recently-appointed Rear Admiral Horatio Nelson to Naples; the Hamiltons had briefly met him in September 1793. At the time of that initial meeting, the Hamiltons had been very impressed by the slight, unassuming young naval officer. Sir William had even predicted, with uncanny precision, that, although Nelson was only a small man and not very handsome, he would live to become the greatest man that England had ever produced. Nelson, on his part, had written to his wife on 14 September 1793 after that brief meeting:

Lady Hamilton has been wonderfully kind and good to Josiah [Nelson's stepson]. She is a young woman of amiable manners, and who does honour to the station to which she is raised.

★

Horatio Nelson was born in 1758 at Burnham Thorpe in Norfolk, where his father was the rector. A slight, sensitive boy, his career was meteoric. Entering the navy at twelve, at twenty he had reached the rank of post-captain. During the taking of Calvi on Corsica in 1794, he lost most of the sight in his right eye. He was knighted in 1797.

Even those who loved and respected Nelson criticized his passion for fame, riches and adulation. His egoism and selfish disposition were tempered with a selfless love of his men that was simultaneously possessive and generous. It was not misplaced; they adored him. He never asked any of his 'brothers' to do something he himself would not tackle, be it swabbing a deck or fighting hand-to-hand against the enemy. In 1787, after several short relationships, he met and married a pleasant widow called Frances (Fanny) Nisbet, whom he had first met in the West Indies three years earlier.

In 1798, Nelson's mission to find and destroy the French fleet had seriously depleted his supplies. With the northern Italian states under French domination and Spain remaining neutral, Naples and Sicily were the only alternatives for revictualling in the Mediterranean – but Naples was under threat from France. One wrong move politically and the French would move in. It was a delicate diplomatic situation requiring astute manipulation. The problem was averted, not through the dallying Sir William, but through his wife, who realized that diplomatic formalities on this occasion could only result in loss of vital time.

Emma immediately sought an audience regarding the revictualling with the queen, who, recognizing the obligation the British would be under, was fully cooperative. Nelson always swore that without this timely and courageous intervention from Lady Hamilton, his astounding success at Abukir Bay on 1 August 1798 – the Battle of the Nile, one of history's greatest sea victories – could never have been achieved. Nelson sank fifteen of the seventeen French vessels, including the greatly prized flagship, *L'Orient*. There were no British losses, but Nelson was shot in the forehead, a wound which possibly affected his brain, and set in motion the bizarre, sometimes unfathomable behaviour that often marred the hero's future reputation. After the Battle of the Nile, the threat to Naples from the French was considerably reduced.

Emma, overcome with the magnitude of the Nile victory, wrote to Nelson on 8 September:

My Dear Dear Sir,
How shall I begin? What shall I say to you? 'Tis impossible I can write for since last Monday I am delirious with joy ... Good God, what a

victory! Never, never has there been anything half so glorious, so complete. I fainted when I heard the joyful news and fell on my side and am hurt, but what of that? I should find it a glory to die in such a cause! No – I would not like to die till I see and embrace the Victor of the Nile!

Nelson returned to Neapolitan waters later in September 1798, thus beginning a momentous chain of events that would drastically affect his own life and that of the Hamiltons. Meanwhile, Sir William showed the sea hero the warmest friendship. The poet and man of letters Robert Southey recorded Sir William's generosity:

'Come here,' said Sir William Hamilton, 'for God's sake, my dear friend, as soon as the service will permit you. A pleasant apartment is ready for you in my house, and Emma is looking out for the softest pillows, to repose the few wearied limbs you have left.'

Naples would greet the sea-lord with a hero's welcome which outclassed even his expectations. The queen openly wept as she hung Nelson's portrait in her private apartment. Emma charged around the streets wearing a headband that vividly proclaimed 'Nelson and Victory', and King Ferdinand abandoned the hunt long enough to proclaim Nelson the kingdom's 'Deliverer and Preserver'. Lady Cornelia Knight, a visitor to the capital, recalled:

I was with Sir William and Lady Hamilton in their barge, which also was followed by another with a band of musicians on board. The shore was lined with spectators, who rent the air with joyous acclamations, while the bands played 'God Save The King' and 'Rule, Britannia'.

Lady Philippina, Cornelia Knight's mother, asked Nelson if he considered the day of the Nile victory as the happiest in his life. With exquisite gallantry he replied: 'No; the happiest was that on which I married Lady Nelson.'

Hundreds of small craft went out to meet the victor, including the Hamiltons' sailing boat. When they climbed on board HMS *Vanguard* Emma is reputed to have stood still for a moment before declaring wildly: 'Oh, God! Is it possible?' and then swooning into the hero's left arm (Nelson had lost the other the year before, in an abortive raid on a Spanish treasure ship anchored at Santa Cruz de Tenerife).

An anonymous edition of the satirical *Memoirs of Lady Hamilton*, published in 1815, offers a markedly different, but possibly tongue-in-cheek account:

> The truth is that, as the boat drew near to the *Vanguard*, Lady Hamilton began to rehearse some of her theatrical airs, and to put on all the appearance of a tragic queen. There was a great swell, at this time, in the bay; and, just as the barge reached the ship, the officer, who saw through her affectation, exclaimed, with an oath, that, if she did not immediately get up the side, the consequences might be dangerous; for that he could not be answerable for the safety of the boat. On this, our heroine laid aside her part, till she reached the gangway, where, instead of fainting on the arm of Nelson, she clasped him in her own, and carried him into the cabin, followed by Sir William Hamilton, and the rest of the company.

Over the next few weeks at the Palazzo Sessa, Emma assiduously nursed Nelson back to health. Apart from the head wound, the hero was suffering from exhaustion and a return of the recurring fever he had contracted on an expedition to San Juan de Nicaragua in 1780.

A grateful kingdom now set about honouring the Englishman whom they regarded as their saviour. Nightly dinners and Court festivities were followed by gigantic firework displays, which splashed Nelson's name across the night sky. It was all vastly appealing to the hero of the Nile, whose vanity was daily suckled on increasing adulation and popularity. The following letter to his wife, Fanny, is particularly interesting in the light of subsequent events:

> *25 [?] September 1798*
> I must endeavour to convey to you something of what passed [meaning the celebrations]; but if it were so affecting to those who were only united to me by bonds of friendship, what must it be to my dearest wife, my friend, my everything, which is most dear to me in this world?

Frequently, in the same letter, Nelson referred to Lady Hamilton in glowing terms:

> I hope someday to have the pleasure of introducing you to Lady Hamilton; she is one of the very best women in the world; she is an honour to her sex.

From their exchange, Lady Nelson was becoming daily more aware of her husband's increasing fascination with the British ambassador's wife. Emma, too, wrote newsy, chatty letters to Fanny:

2 October 1798
The King and Queen adore him and if he had been their brother they could not have shown him more respect and attention ... Josiah is so much improved in every respect. We are all delighted with him ... The Queen has ordered him [Nelson] a set of china with all the battles he has enjoyed in and his picture painted in china.

On 29 September 1798 the Hamiltons entertained, at great cost, 1,800 guests honouring Nelson's fortieth birthday. Robert Southey tells us it was 'one of the most splendid fêtes ever beheld at Naples'. Somewhat pompously, Nelson complained to the naval commander-in-chief, Earl St Vincent, about all the sycophantic praise showered on him by these 'fiddlers and poets, whores and scoundrels'. In truth, he revelled in the adulation, and Lady Hamilton encouraged him.

And what of Sir William? He could not have failed to notice the growing intimacy between his wife and the Nile hero. Courteous and ever the diplomat, perhaps he was relieved. He was now sixty-three and unwell; Emma was twenty-seven and at the peak of her beauty and vitality. When he married her, Sir William had resolved to face the age difference, with its inevitable toll on sexual libido, with stoicism and common sense. That moment, it seemed, had arrived. Who better than Lord Nelson to have a dalliance with his wife – a man he loved and respected, a hero he was proud to call friend? It seemed a civilized solution to an awkward problem.

★

Towards the end of this same year, rashly urged by Nelson, an attempt by the Neapolitan loyalists to oust the French from their northern Italian conquests met with unmitigated disaster. The Neapolitans were unable to face the vastly superior, if smaller, French army. As a result, not only were the Neapolitans beaten back, but a group of radical native extremists (who had styled themselves 'Jacobins' after the violent, 'liberating' French party headed by the bloodthirsty Robespierre) took advantage of this defeat to rise again with encouraged, rebellious hatred.

In a sudden burst of courage, King Ferdinand announced that he refused to be seen to run – that he would defend the palace and his family's lives to the end. Queen Maria Carolina would have none of it. The memory of her sister's gruesome fate under the guillotine lived with her constantly. For her, escape from the advancing French and her own increasingly rebellious subjects was the only solution.

Thus began Emma Hamilton's finest hour. Relying on her friendship with Emma, the queen was able to secrete some two-and-a-half million pounds, crown jewels and treasure at the British Embassy.

Through Emma's intervention, Nelson agreed to convey the royal family and their possessions to the relative safety of Palermo in Sicily. Meanwhile, Emma was frantically busy supervising the boxing and packing of as much of the Hamilton homestead as she could manage – in particular, Sir William's valuable collection of Etruscan vases. Nelson had promised that the two thousand items could be transported on the HMS *Colossus* to England, where Sir William hoped to sell them, ideally to the British Museum.

The royal party left Naples on the HMS *Vanguard* in December 1798, late at night and in great secrecy. A tremendous storm, the worst Nelson could recall, tore at the vessel's masts and sails; several times the ship threatened to keel over. Emma behaved magnificently, cheering the frightened, strengthening the weak and nursing the sick. The queen's six-year-old son was so violently seasick that he died in Emma's arms. Rather than show her distress publicly she escaped to her cabin for a few minutes, where she was appalled to find her husband sitting quietly, two loaded pistols in his hands.

'You know my fear of water,' he said calmly. 'Better this way than drowning.'

'We are not going to drown!' shouted Emma famously, snatching at the weapons. 'We are going to Palermo!'

HMS *Vanguard*, battered and only just afloat, reached Palermo the next day. Thoroughly depressed by the dreary palace which had been unoccupied for years, Maria Carolina wept. 'Life is over,' she wailed, and promptly took to her bed.

The party was to remain in Palermo until June 1799, when the Kingdom of Naples – now ostentatiously renamed by the conquering French liberals as the Parthenopea Republic – would return to its original name. But first, Nelson was commanded by the Admiralty to clean out and crush the French before restoring the rightful rulers.

During the enforced exile, Emma, Sir William and Nelson shared a pleasant villa. There has always been much conjecture about the famous

Tria Juncta in Uno ('Three Joined in One') relationship, which began around the time Emma was nursing Nelson and continued until Sir William's death in 1803. Emma remodelled the motto as 'One Heart In Three Bodies'. Certainly the *ménage* at Palermo raised many eyebrows, not the least because of Sir William's apparent compliance with his wife's blatant infidelity with his best friend. The *Trio* scandal was not the only one to ruffle the displaced Court of Naples. Queen Maria Carolina lost her lover, Sir John Acton, to his own niece, whom he married in 1799. The girl was a child of thirteen – fifty years younger than her aged swain.

Meanwhile, drugged by Emma's physicality, Nelson became increasingly hedonistic at Palermo. Though she could often be coarse and quick-tempered, he was utterly besotted by her. His infatuation did not go unnoticed by his superiors. In 1799, the newly-wed Elgins were requested to stop over in Palermo, on a government-organized break in their voyage to Constantinople, where the earl was to take up ministerial duties. His orders were concise and clear: report back from Palermo on the 'Nelson situation'. He wrote that Nelson looked

> very old, has lost his upper teeth, sees ill of one eye, and has a film coming over both of them. He has pains pretty constantly from his late wound in the head. His figure is mean, and in general, his countenance is without animation.

Not a very encouraging report! However, Elgin was quick to add:

> Nelson, when on business – particularly in private – shows infinite fire. [...] to him and to his officers it is due, that no more mischief has happened in the South of Italy.

Lady Elgin, on the other had, was disdainful of Nelson and arrogantly contemptuous of Emma. Grudgingly, she admitted of Lady Hamilton:

> she is pleasant, makes up amazingly, and did all she could to make me accept of an apartment there, which I should have totally to myself. However, I did not in the least scruple to refuse her Ladyship. [...] It really is humiliating to see Lord Nelson, he seems quite dying and yet as if he had no other thought than her.

Meantime, back in England, Lady Nelson was becoming steadily more alarmed at the gossip concerning her husband – gossip she chose to ignore, though she knew there must be something in it for the lurid stories and calumny to have started in the first place.

Fanny was not the only one growing increasingly worried about the naval officer. A combination of excessive champagne consumption, his support of Emma's indiscriminate gambling (although he hated the tables himself), and a too-physical display in public of their magnetism, caused Nelson's superiors much concern at the Admiralty. Nelson's officers looked on helplessly as their beloved captain, so often like a father to them, became more and more enslaved. Vice Admiral Lord Keith arrived to assess for himself what was happening to the man all England cheered and loved. Hating the frivolous atmosphere in which he found himself, Keith's week with the Hamiltons proved very trying. Chance comments and overheard conversations only confirmed the unsavoury reports concerning Nelson's private reputation. His most galling moment was hearing Lady Hamilton referred to as 'Patroness of the Navy'.

★

In June 1799, Naples was reclaimed: a combination of English naval power and an unrelenting charge through the country by improvised royalist armies had contributed to the lasting defeat of the invaders. Nelson now sailed for Naples on HMS *Foudroyant* to meet in great secrecy with Cardinal Fabrizio Ruffo – one of the royalist army leaders and a staunch warring Calabrian, who had made a triumphant sweep through French-occupied territory with 17,000 motley peasant volunteers. Enthusiasm had incited his men to pillage, murder and rape, all of which Ruffo angrily disapproved, yet he was nonetheless inclined to clemency for his recalcitrant men (the cardinal had, somewhat ironically, named his followers the Christian Army of the Holy Faith), as well as for the rebellious Neapolitan Jacobins, all of whom were at that very moment ready to depart for France. Neither Nelson nor King Ferdinand, however, was prepared to grant free pardon as part of the surrender. As on all important occasions, for his meeting with Ruffo Nelson wore every decoration he possessed. Perhaps in this way he hoped to intimidate the cardinal. (This strange 'peacock' facet of the hero's nature attracted much disdain, causing the Scottish General Sir John Moore to comment that 'the Nile conqueror looked and behaved like a Prince in an opera [...] so pitiful a figure.') Ruffo was singularly unimpressed. Bitter words were exchanged; Nelson, as plenipotentiary for King Ferdinand, further condemned the cardinal's rash promises to both his followers and the Jacobins regarding royal pardons. Ruffo's determination to keep his word ended in deadlock. In keeping with his growing reputation, Nelson behaved badly, pompously dismissing the cardinal, whom he referred to as 'a swelled-up priest'.

Thus the Jacobins and Ruffo's murderous army, having no alternative, were forced to accept unconditional surrender. Soon, near hatred would be heaped upon the Nile victor and his mistress, for their roles and Nelson's uncompromising arrogance in the arrest, trial and execution by hanging of the Baillo Caracciolo, Admiral of the Neapolitan fleet, one of the leading rebels. The prince's request for honourable execution – his right by birth and rank – was denied: thanks, it was said, to Lady Hamilton, who persuaded her lover to show no mercy. She was alleged to have insisted upon being rowed round the ship in order to gain a better view of the suspended corpse. In fact, Emma was nowhere near the hanging, but that did not stop the gossip from spreading. It was Maria Carolina, no doubt remembering her sister's bloody end, who showed no mercy to the insurgents. Some of them wrote to Emma, knowing of the queen's affection for her and thus hoping that Lady Hamilton would be able to save them. But Maria Carolina held firm her decision. It was time to return to Naples. The kingdom reverted to its original name as of June 1799; from this time, French power was finished in Naples.

While condemning the rebels, the queen was munificent to her loyal subjects. With Emma acting as emissary, Maria Carolina distributed gifts of money to the many who had suffered loss of home and possessions during the French occupation. In a separate incident, Emma was successful in obtaining several shiploads of corn from cargo ships putting in at Palermo, which she immediately sent on to a greatly deprived Malta. These humane contributions earned Emma the Order of the Cross of Malta – the first time the distinction had been granted to a woman. In gratitude for all her services, the queen publicly embraced her English friend and then hung a heavy gold chain around her neck, bearing the royal portrait surrounded by precious jewels which glinted *Eterna Gratitudine*. In addition, a further gift of dozens of beautiful dresses arrived at the Palazzo Sessa to replenish Emma's sadly depleted wardrobe, which had disappeared during the troubles. It is hard to reconcile this public show of esteem by Queen Maria Carolina with the Countess of Elgin's withering comments about Emma in a letter to her mother on 4 October 1799:

> I am told the Queen laughs very much at her to all her Neapolitans, but says her influence with Lord N makes it worth her while making up to her.

In fact, Emma, in her own right, had been a favourite of the queen long before Nelson came into their lives. Indeed, their close relationship and Maria Carolina's expansive public gestures brought about ugly rumours at Court that the two were involved in a lesbian relationship – an intimacy entirely separate to 'Lord N'! However, this was very unlikely, and if Maria Carolina and Emma ever knew of the gossip they gave no sign of it.

Emma was not the only one honoured for her loyalty and bravery during the Palermo adventure. Sir William received expensive gifts, as did the officers on HMS *Foudroyant*; Nelson was honoured by the gift of the Duchy of Brontë, with an income of £3,000 a year (Emma instantly nicknamed him 'My Lord Thunder', after the name of the estate); his acceptance of the gift without first receiving permission from England infuriated the Admiralty in London.

The more honours Nelson received the more arrogant he became, which led inevitably to further ridicule and scorn. Absurd cartoons began to appear in the press – pictures that sold as much for their satire as the previous heroic pictures had sold for their glory. Nelson was compared to a Christmas tree by some; Lady Minto commented on the hero's penchant for 'ribands, orders and stars'. Nor did his attitude improve when he discovered that the newly appointed Commander-in-Chief of the Mediterranean was Earl St Vincent and not himself – a choice influenced by his scandalous behaviour with Lady Hamilton. Even Nelson's long-time comrade, Captain Troubridge, became estranged for daring to make pertinent comments, vocal and written, which had been intended for the good of the hero's public reputation. Their friendship never recovered.

★

In 1800 the Hamiltons were recalled to London. Emma must have realized that her whole life was about to change. From the glory of being a celebrated beauty in a tiny kingdom, she was moving into a society that refused to acknowledge her, at a time when she recognized herself loving, but being no longer in love with, her rapidly ageing husband.

About the same time, Queen Maria Carolina decided to visit her daughter in Vienna. Ferdinand had become unusually recalcitrant with her, thus creating personal barriers she considered it best to avoid. Nelson agreed to escort her party and the Hamiltons as far as Leghorn. He would then take his leave of the queen and conduct the Hamiltons to England.

In order to make the journey to Leghorn, Nelson had deliberately ignored direct orders from the Admiralty to proceed to Minorca. He had convinced himself that a further threat to Naples was looming; closer to the truth was his need to be with Lady Hamilton. Upon reaching their destination, Nelson's party was shocked to learn of Napoleon's victory over the Austrians at the Battle of Marengo. Worse, Bonaparte was at that very moment rapidly advancing southwards towards Leghorn itself. This news, and resulting events, were hardly conducive to Emma's physical comfort: she was secretly nearly two months pregnant with Nelson's child. Astounded at Nelson's disobedience, Lord Keith had travelled to Leghorn to discover the reason for the hero's continued audacity. Nelson greeted his stern superior with an ill-timed request to escort the Hamiltons back to England on the flagship HMS *Alexander*, which was refused. Lady Hamilton, fumed Lord Keith, had ruled the fleet long enough.

Instead, the party travelled overland. Their journey was lengthened by a series of spontaneous celebrations along the route. Everyone wanted to cheer the great sea-hero, and to gaze in curiosity at the woman the whole of Europe now knew had him on a lead. In Vienna, there were many dinners, extended invitations and honours – and a final tearful parting with Queen Maria Carolina with mutual promises of eternal friendship. Lord Minto, who was with the party on 23 March, commented:

it is hard to condemn and use ill a hero, as he is in his own element, for being foolish about a woman who has art enough to make fools of many wiser than an admiral. He tells me of his having got the Cross of Malta for *her*.

There were further receptions at Prague and Dresden where, unfortunately, Emma's questionable past stood in the way of her presentation to the Electress. Defiantly (and also because it was the latest fashion), Emma had her hair cut short 'to dress it *à la Titus*', wrote the French portraitist Madame Vigée-Lebrun. She recalled Emma as having had 'an enormous quantity of beautiful chestnut hair, which when loose covered her entirely'. Her shortened hair only emphasized her size, making her, as one frank Scandinavian diplomat put it 'the fattest woman I have ever seen'.

At Dresden, the Hamiltons and Nelson, with Cornelia Knight, spent considerable time with the Earl of Minto's party. One of their guests was a young widow, Mrs Melesina Trench, who was touring Germany. Her *Journal* is interesting in that it exposes some of the stultifying snobbery that pervaded many upper-class families of the early nineteenth century, and of which the Mintos and Mrs Trench were representative. Mrs Trench says on 3 October 1800:

> It is plain that Lord Nelson thinks of nothing but Lady Hamilton, who is totally occupied by the same object. She is bold, forward, coarse, assuming and vain. Her figure is colossal, but excepting her feet, which are hideous, well-shaped ... Lord Nelson is a little man without any dignity [...] Lady Hamilton takes possession of him, and he is a willing captive, the most submissive and devoted I have seen ... Lady Hamilton's mother is what one might expect.

On 7 October:

> [Lady Hamilton's] hair (which by the by is never clean) is short ... her usual dress is tasteless, vulgar, loaded and unbecoming. She has borrowed several of my gowns [one wonders how 'colossal' Mrs Trench must have been!] as her own are so frightful. [...] Mr Elliot says 'she will captivate the Prince of Wales, whose mind is as vulgar as her own, and play a great part in England.'

★

The Hamiltons departed for England on 10 October 1800. As they travelled, the *Tria Juncta in Uno* came under increasingly severe criticism. Concerning Nelson, everyone admired the hero, but many spoke disparagingly of the man. The *Trio*, perhaps determinedly, appeared not to notice anything amiss. Poor Emma, grossly fat as well as being distorted with pregnancy, was often rated coarse, loud-mouthed and common. Yet that most punctilious and refined of composers, 'Papa' Haydn, admired both the lady and her lovely voice and spent much time accompanying her singing his songs.

The party finally docked at Great Yarmouth, where Nelson received a hero's welcome. All ships in the harbour hoisted their flags; the mayor and corporation were on hand to grant him the freedom of the city; later, bonfires and illuminations blazed across the dark night, while the next morning, writes Robert Southey, the 'volunteer cavalry drew up and saluted him as he departed and followed the carriage to the borders of the county'.

At last, in November, Nelson faced his wife Fanny at Nerot's Hotel in London. It was not the happiest of reunions. Sometimes portrayed as a bitter woman with no sense of humour, Fanny Nelson was in fact gently charming. If bitterness was promoted as her future companion, she was led to it by a faithless husband. She had been married to Nelson for thirteen years, in a marriage perhaps lacking in passion but cemented with the bond of genuine affection. Indeed, Fanny was determined not to condemn Lady Hamilton; she clung desperately to the slim chance that everyone was wrong and her husband had spoken the truth in his letters, when dismissing the rumours. When the two women finally met for the first time on 9 November it took Fanny no time at all to comprehend the situation, particularly as neither Emma nor Nelson seemed inclined to disguise their liaison. This flaunting of a new love was the most vicious torment Nelson ever inflicted on his wife. He simply could not help himself; he unashamedly idolized Emma.

A few days later, Fanny, under obvious emotional strain, fainted during a theatre performance the two mismatched couples were attending. Nelson, far from being concerned, was furious; how dare she embarrass him in front of their 'dearest friends'? But, in all honesty, did they *have* any friends? In truth, their whole social circle was compromised by the awkward situation. Cornelia Knight's friends, for example,

> were very urgent with me to drop the acquaintance, but, circumstanced as I had been [as a frequent guest at the Palazzo Sessa], I feared the charge of ingratitude, though greatly embarrassed as to what to do, for things became very unpleasant.

Fanny had hoped that the approaching spirit of Christmas would present an opportunity for reconciliation with her husband. Instead, Nelson accepted an invitation for the festive season from the fabulously wealthy William Beckford of Fonthill Abbey, in Wiltshire. Emma and Sir William, who was a relation of Beckford's, were also invited; Fanny, probably out of delicacy, was ignored. Adoring his relative, the sugar-cane millionaire found Emma vulgar: 'not at all delicate, often very affected'. Later, in his *Liber Veritatis*, his comments were vitriolic:

> Happy it would be, were it possible to banish from all recollection the too seductive Enchantress Sir William Hamilton so far forgot himself as to marry, the termagant cast-off mistress of his own nephew, the boon promotress of tipsy revels, the Circe, who transformed into *tame* Boars so many gallant, *wild* young officers, the prime manager of the capitulation so shamefully violated at Naples, the ready instrument of a ruthless queen's atrocities, the Cleopatra who proved the bane of our

most triumphant admiral and fixed a sound and sanguine spot upon his glorious memory.

However, it must be added that his virulence in no way stopped him from enlisting Emma's aid in an abortive attempt to secure the knighthood he so desperately sought.

Immediately after the Fonthill sojourn, 'our most triumphant admiral' was further honoured by being appointed Vice Admiral of the Blue. Nelson's elevation only emphasized Emma's tenuous social and financial position. She had been correct in thinking that her lifestyle would change considerably once she was back in England. Much of the jewellery she had received from the Neapolitans had to be sold; however, she refused to part with Sir William's earlier gift of diamonds – 'single stones of good water and fair size', and worth £500. These necessary sacrifices distressed Nelson; he blamed Sir William, even though he knew that the retired ambassador still owed several thousand pounds to past creditors in Naples. To add to their troubles HMS *Colossus*, bearing Sir William's precious antiquities to England, foundered during a violent storm. The entire cargo was lost. Sir William had hoped to sell the complete collection for at least £10,000, a fortune at that time. Further expense was incurred when the Hamiltons acquired a house in Piccadilly, a necessary 'good address' upon which Emma had insisted.

Some of this financial stress arose because the Government was so long-winded in arranging Sir William's pension. To tide them over, the knight was compelled to sell some of his pictures, once again exciting Nelson's disgust. Months later, Sir William's pension was settled at £1,200 per annum. Meanwhile, both he and Lady Hamilton were needling the government to acknowledge their losses and essential expenses incurred during the Naples uprisings. Indeed, Emma cherished fond hopes of Sir William being further elevated to the peerage; he had been a loyal servant to the Crown for thirty-seven years. And hadn't she, as the ambassador's loyal wife, also done fine things for her country during the Neapolitan troubles? On all counts the Hamiltons were ignored.

In an attempt to continue life as they had known it in Naples, and hoping to win acceptance in London society, Emma insisted that they lead a fashionable social life. Such extravagant ostentation – it was nothing else – was well beyond their income and it worried Nelson.

If anything, Queen Charlotte was now even more hostile than she had been immediately after the Hamiltons' wedding. However, Emma's acceptance by her lover's family brought a certain standing, especially through the friendship of William and Sarah, Nelson's rather dull clergyman brother and his wife. They represented 'English respectability'; Emma pursued it through them.

*

In January 1801 and in great secrecy, Emma gave birth to Nelson's daughter, Horatia. Nelson was overjoyed. It seems an impossibility that Emma could have hidden from everyone – including her husband – the fact that she carried Nelson's child until the day she was delivered, without anyone knowing or noticing. But this appears to have been the case. Perhaps her increased embonpoint had encouraged the deception. But was Sir William so naïve? It is far more likely, if somewhat bizarre, that he chose to ignore the obvious; for he was truly wearied by the constant social furore on which Emma thrived; the added consequences of acknowledging his wife's illegitimate child by his best friend perhaps seemed that bit too much to bear.

Still under greatest secrecy, Emma took Horatia to a house in Marylebone, where a discreet and kindly Mrs Gibson was paid well to take care of the child, and to ask no questions. Far from duped, she was, however, tactful and cooperative. Horatia would be taken on regular visits to the Hamiltons' town house, but always when Sir William was away on business. At Horatia's baptism Lady Hamilton and Lord Nelson were named as her godparents. Neither was present for the ceremony.

Largely for Nelson's sake at sea, the lovers invented a sailor called Thompson, ostensibly sailing with Nelson. Thompson (Nelson) had permission to write to Emma through Nelson to enquire about his 'wife and our beloved daughter' (Emma and Horatia) with whom Emma was in 'constant touch'.

*

Meanwhile, the British government agreed that their country would have little chance of defence should Russia, Sweden and Denmark support French aggression. For this reason, Nelson received instructions to meet with the Danish fleet and destroy it, thus weakening any added possible threat from the Balkans and Russia. With eighteen ships-of-the-line and thirty-nine smaller craft, Nelson, under the command of Admiral Sir Hyde Parker, sailed to Copenhagen, and on 2 April 1801 audaciously attacked the Danish ships in the shallow waters of the Sound. The Danes were no cowards and put up fierce resistance, both from ship and shore. At the height of one engagement, when the cautious, unadventurous Admiral Parker signalled an unnecessary retreat, Nelson gazed across the choppy water, deliberately putting his telescope to his near-blind eye. He spoke the truth when he said 'I see nothing'.

Before he set out for this encounter, Nelson informed his wife Fanny of his intention not to live with her any longer. In an attempt to soften the blow he added, 'I call God to witness, there is nothing in you, or your conduct, that I wish otherwise.' A final separation quickly followed, after which Nelson settled £1,800 per year – half his entire income – on Lady Nelson.

Despite subduing the Danes, Nelson was reprimanded at home for ignoring Parker's order to retreat; 1,200 men had been lost in a battle many considered unnecessary. Despite the tensions, Nelson found time to send Emma some valuable china for her collection. Ten days later, in a letter announcing his imminent return home, he told Emma in a sudden, passionate outburst: 'I wish for happiness to be my reward and not titles and money.'

★

Nelson was now in mid-life and had a powerful yearning to settle down in a house he could share with Emma and Sir William. (It was never suggested, even when Nelson separated from his wife, that Emma should abandon her husband and the lovers establish a home for just the two of them. The *Trio* relationship, as it turned out, was for life.) The search for a residence fell to Emma. Unfortunately, she failed to locate a house in their preferred location of accessible Chiswick – finally settling instead for a small estate in Surrey. Merton Place was near enough to London to be useful, at the same time far enough away to be recognized as a country residence. Nelson was enchanted with it, despite the surveyor's rather brutal comment: 'It is the worst place I ever saw pretending to suit a gentleman's family.'

Emma's sojourn in Naples now paid dividends. In her hands the house, standing in thirty acres, became a showplace (Nelson always referred to it as his 'farm'). Merton was one of the first houses in the country to have the luxury of water closets and private bathroom arrangements. A dark and gloomy abode when Nelson purchased it, Emma opened it up to let in the light by increasing the number of windows, and by a clever use of mirrors. According to most guests, it was warm and welcoming.

Lord Minto, of course, thought otherwise. In the early spring of 1802 he condemned Lady Hamilton's appalling taste; her vulgarity reaching its nadir, he thought, in the enormous collection of bric-a-brac and 'Nelsonia' with which she had smothered the place. On 22 March 1802 the earl spent the night at Merton:

> [Lady Hamilton] looks ultimately to the chance of marriage, as Sir William will not be long in her way … she and Sir William and the whole set of them are living with him [Nelson] at his expense. She is in high looks but more immense than ever.

Nor did Lord Minto approve of Emma's public persona in the new establishment, condemning both her and Nelson for their continued undisguised show of physical affection: 'The love she makes to him is not only ridiculous, but disgusting.'

The Treaty of Amiens, signed in March 1802, brought an end to the war between France and England. Nelson was now able to return to his new home, where Emma waited patiently for him. It was to be the happiest eighteen months the lovers would spent together. With Merton as a secure base, their love settled comfortably into the kind of domesticity the war hero, understandably, had craved. Emma, however, revelled in filling the house with guests and providing expensive entertainment.

For the very first time, Emma now discovered opposition from, of all people, Sir William. There were several reasons. The knight was tired of the non-stop parties and soirées; like Nelson, he longed for peace and a chance to do the things he enjoyed, instead of enduring the frequently sycophantic life to which he seemed condemned. Also, unaccountably after all this time, he admitted that he resented Emma spending so much time with 'their closest friend'. A short time later Sir William suggested an amicable separation.

The dilemma solved itself most unexpectedly. After a particularly well-attended soirée hosted by the Hamiltons, Sir William was suddenly taken ill. He was well nursed by Emma – and her staunch mother, who had always been on the best of terms with the old knight. However, Sir William died on 6 April 1803. The strange *Trio* were together, Sir William in bed and his wife and 'their friend' on either side, for the last six days of his life. As he breathed his last Nelson was holding his hand and Emma held him against her breast. Afterwards, she insisted on the entire household staff wearing mourning, for which she paid.

Although Sir William kept his promise with a will favouring his nephew Greville, he had left Emma well provided for, with an immediate

£800 and the same amount each year as an annuity (£800 is approximately £40,000 in modern terms). She also inherited the contents of his town house. The house itself had been left to Greville, who, with typical parsimony, ordered Emma to vacate it within a month. Sir William made a further request of the Treasury that, in appreciation of her very valuable services during the Naples troubles, at least half of his pension should also be allotted to her. The government ignored the request, even though Lord Nelson, with his first-hand information of that period, supported it. Nelson wrote officially to Queen Maria Carolina, stating the situation and begging her to support the claim, 'in the name of eternal friendship'. The monarch replied to the 'Deliverer and Preserver' of Naples coolly and reservedly. Eternal friendship was evidently in short supply: the Queen of the Two Sicilies offered no support to her 'dearest friend' other than consolation. It was a most surprising, disappointing and ultimately hurtful rebuff.

After her husband's funeral, Emma ignored propriety and remained at Merton. She was accepted as mistress of the house by everybody except Nelson's father, who strongly supported Fanny.

When four of her northern cousins made contact after so long a silence, Emma had misgivings about their motives. She need not have worried. For a short time, Nelson placed the only boy, Charles, as a midshipman, until he eventually succumbed to madness. Surprisingly, all the girls had received decent educations. (Had Emma, perhaps, been generously inclined in their direction?) As a result, when Horatia came to live at Merton, each of them in turn served as governess to her – a challenge to which they all responded admirably.

After more than a year of rural domestic happiness, Nelson was suddenly recalled to duty in May 1803. Once again, Bonaparte was preparing to invade England. It was to be the Corsican's last attempt, at the cost of Lord Nelson's life. Not long after his departure for the Mediterranean, Emma discovered she was pregnant again. The child, another girl, died a few weeks after birth. After a two-year blockade of Toulon and other French ports, Nelson returned to Merton for three weeks in August 1805, after an unexpected victory off Cape Finisterre. On 15 September, he was urgently recalled; the French and Spanish fleets were showing signs of unrest. On 21 October, as though by premonition, Nelson wrote and signed a heartfelt document, a further codicil to his will, bequeathing Lady Hamilton and Horatia to the goodwill of the nation:

> ... Whereas the eminent services of Emma Hamilton, widow of the
> Right Honourable Sir William Hamilton, have been of the very greatest

service to our King and Country to my knowledge, without her receiving any reward from either our King or Country ...

Nelson supports the unusual codicil by listing the several ways in which Emma was of inestimable value to the Nile victory. Then:

Could I have rewarded these services, I would not now call upon my Country, but as that has not been in my power, I leave Emma Hamilton therefore a legacy to my King and Country, that they will give her an ample provision to maintain her rank in life.

★

The Battle of Trafalgar, on 21 October 1805, was perhaps the greatest sea victory of all time. Thirty-three ships (eighteen French and fifteen of their Spanish ally) commanded by the stalwart Villeneuve encountered twenty-seven ships under Nelson's command. Eighteen of the enemy ships surrendered; four were captured later, off Corunna. There were no British ship losses. The enemy casualties amounted to 14,000; the total British casualties, killed and wounded, numbered 1,500. Lord Nelson was among the dead. As always, he had been in the thick of the fighting. He wore all his medals and decorations, which flashed and glinted in the early light, thus making him an easy target. Captain Thomas Hardy, Nelson's flag captain and friend, was fully aware of this – and of Nelson's vanity. Hardy urged Nelson to change his uniform for something which would not distinguish him. Nelson refused to listen. A French sniper, high up the mast, spotted Nelson and shot him, the bullet passing through his shoulder and chest and snapping his spine. In great pain, Nelson was taken below, where he lived for a further three hours, willing his men on to victory. He was assured of his greatest glory before he died. Typically, his last words were: 'Now I am satisfied. Thank God, I have done my duty. Kiss me, Hardy. Take care of Emma.'

Realizing that he was about to face a critically decisive battle, Nelson must have anticipated that his chances of survival were not encouraging; the codicil certainly points to this. Nelson himself was physically in very poor shape. His sight was rapidly waning; he had lost his right arm; he had recurring attacks of malarial fever; his teeth had rotted; and he had recently suffered several heart attacks – these, more severe than even Emma realized. He had made a decent provision for her and had arranged a dowry of £4,000 for Horatia, on which Emma was to enjoy the interest. Now, having earnestly bequeathed his loved ones to what he hoped would be a grateful government, the hero realized the irony: Emma would be more financially secure if he were dead.

The nation shuddered to a shocked standstill when the death of Nelson was announced. Emma was beside herself with grief. Inconsolable, she took to her bed, hysterical sobbing interspersing the long silences of shocked, mute mourning. Her bed was covered with Nelson's letters. It was left to Captain Hardy to deliver such trinkets and mementoes as there were, including a lock of hair that Nelson had especially asked his friend to deliver to his mistress. It was particularly decent of Hardy, for he had never cared for Emma since the time when she had undermined his authority by successfully interceding for a group of mutinous sailors.

Emma was present at neither the *Victory's* arrival at Greenwich, nor at Nelson's state funeral, held on 9 January 1806. The dead hero's body lay in state for three days in the Painted Hall of the seamen's hospital at Greenwich. *The Times* reported

the carriages of the nobility [...] with the mourning coaches appointed to form part of the procession, began to assemble at eight o'clock, in a line from Hyde Park Corner to Cumberland Gate. By ten, about one hundred and six carriages were assembled, of which number near sixty were mourning coaches, principally filled with Naval officers [...]

In St James's Park were drawn up all the regiments of cavalry and infantry quartered within one hundred miles of London who had served in the glorious campaigns in Egypt after the memorable Victory of the Nile.

To his eternal discredit, George III allowed no royal representative to attend Lord Nelson's funeral. Always fiercely disapproving of the Emma/Nelson liaison, the king refused his son, Prince William (the future William IV), permission to attend in his own right. Nelson and the prince had served at sea together when the prince was in training; the two had remained friends.

The funeral was attended by 'authorized persons only'; these included Nelson's few blood relations, and many state officials, most of whom did not know Nelson other than by name. Emma, closer to the hero than anyone alive and the mother of his daughter, was ignored; she was an embarrassment the officials could not handle on such an historic occasion. As though to balance this ostracism, all the Nelsons offered Emma their full support. Perhaps there was a hint of guilt generated by the handsome state honours they all received.

Nelson's brother, the Reverend William and his wife (who, of course, had contributed absolutely nothing to any of Nelson's great victories) became Earl and Countess Nelson, with an allowance of £5,000 per annum, plus a handsome grant of £99,000 with which to buy a residence suited to the title; Horace (their son) became Viscount Merton of Trafalgar, and Charlotte (their daughter), Lady Charlotte. Lady Nelson, the hero's estranged wife, received a pension of £2,000; each of Nelson's sisters were awarded £15,000. But the mistress and child, both of whom Nelson had always adored, went unrewarded, and his special 'legacy to my King and Country' codicil was completely ignored.

However, Nelson had also willed to his Emma £500 a year to be paid from his Brontë estate, plus a straight gift of £2,000. Emma was also to inherit Merton Place and its contents, and the interest on the £4,000 which was Horatia's dowry. These monies, together with the substantial bequests from Sir William, should have ensured Emma's comfort and independence for life.

But it was not to be.

Unhappiness drove Emma to host gambling parties and lavish entertainments at Merton; she was soon deeply in debt. She also drank considerably more porter than she had done previously. Years before, she had taken to the drink as the 'singer's habit', blaming it for her great size. The habit had increased – but was now more a heartbroken lover's solace. Fearing penury, Emma took up her own cudgels for recognition; it would be a fight which would last until she died.

At a conservative estimate, she owed creditors well over £15,000 just a short time after Nelson's death. Selling Merton Place was simply not to be considered. A special trust fund was arranged by friends; the price for this kindness was to name Merton as security, together with all of its contents and most of Emma's valuables. She had no option. Figuratively, she had lost Merton; soon it would be a reality.

Eventually, for a nominal amount, Emma's friend Lord Queensberry rented her his residence at Heron Court, Richmond, where the three women – Emma, Horatia and Emma's mother – lived for the best part of 1809. Under these distressing circumstances the porter flowed; Emma became extremely coarse. It amused those who derided her; it saddened those who loved her. She left Heron Court and was compelled to move several times more, until she was reduced to hired rooms, then finally lodgings. She was also ill by this stage, suffering from a serious liver complaint.

During 1809, the news that Greville had died did not unduly affect her; but in January 1810, Emma was devastated when her mother – her best friend – passed away. Now, there was only Horatia. Strangely, instead of death bringing them closer, Emma became irritable and difficult with the girl – particularly after her hopes of a decent legacy from the outrageous rake, the Duke of Queensberry, came to nothing when he died in 1810. (Emma, fond of the old *roué*, had dined frequently with him in town; like many women, he had hinted, and she had had fond hopes, of a substantial inheritance.)

The slide was escalating. Although Emma managed to avoid her creditors for a few more months, the authorities finally caught up with her. Early in 1813, Emma found herself in the King's Bench Prison – more a detention centre – for unresolved debts. Emma would reside at the ignominious address of No. 12 Temple Place for a little more than twelve months, on two separate apprehensions. Horatia was with her. Even in these pathetic circumstances, Emma attempted to 'entertain', albeit at what must have been an embarrassingly humble level. On Christmas Day 1813, for example, she gave a dinner, the guests at which included the Duke of Sussex and his mistress, Mrs Bugge. There was the traditional bird, served on hired silver plate – but there were no knives and forks.

Emma had much to thank Alderman Joshua John Smith for. A comparatively new friend, she had met him through a neighbour when she was living at Merton. When she was incarcerated, thanks to his interest in her welfare, he twice obtained her release from King's Bench prison. On the second occasion, both he and Emma realized that her debts were insurmountable. There was only once solution, if she wished to avoid further arrest: Emma must leave for France immediately; it presented no safety concerns since the Treaty of Amiens and Napoleon's ignominious defeat. A few days later, Emma and Horatia sailed for Calais, travelling secretly and at night. Emma would never return.

Although she was desperately poor, Lady Hamilton was never entirely without food and shelter. Occasionally, she sold a few of the trinkets still in her possession so that Horatia might continue her studies with an English teacher Emma had met. She also indulged herself in an essential bottle of wine, albeit of poor vintage. Emma knew she was dying of an enlarged liver, aggravated by years of steady drinking. She saw no reason to stop now.

Death came during the early afternoon of 15 January 1815. Emma was buried, not in England as she wished, but in the cemetery at Calais. A Henry Cadogan, a customs official who had been good to Emma in her last weeks, honoured all the funeral expenses.

One of the surprising things about Lady Hamilton's final months was

Horatia's loyalty. Nelson's family had offered her a permanent home; she could have left her 'guardian' to rot in prison, or in one of the many lodging houses they had occupied. Instead, she stubbornly chose to remain, bearing Emma's frequent drunkenness and resulting coarse insults with dignity. She returned to England almost immediately after Emma's death.

Horatia appears to have inherited her father's determination, coping well with a lifetime of questions and gossip, and the ghost of one of the biggest scandals of the late eighteenth and early nineteenth centuries. In 1822, she married Philip Ward, a young curate for whom she bore nine children. Although she had been informed many times, and despite the incontestable proof with which she was ultimately presented, Horatia could never accept the woman she knew as Lady Emma Hamilton as her mother.

For Emma's part, her love for her daughter never wavered, although this was not always apparent. Even on her deathbed she was still continuing the fight for the pension she truly believed to be her right – and which she now wanted for Horatia's benefit. On her deathbed she wrote to the Prince Regent, requesting that the Government provide for Horatia to help her to 'live as becomes the daughter of such a man as her victorious father was'.

As with Lord Nelson's, Emma's final request was ignored.

George Sand

A Lust for Life

'What a splendid man she was, and what a woman!'

Ivan Turgenev (1818–83)

George Sand was probably the most prominent, controversial literary personality of the nineteenth century, whose considerable talents were surpassed only by her scandalous, unrestricted private life. Today, she is remembered more for the latter than the former – her many love affairs, her brush with lesbianism, and the slur of transvestism; during this period understandably never far from a woman who chose to wear male apparel. Even her close relationship with her son provoked disturbing rumours.

George Sand's defiance of the mores of her age, her fierce feminism, her belief in free love and her extraordinary energy emphasized individuality in a world in which women were expected to be little more than insipid misses, decorative wives and dutiful mothers. She was known by many as the spokeswoman of her age: Henry James revered her; Dostoevski thought she surpassed Dickens; Gustave Flaubert called her 'My Dear Master', while Oscar Wilde considered her an addiction.

Her lovers were legion. In 1855, in his fifty-seventh year, the painter Eugène Delacroix was asked if he had ever been George Sand's lover. 'Certainly,' he replied, 'as everybody else was!' Socially and sexually she demanded, and received, absolute subjection from her lovers. The diarist Albert Vandam detested her, swearing that

> Sand's earlier books had been written with the heart's blood of one of the victims of her insatiable passions – for I should not like to prostitute the word 'love' to her liaisons.

Two warring aspects of her nature fought a constant battle for supremacy. The mother-figure she subconsciously represented to most of her lovers frequently rode roughshod over the mistress-image she longed so much to fulfil. Two men – Frederick Chopin and Alfred de Musset – stand out above the rest, for they played a vital part, both in George Sand's life and in European cultural history.

★

Amandine Aurore Lucie Dupin – the future George Sand – was born in Paris on 1 July 1804, the same year that Napoleon Bonaparte was crowned Emperor of the French. She was the daughter of a twenty-six-year-old army officer, Maurice de Saxe, and a tavern-keeper's daughter, Sophie-Victoire Delaborde, aged thirty, whom he had met in Milan during Napoleon's first Italian campaign, four years previously. When Maurice was posted back to Paris, Sophie unashamedly turned camp-follower; her tenacity was rewarded a few months later when, heavily pregnant with Aurore, Maurice married her.

Aurore was four years old when her father was killed in a riding accident. Her mother was unable to cope with the trials of motherhood, resulting in the child being reared by her paternal grandmother, Madame Aurore Dupin de Francueil, at her country estate at Nohant, in the Vallée Noire, south-east of Paris. This distinguished *grand-dame*, herself illegitimate, had aristocratic forebears in Louis XVI, Louis XVIII and Charles X, as well as the Polish Elector Augustus the Strong. Having narrowly escaped the guillotine during the 1789 revolution, Mme Dupin embodied the haughty spirit of the old aristocracy even as she embraced the freedom of the new order.

At fourteen, Aurore entered the Couvent des Anglaises, at that time one of the three best boarding schools in France. A first-rate student, she was also a *diable* (havoc-maker) – until she decided she wanted to be a nun. The conviction brought an incredulous Madame Dupin rushing to the capital to reclaim her granddaughter. Thus, in 1820, Madame Dupin undertook the rest of Aurore's education, encouraging a lifelong love of music, languages and letters. When she wasn't studying, Aurore explored the countryside around Nohant, either on foot or riding her beloved mare, Colette. During one of her early-morning canters she met Stéphane Ajasson de Grandsagne, a young man from the neighbouring town of La Châtre. For several months they saw a great deal of each other. It was Grandsagne who first taught her to wear men's clothes for comfort when riding. Aurore later described him as 'lacking neither knowledge, intelligence, nor wit'. But young Stéphane did lack financial security, and Madame Dupin was not about to encourage an impecunious grandson-in-law.

Aurore was more striking than conventionally beautiful, with a near-swarthy complexion; her full, sensual mouth sometimes gave her an unfortunate sulky expression, especially when in repose. Her best feature was her dark, luminous eyes. The poet Heinrich Heine thought her plain: 'only her somewhat protruding lower lip suggests sexuality'.

In 1821, Madame Dupin died on Christmas Day, leaving her under-age granddaughter with the responsibility of the Nohant estate, the town house in Paris and an annual income of 25,000 *livres* – a very reasonable sum at that time. At first, Aurore attempted to live with her mother in Paris, but their temperaments were unsuited. Back at Nohant she spent much time with the wealthy Roëttiers; through them, Aurore met her future husband, the dashing but impoverished Casimir-François, an illegitimate but recognized son of Baron Jean-François Dudevant. He was ten years older than Aurore, a fact which did not stand in the way of a mutual attraction, leading to their marriage on 17 September 1822. The following month the couple occupied Nohant where, on 30 June 1823, Aurore gave birth to a son, Maurice.

It didn't take Aurore long to discover the constrictions of conjugal life. At nineteen she had acquired a disgust for the sexual act as performed by a husband whose demands were excessive and crude. In addition, she was spiritually frustrated by this man who was no match for her probing intelligence, something he considered to be the sole right of his own sex, but in which he himself proved singularly lacking.

In 1825, while travelling with Casimir in the Pyrenees, Aurore began an unlikely affair with a young magistrate from Bordeaux called Aurélien de Sèze – unlikely because the affair was 'passionately platonic'. In 1827, when Sèze unsuccessfully urged a physical consummation of the relationship, the letters suddenly stopped. Losing Sèze, and increasingly disgusted by Casimir's crudeness, promiscuity, drunkenness and physical abuse, Aurore yearned for escape and fresh emotional stimulation.

When Stéphane de Grandsagne, now a classics and science scholar, suddenly reappeared on the scene, Aurore grasped hungrily at the rekindled affair, with its excitement, the secret meetings, the fulfilled physical passions. On a supposed social visit to Paris in December 1828, she spent two weeks with her lover. On 13 September 1829 – almost seven years to the day of her marriage to Casimir – Aurore gave birth to a daughter, Solange. Casimir was delighted; such was his ego that it never occurred to him that his wife had been unfaithful.

Left Villiers' lover King Charles II, whom she declared was 'the best-endowed man I've known.' Their passionate liaison lasted more than twelve years.

Frances Stewart, in a portrait by Lely. She was the one woman who allegedly did not fall for the Merry Monarch's charms.

One of Villiers' rivals for the King's attentions, Nell Gwynne. Nellie was the most natural, yet also the most audacious of the King's mistresses.

Above King Louis XIV, by Robert Nanteuill. The King's sexual appetite was voracious, his appeal to women founded upon an intoxicating mix of sexuality and power. Madame de Montespan was determined to become and remain his mistress – whatever the cost.

Right A chilling vision of the Abbé Guibourg and La Voisin celebrating a black mass (complete with slaughtered child) on Mme de Montespan.

Sir Joshua Reynolds painted this typically voluptuous pose of Lady Emma Hamilton. She was a renowned model: every worthwhile artist of the day was anxious to capture her image on canvas.

Lord Horatio Nelson, whom Emma entranced and captivated for so many years. He famously declared, 'My soul is God's, my body Emma's.'

Emma's husband, the patient, long-suffering Sir William Hamilton.

Above Emma's performance in her famous *Attitudes* became a talking point throughout artistic Europe. Here are four of them, as captured by Emma's favourite painter, George Romney.

Opposite George Sand. During the course of her life, she was variously labelled 'nympho', 'vampire', 'slut', 'monster', 'daughter of Sappho' and 'mother'.

Alfred de Musset: just one of Sand's lovers who recognized her as both his 'mother' and his 'whore'. Dangerously passionate, their affair was one of the most destructive of the nineteenth century.

A satirical impression of Sand, sartorially provocative in the men's apparel she made her own, and which added notoriety to her already infamous literary reputation.

Composer Frederick Chopin gives an intimate recital for his mistress, George Sand. They were vastly different personalities, yet their union endured 'nine years of exclusive friendship'.

In July 1830, Jules Sandeau, a young law student in Paris, was visiting his home town La Châtre when he first met Aurore. He was the first of the many men who would play a serious role in her future life. At nineteen, Jules was six years her junior, a lover-pattern that would repeat itself throughout Aurore's life. It took the blond, blue-eyed young man three months before Aurore finally surrendered to his persistence. Later, she wrote to a friend:

> If you knew how much I love this poor child [...] his timid gaucherie towards me [...] gave me the desire to see him, examine him.

Aurore's response to Sandeau's passion only emphasized the limitations imposed on her by a meaningless marriage. When she discovered that Casimir was having an affair with one of his own servants, she said nothing: after all, she was equally guilty. After three wonderful months, Sandeau returned to Paris, determined to quit law studies and become a writer. His departure made Aurore feel more alone than at any time since the loss of her grandmother. Then, one cold morning in November, her life changed drastically. She wrote to Jules Boucoiran, young Maurice's tutor and her friend, on 3 December 1830, informing him of a package she inadvertently discovered, addressed to her in Casimir's handwriting and to be opened on his death.

> I could not find the patience to wait until I became a widow [...] I supposed my husband dead, feeling rather anxious to know what he might think of me while still alive.
> Good God! What a will! Curses for me and nothing else!

After nine unhappy years, Aurore announced her plans to leave Casimir. He demanded reasons. She told him of her lust for life, her disgust with the emptiness of her present existence and the need to change it. She told him bluntly that she wanted an allowance and that she would go to Paris 'forever' – which was Aurore's way of demanding the complete liberty to *be*, and to love whomsoever she may choose!

Casimir knew there would be no retraction. Reluctantly, he agreed that his wife should spend six months in Paris and six at Nohant. She would be allowed 250 francs a month – a piffling amount considering the money came out of her inheritance. Leaving the children behind was her biggest distress, but she knew they would be better off at Nohant rather than sharing the unsettled, unpredictable existence upon which she was about to embark. After ensuring their welfare, Aurore, Baronne Dudevant set off for Paris and a new, independent life.

★

During the 1820s and '30s, Paris was rapidly becoming the centre of the European cultural advance. In a world dominated by men, Aurore was undaunted: the determination to succeed fired not so much by the failure of her marriage as by her new-found freedom. Aurore drifted into journalism, more as a means of earning a few francs than from a burning ambition to be a writer. This happened after working for a time as a hack-journalist for Hyacinthe Latouche, the caustic but kindly editor of *Le Figaro*. Aurore was happy to be working with like-minded people. A bonus was her resumed affair with Jules Sandeau, who also happened to be on the *Figaro* staff, and with whom she would collaborate on work for the paper. The rekindled affair was sexually gratifying for both of them. When she returned to Nohant, Sandeau followed, meeting her clandestinely while Casimir slept off his hang-over. She wrote to Emile Regnault, Sandeau's medical student friend from Bourges:

> I'm a fool. I'm covered with tooth-marks and bruises. I can hardly stand up. I am in a frenzied state of joy. If you were here right now I would bite you till the blood came, just to have you share a bit of our frenzied happiness.

Sandeau and Aurore decided to combine their talents and write a novel. The result, *Rose et Blanche*, or *The Actress and the Nun* (1831) was written in the main by Aurore, although it was autographed 'J Sand', the name the couple chose as a joint *nom-de-plume*. Sandeau, without rancour, had accepted for some time that his co-writer's star was beginning a rapid ascent. Her very industry, so much more dedicated that Sandeau's, augured a professional rupture of their three-year relationship.

Aurore first presented herself before the public as George Sand with her novel *Indiana* (1832). The work was an overnight sensation; a new novelist had emerged, whose career and consequent fame would span the next forty-four years.

'It places you,' said Hyacinthe Latouche, not without pride, 'at the head of contemporary writers.'

All George Sand's heroines are proudly independent. Indiana is a

Créole who had much in common with George Sand's own emancipated life. In the largely autobiographical novel, Indiana leaves her older husband for a new life, and a young, intriguing lover. Edmund de Goncourt, the elder of the two prolific Parisian diarists, sensed in George Sand a ruthlessness, 'a basic coldness which allowed her to write about her lovers when practically in bed with them'. George (her name from here on, curiously anglicized) wrote of her first major success:

> I was initiated between the pages of *Indiana*, which represented my whole future, and a thousand-franc note, which was all the money I had in the world.

George had long ago observed that a man's name bore more assurance of acceptance in the world of letters. She took the observation further, electing to dress as a man on many public occasions. It was an idiosyncrasy born out of necessity: the theatre was expensive. Wearing men's attire assured George admittance without harassment into the cheapest seats at theatres and concerts; alternatively, as an unescorted woman, she would lay herself open to verbal and physical abuse and moral criticism for being at the theatre in the first place. As soon as she dressed as a man she passed unnoticed and without comment (although a confused *restaurateur* called Pinson, whose establishment George frequented, commented: 'when she's dressed as a man I call her Madame, and when she's dressed as a woman I call her Monsieur.')

As her fame spread, what had at first been a means of disguising her sex became her chosen, stylish 'uniform', defiantly reinforcing her new identity. With striking individuality, she emphasized masculine sartorial style by smoking cigars. However, not by any means did George dress exclusively as a man.

The permanent rift between George and Sandeau came early in 1833 when she discovered him in bed with a laundress. Sandeau, now twenty-three, unsuccessfully took an overdose of morphine. George was unimpressed. She wrote to Emile Regnault:

> I desire to have no communication with him [...] I have been too deeply wounded [...] make him understand that nothing can re-unite us in the future.

But was George wounded? Sixty-three years later, on 12 February 1896, Edmund de Goncourt wrote:

Delzant [writer] told me today that Mme Sandeau had left him all her husband's papers, and that [...] there was a letter which this lady always carried next to her heart, and which she showed to her husband every so often; this, as a vengeance for his past love-affairs. It was a letter written by Mme Sand to a medical student while she was living with Sandeau, a letter in which the mother combined with the mistress, and the phrase 'my dear boy' occurred in the middle of the most passionate, frank and explicit references to their happy copulation.

Episodes like this are conveniently forgotten by George in her autobiographical *Histoire de Ma Vie*. 'I swear I will never love again!' she vowed intensely after the split with Sandeau. She would make similar fatuous statements at the end of all her relationships, knowing it was a vow she was absolutely incapable of keeping. Now she amused herself for a time with the Swiss poet Charles Didier, whom she treated appallingly and who wrote of her:

There are depths of ferocity in her. She loves to make others suffer and takes pleasure in the pain she causes.

However, George even surprised herself with her next romantic experience.

★

For some time, the authoress had been a great admirer of Marie Dorval, one of the most talented actresses in the Paris boulevard theatres. In 1831, after watching Dorval's performance in Alexandre Dumas *père*'s tragedy, *Antony*, Sand had impulsively written a short note of congratulation. To her amazement, the actress presented herself at George's apartment the following day, bringing into her life a volcanic energy and the zest for living for which Marie was well-known. The diarist Arsène Houssaye describes the actress as having

a fish-wife's voice, a serving-maid's body [...] Art − sacred Art! − adorned everything she touched.

Despite her hitherto totally heterosexual relationships, George found herself disturbingly attracted to this tiny creature, who was five years her senior, defied convention with a shrug, and who was absolutely true to her own beliefs. She was everything that George longed to be. Typical of her early emotional insecurity, George wrote to the actress:

> Do you think you can bear with me? I'm such a boor, so stupid, so slow in thinking out loud, so gauche and tongue-tied [...] I feel that I love you with a rejuvenated heart, a heart you have remade anew. If it is a dream, don't rob me of it too quickly.

Paris called them 'The Inseparables'. Gustave Planche, acerbic critic of the *Revue de Deux Mondes* and sometime lover of George, tried to warn her of Dorval's sapphic tendencies. A furious George defended her new friend even as she defended her own right 'to love whomsoever I may choose'. She was immensely proud to have 'for my closest friend a woman who has no bridles on her passions'.

Both women were married; both adored men and male sexuality – but these aspects of their lives had nothing to do with the private, singular and intense relationship that rapidly developed between them. It seems they were truly in love during this short, ecstatic period. Without really knowing the exact nature of the relationship, casual comment became salacious gossip. Marie's narrow-minded lover Alfred de Vigny was accusatory (Comte de Viel Castel called him 'an old rose-coloured silk dress, which had been exposed to the sun's rays for years'); perhaps he grew afraid of losing his mistress to 'a man in turn of phrase, language, sound of voice, and boldness of expression'. He had no desire to lose the woman he adored much more than his cold English wife, and for whom he had written *Chatterton*, his greatest play. However, the affair continued unabated. In 1833 George wrote to Marie:

> If you have found no one better, please allow me to be your cavalier and I will come to collect you between six and seven. Just let me know. I love you. *Adieu.*

and later:

> I am not able to see you today, my darling. I'm not that lucky. Monday, morning or evening, at the theatre or in your bed, I simply must embrace you, my girl, or I will go mad. I am working like a convict [so that] this will be my reward.

As is the way with passion, the initial intensity between the two women cooled during that same year – at least, on Marie's side. Ardour would mutate into a friendship both women valued throughout their lives. From the secure comfort of retrospect fifty years on, Arsène Houssaye luridly commented that Marie, returning from the theatre, would find

> the strange woman waiting for her prey as she smoked cigarettes ... A singular amorous duo followed. The dark-haired one loosened the blonde one's hair. The blonde loosened the dark hair of her companion. And these locks of hair were mingled with the kisses and the bites. Both ... were frantic for the unforeseen and insatiable for love.

★

'It is my fate,' George often complained, 'to attract weak men, or men who sense the mother in me.'

The pattern seemed the same each time: she would begin as a mistress and by degrees end up a mother-figure. The lovers were younger, often slightly-built, invariably weaker, somewhat feminine: in short, men who thrived on a stronger personality. There were two notable exceptions: the lawyer Michel de Bourges, and fellow-writer, Prosper Mérimée.

Mérimée in particular was neither weak nor feminine. A superb linguist, noted archaeologist and historian, he became Inspector of Historical Monuments as well as Napoleon III's Master of the Revels at Compiègne. A brilliant young man of letters, at twenty-one he had risen to eminence through the success of his first collection of one-act plays.

The couple met in April 1833. Mérimée's aggressive masculinity fascinated George. She had read his travel essays with great enthusiasm; he had read nothing of hers. She thought him handsome – an exotic with a passion for things Iberian (Mérimée would write his most lasting novella, *Carmen*, twelve years later, in 1845). They met at a performance of Meyerbeer's *Robert The Devil,* after which Mérimée spent the next few days blatantly doing his best to seduce her. But could George live up to what was expected of her? Certainly not in experience – and she was well aware of Mérimée's reputation for following up a boudoir conquest with a public flaunting of his success. However, his unabashed masculinity excited her into a submission which has since become famous – as told to Mérimée's friend, Comte Paul d'Haussonville:

> Very well ... I am willing. Let it be as you wish, since you get such pleasure from it. For my part, I want you to know that I am sure it will give me no pleasure at all.

Mérimée enjoyed nothing better than a sexual challenge from a woman who purported to be cold – until an expert put fire in her blood. They returned to her apartment. His first surprise came when George changed into outlandish male attire, a dazzling wrap and a pair of brightly coloured Turkish slippers. His next surprise was her total lack of coquetry and feminine wiles. These were the sexual weapons that Mérimée had so looked forward to demolishing. There was no pre-coital foreplay. There was no challenge, no love war; she appeared to be resolute in fulfilling her promise merely to tolerate his assault without raising a finger to encourage it. More daunted than he cared to admit, he determined to melt the ice – until he watched her clinically efficient manner (and what a time it took!) in preparing the love-couch with her maid. Then, after a near robotic disrobing of herself, George slipped into bed.

Now thoroughly disenchanted, Mérimée reluctantly joined her, hoping close proximity would do the trick. But George lay absolutely still. This most sexual lion of the boulevards was so utterly disillusioned that he found himself unable to perform. It was not as if he had lost his erection – he never acquired one to lose; nor did Madame Sand intend aiding him. Furious and humiliated, Mérimée left the bed and dressed quickly, trying unsuccessfully to hide his embarrassment. At the door, he turned and said scathingly: 'Madame, you have the innocence of a young girl without her advantages and the pride of a marquise without having her graces.'

George was shattered by her lover's humiliated exit. Later, she blamed herself, admitting how crude and clumsy her handling of the whole episode had been. She wrote to Mérimée immediately, begging for a chance to repair the damage:

> Would you have the courage to come to my door at 9.00 p.m., to know
> if I am here? If the prospect bores you then don't come. I am more
> resigned than you think. I have improved considerably since yesterday …

But Mérimée was not prepared to risk further embarrassment. He told friends: 'Madame Sand has no love in her heart – she puts it all in her books!' To others: 'She is debauched to the core, but more from curiosity than temperament.'

George wrote to her critic friend and mentor Sainte-Beuve on 24 July 1833: 'in the end, at the age of thirty, I did what a girl of fifteen would not have done [and] the experiment failed completely. I shed tears of disgust, pain and discouragement.'

George and Mérimée met only once more. This was some fifteen years later in 1848, at a dinner in Paris given by Lord Houghton. Mérimée stared hard and long at George, who returned his gaze; neither one of them made an attempt to speak to the other. It seems safe to assume that they were made uncomfortable by shared humiliating memories of a single night that both would rather forget. However, to George's surprise and Mérimée's credit, he voted (unfortunately, in the minority) that she should be awarded the prestigious Academy Prize of 20,000 francs. Even more of a surprise was his canvassing of her earlier lover Jules Sandeau on her behalf. After this chance encounter, however, they never met again.

★

Meeting Alfred de Musset in April 1833 played a large part in dulling, but never obliterating, the embarrassment of the Mérimée episode. George had heard and read a great deal about this aristocratic young poet, whose well-known arrogance appalled her; but since he was the golden boy of the French Romantics and the most discussed poet in France, she realized that their paths must ultimately cross. Even so, only the month before, when Sainte-Beuve arranged a meeting George wrote to her friend on 11 March:

> Regarding Musset, and on reflection, I do not wish you to bring him here. He is very much a dandy, we would not be well suited.

Perhaps she had already sensed a high-voltage emotional danger ...

Musset's rise to fame had been rapid. At twenty, he was already something of a *roué*, living largely for the theatre, gambling, and 'easy' women. His nervous, often neurotic temperament with its resultant unpredictable mood swings led to a false rumour that he suffered from epilepsy. He was seriously addicted to the Emerald Poison – absinthe – which led Heinrich Heine to describe him as 'a young man with a promising past'. Handsome and charming, he had rarely been refused anything; consequently, he was selfish and spoilt. Exaggeratedly fashionable, he was the epitome of dandyism, his sometimes misleading effeminacy causing the sculptor Auguste Préault to dub him 'Mademoiselle Byron'.

By chance, around 15 April 1833 both George and Musset were guests at a literary dinner party in honour of François Buloz, editor of the *Revue de Deux Mondes*. A veiled empathy between George and Musset was already in evidence when the dinner party broke up that night – a response not unnoticed by Gustave Planche who, once again, watched his amorous chances with George disintegrate in the thrill of a new attraction. (The great Victor Hugo detested Planche and described him as 'a fungus not afraid of being bitten because it knows that it is poisonous'.)

Musset sent George some quickly scribbled lines. She responded by sending him a copy of *Indiana*. They continued to loan each other their work, George eventually commenting that

> your creations are in themselves far more beautiful than mine. My figures are more gross, more down-to-earth [...] Your portrayals belong to the youth of the soul.

They entered into a passionate affair of minds some short time before their bodies entered into a passionate affair of the flesh. They talked for hours, discussing and arguing in a way George had never known with her husband. Here, in her bed at last, was the essence of why she had come to Paris – a man of ideas and genius, who satisfied her physical desires. And yet, already she was unconsciously preparing for her role as the poet's 'mother', when she wrote on the flyleaf of the first volume of *Léila* (her second novel and the work that really established her as an important novelist): 'To My Naughty Boy, Alfred'.

The lovers shared many opinions: both regretted the fall of the Empire and the Napoleonic Dream; they felt antagonistic towards Victor Hugo's overblown prose; both adored music and agreed that liberty was worth dying for. She introduced him to the Eastern ambience popular at the time, teaching him to smoke Egyptian tobacco while he listened with increasing enthusiasm to her passionate outbursts about life and art. He had to admit it: this strangely powerful and fascinating woman had rekindled within him the hope he had long considered dead.

Musset's last serious affair had been painful and embarrassing. The woman, Madame Beaulieu, was married; unknown to him, she had used him lightly to disguise from her friends a more passionate attachment to a man she really loved. Discovering this, the young poet had lost himself in an endless round of pleasure and degradation which finally left him satiated and exhausted. Now, four years later, he wrote to George: 'I am in love with you. I have been since that first day when I visited you ...'

Paul de Musset, Alfred's elder brother, was distinctly troubled. By reputation alone, he knew the authoress was capable of devouring his sibling. (However, Arsène Houssaye groused, 'He treats his brother like a saint.')

It is easy to understand the young Musset's attraction to the dominating personality of George Sand. World-weary at twenty-two, anyone with the power to relieve the ennui of his existence was worth pursuing. Despite their physical compatibility, the poet told George (wasn't she expecting it?) that he also saw her as a mother-figure, an image no doubt encouraged by the six-and-a-half years difference in their ages. He confirmed the impression in another letter, in which he told her, 'I love you with the love of a little child'.

The affair with the poet was the most romantic, as well as the most doomed, love that George Sand ever experienced. The pair spent two short 'honeymoon' periods near Fontainebleau, after which Musset moved in with the authoress, on the Quai Malaquais. It was the spring of their happiness; even Paul de Musset was impressed.

George was hyperbolic, as always at the beginning of an affair. 'At last! I have met my destiny. Never have I been happier, or more secure in love.' On 25 August she wrote to Sainte-Beuve:

> I have fallen in love, and this time very seriously indeed, with Alfred de Musset. It is not a caprice; it is a devoted attachment [...] It is the love of a young man together with the friendship of a comrade.

George Sand's industry was still unflagging; she had no trouble working from seven to thirteen hours daily, usually throughout the quiet hours of the night. The writer Charles Yriarte, commenting on George's indefatigable energy, wrote:

> She would write the last lines of a novel, say, at eleven; put the page aside; take another piece of paper and begin another novel at eleven-five; and this was not an exception, but her habit.

Musset, on the other hand, was inclined to be spasmodic, his inspiration coming in short, energetic bursts. Discipline counted for nothing with him; lack of it, artistically, was a large part of his genius.

It was a need for fresh locales and new inspiration that turned the lovers' thoughts to Italy, especially since George's next planned novel would be set in that country. Poor Madame de Musset was aghast that her son should even consider such a sojourn with a woman as scandalous as Madame Sand. Having convinced him of the madness of such a venture, her victory was overturned by an impromptu visit and a charming imploration from a determined George, who had no intention of being refused:

She employed all the eloquence for which she was famous and persuaded me to entrust my son to her, repeating to me that she would love and care for him like a mother … even more than myself! What could I say? The siren tore a consent from me!

The lovers departed on 12 December 1833, just after Musset's twenty-third birthday. They were seen off by Paul de Musset, who wrote in his brother's biography:

On a misty, melancholy evening, I saw them enter the stagecoach amid circumstances of evil omen.

★

A series of mishaps left the travellers exhausted by the time they reached Pisa. On the flick of a coin, they changed their plans and headed straight for Venice instead. Venice! For lovers, probably the most romantic city in Europe. They arrived on 1 January 1834, both George and Musset instantly in rapport with the city of canals. They stayed at the Albergo Reale (known today as Hotel Danieli) in Suite No. 13. Their days and nights were filled with novelty and joy in each other's company, until George suddenly began complaining of persistent headaches. At first, the poet was solicitous and considerate; but the selfish, spoilt *enfant* soon came to the fore, showing a lack of tolerance and understanding. Hurt by her lover's selfishness and angered by his petulance, George was further distressed when her 'golden child' began to seek diversion by himself – or rather, in the company of the French Consul, a family friend of the Mussets, who encouraged his debauchery. Very soon, the poet was wishing he had made the Italian journey alone.

It soon became evident that when things went smoothly, Musset was in love; when problems arose, Musset fell out of love. It was an essential part of the schizophrenia from which he suffered, making him the most passionate and romantic of lovers, or the foul-mouthed, debauched, unpleasant youth George had not yet encountered, but who was about to lurch into her life. As her headaches became increasingly debilitating, so Musset became progressively more objectionable until suddenly, on 9 January, he announced quite coldly: 'I am unable to love you any longer. I ask you to forgive me.'

It was only one of his moods, but George had no way at the time of recognizing this. (She would, however, remind him of these words in a passionate, reproving letter written the following October.) Bitterly hurt and with all thoughts of her 'destiny' shattered, George's anguish mutated into defensive anger. She wanted to leave Venice as quickly as possible. In a last effort to escape the painful emotional trap they had fallen into, she asked the hotel manager to send a doctor to bleed her, thinking that curing her headaches might return the relationship to its former Edenic state. Neither George nor Musset could know that the arrival of Doctor Pietro Pagello was the true beginning of their end. Pagello banished George's headache, substituting in its place an emotional migraine stemming from mutual attraction. The doctor was handsome, strong and susceptible to feminine charm; George made no attempt to discourage him. In truth, it was not their first encounter; days before, Pagello had seen this 'young woman of somewhat melancholy countenance' on the balcony of the Albergo Reale. For her part, George had been all too aware of the stranger's admiration.

Headaches banished, George snapped back to reality. They had come to Italy to *work*; indeed, they were living in Italy on the 5,000 francs' advance she had been paid in unfulfilled commissions. Musset was scathing. He fully expected his mistress to live for the moment and join him in continued hedonism and love-making. Instead, she paid her first respects to her pen!

Ignoring the tirade, George settled down to hard work behind closed doors. Her determination and discipline only succeeded in making the poet feel emotionally dismissed and artistically guilty; he simply lacked the will or the desire to follow her example. Five years later, in a letter to the painter Eugène Delacroix dated 7 September 1838, George would say of retreating love:

> Love, when one's star is glowing at its fullest; art, before all, when that star is in decline!

Numbed by the chill of their declining affair, George turned to her art for solace and emotional survival. For his part, a piqued Musset flounced off on a childish revenge-spree, only to return days later, clearly chastened and upset, to inform George that he was suffering from *une mauvaise maladie* – an unpleasant disease (referred to in a condemnatory letter to Musset in October 1834). Musset's licentiousness made him an easy prey for one of the many sexual diseases which were common at that time. They would have left Venice immediately, had George not been suddenly stricken with severe dysentery. The attack lasted for the best part of a week. As she recovered, Musset now fell ill with a serious case of 'typhoid fever complicated by alcoholism'. To add to their problems, money was running out. Their extravagances and George's generosity (she was paying all Musset's expenses) left her monetary reserves very low. Eventually, they were compelled to move to cheaper lodgings.

At the beginning of February 1834, Musset became worse. George wrote urgently to Dr Pagello: 'I beg of you to come immediately, bringing with you a specialist … I fear for his sanity more than his health.' Pagello, together with a colleague, spent two days fighting to quiet the invalid, who had succumbed to one of his peculiar hysterical fits. On 8 February, George wrote to Jules Boucoiran:

> last night was horrible. Six hours of such powerful madness that, in spite of the efforts of two strong men, he ran around his room stark naked. Cries, songs, howls, convulsions … my God! my God! What a spectacle! He tried to strangle me in his embarrassment.

Musset now worsened when he developed a severe bronchial infection, which climaxed in the poet coughing blood. Throughout these traumatic days, the poet was demanding, impossibly selfish, alarmingly insulting and foul-mouthed. 'Bitch', 'slut', 'whore' were epithets George now heard so frequently they no longer hurt.

Resigned, and with the mother-image now well to the fore, George sat with her deranged lover for well over a week, acquiring what rest she could, sleeping by his side on a couch. Dr Pagello was most solicitous; vulnerable from exhaustion, George found herself falling in love. If the handsome Italian needed a push in the amatory direction, George surpassed herself when she sat down impetuously in front of him one evening and scribbled furiously, in silence, for an hour. She handed him the missive in an envelope; he saw it was addressed 'To the not-so-bright Pagello'. The doctor was overwhelmed later that night as he read the outpourings of a frustrated woman:

> Am I to be your companion or your slave? Do you love me or do you only desire me? When your passion has been satisfied will you have the grace to be grateful? If I give you great happiness, will you be able to make me feel that I did? Do you realize *what I am*, or will you take good care not to realize it? Do the pleasures of passion stupefy and brutalize you, or do they throw you into an ecstasy which is divine? You may be the best or the worst of men, but I love you without caring whether or not I can respect you. I love you only because I love you, but perhaps before long I shall be constrained to hate you …

Surely, an invitation to bed her! George's next letter was even more direct:

> Not one of my friends, if I consulted [them], would advise me not to close my soul to all strong passion; but this would not prevent me from handing myself over to you and sleeping peacefully in your arms.

Pagello was drugged; how could he resist? George's frankness simply swept the suburban doctor away on an emotional tide he had never before experienced. Later, he wrote:

> There is no denying that this woman's genius astonished me and overwhelmed me. I would have given anything to see her at once, throw myself at her feet, and swear undying love to her.

Pagello felt guilty about Musset, but, suddenly, discretion was of no concern; they fondled, cuddled and even drank tea from the same cup – all of which the recuperating invalid witnessed, or sensed. Musset was beside himself with rage, screaming insults and accusations of treason. In June he would admit to François Buloz that he'd said to George:

> You are a slut. My one regret is that I did not leave you twenty francs on your mantlepiece the first time I had you.

Physical weakness and insecurity led Musset into a fantasy world where many intimate moments he thought he witnessed between the doctor and George were the product of his fertile, fevered imagination. Unlike Musset when she was ill, George nursed him without complaint. Having exhibited the darker, uglier side of his nature, Musset now became so insulting and violent that the long-suffering George finally snapped. In uncontrolled rage, she threatened to have him committed to an insane asylum. Musset later told his brother that he knew she meant it. Purely by chance, they were now living next to a mental institution! Musset was frightened; '[I] returned to my room without daring to answer her.'

In fact, Musset's rages and paranoia were not muted in the slightest by the threat. On one occasion, George was in the midst of writing to Pagello for advice concerning Musset's well-being. When the poet entered the room, suspicious as to George's occupation, she tore up the missive and tossed it through the window, afraid of the poet's reaction. What followed was in the best farce tradition, as later admitted by

Musset. Sensing physical danger, George rushed outside to gather up the fragmented letter. Then she leapt into a nearby gondola and ordered the gondolier to take her to the Lido. Quick as lightning, Musset jumped in beside her. George remained silent; Musset simply stared at her. At the Lido, she leapt out of the gondola and headed directly for the Jewish cemetery, 'leaping from tomb to tomb'. Musset followed, 'leaping as she did'. When George finally stopped and sank on to a gravestone and began to cry in rage and frustration, Musset advised very quietly: 'Confess now that you are a [whore].'

'Yes, I am,' she answered.

After Musset's appalling, strange behaviour, George now felt she had the right to pursue the phoenix of a new love born out of the death of the old, without any secrecy or deceit. Curiously, within days of the episode above, the poet had 'stablized', accepting the *status quo* as something he had brought about himself. As gracious as he had been vile, Musset, showing only affability towards the doctor, calmly finalized plans for an honourable departure for Paris (with George's financial aid) on 29 March. The recriminations had ceased on both sides – as though the many insults the poet had spat at his mistress were no more than a sick man's hallucinations. Both knew differently. Before George and Musset finally parted, this curious *ménage* shared a strained farewell dinner, during which Musset gave his successor his blessing.

George admitted, as she watched her young poet's gondola disappear into the pale lagoon mists, that she felt part of herself going with him. Amazingly, a steady correspondence between the pair resulted, from which the following are extracts. The first letter from Musset was penned on 24 March 1834:

> ... as I had stepped outside your door, with the thought that I had lost you for ever, I felt that I deserved to lose you, and that no punishment is too hard for me.

George wrote to him on 3 April:

> How shall I exist without the happiness and the distress that you caused me? [...] Do not believe that I can be happy with the thought that I have lost your heart. Whether I was your mistress or your mother matters little. I know that I love you now, and that is all.

Two days later, on 5 April, Musset inscribed:

You thought you could be my mistress, but you were really my mother. [...] we have committed incest, you and I.

The Venetian episode left its permanent mark on both of them; Musset, especially, was never the same again.

George remained in Italy for another five months, writing the novelettes *Andre, Mattea, Jacques, Leone Leoni,* and the first of what would later be recognized as minor works of genius, *Letters of a Traveller.* The affair with Pagello continued, but both knew they were already in the autumn of the liaison. With the excuse that her children needed her, George left for Paris on 24 July 1834. Pagello agreed to accompany her, he having sold most of his possessions to cover his expenses. 'I realized that if I should go to France,' he wrote, 'I should return without her.'

From 15 August, when they arrived in Paris, the wild ungovernable passions that had fuelled her relationship with Pagello during Musset's illness rapidly dwindled into indifference. George treated her lover disgracefully. 'For the first time in my life I love without passion,' she wrote to Musset after only six weeks. Without the threat of exposure, without the clandestine nature of their love, there was no excitement. Dr Pagello, good looks and all, paled into insignificance.

When Musset discovered that George had returned to Paris, he insisted upon seeing her just once more, declaring that he was hers, 'body and soul'. Regardless of making Pagello look a fool, she visited Musset. Their fervour, fired by months of separation and stress, exhausted both of them. Within days, however, they had parted bitterly, Musset's jealousy having been roused by his friend, Alfred Tattet, a wealthy banker's son who loathed George. The spiteful young dandy quickly convinced the poet that a drunken Pagello had acknowledged his affair with George while Musset lay seriously ill. Deeply distressed by this exposé, Musset departed for Baden on 25 August. Abandoning poor Pagello, George left for a three-month sojourn at Nohant.

The Pagello affair was over; George firmly closed the door on the whole episode when the Italian returned to Venice on 24 October 1834. In retrospect, Pagello followed the same pattern as George's other lovers. Franz Liszt, the Hungarian pianist and composer, found his initially close friendship with the writer gave him ample opportunity to observe the routine:

Mme Sand caught her butterfly and tamed it in her box by giving it grass and flowers – this was the love period. Then she stuck her pin into it when it struggled – this was the *congé*, and it always came from her. Afterwards, she vivisected it, stuffed it, and added it to her collection of heroes for her novels. It was this traffic of souls which had given themselves up unreservedly to her which, eventually, disgusted me with her friendship.

Liszt grew to despise George Sand because he considered her a collector of men; a somewhat hypocritical opinion from a man whose own amatory notoriety matched his pianistic fame.

In November 1834, George began the remarkable diary which became famous as *Journal Intime*. In it she expressed openly the arguments for and against her passion for Musset. She wrote as herself; then she sublimated self to speak from the poet's point of view, dissecting the opinions of both friends and enemies in the process. What is evident in this 'crucifixion' is that George still loved her poet – and if loving him as 'her child' is dominant, there is no question that she also lusted for him. She attempted to explain her Venetian subterfuge in the *Journal*:

> If I had not lied to you in Venice, your own fury would have killed you. Then, as you grew better, I had to keep on lying, otherwise you would have died of wretchedness.

It was the sort of self-vindication at which George Sand excelled. She 'told' Musset on 25 November, via the *Journal*: 'I love you. To be loved by you I would submit to any torture.' Soon, all Paris knew of George's confused grief. Sainte-Beuve was so concerned about her that he wrote to Musset towards the end of November:

> I […] beg you not to see nor receive the person I have seen so distressed this morning.

Disdainfully, Musset replied:

> I confess that I do not understand what her reason can be when last night I positively refused to receive her at my house.

In vain did George try to see Musset, cutting off her fine thick hair and delivering it to him. Musset is reputed to have buried his tear-stained face in it. George escaped to Nohant, having handed the *Journal* to Jules Boucouran to deliver to the poet. Predictably, Musset made abject apologies. George wrote to Sainte-Beuve on 15 December:

Alfred has written me an affectionate letter, repenting his many violences ... [but] I have no wish to see him again; it makes me ill.

They parted finally in August, after a particularly violent quarrel which had driven George to attempt to stab her lover. But Musset had snatched the dagger from her and had held it to her throat. It was the moment of truth for both of them.

In 1836, Musset's *La Confession d'un Enfant du Siècle* was published. It is a tortured autobiographic novel which vividly describes one of the most traumatic love affairs of the nineteenth century. Musset did not spare himself; he took the blame for everything that had gone wrong:

> Only spotless lilies will grow on your tomb [...] People will always remember us as Romeo and Juliette, and Eloïse and Abelard ... never one without the other.

Between 1835 and 1837, however, Musset wrote a collection of poems called *Nuits*, exploring the same situation, but with the poet no longer regarding George as the innocent. He condemns her for darkening his youth and his future with her all-enveloping passions. Ten years later, in 1847, the actress Madame Judith Bernât of the *Comédie-Française* met the erstwhile lovers individually during the course of her work. She commented:

> Shall I confess it? The impression he made on me was a very ambiguous one, for good and bad were strangely blended, or rather conflicted, in his nature. He was but thirty-seven years old then, but he looked nearly sixty.
>
> I found it difficult to believe in his romantic relations with George Sand. It is true that when a little later I had an opportunity of seeing the latter close to I was just as much struck with the ugliness of that masculine-looking creature ... Her chin was linked to her neck by three rolls of fat from which grew scattered hairs, her cheeks were flabby and drooping. She had very slovenly habits. Nature certainly made a mistake in her case, for she ought to have been a man.

But this was 1835. While George would go on to love again, Musset never recovered from the affair. Despite the countless other women who crossed his life, Musset loved George until he died, aged forty-seven, in 1857. It was said that he died of a broken heart; that he drank to obliterate the pain of losing the one woman he had truly loved. In fact, Musset's demise was the result of further debauchery and the pleasure/pain he derived from inebriation. Sainte-Beuve told the Goncourts of an occasion he went to dine at Véry's, which they recorded on 12 September 1864, seven years after Musset's eventual demise. Musset had been at the restaurant on this same night; he had been paid in advance for a new serial and the poet was celebrating by spending his fee on a private orgy. The Goncourts' diary reveals:

> There was a whole brothel upstairs, on which Musset was spending his 4,000 francs. By the time the women arrived he was already so drunk that he could not enjoy his own orgy.

Long before he died, Musset was a well-known fixture at the Café de la Régence. According to a friend of the Goncourts, a Dr Martin, here Musset would drink 'absinthe that looked like thick soup [...] after which the waiter gave him his arm and led him, or rather half-carried him, to the carriage waiting for him at the door.'

A year after Musset's death, George wrote *Elle et Lui* (1859). Based on her affair with the unhappy poet, it was 'an act of posthumous literary vengeance', to quote Curtis Cate, George Sand's biographer. In it, the hero is irresponsible, lazy and something of a gigolo (Musset), while the heroine is hard-working and gifted (Sand). The inference was obvious. Infuriated by her cruel impertinence, Paul de Musset immediately retaliated by writing *Lui et Elle*, neatly reversing the characters: the heroine is an untalented singer (Sand) while the hero is a composer touched with genius (Musset). Both novels were too transparent for the public to take kindly to them.

★

George Sand met Frederick Chopin for the first time in 1836, two years after her disastrous Venetian experience, and her legal separation from Casimir. They were introduced at the *salon* of Countess Marie d'Agoult, Franz Liszt's mistress and the mother of his three children. There was a mutual indifference, even dislike. To the fastidious pianist and composer, George was unattractive, masculine and irritating; even her features antagonized him.

'Who is that peculiar woman with the disgusting cigar in her hand?' Chopin asked his composer friend, Ferdinand Hiller, and then added, 'but is she truly a woman?'

Later, Chopin wrote to his parents in Poland that George Sand's face repelled him. George had an equally poor opinion of the composer; she considered his playing remarkable, as were his features, which she described as androgynous. When they parted that night she added cold reserve and snobbishness to her summation.

Slight, small-boned, gentle and weighing less than seven stone, Chopin was indeed as feminine as he was masculine; he would be compared to Shelley's *Hermaphroditus*. Liszt wrote:

> His blue eyes were more spiritual than dreamy; his bland smile never writhed into bitterness. The transparent delicacy of his skin pleased the eye; his fair hair was soft and silky; his nose slightly aquiline; his bearing so distinguished and his manners stamped with such high breeding, that involuntarily he was always treated *en prince*.

The antagonists were not to meet again for fifteen months, on 13 December 1837, at the *salon* of their mutual friend, Countess Charlotte Marliani, when each was compelled to revise those first impressions. Chopin played frequently that evening. Lacking the theatrical bravura of Franz Liszt and the stamina of Sigismund Thalberg, he nevertheless possessed a flawless pianistic technique which, coupled with his refined, delicate interpretations, would place him as the leading pianist in Europe during the 1840s. Loathing the concert platform ('The public frighten me and their breath stifles me, their curious gaze paralyzes me'), he became the darling of the Parisian *salons* and drawing rooms of Europe. Amazingly, he gave fewer than thirty public piano recitals during his nineteen years' residence in western Europe; his constant poor health also had something to do with this. Now thirty-four, George was acutely aware of her six years' seniority over the man she now determined to enmesh as her next lover. Chopin, for his part, began to recognize in George a woman whose outlandish dress and revolting cigar habit disguised a sensitive heart and a sharp intelligence.

As with Musset, when he first met George Chopin was slowly recovering from a complicated, unhappy love affair; his pending engagement to Maria Wodinska was thwarted through parental opposition on Maria's side. Also like Musset, he was newly recovered from 'an unpleasant disease'. Chopin was open to new adventure – yet while it was evident that he was increasingly attracted to the novelist, he balked at the bedroom door. Frustrated, George penned a very long, hypocritical letter to Chopin's friend, the patriot Albert Grzymala, whom she liked and trusted (but who, recognizing the vampire in George, and being protective of the gentle Chopin, never fully returned the compliment). She told him she loved the pianist, but that their union could only ever be spiritual since she was as good as married to the playwright, Félicien Mallefille (an ongoing liaison which turned out to be of very short duration). George declared:

> I have no wish to abandon myself to passion although there is still a furnace smouldering in my heart which at times is very threatening …

Then, contradicting herself, she determines to convince Grzymala that she is quite happy to share

> [just] a few hours of passion which is pure poetry at intervals […] if marriage (or any union resembling it) would be the grave of his artist-soul.

Such reasoning exposes George Sand at her most conniving and devious. Would there have been an affair if George had not set out to claim Chopin for her own? It's doubtful. They were vastly different personalities: she was aggressive and a go-getter, loving the outdoors and fighting for just causes; he was happiest surrounded by the sophistication of the *salon,* the privacy of his music room and the presence of close friends of like mind. She was essentially physical, lusting (never her word, but the right one) after any man she fancied; his sexual drive was never equal to her demands. She was a republican and for the people; he was a snob and courted the rich and titled. Her sense of dress dangled between the slipshod and the 'exotic'; his was the essence of *bon ton*: a study in sartorial elegance. ('His glove collection rivals Delacroix's waistcoat collection and mine put together!' confided Balzac.)

Through friends, George sent blatant messages to Chopin – 'tell Chopin I admire him'; 'I worship him'; 'I adore him' – all of which softened the pianist's resistence. Aglow at the prospect of amorous battle, George set out for Paris where, sometime around 8 June 1838, complete victory was hers when she claimed her victim between the sheets. Experience soon made it apparent to George that her new lover was no bedroom athlete. 'How can one love without a single kiss?' she argued irritably. Thoroughly frustrated, she now told Chopin he made love like an exhausted old woman. She recalled, writing to Grzymala:

> He seemed to despise (in the manner of a religious prude) the coarser side of human nature … and to fear to soil our love by a further ecstasy.

At last, George was forced to accept that her lover would never be a Lothario – that theirs was meant to be a spiritual union which transcended the mere physical. This was her self-delusory manner of disguising the fact that Chopin simply couldn't satisfy her carnal needs. Chopin, only too aware of this, explained their unusual relationship to his erstwhile mistress Delphine Potocka four years later, on 19 November 1840:

> My affair with her [George] didn't last a year; it ended in Mallorca when I was so ill. I swear by my love for you and by my love for my mother – what I have just said is the sacred truth. I was not [passionate?] enough to satisfy her. My illness served her as a pretext for a break with me. From that time she has given me only maternal love. She takes care of me devotedly [...] All those who go to Nohant know about her lovers, and in Paris too it is known who is her favourite [...] this unquenched passion of hers is a real disease.

★

Chopin's sexuality has always raised a moot point. During late adolescence, he had shown a marked preference for the companionship of his great friend, Tytus Woyciechowski, who, if we are honest, was Chopin's first love, although there is not the slightest proof of homosexuality on Tytus's part. (Had there been, judging by Chopin's early letters, there seems little doubt that the composer would have responded.) To Tytus, Chopin wrote obsessive letters and notes, many of them homoerotic:

> 'You don't like to be kissed. But let me do it today' (27 December 1828); 'I affectionately embrace you, and kiss your lips, if you allow me.' (12 September 1829); '... but I want you, and I expect you clean-shaven.' (5 June 1830); '... don't kiss me now for I haven't washed yet. How stupid of me! You wouldn't kiss me even if I were smothered in all the perfumes of Byzantium ... Tonight let me dream you are kissing me.' (18 September 1830).

On the other hand, letters to Countess Delphine Potocka, his former pupil and short-time mistress, indicate a strong heterosexuality. Chopin sought to woo her through music, but Delphine had far more elemental plans; as Guy de Pourtalès wrote, 'she gave him what was in his mind long before he had ever dreamed of asking her for it.' Delphine aroused

Chopin's sexuality more than any other woman during his lifetime. All inhibitions swept away, he penned these words to her in 1835, only a year before he met George Sand:

> When, with passion, I have emptied my fluid into a woman until I am pumped dry, then inspiration shuns me. A man wastes this life-giving precious fluid for a moment of ecstasy. The creator must abjure woman, then the forces in his body will accumulate in his brain in the form of inspiration. Sweetest Fidelina, how much of that precious fluid, how many forces have I wasted on you! Who knows what ballades, polonaises, perhaps an entire concerto, have been forever engulfed in your little D flat major ...? [their soubriquet for Delphine's sexual organs]

Chopin was not alone in his 'wasted-precious-fluid' theorem. The Goncourts recorded in their *Journal*

> Balzac's thriftiness in the expenditure of his sperm. He was perfectly happy playing the love game up to the point of ejaculation, but he was unwilling to go any further. Sperm for him was an emission of cerebral matter and, as it were, a waste of creative power. [30 March 1875]

However, since Chopin's letters to Delphine originally came to light in the 1950s, the authenticity of them has been severely queried. Leading authorities on Chopin disagree violently about both content and handwriting. Delphine admitted after Chopin's death that she still possessed many of the composer's letters to her; the Potocki family are said to have refused posthumous publication because the letters were too explicit. While there is much to support the forgery theory, the truth will never be known. This very uncertainty adds a further intriguing facet to the Chopin legend.

★

It was largely on account of her son Maurice's health that George had decided to spend the winter of 1838/9 in Mallorca. Chopin thought that he, too, would benefit from the milder climate. Together with ten-year-old Solange, George's daughter, the four of them set off, arriving at the capital Palma on 8 November. As with the Venetian trip with Musset, it was planned as an idyllic working-holiday; perhaps George also felt that an exotic climate might encourage and ignite Chopin's romantic ardour. The reality became a nightmare.

The first three weeks were magical, although their accommodation was, at best, primitive. After the first week they left Palma and went to stay at Establiments, not far from the capital. Chopin's health improved and George wrote that the island was 'the most perfect place on earth'. Then the weather broke suddenly. It rained without ceasing; Chopin's health deteriorated to such an extent that George, growing alarmed, was compelled to seek medical help. Her autobiography tells us that the doctors only confirmed what she already knew: Chopin was suffering from advanced consumption.

George catered daily for the children's education, also managing all the cleaning and cooking, and devotedly nursing 'little Chop'. (Years later, in her autobiography *Histoire de Ma Vie*, she would refer to Chopin at this time as a 'detestable invalid'.)

To add to their burdens, the Mallorquins had discovered the type of bohemian guests their island was hosting; they were less than pleased. The visitors ignored the Holy Day, and George insulted her sex by dressing herself and her daughter as men. To top it all, she was cohabiting with a man who was not her husband, and who was infecting the island with a highly contagious disease. Much later, George wrote scathingly about the natives, angrily dismissing them as 'peasant[s] who understand nothing except how to pray, sing and work – and who never *think*!' The Sand party was ordered to quit the villa, but not before paying for total redecoration, plastering, fresh mattresses and linen. Anything else touched by the sick man had to be destroyed and replaced. This was the law in Spain at the time.

During the good weather they had visited a remote Carthusian monastery at Valldemosa, seventeen kilometres from Palma. They went there now, travelling on 15 December. Only three other people were in residence. Their accommodation was bucolically simple. George and the children enthused; Chopin did not. However, despite his weakening physical state, Chopin worked. Later, in Paris, George reminisced: 'Oh, with what poetry his music could light up that sanctuary, even when he suffered most!'

Here, Chopin completed the major part of the *Préludes*, Opus 28, begun two years previously. A collection of twenty-four miniatures, they rank among his greatest lyrical creations. His achievement is all the more amazing because he had no piano – 'an uncivilized country in this respect', he commented. He was compelled to write directly, without the benefit of actually hearing his music, until, eventually, he was able to hire a local upright 'which irritates more than relieves him', snapped George.

He had almost given up expecting his imported Pleyel instrument to arrive and was pleasantly surprised when it did. (Today, both instruments, greatly revered, are on display at the Charterhouse at Valldemosa, together with the world's most important private collection of Chopin's manuscripts, letters and personal objects.)

Years later, George recollected that:

His agreeableness and cheerful amiability in society were frequently matched by the gloominess and peevishness of his behaviour to those around him at home, whom he sometimes drove almost to despair.

George and Chopin now accepted the services of Maria Antonia, a neighbour, who insisted upon caring for their needs. It was the only kindness they had so far experienced on the island. Deliberately charged ridiculous prices for food, it was only through the kindness of the French Ambassador that George eventually stocked her cupboards with supplies sent out from Palma. Although she had bought a goat to combat the short supply of milk, the animal yielded little – until George discovered the 'good' Maria Antonia helping herself, then topping up the can with water. She also stole from their supplies.

When, at last, the weather changed for the better, the party left for Palma. They had resided for ninety-seven miserable, hungry, despairing days at Valldemosa. Import tax and transportation of Chopin's Pleyel piano had been extortionate; now, Mme Hélène Choussat, the wife of George's banker and not steeped in island superstition, bought it for 1,200 francs.

Haemorrhaging badly, Chopin was delighted when they finally set sail for Marseilles. From Barcelona, on 15 February 1839, George wrote to her friend Charlotte Marliani, wife of the Spanish consul in Paris, relating their Mallorcan experience in no uncertain terms:

We had three leagues of rough road to cover between our mountain retreat and Palma. We knew ten persons who owned carriages, horses, mules, etc, but no one would loan us them. We had to make this journey on an unsprung cattle-cart, and of course, Chopin had a frightful attack of blood-spitting when we reached Palma. And the reason for this unfriendliness? Chopin coughs, and whosoever coughs in Spain is declared a consumptive; and he who is consumptive is held to be a plague-carrier, a leper … We were treated like outcasts at Mallorca – because of Chopin's cough and because we didn't go to mass. My children were stoned in the streets … I should have written ten volumes to give you an idea of the cowardice, deceit, selfishness, stupidity and spite of this thick-headed thieving and bigoted race ...

The writer Robert Graves (who lived for some time on the island and loved the Mallorquins) tells us that George Sand quarrelled with workmen, behaved very badly to the island's hierarchy, flaunted her bohemianism and made absolutely no attempt to remember her position as a visitor to the island. Maurice hung a copy of Goya's *Monastic Orgy* on a wall of their accommodation, which was duly reported to the townsfolk by a visitor.

George gave full vent to her fury against the Mallorquins in an extended résumé, *Un Hiver à Majorque* (*A Winter in Mallorca*, 1840), a vicious, sarcastic attack, which no amount of excellent descriptive writing on Mallorquin customs and terrain can disguise. No fewer than forty of the island's lawyers decided a mass revenge on the French authoress. It finally fell to the historian José Maria Quadrado – a powerful puritan who loathed all that George represented – to reply with equal hatred in his *Refutation of George Sand*, which appeared in an edition of *La Palma* in May 1841. His arguments are very convincing. He ends with personal insult, more viciously direct than anything George Sand had written about the Mallorquins:

George Sand is the most immoral of writers and Mme Dudevant [George's married name] the dirtiest of women.

George suffered severe physical reaction from the Majorca experience; for several weeks she was ill. Unlike Musset in Venice, Chopin proved a good and kind nurse.

★

In the late spring of 1839, George returned to Nohant with Chopin, both of them fully recovered in health and energy. This was Chopin's first visit to the estate and he was happy, even relaxing sufficiently to treat the assembled guests to a display of his brilliant gift for mimicry. Delacroix, Chopin's close friend, loved the estate but nonetheless commented, 'I would soon become antediluvian at Nohant!' The critic and writer Théophile Gautier thought it 'as amusing as a Moravian monastery'.

It was during this summer that George decided to curtail physical relations with her lover; they had been together less than a year. To

Grzymala she wrote, 'it is my concern for Chopin's health'. In fact, it was her way of easing herself out of a situation she had long felt to be irksome. Years later, in *Histoire de Ma Vie*, she stated that the only reason she didn't leave Chopin on their return from Mallorca was her fear of his suffering an adverse physical reaction. Chopin seemed to accept his *congé*; unlike George's, his battle against carnality was not difficult.

★

'No more than a smoking room', was how the diarist Houssaye described George Sand's *salon*. However, it became one of the most controversial *salons* in Paris. Liszt was a frequent visitor, although Chopin had become tired of the Hungarian's superficial airs and irritating bombast. He was particularly angry when he discovered that Liszt had used his apartment for a sexual assignation with the nymphomaniac Marie Pleyel. George and Marie d'Agoult had also become disenchanted; Marie resented George 'feeding' Balzac information concerning her stormy life with Liszt, which eventually resulted in Balzac's *Beatrix* (1839).

Comte Horace de Viel-Castel wrote mysteriously in his memoirs: 'I know that Madame d'Agoult was deeply corrupted through her intimacy with George Sand.' Perhaps he was referring to the many rumours that, where George had failed to sexually ignite Liszt, she succeeded with his mistress when they first met. (George Sand's attraction to Liszt was well-known. Richard Lewinsohn writes of George admitting that she would like nothing better than to 'lie under a piano on which Franz Liszt was hammering with a force that no instrument could resist'. The image speaks for itself.)

The next years for George Sand seemed comfortably settled; she had literary success and international fame, a wide circle of influential friends, Chopin's health seemed fairly stable, and she was mistress of a very popular *salon*. That was the impression; the facts were somewhat different. It was in 1841 that George finally accepted that her relationship with Chopin had become seriously onerous and must be terminated. Her diary of this period is full of hurtful, irritable remarks. In the beginning, his melancholic nature had been 'soulful' and 'a gift from the Muse'; now it was simply 'an affected malady'. She frequently referred to him as 'naughty'. At thirty-seven, the mother-image had now fully emerged; Chopin, six years younger, had become her 'child', her 'little one' … even her 'son'! Such euphemisms, tinged with disdain, only emphasized the shifting rhythms of her feelings for the composer. They presaged her boredom and the inevitability of the true end of the affair, and the beginning of a barely-tolerable friendship which would last through the next five years, until the sudden brutal parting.

The summer of 1846 throbbed with tension, aggravated by Chopin's serious altercations with George's son, Maurice. Further unpleasantness occurred when George flatly refused (seconded by Maurice) to entertain Josef Nowakowski, a composer friend of Chopin, at Nohant. Chopin refused to accept the excuse that there was no spare room; he felt humiliated and offended, a state exacerbated by the appalling treatment meted out by George (in jealousy) to his beautiful friend and compatriot, Countess Laura Czosnowska, during a recent visit to Nohant – ironically, as George's personal guest.

Meanwhile, George continued with *Lucrezia Floriani*. When this novel was published in 1847, she vehemently denied that Prince Karol was a cruel portrayal of Chopin. No one believed her; indeed, her descriptions of the Prince were just too close to home:

> Gentle, sensitive and very lovely, he united the charm of adolescence with the suavity of a more mature age; through the want of muscular development he retained a peculiar beauty, an exceptional physiognomy, which, if we may venture so to speak, belonged to neither age nor sex …

Later, she paints the Prince as 'a high-flown consumptive, and an exasperating nuisance'; the description could have come directly from a page of her autobiography. The novel was a vindictive and cruel comment on a soured affair. Oddly enough, Chopin took no offence, but those present at the first reading were embarrassed. The painter Delacroix squirmed. In his *Journal* he wrote:

> Executioner and victim both amazed me. Madame Sand seemed absolutely at her ease, and Chopin never stopped admiring the story.

Darkly, among friends, 'Lucrezia' became a new soubriquet for George Sand. The biographer Adam Zamoyski summed it up admirably:

> George Sand had carried out vicious autopsies on most of her dismissed lovers, but she had never until now gone in for vivisection.

Chopin's acceptance of what friends had seen as a degrading character-portrayal would assume bitter importance in the final break-up. This was initiated from an unexpected quarter. George was at Nohant when her daughter Solange – married but two weeks to the talented but uncouth sculptor Jean-Baptiste Clésinger – contacted Chopin in Paris, where he had remained in order to work with his students. Solange told the composer that there had been a blazing quarrel between her new husband and Maurice in George's presence, during which Clésinger had threatened Maurice's life. A struggle with a gun ensued, during which the sculptor had struck George. Aghast, George had thrown both him and Solange off the Nohant estate immediately. The Goncourts were told of a bitter exchange:

'I'll publish a full account of your disgraceful behaviour,' shrieked Madame Sand.
  'If you do, then I shall make a carving of your arse, and everybody will know it!' retorted Clésinger.

Solange, always inclined to a wilful selfishness, knew that the best way to avenge herself was to expose her mother to Chopin. Thus, she informed Chopin only of her version of the fracas. Fanning the flames, she told him how relieved her mother was that he was unable to visit Nohant; his absence allowing her to carry on a holiday affair with a journalist guest called Victor Borie. Chopin, who was now seriously ill and constantly haemorrhaging, did not need this stress. However, he was loyal and supportive of the duplicitous Solange and her crude husband. He wrote to tell her that 'his carriage was at her disposal'.

So simple a gesture finally and irrevocably doomed the Sand/Chopin relationship. George believed that Chopin had abandoned her in favour of her daughter. She did not understand that Chopin's action was one of compassion, not defiance, and certainly not with the aim of further alienating mother and daughter.

Angry and hurt by supposed betrayal, George sat down and wrote a letter to her writer/lawyer friend Emmanuel Arago. A prodigious letter-writer throughout her lifetime (she wrote over 19,000) this one, running to seventy-one pages, must be one of the longest letters in existence. She accused Chopin of disloyalty; she then made herself ridiculous by accusing him of having been in love all along with Solange and not her – that he had shown not passion for her, but hatred, accusations of which she herself was later ashamed. The letter also contained some thoughtless, crude, absolutely unwarranted sexual innuendos, the product of her resentment and bitterness.

Told of the letter, Chopin was hurt and disgusted. On 28 July 1847, George Sand wrote what would be her last letter to her erstwhile lover. It ends:

> ... and I shall thank God for this strange resolution to our nine years of exclusive friendship. Let me hear from you occasionally how you are. It is pointless ever discussing other matters.

Chopin's *congé* was complete. Greatly distressed, he rushed to his friend Delacroix and read him the letter. The painter was appalled:

> It really was atrocious. The cruelty of her passions, the impatience so long repressed, come clearly to the surface in it.

George Sand undoubtedly broke Chopin's heart. Respecting order, he had become used to a rhythm of living, of companionship, a mutual circle of friends, of being looked after during his frequent illnesses. Reflecting on this episode in her autobiography, George, to her discredit, described Chopin as 'a hopeless neurotic [with whom] my relationship was pure and motherly'. With brutal finality (and Maurice's help), she now slammed the door on the affair and indeed the friendship by destroying all of Chopin's letters to her. Chopin, by contrast, kept everything George Sand had ever written to him, even carrying her first letter wherever he went until his death.

Meanwhile, George made the twenty-eight-year-old Victor Borie, the journalist with whom she had been enjoying a holiday fling, her new lover/secretary. Within a year, however, Borie had fled to Brussels, threatened with prison for editing a subversive newspaper.

But for the generosity of an immensely rich Scottish ex-pupil, Chopin would have ended his days in penury. Jane Stirling began studying with Chopin in 1843; soon, she became a victim of unrequited love. She and her widowed sister Mrs Erskine were generous to a fault, at one time sending a parcel to the ailing, near destitute composer containing a gift of 25,000 francs. Chopin's pride forbade acceptance of such munificence until, desperate, he finally agreed to accept a loan of 15,000 francs. Jane Stirling seemed to take over from George the role of protective mother. She used her influence to lure the sick man to England and Scotland, where he completely exhausted his strength playing before Queen Victoria, the famous and the wealthy. He should have been happy; in fact he was wretched. He hated the claustrophobic omnipresence of the sisters; he was bored, lonely and ill. Although he dedicated two nocturnes to Jane,

Chopin – unusual for him – commented most ungraciously behind his benefactors' backs:

> One day more here and I shall go mad. No; I shall perish! My Scotch-women so dreary – may the Divine power preserve them.

At last, on 24 November 1848, he returned to Paris; desperately ill, the shadow of death was already upon him.

Chopin met George only once more, and that by chance. She had been invited to dine with Countess Marliani; as she arrived, Chopin was about to leave. Both of them were shocked by the encounter, but they managed to stay controlled and formal to the point of chilliness. Both of them had so much to say and were too proud to speak. They never saw each other again.

The finality of this meeting seemed to sap the composer of the will to live; he was, indeed, dying. Near the end, he told his dear friend Grzymala: 'I have never cursed anyone but life is so unbearable now, that I am beginning to think I might feel better if I could curse Lucrezia [George]!'

Chopin died on 17 October 1849. It fell to Solange, who had been watching over him, to close his eyes. Delacroix mourned:

> What a loss! What miserable rogues fill the squares while that beautiful soul had burned itself out!

Officially, the cause of Chopin's death was phthisis, an advanced state of consumption; those who knew him well thought otherwise. When they had realized his death was imminent, mutual friends had begged George to make her peace with her former lover: in vain. However, when she received Charlotte Marliani's letter informing her of Chopin's end, the novelist was ill for days. Grzymala was unimpressed by her show of grief. He wrote to his friend Auguste Léo:

> If he [Chopin] had not been unlucky in knowing George Sand, who poisoned his life, it's possible he would have lived to be as old as Cherubini.

The composer lies buried near to that same Cherubini (he died at eighty-six) at the cemetery of Père-la-Chaise. The funeral service, on 30 October, was attended by more than three thousand mourners. George was not present. Chopin's own *March funèbre* from the Sonata in B-flat minor was among the chosen music, as well as an organ arrangement of two of the *Préludes*. The German composer Meyerbeer and Prince Adam Czartoryski headed the funeral procession from the Madeleine. By a bizarre irony, Solange's husband Clésinger was made responsible for a death mask of the composer.

Apart from extolling Chopin's musical genius, in *Histoire de Ma Vie,* George nebulously condemns their relationship: 'We could never really mix when we were separated by a whole world,' she concluded.

★

George Sand lived for a further twenty-seven years after Chopin's death, during which time she led a busy, relatively peaceful life, writing bourgeois pastoral novels and plays, which received mixed reviews and varied success. They are rarely read today. After the fall of the French king Louis-Philippe, in February 1848, George stayed in Paris for a time, writing most of the official bulletins for the new Republic; with nationwide distribution many saw her as the unofficial Minister for Propaganda. Marie d'Agoult had a point when she condemned her erstwhile friend's political writings as 'purely agitational'.

But to her credit, George fought tirelessly for human rights. She encouraged many writers, not least Gustave Flaubert, who became a lifelong friend even though their writing skills were polarized. ('You paint people as they are,' she told him, 'while I paint them as I would like them to be.') There were fewer lovers now, all of them of a transitory nature, until she met Alexandre Manceau in 1850. He was thirty-two to her forty-six; he had been an engraver before becoming George's private secretary and final lover. Manceau was more devoted than passionate, in a liaison that lasted until his death in 1865.

During those fifteen years, Balzac died (in 1850), followed three years later by another of George's erstwhile lovers, Michel de Bourges. Solange and Clésinger separated after a marriage that had been stormy from the first day. George continued to churn out several major works each year, including her 20-volume autobiography, *Histoire de Ma Vie*. ('She canonizes herself in the history of her life,' wrote a disgusted Comte de Viel-Castel, on 8 June 1855.) During that same year George Sand entertained Charles Dickens. He thoroughly enjoyed the encounter, although he found it difficult to imagine her other than as

> the Queen's monthly nurse. Chubby, matronly, swarthy, black-eyed – a singularly ordinary woman in appearance and manner.

In 1857, George's son Maurice was married. Unfortunately, Maurice and the current favourite Manceau (as with Chopin) had never agreed. After a particularly unpleasant quarrel, Maurice insisted that his mother choose: him or Manceau. She had chosen her son above Chopin years ago; now, with no fault to find in her lover, she stood by Manceau. It was a painful day in January 1864, when George left Nohant to go and live with her lover at Palaiseau, near Paris. It would be a short sojourn, for Manceau died of consumption on 21 August the following year. Never far apart, the way was open for a reconciliation between mother and son.

Surprisingly, and despite their full involvement in the literary life of Paris, the Goncourt brothers only met George for the first time on 30 March 1862, when she was fifty-eight. Then, they remarked, 'She looked like a ghostly automaton ... or perhaps the mother superior of a Magdalen hospital.'

Visiting Nohant in 1863, Théophile Gautier later informed the Goncourts about the singular mode of living at the manor house:

> Mme Sand arrives [for breakfast] looking like a sleepwalker and stays asleep throughout the meal ... Conversation varied, but there was a distinct enthusiasm for scatology ... all their fun comes from farting. [The painter] Marchal was wildly popular with his wind.

During the Franco-Prussian War of 1870, George's estranged husband Casimir Dudevant died. George was unmoved; she was too busy writing against the bloody outcome of the Paris Commune. She found it difficult, anyway, to take seriously a man who had only recently written to the Emperor, stating that his life, burdened by being the husband of George Sand, surely merited his being awarded the Cross of the Legion of Honour!

In 1872, George entertained the opera singer Pauline Viardot and her lover, the acclaimed Russian writer Ivan Turgenev. He would return to Nohant again, mutual admiration paving the way to a deep and lasting friendship between two of the most famous writers of the nineteenth century.

Twelve years later, on 25 August 1884, Edmund de Goncourt wrote of Dumas *fils*:

> [He] talked to me a lot about Mme Sand, whom he described as a monster unconscious of her depravity, her egoism, her good-natured cruelty. Summoned to Nohant when Manceau died, he had asked her,

with the dead man still awaiting burial, how she felt. 'I feel,' she replied, 'like a good bath, going for a long walk in the woods, then going to the theatre this evening.' [...] Going to stay in Paris for a while the old woman started going out to supper, drinking champagne and making love; in fact living the life of a girl student.

Apparently, George's post-Manceau debauchery laid her so low that her doctor told her bluntly she would kill herself if she carried on.

The novelist's last years were spent peacefully at Nohant, where she died on 8 June 1876, of a painful intestinal blockage. Her wish for a civil burial was countermanded by her son, who arranged for a religious ceremony. Among the illustrious friends who came to mourn the greatest female French novelist of the nineteenth century were Flaubert, Alexandre Dumas *fils*, and Prince Jérôme Bonaparte. Of her many ex-lovers, only Victor Borie was there to pay last respects.

★

Charles Yriarte, a man of letters and a respected writer, detested George Sand. He moved in the same literary circles and knew the authoress well. He considered her to be absolutely devoid of heart, except for her children:

> She was an absolute Messalina – *lassata sed non satiate*[1] – who took to her arms men like Sandeau, Musset, Chopin and Liszt, merely for the notoriety such liaisons brought, much preferring hall porters, car-men and the like. This is not scandal, not merely the appreciation and opinion of one man, but the *consensus omnium* of all who were intimately acquainted with that strange genius, who would write in the most elevated and romantic tone of love, and then throw her arms around the neck of the porter who carried up her boxes.

Gustave Flaubert disagreed:

> One had to know her as well as I did to understand how much of the feminine was present in that great man. She will live on in a unique glory as one of the great names of France.

---

[1] *Exhausted but not satisfied*

These polarized, passionately conveyed opinions are expressed by writers who possessed an intimate knowledge of the authoress. Whatever it was in George Sand's personality that could fuel such diversity, it contributed to make her a legend in her own lifetime. That legend has continued to the present day.

Lola Montez

Adventuress with a Whip

'She is fatal to any man who dares to love her.'

Alexandre Dumas, père

Arriving at New York on 5 December 1851, Lola Montez watched her fellow passengers disembark from the upper deck of the SS *Humboldt*. Suddenly, there was a cry of recognition from a group of reporters standing on the quayside.

'Lola has come!'

A single utterance announced the arrival at last of one of the most intriguing, most talked-about women of the mid-nineteenth century. During the following months, as the notorious adventuress danced her way across America, 'Lola has come!' would gradually acquire meanings synonymous with danger and formidable problems; Lola's outrageous unpredictability was capable of presenting both at once. Stories of her legendary beauty had preceded her; portraits and contemporary accounts show her to have been extraordinarily beautiful, with luxuriant black hair complementing pale golden skin, a small waist accentuating a voluptuous bosom, and a generous red mouth offsetting the magnetic blue of her eyes, which were particularly compelling. Credited with combining 'the wit of a pot house with the carriage of a duchess', Lola was not easily forgotten.

An inveterate liar, Lola's biggest and longest-sustained lie must be her reinvention of herself when she returned from India in the winter of 1841, escaping a loveless marriage and an ambitious mother to whom she was a burden. This reinvention would change not only her name, but also her destiny.

★

The woman who would become a legend in her own lifetime as Lola Montez was probably born in February, 1819 or 1820; the actual date has been lost in time. The daughter of Edward Gilbert, a petty army officer, and Eliza Oliver, a milliner's assistant, Maria Dolores Eliza Rosanna Gilbert was born in Limerick, Ireland. After three years in the police force, Gilbert secured a transfer to India, under the auspices of the British East India Company. He and his family set sail on the four-month voyage to Calcutta on 14 March 1823. Within days of arrival at the garrison at Dinapore, however, Gilbert died of cholera. His widow wasted no time in marrying her husband's friend and colleague, a Scotsman named Patrick Craigie: the pair were married less than a year after Gilbert's death. Left largely in the care of her easy-going *ayah*, the young Eliza's formative years were sadly lacking in discipline – a neglect that would strongly influence her adult behaviour.

In 1826, Eliza was bundled off to school in England, where she was enrolled at the Misses Aldridges' Academy for Young Ladies, an exclusive boarding school at Bath. These next years were probably the happiest, steadiest period in her life. Eliza received a wide general education which included a mastery of the obligatory accomplishments expected of a well-brought-up young lady, as well as a solid grounding in languages. She later admitted she could happily have stayed at the school forever.

She was sixteen when her ambitious mother arrived unexpectedly to escort her back to India – to be married 'to Sir Abraham Lumley, a rich and gouty old rascal of sixty, and a Judge of the Supreme Court', an appalled Eliza wrote later (as Lola Montez) in her autobiography.

But Mrs Craigie's social aspirations were thwarted, largely by her own hand. On the voyage to England, she had met Lieutenant Thomas James, an attractive young Irishman, going home on indefinite convalescent leave. The lieutenant was delighted to accept his shipboard companion's invitation to meet mother and daughter at Bath. Eliza, desperate, now confided her fate to the visiting stranger. With an impulsive surge of protection and desire – he was genuinely smitten by the girl – James decided on immediate elopement. That very night, he whisked Eliza off to Ireland where, not far from Dublin, they were married a few days later by the bridegroom's brother, the Revd John James. Mrs Craigie was aghast; her schemes had ended in a completely unexpected double betrayal.

The marriage was unhappy from the beginning. Eliza was too young and inexperienced to grasp fully the commitment she had made. Although Lt. James genuinely cared for his bride, their widely different temperaments soon became apparent. Petty bickering developed into physical abuse, a situation which temporarily improved when, in 1838, the Jameses returned to India and were able to enjoy the exotic, if limited, social life available. Mrs Craigie, now living in Calcutta and never having forgiven her daughter, was badgered by the other officers' wives into inviting the couple to escape the summer heat of Afghanistan and join her for a month in the cool hills at Simla. The Honourable Emily Eden, who was also visiting the hill station, wrote in her diary:

Sunday, Sept 8
Simla is much moved just now by the arrival of a Mrs J[ames], who has been talked of as a great beauty all the year, and that drives every other woman, with pretensions in that line, quite distracted.

But beneath gay outward appearances, the Jameses' marriage was rapidly floundering. The quarrels and physical abuse resumed. With her life so unendurable, it must have been a great relief when, according to Eliza's autobiography (curiously written in the third person), 'Capt. James ran off with a Mrs Lomer, eloping to the Neilghery Hills.' Leaving James behind, the abandoned wife sought solace from her mother in Calcutta. Mrs Craigie, however, was blunt and unsympathetic. Eliza had made her bed; now, she must learn to lie on it.

But Eliza was adamant that the marriage was over. A contrite Captain James not only booked her passage back to England, but also made her a fair allowance. Perhaps he hoped that a respite back home might smooth away all problems. Eliza sailed at the beginning of October 1840. As she watched the exotic coastline disappear for the second time in her life, she made herself a promise, swearing that she would be answerable to no one in future except herself; she would be subject only to her own whims, sensations and pleasures from now on.

Thus determined, she immediately plunged into a brazen, flaunted affair with Lieutenant George Lennox, an army officer of her own age, who joined the ship at Madras. Their outrageous behaviour ostracized them from the other passengers, while the outraged captain refused to receive them at his table. Brazenly, they disembarked together and made their way to London. The affair continued for a short time until pressure brought to bear by Lennox's family led to a parting. All but penniless, Eliza journeyed to Scotland to stay with her stepfather's relations. After a few days, she was summoned to appear at court in London to answer to a charge of adultery: her lover, Lieutenant Lennox, was apparently a married man.

Shock and her survival instinct now galvanized Eliza into managing her own destiny. In the early 1840s, a lone, penniless girl had but two options: the first – becoming a governess – she was unsuited to by temperament (and anyway, her present predicament would ensure that all doors would be slammed shut in her face). The alternative was to go on the stage.

★

It is difficult to imagine an educated, twenty-one-year-old lady of the late 1830s contemplating an entire change of persona *and* presenting herself for public approval as a dancer in the theatres of Europe. But that is what Eliza did. For a short time she studied at an acting academy, but her teachers convinced her she would be more successful as a dancer. Far too old for classical ballet, she took herself off to Spain where she concentrated on a small – very small – repertoire of national dances which required a less demanding technique. At the same time, she studied the language.

Eliza returned to London shortly thereafter – as Maria Dolores de Porris y Montez: soon simplified as Lola Montez. She had schooled herself in the customs of Spain and now affected an intriguing if somewhat confusing 'accent', which would cause a few awkward questions. Completing her metamorphosis by smoking cigarettes or thin black cigars, she framed her new creation in several invented, gloriously dramatic pasts – all of them useful accessories for a woman of mystery. They intrigued the press for years.

Asked where she was born, Lola would shrug vulnerably, and spin a colourful tale of abduction ... snatched from her cradle when she was very young by a band of gypsies in Andalucía. From them, she had learned to dance and sing, talents she was forced to put to use to earn a living. On another occasion, she became the widow of a *hidalgo* who had fallen on hard times.

The Earl of Malmesbury wielded considerable power at Her Majesty's Theatre, in the Haymarket, London. A few well-chosen words with the manager, Benjamin Lumley, and it was agreed that this ravishing 'Spaniard' (whom the consul at Southampton had requested the earl to escort safely to the capital) should début within a few days. It was typical of the speed with which Lola Montez won support.

Thus, having flagrantly ignored the charge of adultery to which she was answerable in that city (and of which she was later found guilty *in absentia*), she opened at Her Majesty's Theatre on 3 June 1843, appearing between the acts of Rossini's opera *The Barber of Seville*. Dazzling beauty and a powerful stage presence turned a disappointing technical performance into theatrical success. Lola's magnetic personality and exotic beauty, enhanced by ravishing costumes, hoodwinked many people into believing her performance to be better than it was. The *Morning Herald* reported, 'The young lady came, saw, and conquered', while the *London Illustrated News*, dated 10 June 1843, commented mysteriously:

> On Saturday, a new *danseuse,* named Donna Lolah Montez, appeared, created a most novel and delightful sensation and – has not been heard of since.

The reason was simple: Lola had been recognized by one of the audience. Lord Ranelagh, who had received an embarrassing rebuke from an affronted Lola some months previously in Madrid, exclaimed loudly: 'Why, it's Betty James!' and proceeded to hiss the dancer loudly. Others, sheep-like, joined him. Lola allegedly froze, then dashed her bouquet on to the stage, sending it into the orchestra pit with a furious kick. When challenged by the gulled manager about Ranelegh's revelations, Lola haughtily denied the accusations. They were lies – she insisted she was a Spaniard of noble birth. Since life had been unkind to her and her family, she had been forced into earning an honourable living in the only way she could, by performing the dances of her country.

But an embarrassed Lumley was not prepared to risk a possible scandal. Imperiously, Lola threatened to take her 'cause' to the press. Meanwhile, *Age* wrote a scathing piece, identifying the dancer 'in the nomenclature of Mrs James'. Lola hit back, as she always would. She had no scruples about bending the truth to suit her needs, as in this extract from her open letter which appeared in *Era*:

> I am a native of Seville [...] sent at the age of ten to a Catholic lady at Bath where I remained seven months.

Unequivocally, she informed *The Times* that 'my name is Maria Dolores Porris Montez, and I have never changed that name'. Thus, an Irish girl went to the English newspapers to confirm, once and for all, the validity of her Spanish birth. This one-night fiasco at Her Majesty's

Theatre marked the triumphant début and the inglorious end of Lola's London theatre 'season'. She appeared once more, when playwright Edward Fitzball watched Lola in a charity performance and described her

> splendid white and gold attire, studded with diamonds ... so original, so flexible, so graceful, so indescribable ... How rapturous and universal was the call for her re-appearance ...

Lola shrugged and left for Europe. There were other theatres, other horizons to conquer. There was also history to shape.

★

If Lola's future notoriety was born on that warm summer evening in London, it was consolidated worldwide after a dramatic incident in Berlin. She had arrived after artistically stormy visits to Dresden and Brussels, 'where,' she later told the English diarist Albert Vandam, 'my money had all been spent, and I was obliged to part with my clothes first, and then to sing in the streets to get food.'

In Berlin, Lola was quite determined to join her 'friends', Czar Nicholas I and his brother-in-law King Friedrich Wilhelm IV, in the royal enclosure from whence they were attending a military ceremony. (The czar, as visiting guest of honour, was due to stand by the king and, from the enclosure, take the salute of some 30,000 troops.) It mattered little to Lola that she had not been invited, much less that she had never formally met the distinguished gathering. Superbly seated on a spirited saddle horse, she charged at the entrance, only to be apprehended by a harassed police officer. Furious, Lola raised the whip she invariably carried with her and slashed him savagely across the face. The incident was seriously insulting but although much was said – indeed, Lola did actually receive a summons which she tore up and insolently tossed back at the court representative – no action was taken. Worldwide, the adventuress with the whip was suddenly being written about, lampooned and caricatured.

'Courage, and shuffle the cards!' Lola consoled herself, voicing her favourite motto as she invented an invitation from the czar to perform in Russia. Without elaborating, her autobiography mysteriously insists that at some point in Russia, she had been invaluable to Czar Nicholas concerning 'a delicate diplomatic affair'.

Lola had progressed towards St Petersburg via Russian-governed

Poland where she was booked to appear at the Grand Theatre in Warsaw. Inevitably, she ran into more trouble.

Prince Paskewich, Russian Viceroy of Poland, was an old man who 'fell furiously and disgracefully in love with her'. The Grand Theatre was managed by Colonel Ignacy Abramowicz, who also happened to be chief-of-police. He had spied for Russia; consequently, the Poles hated him. While the colonel, a serious balletomane, quickly recognized the dancer's inferior talent, both men recognized Lola as an eminently desirable woman. She rejected both of them. In revenge, Abramowicz undermined her performances with organized disruption, resulting in a cacophony of hisses and boos warring fiercely with the cheers from Lola-supporters. When a furious Lola publicly exposed Abramowicz from the stage, the public, especially the young, were ecstatic. For them, Lola's persecution at the hands of the colonel epitomized Russia's tyranny over Poland, and symbolized the need for rebellion. Unintentionally, Lola had become a political symbol; a nuisance who was ordered to quit the country immediately. Defiant to the end, Lola barricaded herself in her room, threatening to shoot any policeman who tried to arrest her. Eventually, however, she allowed herself to be officially escorted to the border.

At the health spa at Baden-Baden, she publicly – and controversially – demonstrated the suppleness of her physique to a group of young men by tossing a provocative leg over the shoulder of one of them. Disentangling herself, she proceeded to tantalize by lifting her skirts above her thighs to prove the length of her perfect legs. An enraged mayor demanded Lola's immediate withdrawal from Baden and the surrounding areas.

Thus, Lola danced a little and loved a lot, her income most certainly supplemented by the many casual lovers she enjoyed along the way. She writes of receiving several marriage proposals from men of wealth and title, all of which she refused. Since Lola's ambition was to marry a wealthy title, this would seem to be more invention.

Scandal always clung to Lola like wet silk to smooth flesh. Inevitably, news of Mrs Craigie's notorious daughter reached the outposts of India. Poor Mrs Craigie saw nothing for it but to don severe black, send out black-edged cards and pronounce her offspring dead.

★

Lola met Franz Liszt in east Germany in 1844. She had deliberately set her sights on the phenomenal pianist as someone who could be enormously beneficial to her career. She had read that he would be performing at Dessau, so to Dessau she went. She attended Liszt's performance and then sought him out to pay tribute to his playing. Liszt, always susceptible to lovely women, was immediately captivated. Lola persuaded him that, as itinerant performers, they should combine work and pleasure. She informed the pianist that she had only ever known one other lover. Not to be outdone – and conveniently forgetting Marie d'Agoult, his mistress of the previous thirteen years and mother to their three children – the pianist declared that 'Lola is my first great love' and promptly wrote her a sonata. Hearing of the affair, Countess Marie d'Agoult is alleged to have challenged the dancer to a duel; the weapons to be fingernails. The challenge was never put to the test. Frequent quarrels and sapping demands, coupled with Liszt's friend, Richard Wagner, showing his open dislike of 'the woman with the bold bad eyes', led to increasing estrangements, which finally erupted in Dresden. After a particularly virulent upset, Liszt simply deserted Lola. He allegedly handed their puzzled hotel manager a sheaf of banknotes – to replace the furniture destroyed in the room, when Madame Montez awoke and realized her desertion.

★

Lola arrived in Paris a few weeks later, with a handsome Englishman, Francis Leigh, in tow. Despite presenting her with an expensive collection of summer dresses, she was irked by his stinginess and enraged by his pettiness. She attempted to shoot him before dropping him.

With the audacity of youth, and confident in her exotic beauty, she set out to charm the director of the Opéra into engaging her. Was she aware that this hallowed theatre was the acknowledged leading ballet venue of the world, where names as illustrious as Elssler, Grahn, Cerrito, Grisi and Taglioni regularly performed? Probably not; and although she was not blind to her paucity of talent she was fully convinced of her success in this city where sin was a pastime and the *foyer de la danse* at the Opéra the acknowledged rendezvous for achieving it with one of the many wealthy patrons seeking feminine diversion.

Despite a certain scepticism, Léon Pillet, Director of the Opéra, was persuaded; he sensed this beautiful unknown Spanish dancer had 'something'. What he didn't know was that 'something' was a handful of indifferent performances to her credit, from a dangerously small repertoire, exposed in a public career that spanned less than nine months. When Lola, missing no opportunity, mentioned Liszt's name as her sponsor, M. Pillet was convinced. One did not question the support of the greatest musical talent in Europe!

Unfortunately, Monsieur Pillet lived to regret his decision. Lola's performance was treated with amused disdain, even though the critics, as always, raved about her ravishing beauty. Pillet cancelled her contract after two appearances. Théophile Gautier, the foremost dance authority in France, wrote witheringly in *La Presse* on 28 March 1844: 'Having heard of her equine exploits, we suspect Mlle Lola is more at home on a horse than on the boards.'

Despite her disastrous début, Lola identified with Paris. She felt a free spirit in a city where a new liberalism was developing faster than anywhere else in Europe. She blossomed rapidly in style and sophistication in a city which was recognized as the centre of fashion and serious artistic endeavour. The diarist Albert Vandam was one of the few men who recognized, understood and respected Lola for what she was. His memoirs show her to have been remarkably aware of her own limitations:

> … there was nothing wonderful about her, except perhaps her beauty and consummate impudence. She was not in the least reticent about her scheming, especially after her scheming had failed. She fostered no illusions with regard to her choreographic talent; in fact, she fostered no illusions about anything and her candour was the best part of her character.

Later, a chink of vulnerability was exposed ('I remember every word of it,' wrote Vandam) when Lola confessed:

> The moment I get a nice round sum of money I'm going to carry out my original plan; that is, trying to hook a prince. I am sick of being told that I can't dance. They told me so in London, they told me in Warsaw, they told me at the Port Sainte-Martin where they hissed me. I don't think the men, if left to themselves, would hiss me; their wives and their daughters put them up to it.

Vandam brought her to Alexandre Dumas *père*, a prince of literature – not the sort of royalty Lola planned to hook. Dumas promptly seduced her as easily and as temporarily as he had many other beautiful women. He also introduced her to the salon of the controversial feminist writer, George Sand. Famously known for its liberal ideology, her salon was open to artists, visiting intellectuals and the intelligentsia of Paris. Lola quickly adapted to the atmosphere. Out of her depth much of the time, she became a willing, avid listener and apt pupil. During this intellectual odyssey, she soaked up everything, tentatively asking questions that received ready answers and, finally, joining in heated discussions. She was popular with Chopin; Delacroix admired her; Gautier lusted after her; Victor Hugo offered her advice.

But the man who would have the most influence on her increasingly liberal thinking was Father Felicité Lamennais. Lamennais' anti-Papal views had made him an outcast of the True Church. His determination to expose clerical corruption in governmental positions fired Lola's spirit. By the time the season ended, Lola had developed a passionate love of democracy, coupled with a hatred of the Church as a governing body, as fervent as her mentor's. In particular she acquired a peculiar hatred for the Jesuit order. Influenced by Lamennais, she would soon be wreaking havoc by overturning an entire Jesuit government.

Meantime, Lola had been refining her dance technique under good teachers. Almost a year after her inglorious début at the Opéra, she appeared at the Théâtre de la Porte St-Martin in early March 1845. If Lola's dancing talent had improved somewhat, then her grasp of audience psychology and the art of presenting her physical assets to best advantage had matured enormously. Thus, seductively extending a shapely leg, peeling off a garter and tossing it nonchalantly into the midst of a boggle-eyed, admiring male audience, had nothing to do with art but a great deal to do with showmanship and sex appeal.

This time the majority of the critics were unanimous: Mlle Lola Montez had greatly improved. Even Gautier enthused about her performance.

'Your début, Mademoiselle, gave me cause to doubt your heritage,' the critic said frankly, 'but after tonight, I am entirely convinced of your Andalusian blood.'

Duped by beauty, Gautier would become a powerful friend.

★

Throughout her lifetime, Lola would truly love only one man. His name was Alexandre Henri Dujarier, a critic and colleague of Gautier's on *La Presse*, and half-owner of that newspaper. At twenty-nine he was handsome, gentle, educated, well-liked and wealthy. One night he accompanied Gautier to see Lola perform. Gautier confessed to his friend that he had been attending the theatre nightly, 'solely to watch her because she is the most beautiful creature I know'.

Dujarier also watched – and concurred. Backstage, he found Lola stimulating, intelligent and with a razor-sharp wit. Already, he was falling hopelessly in love. He gave no immediate sign of his escalating emotions. Lola, for the first time in her life, recognized she was being courted. She was awed by Dujarier's range of knowledge but, above all, she loved the peace he had brought to her life and the security he promised for a developing future together. They became lovers in March 1845, after Dujarier had asked her to marry him. Lola was ecstatic. In looking for a prince, she had found true love. According to her autobiography, 'in his society [Lola] rapidly ripened in politics and became a good and confirmed hater of tyranny and oppression.'

Everything seemed set for a happy ending – but this was not to be. She and Dujarier were invited to attend a party at the fashionable restaurant Les Trois Frères Provençaux. Slightly puritan-minded, Dujarier did not want his future bride to associate with the types he knew would also be on the guest list. He attended the party alone.

Also invited was Jean de Beauvallon, a twenty-six-year-old Créole by birth, and a journalist on *Le Globe* (a rival paper) by profession. He had long hated Dujarier, since the latter had once sued (honourably) Beauvallon's brother-in-law, thus causing Beauvallon's sister to consider herself socially humiliated. The Créole swore he would avenge her.

After supper a group, including Beauvallon and Dujarier, sat down to play lansquenet. The stakes were high and the evening ended with Dujarier owing Beauvallon 13,000 francs, which was settled immediately, despite Beauvallon's polite remonstrances.

The next day, an incredulous Dujarier was visited by two seconds; he had been challenged to fight a duel. Apparently, Beauvallon had taken offence by the prompt settling of the debt. Dujarier, well aware that 'bruised ego' was an excuse to promote a duel, allowed his pride to overrule his intelligence and accepted the challenge. He had never fired a pistol or used a rapier in his life; Beauvallon, on the other hand, was one of the best shots in Paris. Dujarier, knowing his survival chances were slim, told Lola nothing. (When Dumas *fils* insisted on taking him to a shooting gallery in an attempt to teach him the rudiments, poor Dujarier scored two hits out of twenty-four.)

On 11 March 1845, the hapless man wrote to Lola:

> I want to explain why it was I slept by myself and did not come to you this morning. It is because I have to fight a duel [...] A thousand fond farewells to the dear little girl I love so much, and the thought of whom will be with me for ever ...

Beauvallon shattered his opponent's nerves by arriving more than two hours after the appointed time. Thus, when Dujarier fired, his shot travelled twenty metres wide of his challenger. Beauvallon then took slow, careful aim, so deliberately precise that his own seconds were embarrassed.

Dujarier was struck in the face and he was dead within minutes. A cold-blooded murder had been committed under the guise of a gentleman's settlement. Lola was beside herself with grief and hatred.

But the affair didn't end there. Beauvallon had broken the rules of the duelling code by practising with the very pistols utilized in the duel. Uncovered, he left the country. He couldn't stay away forever though, and, thanks to Lola's untiring efforts, Beauvallon was brought to court the moment he returned to Paris.

On the morning of 25 March 1846, the courtroom at Rouen, where the case was to be heard, was packed. When Lola took the stand there was a murmur of respect and approval. Her clear voice and concise delivery of the facts won her enormous admiration. ('That is why she had undertaken the journey to Rouen,' wrote Vandam, maliciously, 'and verily she had her reward.') Dressed in black, veiled for tragedy, her voice broken with grief, she ended with quiet menace.

'If I had known the name of the man poor Alexandre must face, I would have taken his place, for, unlike him, I am an expert shot. I would have faced Monsieur de Beauvallon on equal terms.'

The public was enslaved. Dumas *père* nodded approval. Gustave Flaubert wept. Someone in the next seat remarked that she looked like the heroine of a novel.

'Yes,' he replied, 'but the heroines of the real novels enacted in everyday life do not always look like that.'

Despite the damning evidence, Beauvallon was acquitted of murder. He was, however, mulcted of 20,000 francs in damages. Untiringly, over the next weeks Lola and Dujarier's friends unearthed a Monsieur de Meynard who had actually witnessed Beauvallon at shooting practice, *firing the same guns used in the fatal duel.* At the new trial, Beauvallon broke down completely. On 8 October 1847 he was found guilty of perjury and given an eight-year prison sentence.

Lola never fully recovered from Dujarier's murder. She admitted that he haunted her throughout her life, often claiming she felt his presence nearby. Understandably, Paris no longer meant the same to her. Once again, it was time to move on.

★

The people of Bavaria loved their king and queen, an understandable reaction in a kingdom where the queen was gracious and the king so lovably eccentric that he insisted on mingling daily with his subjects, hoping to be addressed simply as Mr Wittelsbach. In January 1848, George Henry Francis of *Fraser's Magazine* considered that King Ludwig I had done more to secure the political and social well-being of his people than any ruler the country had ever had from the twelfth century onwards.

At this time, Ludwig was tall and well-proportioned, his lined face still bearing traces of good looks. He seemed utterly indifferent to what was passing by and around him; perhaps because he lived in a strange half-world caused by an increasing hereditary deafness. His singular appearance was emphasized by the somewhat bizarre clothes he wore. *Fraser's Magazine* continues: 'He had the air of one of the fine old breed of fox-hunting country gentlemen.'

Lola arrived in Munich during September 1848 and headed straight for the luxurious Goldener Hirsch, where she took rooms. The city overwhelmed her – a neo-classical capital in the making, created with a king's love and his subjects' money. Ludwig's greatest pleasure was to pass time in his favourite creation, the *Schönheits-Galerie*, the Gallery of Beauties, which he had built to house the portraits of the most beautiful women he had ever seen. Aristos hung side by side with commoners, social status playing second fiddle to physical perfection. Soon, a new portrait would take pride of place.

Lola first met King Ludwig I when she failed to win a contract from the management at the Court Theatre in Munich. Her reputation, both theatrical and amorous, had preceded her, as from henceforth it always would. The angry dancer swept off to plead her cause with the bourgeois monarch. Granted an audience, she was kept waiting for so long that the mercurial Montez temper erupted. (There are several versions of what happened next; given Ludwig's fascination with lovely women what follows is no doubt true in essence …) It seems that in trying to reach the king's study, Lola scuffled with a guard who accidentally tore the bodice of her dress. Embarrassed, he released her immediately. Lola shot through the study door to find herself facing the king. Ludwig allegedly stared at the half-disclosed bosom and immediately enquired, 'Nature, or artifice?'

'It is for Your Majesty to make up his own mind,' replied the quick-witted Lola, quickly grabbing a convenient pair of scissors from the royal desk with which to further slash her dress.

Lola danced at the Court Theatre that same evening; and only the churlish would enquire how the dancer made a dignified exit from the palace with a dress slit down to her waist.

★

For years the dreamer-king had been content to leave administration in the capable, if somewhat austere hands of Mother Church; that is, through his Jesuit-dominated government, but under his autocracy. At the same time, Ludwig would not sanction a strengthening of the order in his realm. The ultramontanes, a group that fervently supported a centralized authority headed by the Pope, instead of localized independence, had stepped up its campaign for further dominance in the country. Recognizing the threat to autocracy, Ludwig was both wary and suspicious, especially of his prime minister, Baron Karl von Abel. The minister had served Ludwig faithfully for over ten years. Now, the king was increasingly aware of the minister's devotion to a more severe order of Catholicism, and of his determination to enliven Jesuit causes.

It is at this point that Lola enters the Bavarian history books. The Bavarians had long tolerated their king's occasional moral lapses with beautiful newcomers; they knew that the fling would culminate in a new addition to the *Galerie*, but more importantly, they knew that the attachment would be short-lived. These were also the sentiments of Queen Theresa, an amiable woman, who turned an obliging blind eye to the king's amorous peccadilloes. There was no reason to doubt that his latest infatuation with a Spanish dancer would be any different.

For once, both the queen and the people were wrong; more than smitten, Ludwig was enslaved. Daily, he spent hours with Lola and, predictably, set his chief court-painter, Joseph Karl Steiler, to work on the latest royal commission for the *Galerie*. The new portrait would be Steiler's most enduring work and the *pièce de résistance* of the *Galerie*.

Lola talked politics with Ludwig, expounding all the theories and ideas she had heard and digested in Paris under the powerful tutelage of Father Lamennais. It was ironic that Lamennais had been disgraced in Munich and had failed to open the king's eyes to his country's administrative problems; now, his 'pupil' would succeed for him.

Within days, the king presented Lola to his ministers. 'Gentlemen, you have the honour to meet my new best friend,' Ludwig announced proudly. 'Please oblige me by treating her at all times with the same respect you have always shown me.'

The adventuress needed only seconds to realize that respect was the last thing she could expect from these dour individuals; she recognized implacable enemies who sensed they would have good cause to hate and fear her. Bluntly, Lola warned the king. She emphasized that the government, all Jesuits except for one, held their monarch under the thumb. Ludwig was uneasy; Lola must be mistaken. But Lola, with supreme gall, pointedly mentioned Karl von Abel as particularly untrustworthy. Ludwig gasped, amazed that in four weeks she had recognized what he had been silently questioning for the last four years.

This revelation came as a great boost to Lola's credibility. For no accountable reason, she had settled a special hatred on von Abel, probably because he was the minister for the religion she detested so violently. The government watched helplessly as the dancer insinuated her views, poisoning – or liberating? – the mind of their totally bewitched monarch. He smothered her with sentimental poetry and diamonds; in return, she fed him hours of liberal dogma. He considered it a marriage of like minds; she readily agreed, knowing the king's mind was also in his breeches. He was in love with her; she loved him back, but as one loves a father. (Even so, and regardless of Lola's later protestations to the contrary, there is no question of her not being Ludwig's mistress. Many of his poems and letters bear proof of consummation.)

Ludwig was impervious to any suggestion that his Lolitta (as he called her) was capable of any political skulduggery. For her part, Lola truly believed that she was releasing the king's mind from the musty conventions of a tired, outmoded governing system. She saw herself as the people's liberator, symbolizing a new freedom in a new age – and, for a short time, the Bavarians actually saw her as their benefactress. The world's newspapers were quick to suggest, perhaps provocatively, that Lola spelled Freedom for the People. Lola, in turn, extolled the wisdom of the king. In her autobiography, she referred to Ludwig as 'one of the most learned, enlightened, and intellectual monarchs that Europe has had for a whole century.'

She pointed out to Ludwig the drastic changes taking place across an unstable Europe, emphasizing the importance of moving with the times before the times left him behind. Ludwig must break the Papal bonds which had stultified his realm for so long. The Jesuits referred to her as the 'Apocalyptic Whore'; Lola shrugged dismissively, knowing she could do and say as she wished with the absolute support of 'her friend, Louis' (Lola's pet name for Ludwig).

Prince Metternich of Austria, a powerful force in the suppression of liberal ideas, offered Lola four million francs and a title if she would convince Ludwig to follow the advice of his government. She was further offered a pension of 50,000 francs annually, provided she packed up and left Bavaria immediately and never returned. Lola refused, determined to help Ludwig – and not unaware, through him, of the unlimited lucrative gain within her reach.

When Prime Minister Abel discovered that the Spanish dancer was seeking Bavarian citizenship he exploded. He informed Ludwig that the creature was not what she seemed; that she privately entertained young men at her hotel. Had a mere Spanish dancer subjugated a great king to her whims and caprices? Ludwig didn't deny the allegation. Taken aback, Abel asked bluntly:

'She is king, then?'

'Yes, she is king.'

Within days, Abel was asked to resign. When the *Hauptmann der Polizei* of Munich complained bitterly that Lola's lies and barefaced effrontery were the cause of Abel's dismissal, she publicly boxed the man's ears before Ludwig banished him from the kingdom. Jealous, Ludwig now questioned Lola about the intimated lovers. Her furious denials left him in no doubt as to her fidelity. Always the supreme liar, Lola had no scruple in concealing her passionate involvement with a handsome lieutenant called Friedrich Nussbammer. He paid dearly for his adventure; eventually banished, his disgrace and shame led to insanity.

Ludwig was, however, fully aware of Lola's wilful nature and frightening temper. At times, she would indulge 'in expressions and gestures only to be heard or seen at Billingsgate, or in the purlieus of Covent Garden'. He didn't care; he was in the throes of his greatest love affair – possibly, at sixty, his last.

By this time, the whole Bavarian situation had become an *affaire de scandale*. Europe waited with bated breath. Once again, the question of her birth and nationality occupied the press. Tired of it all, Lola decided on direct action, through the 10 April edition of the *Illustrated London News:*

> I beg of you, through the medium of your widely circulated journal, to insert the following: I was born in SEVILLE in the year 1823. My father was a Spanish officer in the service of Don Carlos; my mother, a lady of Irish extraction, born at Havana, and married for the second time to an Irish gentleman, which I suppose is the cause of my being called Irish, and sometimes English, Betsy Watson [the surname of her Irish sister-in-law], Mrs James, etc. I beg leave to [say] that my name is Maria Dolores Porris Montez, and I have never changed that name. As for my theatrical qualifications I never had the presumption to think I had any;

circumstances obliged me to adopt the stage as a profession, which profession I have now renounced for ever, having become a naturalized Bavarian and intending, in future, making Munich my residence.

How can one not admire such audacity? Lola's arrogance, her loathing of the Jesuits and her blatant acquisitiveness were the talk of Europe. Her public behaviour was increasingly shocking. Her visits to the opera, or simply walking, or riding, were occasionally lightened

> by spitting in the face of a bishop, thrashing a coal-heaver, smashing a shop window, or breaking her parasol over the head and shoulders of some nobleman adverse to her party. [Reported *Fraser's Magazine*, January 1848.] In Munich itself, stories of her private conduct are freely circulated. As, for instance, that she is constantly deceiving the King; that she beats her domestics and friends, or occasionally amuses herself by tearing with her nails the flesh from the face of someone or other of those cavaliers who number themselves in her train of admirers.

Much of this was true. She was by now hated both at Court and by the people; so much so that Ludwig insisted on an armed guard for her wherever she went. On more than one occasion she had cause to threaten an ugly crowd with her whip, pistol or dagger. Within eight weeks of her arrival in Bavaria, Lola had instigated an entirely new liberal government. The *American Law Journal* (1848) said

> Under her counsels, a total revolution afterwards took place in the Bavarian system of government. The existing ministry were dismissed; new and more liberal advisers were chosen; the power of the Jesuits was ended; Austrian influences repelled, and a foundation laid for making Bavaria an independent member of the great family of nations.

English and Prussian representatives made it clear to their respective governments that 'this most enviable achievement' was the work of the dancer, Lola Montez. The ministers who had been elected had shown Lola their support. Unfortunately, they quickly forgot the part she had played in their elevation by refusing to acknowledge her, or even to pay her a conventional visit, despite the king's request. The new government was known, not without bitter irony, as the *Lolaministerium*, Lola's Ministry.

Lola spent extravagantly, but Ludwig was even more extravagant, building her a small palace in the Bärerstrasse. Given his previously steadfast parsimonious nature, the sheer luxury of this particular classical edifice was bewildering. He crammed the interior with sumptuous hangings and priceless art treasures, indulging his Lola in every luxury she craved – including guards in 'operetta' uniforms to parade in front of the building. Ludwig also engaged servants and a language teacher (unknown to Ludwig, a spy for the Jesuits) for her. In addition, he made her a stipend of 10,000 florins a year, an amount Ludwig would double at the end of their first year together. *Fraser's Magazine* reported that

> the house of Lola Montez presents an elegant contrast to the large, cold, lumbering mansions, which are the greatest defect in the general architecture of the city. It is a *bijou*, built under her own eye, by her own architect [actually, Metzger, the king's architect] and is quite unique in its simplicity and lightness. Any English gentleman can, on presenting his card, see the interior [...] which surpasses every thing, even in Munich, where decorative painting and internal fitting has been carried almost to perfection. Such a tigress, one would think, would scarcely choose so beautiful a den.

Lola had everything. Everything, that is, except a father confessor, for not one of the large clerical community in Munich would 'risk his virtue' for her. Indeed, the priests declaimed from the pulpit that 'there was no longer a Virgin Mary in Munich ... Venus had taken her place.'

Ludwig, turning a blind eye to the threatening storm clouds, concentrated instead on a few poetic lines to accompany Lola's breakfast tray each morning, such as:

> If, for my sake, thou hast renounced all ties,
> I, too, for thee, have broken with them all ...

Lola had been in Bavaria for just five months when, despite intense opposition, Ludwig used the royal prerogative to grant her Bavarian citizenship. The diarist, Arsène Houssaye, admirably summed up Lola's triumph:

> That theatrical heroine, armed with her legendary riding crop, went on, via a thousand and one beds, to conquer the King of Bavaria.

Even the liberal students now hated her; they felt she had betrayed what she had come to represent to them. Thus, when Lola set her bulldog on Professor Ernst von Lasaulx, a much respected university professor of philosophy and aesthetics who had done her no harm, she unwittingly set in motion her own downfall in Bavaria. The students were tremendously supportive of von Lasaulx, and of the growing number of professors who were being dismissed. Knowing the cause, a vast crowd marched on Lola's palace to protest. Impudently cool, she stepped out on to her balcony, raising a glass of champagne in an audacious toast. It was too provoking for the students, who pelted her with stones and fruit. The crowd's fury hardly abated when the king arrived, greatly distressed and saddened. Hatred of Lola could no longer be ignored. Lola, believing every word she uttered, railed against the ingratitude of a people for whom she felt she had done so much; when in fact it was the people's money that was providing her with an enormous stipend and untold luxuries.

Now, with supreme gall, she made a mighty effort to curry favour at the university by extending several invitations to the students. The majority shunned her. The few who accepted, about twenty, were charmed by her. They defied their own kind and formed their own union when they were ostracized for associating with 'the king's woman'. Known as the *Alemannen*, and dressed in specially designed uniforms, they became her devoted bodyguard. Inevitably, word soon spread that these young men, nicknamed 'Lola's Harem', were much more personally involved with the adventuress than appearances suggested (they were, after all, living in a house at the bottom of her private garden). Lola vehemently denied the accusations, although she took at least three of them to her bed – even encouraging one of them, Elia Piessner, to believe that she would marry him.

Meanwhile, Ludwig's letters of this period reveal that by far the most intimate reward he could expect from Lola at that time was to be allowed to suck and lick her toes and feet, preferably unwashed at his request. Meantime, in order to be the equal of her enemies at Court, Lola bullied Ludwig into granting her a title. He granted her two. Despite great opposition – Ludwig was the only one who condoned the elevation – on 14 August 1847, Lola became the Baroness Rosenthal and Countess of Landsfeld, the latter honour with 'feudal rights over some 2,000 souls'. She toyed with the idea of having a riding crop emblazoned on her coat of arms.

According to Arsène Houssaye, Lola's charm even penetrated the domestically minded Queen Theresa, who conferred on her Bavaria's greatest honour: the Order of Saint Theresa. However, with the whole country now seething with hatred for the king's whore, Lola's palace began to suffer continual attack. On one occasion she bravely, if stupidly, faced the crowd by herself, going out to meet them with only her whip. She soon retreated, trading insult for insult.

Finally, in desperation, on 8 February 1848 Ludwig shut down the university, a mistake that led to a new sport: Lola-lashing. Crowds, no doubt inflamed by alcohol, actually set out to find and molest her; Lola would have faced possible death had it not been for the staunch *Alemannen*.

Heartbroken, even Ludwig now realized that Lola would have to go.

His mistress, suddenly aware that her power and lucrative position were in serious jeopardy, persisted in avowing her love for Ludwig.

The world's politicians and royal families followed the fracas with amusement flavoured with some concern. The bloody outcome of the French Revolution was still sharply etched on the European mind. Now, a full-scale uprising was threatened in a normally peace-loving country. This could happen to any one of them. For once, Queen Victoria *was* amused.

'This whole silly affair is a contest between the Jesuits and Lola Montez, not between Royalty and Republicanism,' she is said to have announced, smiling benignly.

Lola's eventual escape from Bavaria was dramatic, involving several coaches, the loyal protection of the *Alemannen*, disguises and near capture. The Spanish dancer with limited talent had dominated Bavaria and enslaved its king for nearly two years; during the process she had managed to fleece the treasury of nearly two million florins. By the time she escaped unhurt into Switzerland, she had brought Bavaria to the brink of civil war and succeeded in bringing about a state of undiluted antagonism between Austria and Bavaria; there could be no retraction.

★

When, over the next few weeks, she didn't hear from Ludwig, an undaunted Lola once again resorted to disguises in an attempt to see the king. She was recognized and kept under close guard until Ludwig arrived; he confirmed that her stipend, which he had doubled only weeks before, would continue. Unable to bear the loss of his great love and counsellor, and hoping to resume their former relationship as a private citizen, Ludwig abdicated in March 1848, on a fixed income of 500,000 florins annually. This was threatened immediately he attempted to join Lola. Ludwig may have been lovesick but he wasn't prepared to lose his lifestyle. Meantime, Lola relieved her boredom in a series of affairs which included Auguste Papon (a bogus marquis), Robert Peel, the eldest son of Sir Robert Peel who was in Switzerland on diplomatic duties, and a number of dubious young men. She also continued her affair with Elia Piessner after the *Alemannen* had disbanded. Eventually, the misguided student was dropped; he returned to Bavaria, completely disillusioned.

Lola soon asked for, and received, an increase in pension, although Ludwig had told her she must 'learn to budget'. He forwarded her furniture – two tons of it – together with her jewels, some of which were taken from the ravishing Wittelsbach collection. The pair exchanged letters frequently, he preserving hers within the cornerstones of the new buildings he erected. (Some of them were revealed during heavy bombardments of Munich during World War II.)

Distance, time and suspicion all had a part in the cooling of Ludwig's ardour; but the death blow to his passion came when young Piessner, begging for financial help in order to finish his studies, bitterly exposed his own affair with Lola, and her involvement with other favoured members of the *Alemannen*. Lola denied everything, expressing eternal fidelity to the only man she had ever loved: Ludwig. Of course, her handsome pension had nothing to do with her passionate avowal.

★

Lola duly left Geneva for a short visit to London, where she was being portrayed in a farce at the Haymarket Theatre, called *Lola Montez, or Countess for an Hour*. Immensely successful, it was mysteriously taken off after a few performances, possibly to avoid a delicate situation between Bavaria and England. In 1849, in her early thirties, Lola returned to the English capital and moved into Half Moon Street. During her daily drive in fashionable Hyde Park, she became aware of a young man with a delightful dog. The dog became a gift and the owner, George Trafford Heald, a twenty-one-year-old cornet in the Second Life Guards, Lola's second husband. Benjamin Disraeli, writing to his sister, commented that 'Lola Montez's marriage makes a sensation.' Subsequent events would prove even more sensational.

Heald's income, by today's standards, was well in excess of £700,000 a year. As their only relative, the young man would also eventually inherit the fortunes of each of his many aged uncles and aunts. Lola, it seemed, had finally hit the jackpot. Yet, despite this new financial security, she wrote to Ludwig and begged him to continue her pension.

After only nineteen days as Mrs Heald, Lola was summoned to court on a charge of bigamy. Heald's guardian, Miss Susanna Heald, had sensed the gold-digger in her ward's bride and was determined to have the marriage annulled. She spent time and considerable money to find the inevitable skeleton in Lola's closet; there were plenty to choose from. But even Lola was shocked with an exposure of bigamy. She mistakenly believed that her separation from Captain James had been finalized in divorce through a special Parliamentary Act. The whole case rested on a clause, issued in 1842, that neither Captain James nor Lola could marry again as long as the other was alive. Miss Heald had discovered that Captain James was very much alive and serving his country in India. At the trial – a watershed in British divorce history exposing long-outmoded laws – Lola was placed on bail.

Realizing that the dice were rolling against her, Lola fled the country with her new husband, thus forfeiting bail-money of £2,000, a small fortune in those days. Nor did Heald show the slightest bitterness when Queen Victoria resigned his commission *in absentia*. They tore around Europe, avoiding the wrath of Miss Heald, until strain and worldwide reportage took their toll. In Spain, they quarrelled frequently; on one occasion, Lola stabbed Heald's hand. On another, in an exclusive casino, she beat his head when he had run out of ready money. In Cadiz for Christmas, he took a leaf from Franz Liszt's book and walked out on her without telling her. She wrote to Ludwig expecting sympathy; he replied, rather irritably: 'If you could only stop for a moment to look at yourself, you might begin to understand why you always end up alone.' Clearly, the king no longer trusted her, but being a man of honour he could never totally desert her.

Heald soon returned to Lola, unable to live without her. He would abandon her several times more, only to return each time, until finally, in August 1850, he left for good. He was twenty-eight when they found him dead in a hotel room in Folkestone, England, where he had steadily drunk himself to death. Only weeks after this tragedy, Lola discovered, too late, that Captain James had also died, in India. She was now a widow! All the running would have ceased; she would have been free to marry Heald, and make a new start.

Faced with new financial problems, Lola decided to write an intimate autobiography, making use of Ludwig's highly personal letters to her. Ludwig was appalled; even more so when Lola demanded an annual pension of 25,000 francs in return for her silence. Recognizing blackmail, Ludwig threatened to cut off all allowances. Unpredictable as ever, Lola returned Ludwig's letters to him, making no demands. In the event, the first instalment of Lola's autobiography was not a success when it appeared in *Le Pays*. With a change of editor, the serialization of the memoirs ceased.

At this point, Lola returned to the stage after strenuous work under the noted choreographers, Charles and August Mabille. Her début – a private affair for several hundred men and a few women – took place at the Jardin Mabille and was very well received, enough for Lola, after a difficult tour, to contemplate an assault on America. She boarded the SS *Humboldt* on 20 November 1851. The New World awaited her.

★

Lola had been thinking about America for some time. A well-known dancer, an acknowledged beauty and a countess to boot: she could hardly fail. Her indignation can be imagined when she was offered a contract with P. T. Barnum, the circus proprietor.

'I may have seen better times,' she said haughtily to Edward Willis, her new American manager, 'but I draw the line at appearing in a sideshow.'

Nevertheless, visiting America proved a wise decision. Combining a new career in acting with her established dance programmes, Lola's appearances all over the country were sell-outs. At the Broadway Theatre in New York, for example, she made over $4,000 in one week and had the distinction of having generated the highest box office receipts in the history of that theatre. She was not a fool. She would never deny that her reputation as a king's mistress, her notoriety with whip, dagger and pistol, and her infamous boudoir reputation were the real box office draws. American society expected a shameless, untalented king's whore; instead they were charmed by Lola's seriousness and good taste, qualities expected in a countess.

However, her infamous Spider Dance remained controversial. Many Americans considered it indecent, especially those devotees of the great Fanny Elssler, who anticipated from Lola something akin to Elssler's famously classical *La Tarentule*. Shaking spiders from the upper regions of a full skirt in order to stamp on them was prurient, declared the moralists, who thought Lola exposed too much of her legs. Despite knowing the dance to have originated in southern Italy, Lola insisted that she was performing a genuine, authentic Spanish folk dance from the land of her birth.

Everything she did was news, from her great love of animals to her violence with a whip. She dressed almost invariably in black. Her answers to questions about her relationship with Ludwig were flamboyant, often untruthful, but always fascinating. Embellishment came easily to the dancer, so that with each new account of her Bavarian period she appeared increasingly as an angel of deliverance. Lola considered it good box office.

Her immense success in America produced two sensational 'autobiographies': one penned by the bogus Marquis Auguste Papon, Lola's former lover; the other by her vengeful ex-agent, who also sued her for $65,000, for breach of contract (Lola had walked out halfway through a contracted tour, in order to go to America). Lola cross-sued; nothing was heard again of either case.

Having appeared successfully in several classic plays, Lola brought out a full-length starring vehicle entitled *Lola Montez In Bavaria*, in which she played four different versions of herself. It was a trite, third-rate work – but highly successful with the public. She performed it in Manhattan earning over $1,000 a week at a time when $500 *a year* was considered a good salary. She was now attracting much interest as an actress, accruing more serious critical attention than ever she had as a dancer.

The famous Montez temper had many opportunities to express itself across the country, particularly during her dance performances. Some of her audiences deliberately baited her, purely to enjoy her histrionics. In New Orleans, she slapped and beat her maid for insolence; the girl successfully sued Lola. Officers who tried to arrest her were punched; others found themselves at the point of her dagger. On one occasion, when the police successfully disarmed her, she grabbed a bottle marked 'Poison', drank the contents and declared that she might now gain peace. She collapsed, not dead, but in a faint; the bottle was a stage property, containing only water. Another time, she slapped and kicked a stage prompter – who promptly kicked her back and sued her. The courtroom rang with peals of laughter at her many quips: 'I could have been content to have been kicked by a horse; but by an ass ...'

Montez met Patrick Hull on board the SS *Northerner,* sailing to San Francisco from Panama. A good-looking man, he not only bore a strong resemblance to her great love Dujarier, but he was also half-owner of a newspaper. The couple were subsequently married on 2 July 1853, with Lola automatically becoming an American citizen – and conveniently losing six years off her age. Her arrival in San Francisco was nothing less than adulatory. California was a far cry from the more sophisticated East Coast. Communications being slow, little was known of Lola Montez beyond her unique beauty and her role as a king's ex-mistress. The *San Francisco Herald* rhapsodized:

Everybody is in a fever to catch a glimpse of the lioness [...] Whether she comes as danseuse, politician, beauty, blue-stocking or noble lady, she is welcomed, so she permits herself to be seen, admired, sung, courted and gone mad over here as elsewhere.

Lola was credited with drawing the largest audiences of any theatre, ever, in San Francisco's history. Tickets were going at ridiculous prices. She was scheduled to make her San Francisco début as Lady Teazle in Sheridan's *School For Scandal* at the American Theatre. Her season, a total of five plays and several dance divertissements, played to full houses, and netted her a personal profit of $16,000. Of the Spider Dance the *Alta California* wrote:

Witty, spirited, sparkling. If we could know the wishes of a heart which is, we are inclined to believe, that of a noble woman, the knowledge would doubtless turn the lip that whispers busy scandal white with shame.

Mrs Mary Jane Megquier, wife of a doctor turned gold-prospector, remembered Lola,

dancing the Spider Dance [in which] some thought she was obliged to look rather higher than was proper in so public a place ...

Lola felt so at home in California that she decided she would settle in the 'golden state'. When asked, she denied that her enormous success in San Francisco had influenced her decision to live in California. She explained that the state epitomized for her what she understood about freedom and equality. Meantime, for a dollar a shake, her many adoring fans formed long queues for the honour of shaking the hand of the Countess of Langsfeld.

But it was not all adoration. She faced her worst audiences in Sacramento and Marysville which, at that time, were little more than frontier towns. The Sacramento audience laughed at her and heckled her finesse. On several occasions she left the stage in tears of fury. Things were thrown at her; they were not bouquets. On some nights, she bounded into the auditorium to face the audience on its own level. Admiring her pluck, the crowds became even more rowdy. They were out for a good time and Lola's very refinement gave them the chance to let off steam, during which they wrecked the theatre. Escaping from the building, Lola was pursued to her hotel where the crowd harangued her underneath her window, banging pots and pans and yelling ugly remarks. When the editor of the *Daily Californian* wrote objecting to her manners, her morals *and* her dancing, she challenged him to a duel in which he would

> … don petticoats. I have brought some with me for the occasion. I leave the choice of weapons with you, for I am very magnanimous. You may choose between my duelling pistols or take your choice of a pill out of a pill box. One shall be poison and the other not and the chances are even.

The challenge was not accepted, but the story was printed across America and the world. For a long time people jokingly settled arguments with what became a famous catchphrase: 'Pistols, or Pizen?'

In Marysville, Lola flopped badly. She surpassed herself in anger and unpleasantness, lashing out at her fellow artistes and in particular at her husband, finally hurling all his clothes from their hotel window. He left immediately. It says much for Lola's personality that she finally wooed the rough element of the audience over to her side, and was reconciled with both her company and her husband.

Forty miles from Marysville and lying at the foot of the Sierras was Grass Valley, a flourishing mining town and the site of the highly lucrative Eureka mines in which Lola, for some years, had held shares. Inexplicably, she was impressed and now saw herself as part of the growing community. She and Hull bought a picturesque cottage and settled down to a life of domestic bliss. He was most impressed; so was the community, naming a mountain and a gold mine after her. Lola made preserves, tended the garden, paid visits and increased her animal collection to include dogs, a horse, a goat, birds, a wildcat and a grizzly bear. She wrote to Ludwig, asking him again to ship out her furniture. This the ex-monarch did, adding extra pieces and some jewellery he knew would surprise and please her. Hull was riled by the gesture, especially the jewellery. But the acquisitive gold-digger in Lola could never refuse such gifts. Increasingly estranged, Hull now resented Lola's enormous popularity, and even more his acquired soubriquet, 'the Count of Langsfeld-Hull'. Within months they were divorced.

Thinking of Dujarier, Ludwig, Heald and now Hull, Lola was forced to recall the damning prediction of Alexandre Dumas, *père*: 'She is fatal to any man who dares to love her.'

In November 1854, Lola's world-famous temper sprang into action once again when Henry Shipley, the editor of the *Grass Valley Telegraph*, insulted three itinerant vocalists whom Lola had befriended. He had boasted that he intended 'to roast them, even before they had performed'. Lola begged him not to be unkind. When he refused, she threatened to shoot him.

'I said I'd shoot him,' she later added, 'after he had threatened to cut my throat!'

Lola now sought him out and publicly whipped him in the saloon where he was drinking. When he tried to punch her, she was too quick, giving him a black eye; '... thanks to some rings I had on at the time, I made a cutting impression.' Shipley resigned not long after the incident. Once again, Lola's name was emblazoned across the world. She had reached that point of notoriety where cartoons of her in action with her whip and/or pistol appeared in the world's newspapers; some were funny, some ridiculing, many were waspish.

During this period she befriended a talented little girl called Lotta Crabtree who, under Lola's training and encouragement, eventually became a very famous actress. Lotta repaid Lola's kindness in 1866, by performing a cruel burlesque based on her mentor at the Howard Athenaeum in Boston.

On 20 June 1855, the mercurial, highly talented actress Caroline Chapman (who often performed with her equally talented brother) appeared in a burlesque written, surprisingly, by Lola's friend and sometime co-star, Dr William Robinson, called *Who's Got The Countess?*, in which Lola's characteristics were exaggerated to absurdity. For some reason, the Chapman brother-and-sister team were aggressively anti-Lola. The Spider Dance – renamed 'Spy-Dear' by the Chapmans – was brutalized. Caroline didn't miss a trick and, although the audience hated it, they laughed because it was very observant. Robinson soothed Lola's humiliation by explaining that burlesque 'was often a compliment, always an advertisement and here [in America] a native custom'. He then proceeded to build the piece up until it included the whole cast at the American Theatre in San Francisco, where Lola had been playing and where she had employed George and Mary Chapman (relatives of the infamous Caroline) in her troupe. The enlarged work became a sharp, glittering satire against Lola. The critics savaged the piece. A letter appeared in the *Herald,* calling the show:

> an exceedingly coarse and vulgar attack on one who, whatever her faults and foibles may have been, has proved herself a noble-hearted and generous woman [...] and who little deserves [...] ridicule and scurrility.

Lola's incurable need for adventure heightened her growing disenchantment with life at Grass Valley. She had grown stale and she knew it. She longed for new climes, new faces. Once again, it was time to move on.

★

In June 1855, Lola set sail for Australia with a small company, which included Noel Follin, a handsome actor and Lola's current lover, who appeared onstage as Frank Folland. She arrived at Melbourne on board the *Waratah*, and was met with flowers by the writer, poet and Commissioner for Crown Lands, Richard Hengist Horne. He reputedly saved young Follin's life one night when Lola rushed at her lover brandishing a pair of scissors.

After two weeks' successful engagement in Melbourne, the company moved on to Ballarat, a fair-sized township north-west of Melbourne, where Lola's reception was even more enthusiastic; some of the miners there even flung gold nuggets on to the stage to show their appreciation. Invited to inspect the Victoria Reef mine, Lola shunned the specially rigged armchair and delighted the miners when she slipped her foot into the rope 'noose'(as they would do) and, holding on with one hand and a glass of champagne in the other, made her descent to deafening cheers.

Unfortunately, Henry Erle Seekamp, the editor of *Ballarat Times,* considered Lola's performance and morals 'fostered unhealthy excitement'. Once again, whip in hand, Lola arrived to give him the beating of his life – with a new riding crop, won that very day at a bazaar lottery. She found him sitting in a local bar; anticipating Lola's reaction, he had brought along his own whip. Storming across to Seekamp, Lola recalled that she

> applied it [the whip] most vigorously to his head and shoulders. Mr Seekamp was not unprepared [...] and for a short time the combat raged with more than Trojan fury.

The two finally abandoned the lash in favour of fists and tearing at each other's hair. A crowd began to pelt the editor with fruit as they cheered Lola to victory.

In Geelong, a thriving town south-west of Melbourne, the mayor closed the theatre and the company could not perform. Returning to Ballarat, Lola took the whip to her manager, James Crosby, whom she accused of 'fixing' the box office receipts. But Crosby's wife had learned from Lola's previous Ballarat assault; she had brought along her own whip, intent on defending her husband. For the first time in her life, Lola met her match. Mrs Crosby lashed her so fiercely that she snapped the whip in two. Tossing it to one side, she grabbed at Lola's hair, beating her mercilessly about her head and neck. That night, there was no performance. Ever after Crosby referred to his wife as the 'whippress of the whippress of the whippers'. Lola never used a whip again.

In more ways than one, therefore, the tour was far from being wholly successful. After performing in Sydney, Lola was warned against a profitless tour through China and India, and subsequently dismissed her company at the end of the Sydney engagement; all except for Follin and her conductor. Perhaps 'deserted her company' would be a more accurate phrase however, following the opinion of her company as angrily expressed in the *Sydney Morning Herald* on 11 September 1855:

> This is the *good-hearted* Lola Montez, so widely eulogized throughout Sydney [...] away with such false twaddle as I have seen about her [...] Her conduct in deserting her company is as wrong as wrong can be.

Lola would subsequently be sued for breach of contract by them, just as she was about to sail out of Melbourne, having completed the final leg of the tour. Handed the writs, she promptly stripped naked and leapt into bed, daring the Sheriff's bailiff to 'arrest her as she was'.

Unhappily, tragedy struck on the return voyage, during Follin's twenty-ninth birthday party. A jolly affair with lots to drink, Follin became slightly intoxicated and went up on deck to clear his head. Lola followed shortly afterwards. A piercing scream sent the guests rushing on deck, where they found Lola unconscious; Follin was nowhere in sight. When she regained consciousness, Lola became hysterical, convinced her lover had fallen overboard. Follin was never seen again. Devastated, Lola was determined to help Follin's family, especially his two children. His wife refused to see her, but the dancer had more success with his stepmother. A notice appeared in August 1856, announcing the auction of Lola's jewels; they fetched $10,000, a fraction of their true worth. Lola gave the money to the family, ensuring for both children an exclusive education.

On the same day as the auction, another rumbustious Chapman burlesque on Lola opened, called *A Trip to Australia*. It was not popular. Audiences were aware of the Follin tragedy and of how deeply Lola had been affected and her ensuing generosity. Coincidentally, Lola opened

Previous page The most famous portrait of Lola Montez, painted by Joseph Karl Steiler. 'She is fatal to any man who dares to love her,' warned Alexandre Dumas, *père*.

Above Montez's most famous and enduring conquest, King Ludwig I of Bavaria. He gave her millions and changed the entire governing system of his country for her. He also loved to lick her toes…

Lola Montez, of her own admittance, was an indifferent dancer. This lithograph shows a regrettably typical audience response to her performances.

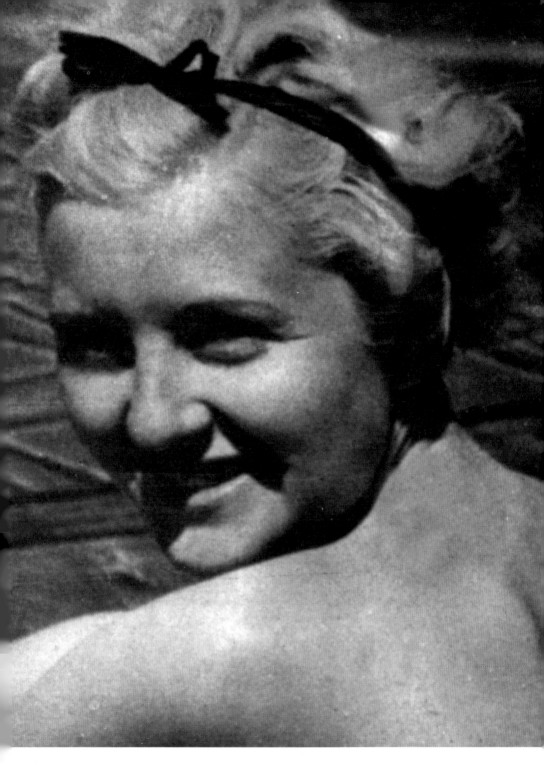

Eva Braun. She met Hitler when she was just seventeen years old. They became lovers when she was twenty. At thirty-three, she died beside him in a mutual suicide pact.

Above An informal photograph of Hitler and his mistress, Eva Braun.

Left Hitler and his niece Geli Raubal. Questions were raised about the nature of his relationship with the young girl, who later committed suicide. Or was she murdered?

Left Marion Davies in the early 1920s, just after she had left the Ziegfeld *Follies* to begin a movie career as the protégée of newspaper magnate William Randolph Hearst.

A publicity shot of Davies during the making of *Polly of the Circus* (1932). At her peak, she was considered the world's fifth most popular actress. Her parties with Hearst made Hollywood history.

Left La Casa Grande, San Simeon. Hearst's proudest architectural achievement, where he and Davies spent their best years entertaining the world's most famous names, including Churchill, Beaton, Gloria Vanderbilt and Einstein.

The love of Davies's life, press tycoon William Randolph Hearst. Their relationship, which endured for over three decades, was terminated only by Hearst's death.

Davies with literary genius George Bernard Shaw and actor Charlie Chaplin, at the MGM studios in 1933.

La Belle Otero, appearing on one of the many posters that glorified her talents during her ten-year contract with the Folies Bergère.

Above A dancer who was rated and admired above all her peers, Caroline Otero took the world's theatres by storm, winning rave reviews wherever she appeared. The Japanese emperor gave her a Pacific island in appreciation of just one performance in Tokyo.

Above As well as being one of the best-known performers of her day, Otero was also one of the world's most expensive courtesans, and could charge up to £8,000 for a night in her bed. 'Sem', the successful cartoonist, once commented after one of her theatrical presentations: 'As I watched her, I could feel my thighs blushing!'

during the farce's run and was gratified to find herself playing to full houses while the offending piece was very sparsely booked.

Lola, now thirty-six, had become immensely fond of Noel Follin's half-sister, Miriam. She saw much of her younger self in the girl, who was spirited, beautiful and ambitious. In a bizarre arrangement, Lola suddenly acquired a 'sister' when Miriam changed her name to Minnie Montez. Their working relationship was happy and successful, 'Minnie' learning 'much about audience rapport as she heard her "sister" hurl invective at the gallery for mocking her'.

Inevitably, the time came when the younger girl wanted to make her own way – via a married bank president's bed. Her future life, in its way, was as turbulent as Lola's, involving fortunes won and lost, royal suitors and marriages. She ended up a very wealthy woman, of considerable importance in the publishing world.

With the 1855 American recession, which greatly reduced theatre audiences and, therefore, takings, Lola realized that her day had come and gone. On 13 October 1856, she began a five-night farewell season, appearing in her favourite plays. On 18 October, she danced the Spider Dance for the last time. But the public had not seen the last of Lola.

★

During the late nineteenth century, amusing, entertaining lectures were very popular both in England and America. In 1857, after a stage career lasting thirteen years, Lola embarked on her first lecture-tour. Tentative at first, she began to draw capacity houses. She had commenced another brilliant career! With it, pretence to Spanish blood disappeared. She became an assured, delightful speaker, talking about 'Beautiful Women', 'Comic Aspects of Fashion' and 'Comic Aspects of Love', among other topics. The *New York Herald* named her one of the principal lecturers of the day.

After delivering one of these lectures one day, Lola was approached by a pleasant, well-spoken woman, who claimed to have been at school with the lecturer during her short sojourn in Scotland. Lola had no recollection of Mrs Isaac Buchanan. They were to meet again quite soon under vastly different circumstances.

During 1857, Lola made a mysterious voyage to France. She soon returned, but steadfastly refused to talk about the trip. The story was not a pleasant one: Queen Theresa, Ludwig's wife, had died; now, despite everything, the ex-king wanted to marry his Lolitta. He was seventy-one and she thirty-seven. Unable to resist securing her future, Lola entered into a morganatic marriage with the ex-king, who took his bride to Italy for their honeymoon. Unfortunately, he also took along some of his family, who made Lola's life a misery with insult and vicious innuendo, none of which Ludwig heard due to increasing deafness. But worse followed when, after consummation of the marriage, Lola discovered her husband had been suffering from syphilis for well over ten years. She was disgusted and horrified, particularly when she discovered that she, too, had contracted the disease. She left Ludwig immediately and returned to America, never mentioning the marriage again.

Her constitution being nowhere near as robust as Ludwig's, her once-fabulous good looks deteriorated rapidly. Well aware that she was doomed, Lola's concern with her spiritual welfare increased considerably. She read the Bible constantly and became a 'figure', stopping people in the street, speaking about the Good Book and handing out tracts. She went back to London with the idea of starting a boarding house, which she hoped would provide her with a useful income; unfortunately, her religious fervour turned prospective guests away. She became seriously ill and regained some of her strength only through the kindness of two total strangers from Derby, who had heard about her plight and straightaway, very generously, invited her to stay with them for as long as she wished.

With great resilience, Lola returned to America and a new progress of lecture appearances which continued to draw full houses. One day, walking down Broadway, she bumped into Caroline Follin, Noel's daughter. The girl deliberately ignored her. When Lola spoke to her, introducing herself as Caroline's benefactress, the arrogant girl still refused to acknowledge her, threatening instead to summon a police officer, if Lola did not stop harassing her.

Lola was bitterly aware that she had auctioned her jewels only to educate and encourage a social snob. In 1860 she suffered a sudden, massive stroke, attributing it to the great shock she had received with Caroline Follin's cruel snub. Her will to survive was tremendous. Despite being paralyzed down her left side and suffering slight facial distortion, within a few months she had recovered sufficiently to be able to walk and talk almost naturally. Against Lola's wishes, her mother crossed the Atlantic, ostensibly to see her sick daughter. Lola knew differently: her mother had come to visit only to determine what pickings there would be in the event of her offspring's death. Lola was dismissive, telling her mother that though she knew she would have welcomed a famous daughter, Lola had never been famous: only notorious. Within a few days,

Mrs Craigie returned to England, leaving her daughter ten dollars 'to help you along'.

Shortly afterwards, Mrs Buchanan, Lola's purported old school friend, suddenly resurfaced. Like a ministering angel, she had arrived at the right time to take care of the ailing adventuress. She insisted that Lola should stay with her and her husband at their house in Astoria, Long Island; an invitation Lola accepted gratefully. For some time, she had had a presentiment that she had not long to live. The Buchanans gave every indication that they were willing to take care of Lola until she passed on. They engaged doctors, sought second opinions, and engaged private nurses. In gratitude, Lola made a will in their favour.

History seems to have been unkind to the Buchanans. The press made allegations that these generous people had set out to cheat Lola of whatever she possessed. True, the Buchanans had moved Lola to a less-expensive abode three blocks away, after the signing of the will; but they had continued to engage a nurse. There were reports that the nurse abused Lola; that the famous ex-mistress of a king was dying in 'a dingy tenement room'; that the parish priest was 'disgusted by the filth and squalor, and [...] wasn't surprised when Madame Montez suddenly died'. The truth of these allegations, however, is far from certain.

It was also rumoured that Lola still had in her possession a diamond necklace worth around £10,000; this was not discovered among her effects. Was it conjecture? Or was the necklace stolen? A gift from Ludwig, it was Lola's last link with her illustrious past. Did the Buchanans scheme to possess this trophy, as well as the few jewels the ex-dancer still cherished?

Over the preceding weeks, Lola had become the repentant Magdalene. Her belief in 'my beloved Saviour' was transcendental. Not long before she died, Lola felt wholly secure in the knowledge that her sins had been forgiven.

*

On 17 January 1861, Lola Montez died of pneumonia. Californians first heard of her demise when the Pony Express flashed into San Francisco from St Louis, with the stark news: 'Lola Montez died in New York on the 17th.' She was forty-three. The minister present during her last moments wrote:

> In the course of a long experience as a Christian minister, I do not think
> I ever saw deeper penitence and humility ... than in this poor woman.

Ludwig survived her by another seven years, happy in the knowledge that his Lolitta had died 'as a Christian'. She left around £750 which barely covered the doctors' many bills and her burial plot at Greenwood Cemetery, New York.

There was one final irony which Lola would have enjoyed: the woman the whole world knew as Lola Montez was buried quite simply as 'Mrs Eliza Gilbert'.

Eva Braun

Mistress in the Shadows

'The stupid cow!'

Angela Raubal, Hitler's half-sister (1883–1949)

Germany's twelve-year suppression under the Nazi Party was the most violent, devastating period in the history of the twentieth century. Between 1939 and 1945, fifty-five million people died, most of them brutally, in a war which was precipitated by a man with a misplaced sense of his own destiny and an insatiable appetite for power. His private life was lonely; he had little ability to make friends. Sexually, his persuasion was bizarre and utterly revolting to his partners. The world and history remember him as Adolf Hitler.

According to Heinrich Himmler, Reichsführer-SS, the Head of the Gestapo, one woman, and one woman only, was capable of coping with the many peculiarities in Hitler's strange and complex personality. At seventeen, Eva Braun was a pleasant, well-adjusted teenager, happily adhering to the conventions of her middle-class, Catholic upbringing. No doubt her life would have followed the same pattern as that of all her friends, but for a chance encounter with 'a man of certain age' one warm Friday afternoon in October 1929. That man was Adolf Hitler. It was a meeting which would change her life forever.

★

Eva Braun was born on 6 February 1912, in a comfortable house on the Isabellastrasse in Munich. Fritz Braun and his wife, Franziska, already had one daughter, Ilse, who was born in 1909. Another daughter, Margurete (always known as Gretl), would complete the Braun family three years after Eva's arrival. All three girls were raised under very pleasant conditions, despite the inevitable deprivations brought about by the 1914–18 war. Eva completed her education at a convent in Simbach and then she returned to Munich. Around this time, in 1929, Fritz Braun inherited a sizeable fortune from an aunt. He happily informed his daughters that none of them needed to work again; but none of them wanted to be beholden to a father who was, at best, severe and over-protective. Thus, in September 1929, after a series of other occupations, Eva began to work for Heinrich Hoffmann, a professional photographer whose rather nondescript studio belied his success with several famous clients. These included Kaiser Wilhelm II and the internationally famous Italian operatic tenor, Enrico Caruso. Despite the poor salary, Eva was happy as bookkeeper and general saleslady.

She had been with the studio for around three weeks when one day, as she was standing at the top of a ladder filing invoices, the door opened and in walked a stranger. He was far from prepossessing, dressed in ill-fitting, uncared-for clothes, his dark hair lank and oily, and sporting an unusual 'toothbrush' moustache above his upper lip. From the top of the ladder, Eva was acutely aware of the stranger's intense blue eyes roving over her legs. It remained Eva's earliest recollection of Adolf Hitler.

Heinrich Hoffmann had known Hitler for some time, both politically and socially. Sensing Hitler's interest in his assistant, he introduced 'our good little Fraülein Eva' to Herr Wolf, the pseudonym Hitler insisted upon in his early career, when meeting strangers for the first time. Eva was sent out to buy a sausage snack for the men; when she returned, her boss invited her to sit with them and share it. 'Herr Wolf' made no attempt to disguise his attraction to the young girl facing him. Disturbed, but unaccountably excited, Eva escaped as quickly as she could and hurried home. Quizzed as to why she was late, Eva apologized, then proceeded to describe her unexpected meeting with the strange man with the sharp blue eyes. Though the boss had introduced him as 'Herr Wolf', she explained that the man had later revealed to her his real name: Adolf Hitler. Eva admitted she had never heard of him.

But her father had. As Eva had been relating her day, Herr Braun had entered the room unobserved. Now, he addressed his daughter sharply, but not unkindly, calling Herr Hitler a fool and an imbecile, who had set his heart on reforming the world. He warned 'Effie' (his pet name for Eva) to be on her guard against him should he return. Germany, he added, would be a lot better off if he took himself back to Austria.

★

Adolf Hitler was born in Braunau-am-Inn, Austria, on 20 April 1889. His illegitimate father, Alöis Hitler, married his third wife Klara Pölzl in 1885 – she was a first cousin, twenty-three years his junior. Of their six children, only Adolf and Paula (who was soon discovered to be slow-witted) reached adulthood.

While his mother understandably lavished affection on him, Adolf's bullying, drunken father ill-used both her and his son. Adolf loathed him and never forgave him for the ill-treatment, including drunken rape, that he meted out to his beloved mother. The fourteen-year-old felt no grief when his father died in 1903.

Even at this age, Adolf loathed all authority except his own; his arrogance was insufferable. Not unintelligent, his progress was considerably marred by innate laziness; thus he took five years to complete a three-year educational course. His awkward personality and open disdain for his teachers and fellow students led to his mother being requested not to send him back after the holidays. At his new school, some twenty miles further away in Steyr, he fared even worse. As his loathing for school and conformity increased, he managed to persuade his doting mother not to send him back to finish his education; the plea was illness. With a final show of supreme arrogance he is alleged, during a drunken spree, to have wiped his backside on his report form before posting back the desecrated document to the headmaster.

Hitler twice failed to win a place at the Vienna Academy of Fine Arts. (Much later, the refined Albert Speer, Hitler's architect and town planner, would be 'stunned by what met with [Hitler's] approval' in art, which included paintings of 'tipsy monks and inebriated butlers'.) For a time, Adolf lived like a tramp, sleeping rough and often going without food.

When the First World War was declared in 1914, Hitler volunteered for service with a Bavarian regiment. It has been rumoured that he rose no higher than the rank of corporal due to being court-martialled on a charge of illicit relations with a senior officer. However, he was twice awarded the Iron Cross for bravery in his service as a runner on the Western Front. In 1918, when Germany surrendered, the corporal was lying in a military hospital at Pasewalk, wounded and temporarily blinded by gas.

A year after the war ended, Hitler became involved with the National-sozialistische Deutsche Arbeiterparte – the Socialist German Workers' Party. His manic enthusiasm and untiring energies, plus a startlingly hypnotic, oratorical talent quickly placed him at the forefront of the movement. Within a short time, the SGWP had become the Nazi Party (an acronym of '**NA**tionalso**ZI**alistische'), with Adolf Hitler as its undisputed leader.

In 1923, his arrogance again came to the fore, when he led a squalid, ill-timed *putsch* in an attempt to overthrow the government of Bavaria. Sixteen Nazis were killed during the affray; Hitler dislocated a shoulder. Brought to trial for what amounted to high treason, he was jailed for five years but was mysteriously released after only nine months' incarceration. During his imprisonment, Hitler dictated much of his massive autobiography, *Mein Kampf* ('My Struggle'), to fellow inmate Rudolf Hess (whom Hitler would later appoint as his deputy, when he became Führer). The ill-informed, badly written and biased book, in which Adolf emphasized the superiority of the Aryan race and the inferiority of the Jews, became the political lodestar among the rapidly increasing number of Nazi supporters; by 1939, over six million copies had been sold.

★

In 1929, Eva Braun was seventeen – a healthy young woman whose world was dominated by gymnastics (at which she excelled), mountain climbing and reading popular romantic novels. She fantasized about Hollywood and she adored ballroom dancing. It ran in the family: over the next few years, her sister Ilse became a competitor on the international exhibition ballroom-dancing circuit.

Herr Wolf's obvious interest in her had alerted Eva's attention to her body and her looks. Scrutinizing herself, what she saw pleased her. She was taller than average (she said she was as tall as Napoleon), with a full pleasant face which was pretty rather than beautiful; it was framed in an abundance of chestnut-blonde hair. She liked her body, but wished her breasts were more prominent.

In the weeks following their initial meeting, Hitler came into the photographer's occasionally, sometimes bringing small gifts of flowers or chocolates for Eva. She accepted them shyly. Was Herr Hitler courting her? She felt certain of it when one day he presented her with a signed photograph of himself.

Abruptly, the visits ceased for twelve months. Then, as 1930 drew to a close, Hitler just as suddenly resumed contact with the little shop girl. He offered no explanation for his absence but Eva didn't care: she was so happy to see him again. If she had known why Hitler had disappeared from her life for the previous twelve months, or even suspected the nature of the dark sexual perversions which were at the root of his psyche and which, at that very time, were rapidly driving another young girl to her death, she would have turned away from him in disgust. As it was, she happily accompanied him as he escorted her to the opera – his favourite relaxation – to the theatre and occasionally to a restaurant. His behaviour was always very correct. Sometimes, there were long gaps in between their trysts, but Eva no longer worried. By now, she couldn't help but be aware of Hitler's growing importance as a revolutionary politician and she was proud to be the girl he seemed to favour. Guiltily, she hid all signs of the relationship from her parents, knowing from her father's earlier outburst that they wouldn't be supportive of the courtship.

When Hitler spoke to her of his genius, and of his great destiny as Germany's 'chosen' leader, Eva paid little heed. It might all be true, but frankly, Eva didn't give a hoot about politics. She was eighteen; she wanted to dance and have fun. It says much for Adolf Hitler's strange charisma that Eva was willing to forgo these simple pleasures just to be with him. Throughout the course of their relationship, all his opinions were sacrosanct, his plans inviolate and his orders unquestioned. In all things, if he sought advice he rarely followed it and, rightly or wrongly, everybody jumped to obey his command. He had, Eva realized, one true love: the people. She knew instinctively, almost from the beginning, that she would always take second place to his public life; she would always remain a lady in the shadows. It didn't matter; Eva was in love.

The weeks went by and Eva was happy enough with her lot, until she chanced to hear of a serious rival.

Her name was Geli Raubal.

★

Angela Raubal was Hitler's half-sister by his father's second marriage. Back in the late 1920s she had joined the emerging politician as his housekeeper, both at the Berghof, Hitler's private retreat on the Obersalzberg, and at his large apartment in Munich. Her two daughters, Friedl and Angela (known as Geli), went with her. Although both daughters were equally attractive, it was Geli to whom Hitler felt a powerful sexual attraction. Born on 4 June 1908, she had grown into a beautiful, vivacious girl with the Nordic good looks that Hitler idealized. His increasing infatuation was the reason why Eva had been ignored for most of 1930. He lavished attention on the twenty-one-year-old Geli, proud to be her escort, especially since their blood-ties instantly blocked any gossip.

When Hitler's obsession with his niece began to interfere with his work, Party members grew disturbed. There was also resentment concerning escalating expense – for Geli dressed extremely well and the Party paid. Ernst Röhm, the homosexual chief of the Sturmabteilung (SA[1]), who was a founder-member of the Party and one of the few people with whom the Führer felt any affinity, was given the task of making known the Party's unrest. Hitler was adamant about the innocence of the relationship; Geli Raubal was his niece as well as his ward (for Hitler saw himself as her guardian). These were facts not to be challenged. But Röhm persisted, pointing out that there were dark rumours; people were talking. Hitler ignored the arguments. Geli meantime continued to bask in the attention and the reflected glory of her uncle's escalating popularity. When Hitler moved into a new apartment on the Prinzregentenplatz in Munich, in September 1929, Geli was allotted the room next to his. She was delighted with the new arrangement, largely because she was already half in love with her uncle, despite the nineteen years' difference between their ages.

Then, suddenly, things changed. Her uncle began asking direct, intimate questions about herself, her body and her private life. Geli felt uncomfortable and resentful, particularly when she found her freedom being restricted 'for her own protection'. On the one occasion she stayed out until dawn with some old friends, Hitler became paranoid. For days he harangued and insulted the girl, incensed that she might be having a secret affair. He lectured her for hours on the vileness and dangers of promiscuous sex; when she indignantly denied his accusations and the slurs on her virginity, his voice grew shrill and frightening. He insisted that her mother should have her medically examined. Although Geli was pronounced *virgo intacta*, Hitler now insultingly referred to her as a *demi-vierge* and began locking her in her room at night. During the day, she was under the constant surveillance of various powerfully built SA guards. Humiliated, the bubble had burst for Geli: her fascination for her uncle rapidly disintegrated in a combination of misery, fear and disappointment.

Perhaps this sudden repugnance in the truculent and wayward Geli encouraged Hitler to seek some sort of revenge. Meeting a pretty, susceptible girl like Eva Braun not only appealed to his male ego; she made him aware that Geli was not the only attractive girl in Munich. Thus Hitler conducted a double relationship for the next year or so: in Eva, four years younger than Geli, he sought innocence, while his darker psyche was taunted by an uncontrollable, unhealthy desire for his niece.

Angela Raubal was increasingly aware of her daughter's acute misery.

---

[1] Literally translated, '*Sturmabteilung*' means 'storm division', so these organised thugs were also known as the storm troopers, or sometimes, after their uniforms, the Brownshirts.

Perhaps she experienced a degree of guilt. In *Hitler: The Missing Years*, Ernst Hanfstaengl, sometime foreign press secretary in the Führer's entourage and his close friend, assumed Frau Raubal's 'tacit acquiescence' in whatever 'particular combination of arguments [Hitler] used to bend [Geli] to his will'. Now she confronted her half-brother, demanding to know his intentions concerning her daughter. Did he intend to marry the girl, for instance? There had been rumours. However, Hitler only made a promise not to harm Geli in any way; later being more specific, he swore never to violate the girl. Angela was placated; her half-brother was, after all, Geli's self-appointed guardian. But regardless of his promise, Hitler began to make urgent, unusual demands of Geli which left her filled with disgust and revulsion – so much so that she was unable to express it to others. Hanfstaengl heard from a third-hand, but reliable, source, how Geli had confided to a girlfriend that her uncle was 'a monster. You'd never believe the things he makes me do.' Collaboration and further evidence was supplied by Wilhelm Stocker, allegedly one of Geli's guards and subsequent lovers.

In his admirable book *Geli and Hitler*, Ronald Hayman writes of what Geli eventually revealed only to Otto Strasser, a Party member who was about to be expelled for his left-wing political views. Apparently, Geli had spoken openly to Strasser, who later admitted that what she revealed he had only read about previously, in Krafft-Ebing's *Psychopathia Sexualis*. Against her nature, but because she loved him, Geli confessed to satisfying her uncle's sexual demands by squatting across him, naked, as he, also naked, lay squirming on the floor. He spent much time gazing in fascination at her most intimate parts. This humiliating subjugation greatly stimulated him; his growing excitement led him to an orgasm that was achieved only after the girl had urinated or defecated on his naked body. (Later, other women who were fated to cross the Führer's amatory path fared in much the same way, subjugated through fear into varying acts that disgusted and revolted them.) That Geli satisfied these bizarre needs was verified later by various household staff, who spoke of 'unspeakable things' they had been far too afraid to mention until after Hitler's death (although, even at the time of the affair, disturbing rumours circulated).

Around the time that Hitler was introduced to Eva Braun, the future leader of Germany wrote a particularly graphic letter to Geli, describing in intimate detail his sado-masochistic sexual gratification with her. She never received it because it was purloined, with blackmail in mind, by a Dr Rudolf, the son of Hitler's then landlady. Rudolf's price was high; the Party paid up. Only months later, Hitler was blackmailed again, this time concerning a set of obscene paintings he had made of Geli's genitalia. The pictures left the viewer in no doubt as to Hitler's coprophilic inclinations. After the transaction, one of the negotiators, Father Bernhard Stempfle, was discovered with three bullets in his heart. Death would be the fate of several others who were unfortunate enough to know too much about the Nazi leader's unhealthy sexual relationship with his niece, and others.

By 1931, Geli was desperate to escape her bizarre involvement. The unhappy girl blurted out her intention of leaving Munich immediately, in near panic deciding to go to Vienna to continue her music studies. Acquiescing at first, Hitler reneged suddenly, refusing permission on the grounds that he was her guardian. Geli lost her temper; she was over twenty-one with a right to independence. Her uncle insisted that she would have no life without his guidance; that he would not be in a position to protect her from lustful men if they were parted. He ordered his niece to go to her room immediately. With an important speech to deliver that evening in Hamburg, Hitler then stormed to his waiting car and drove away. He never saw Geli alive again. She was found the next day, 18 September 1931, in her room, apparently having shot herself with her uncle's 6.5 mm calibre Mauser pistol; and with her nose mysteriously broken. She was just twenty-three. There was never enough concrete evidence as to why this vital, attractive girl should suddenly take her own life. Surely, Geli would not have announced her plans for Vienna and for the future, if she had been entertaining thoughts of committing suicide? Police inquiries led the authorities to point a vague and shadowy finger in Hitler's direction as her suspected killer. But conjecture alone was not enough to make an arrest.

And of course, on the surface, it was a preposterous theory anyway! Why, they asked themselves, would a devoted uncle, the girl's guardian and a well-known public figure with everything to lose, commit such obvious folly? Perhaps Hitler had ordered the murder of Geli by one of his mindlessly obedient aides? Some suspected that Geli had become an embarrassment to the Nazi Party and had been liquidated under Himmler's orders. Or had a jealous boyfriend crept in and killed her? Theories abounded; nothing was finalized.

Ernst Hanfstaengl, who had never liked Geli, was unsympathetic. He thought her 'an empty-headed little slut, with the coarse bloom of a servant girl, without either brains or character'. Several other people, without the cold disdain of Hanfstaengl, were now able to admit their awareness that Geli had given herself freely – namely to healthy minded young men of her own age, who could for a time obliterate the nausea and disgust she felt about her stifling, obscene relationship with her uncle. These lovers included Hitler's trusted chauffeur and bodyguard, Emile

Maurice (at one time he and Geli had planned to marry), and the several young SA guards assigned to watch over her at all times. Geli's powers of attraction must have been considerable for those guards to have risked their lives in pursuit of her favours; had they been exposed, Hitler would have shown no mercy.

There were no answers to the many questions surrounding Geli's death; only supposition. Fourteen years later, in 1945, the US army paper 'Stars and Stripes' reported authentic discovered documents which were said to prove Hitler himself killed Geli. At the time, the strongest evidence to support the suicide theory was supplied (or was it planted?) by the discovery of a letter on blue paper which lay near to Geli's body; it had been torn up. Reassembled, it contained a short message, thanking Hitler for a memorable evening, and hoping for the joy of another meeting soon.

It was written by Eva Braun.

★

The suicide verdict was sufficiently indeterminate for Geli to receive a Christian burial in Vienna (official suicides could not be buried in consecrated ground). Hitler was not permitted to attend the ceremony; the country of his birth had marked him as an undesirable. He was, however, later allowed to visit Geli's grave under cover of night to pay his last respects. Eva's employer, Heinrich Hoffmann, believed that with Geli's death 'the seeds of inhumanity' were sown in Hitler. He became very concerned that the grief-stricken leader would try to take his own life. He arranged for him to attend a few outings and intimate dinners surrounded by congenial company. The photographer's studio and home had become well-known venues for weekly social gatherings for discussion on the arts and politics. The assemblage included many artists and cultured figures, many of whom were homosexual. Hitler apparently enjoyed himself enough to become a regular. Hoffmann also advocated the charms of Eva Braun; Hitler began to spend much of his time with her.

In many ways, it was Geli's death that brought Hitler and Eva Braun to a new understanding. However Geli had died, there was no denying Hitler's intense grief; Eva witnessed his pain and discovered a different man to the arrogant, ambitious anti-Semite she had grown used to. For his part, over the next few weeks Hitler found unexpected solace in the company of this pleasant suburban girl who asked no questions and was always available for him. It also helped that she did not object to him photographing her naked. The shots were always from behind, nearly all close-ups of Eva's buttocks, Hitler's explanation for the unusual angle being that he did not want anyone identifying her.

Eva Braun became Adolf Hitler's mistress during the first months of 1932. The nature of their relationship is enigmatic. He was twenty-three years older than she was. Physically, his scraggy legs supported a puny, soft-muscled body which was narrow shouldered and wide hipped. His pigeon chest was later disguised with clever padding in his jackets. He had powerful body odour ('Appalling,' shuddered Lina Basquette, the American film actress Hitler attempted to dominate), a mouthful of yellow teeth, bad breath ('I could never have kissed Hitler; he had yellow teeth and his breath smelt,' exclaimed Frau Schröder, his one-time personal secretary), and a lifetime of severe flatulence. He allegedly bathed only once a month (although he is said to have 'washed himself thoroughly' in between times) and detested aftershaves and colognes.

Sexually, there were complications. Hitler had a certain effeminacy which led many to suspect him of being a latent homosexual. There were veiled rumours of homosexual liaisons; one in particular with an army officer during the 1914-18 war. The affair was exposed and, although the episode supposedly then went on file, a careful search in the official records revealed nothing. Before Hitler became Chancellor, a similar records-search was conducted by the Nazi Party – the aim, apparently, to locate and suppress documented proof of the leader's sexual misdemeanours.

In addition to these uncertainties about his sexual orientation, Hitler reportedly suffered from a number of physical ailments which would have complicated any sexual relationship with the young Eva. He was a victim of phimosis, an over-tight foreskin condition that caused pain during erection and, on occasion, made it impossible. Ironically, being violently anti-Semitic, Hitler would not submit to the usual circumcision which would have solved the problem. He apparently had only one testicle[1] and suffered bouts of embarrassing impotency. At seventeen, he had picked up syphilis from a Viennese prostitute, which was never properly treated. Later, it would result in a weakening of his hearing, the threat of blindness and a loss of muscle control, leading to slow but progressive paralysis, which commenced around 1937.

[1] During the Second World War, the following morale-boosting song, sung to the tune of 'Colonel Bogey', was popular with the British army:

Hitler – he only has one ball!
Goering has two but they're quite small;
Himmler, is very similar,
And little Goebbels has no balls at all!

This, then, was the man who was increasingly regarded as the future saviour of Germany, and whose strange charisma dominated not only Eva Braun, but thousands of susceptible young women across the country. Indeed, there is ample proof that Adolf Hitler's somewhat bizarre attractions and his gift for oratory were sexually stimulating to thousands of women. Nigel Cawthorne in his *Sex Lives of the Great Dictators* (1996) relates how some women freely admitted to reaching orgasm at the climactic moments of the Führer's speeches. It was well known that many women fainted and required medical attention during the Führer's orations; also that wives and girlfriends, at the moment of climax with their husbands or boyfriends, would shout out Hitler's name. During some of his more violent speeches, some women had also, on occasion, been known to lose control of their bladders. In Munich, the middle-aged matrons who invariably occupied the front row of a Führer lecture left their seats and the floor immediately around them wet with urine. One woman, in desperation, even attempted to eat the pebbles Hitler had stepped upon! Despite such idolatry, Hitler was never once known to take sexual advantage of his aroused electorate; many said he was actually afraid of them.

Initially, it is thought that Eva contributed to the sexual difficulties in the relationship, as she reportedly suffered with an unusually tight vagina. Later in the liaison, she underwent a series of difficult, complicated operations under Professor Scholten, an eminent gynaecologist. Of necessity, the operations were spread over some months and caused Eva considerable pain. However, they were ultimately successful. A few days after announcing the positive prognosis, and now knowing far too much about the private life of the Führer and his mistress, Professor Scholten conveniently met with a mysterious and fatal car accident.

The sexual relationship between Eva and Hitler has always been a subject for controversy. Was it physical, or was it simply a close platonic friendship? The fact that Eva underwent a painful vaginal operation suggests the former, but noted historians such as Anton Joachimsthaler (and even the sadistic SS leader, Heinrich Himmler) are convinced that the relationship was not physical. Some adhere to the belief that the Führer enjoyed Eva's companionship because she was undemanding, uncomplicated and had not the slightest political ambition. Unlike many beautiful women of Hitler's acquaintance, she never made him feel sexually challenged – and the fact that the Führer suffered from impotency on occasion made this a constant tension. It is certain that Eva never experienced the revolting demands made of Geli and others. With her, Hitler's sexual titillation appears to have gone no further than the eroticism provided by photographing her buttocks, or having her dress in the chamois leather underwear he selected. Then there is the unlikely theory perpetuated by some that Eva was simply a gold-digger, caring only for concrete rewards and nothing for he who provided them. Such a premise would make sense of Eva turning a blind eye to the Führer's many defects and sexual peculiarities. Whatever the truth, Eva Braun was the one woman with whom Hitler was able to sustain a steady relationship.

★

Late in 1932, Hitler's political position was strongly consolidated, with increasing support not only within the Nazi Party, but also on a national level. Eva now expected to spend more time with her lover, but this was not to be. For weeks, sometimes months, she would hear nothing from Hitler, know nothing of his commitments and only discover his whereabouts from the press or over the radio. She confided to her older sister that she could no longer bear the endless, empty waiting; but when Ilse suggested her sister should break with her lover, Eva grew angry and warned Ilse never to suggest such a thing again.

At last, though, even the long-suffering Eva's patience gave out. At midnight, on 1 November 1932, Eva Braun attempted suicide by shooting herself with her father's pistol. She had been Hitler's mistress for less than a year. The bullet, which lodged itself in her neck, had been aimed at her heart, but the gun had misfired. Hitler was appalled when he heard the news. Whatever his role was in Geli's death, he had not yet fully recovered from her demise of less than twelve months ago; now, Eva had tried to take her own life. Hitler made a promise to himself to take proper care of her in future. Because of heavily censored radio and· press, the incident was never made public. Meanwhile, Ilse managed to convince their parents that her sister was the victim of an unfortunate accident.

Though Eva was upset by the infrequency of Hitler's visits and angry at being kept in the dark about his schedule, she was generally confident that the majority of the women who crossed her lover's path – especially the actresses and dancers to whom he seemed particularly drawn – were ephemeral and in no way threatening to her position. There were, however, a few notable exceptions. One was Winifred Wagner, the English-born wife of Siegfried, the son of the famous composer Richard Wagner. Winifred had been a friend and near-fanatical supporter of Hitler for at least seven years before Eva appeared on the scene in 1929.

The Wagners' marriage was hardly ideal; Siegfried was twenty-eight years older than his wife, and homosexual. He had little time for Hitler, who annoyed him intensely by conducting a very open, if frivolous, flirtation with his wife. Eva had been informed of this earlier attraction and had felt no threat until Siegfried Wagner died in 1930. The girl had known Hitler less than a year, but she considered her would-be lover's condolences to Siegfried's widow somewhat over-ardent, and was understandably concerned when she later learned that Hitler had for a time seriously considered marrying the widowed Frau Wagner.

To the Führer, it made perfect sense. For him, Richard Wagner had been the forerunner of the National Socialist movement, his music being symbolic of the might of the New Reich – just as Hitler represented the fight for the perfect Aryan Germany. Appalled at Hitler's proposal, Ernst Hanfstaengel tactfully suggested that Frau Wagner might not yet be ready for another commitment. As a well-educated sophisticate, Hanfstaengel saw the funny side of a protracted union between the short, puny man sitting before him and the gross, overweight Winifred. At Hanfstaengel's mention of possible distress caused to Eva Braun, Hitler's eyes narrowed. Had he not made it clear to her from the start that he would always place the good of Germany before any personal consideration?

The Chancellor obviously had no idea Eva had recently confided to Ilse that *she* was hoping soon to receive Hitler's marriage proposal herself! In the event, Eva's loyalty was never put to the test. Hitler's marital enthusiasm abated considerably when it was pointed out that such a union would undoubtedly lose him a large slice of the female vote.

For this same reason, Hitler continued to impose on Eva the necessity for secrecy about their relationship. The German people must know nothing about her; they must never feel that he had allowed a mistress to separate him from his total commitment – not so difficult a task under the rigid censorship imposed on the press by the Nazi regime. Indeed, the Hitler/Braun liaison was one of the best-kept secrets of World War Two.

★

In January 1933, despite being regarded by many as no more than a rabble-rouser, Adolf Hitler was appointed Chancellor of the Reich – a victory that occasioned Eva Braun great elation as she watched the famous, 100,000-strong torchlight procession welcoming her lover to Berlin. On 6 February, she linked this grand occasion with her twenty-first birthday. Hitler celebrated his victory and his mistress's coming-of-age by presenting Eva with a mediocre, inexpensive ring of small tourmalines, with matching earrings and bracelet. It was the cheapest jewellery Eva ever possessed; it was also her most favoured. Later, Eva was wrongly assumed to possess a considerable amount of valuable jewellery. Albert Speer, Hitler's chief architect and, from 1942, Germany's Minister for Armaments, who spent much time with her, said 'she wore nothing of the sort'. Certainly, there is little evidence of costly adornments in her many photographs, although Hitler is known to have instructed his private secretary, Martin Bormann, to supply her with certain 'valuable objects'. Speer added a codicil, 'At any rate, she never used for personal ends the power which lay within her grasp.'

On 27 February 1933, the Reichstag, the seat of the German parliament, was burned to the ground. The incident became known as 'the funeral pyre of democracy'. Was Eva really unaware of the whispered insinuations regarding arson, and the openly hinted at complicity of her lover and his gang of thugs – the Sturmabteilung – in the burning? World fascination eventually led the Nazis into providing a scapegoat, when they arrested and executed a poor, half-witted Dutchman, Marinus van der Lubbe, for the crime. Was she ignorant of the mindless book-burning in front of the University of Berlin on 10 May 1933, when hundreds of students on a rampage were encouraged to find and destroy all erudite and controversial works by Jews, Marxists and Bolshevists – a senseless 'burning of learning' campaign that outraged the entire world? Eva's views on these events are unknown.

At this tumultuous time, Eva's loyalty was unquestioned. However, it was not fully returned by the Führer who was unfaithful within months of Eva becoming his official mistress. If she suspected, she said nothing. Too many of the Führer's amorous encounters had died in questionable circumstances, or had died a victim of their own hand. These included Mimi Reiter, Suzi Liptauer, and the lovely prima ballerina, Inge Ley. Others had attempted suicide. There were ugly rumours of deliberate execution. Then there was the sinister interlude involving Renate Müller …

★

Renate Müller was one of Germany's most talented, popular, international film actresses. Glamorous and amusing, her charms had attracted Hitler and he had admired her from afar for some time. In early 1933, Eva knew little of Hitler's fascination with personalities from the world of entertainment. Eventually, the Führer contrived a meeting with the actress, who found him awkward, clumsy and overloquacious. But Hitler persisted. He made her gifts of expensive jewellery, which she found embarrassing to accept, but was unable to refuse without risking antagonism. Renate was quick to recognize the new Chancellor's power and his ability to influence her career.

One night in 1933, after an elegant Party reception to which she had been invited, Hitler manipulated the actress into staying behind when the other guests had gone. She knew what was expected of her – or thought she did. To her amazement and acute embarrassment, when both of them had stripped, the leader of the Third Reich suddenly flung himself on the floor and beseeched her to chastise him. Many people find sexual stimulation through pain, be it physical or mental. Given Hitler's bizarre sexual persuasion, it is possible that this total abasement was his sexual response to the gruesome and horrendous stories he had just shared with the actress – incidents dealing with tortures administered under his orders, to the Jews and other recalcitrants, by his newly formed Gestapo.[1]

Revolted, but quick to recognize the potential danger she had innocently fallen into, Renate Müller complied; she was very frightened. She now knew too much about Hitler's private sexual aberrations for her own safety. Eventually, she confided in her friend, the film director Adolf Zeissler, that she had been forced into obscene swearing, and kicking, verbally insulting and whipping the Führer with one of his three favourite whips – enforced punishments which disgusted her, but had excited the Nazi leader to sexual climax.

The actress told Zeissler there was more but, although he urged her to tell him the details, she would say nothing further – except that she was enormously ashamed and embarrassed at what had taken place. Afterwards, she said, Hitler had acted as though nothing untoward had happened.

Frightened, when Hitler called she now obeyed. Aside from her intimate knowledge of the Führer's sexual persuasion, the Gestapo had discovered that, years before Hitler's rise to power, she had had a Jewish lover. As a result, Renate Müller suddenly found herself on an entertainment black list and was told that she must face a 'trial' for her involvement with a Jew.

The strain of all these burdens broke the star's health; to recuperate, she lodged herself in a sanatorium. One morning, she was found dead, having supposedly leapt from a third-floor window. But had this beautiful, successful, thirty-year-old actress, who had everything to live for, killed herself during a fit of depression? Or had the Gestapo arrived

---

[1] '*Geheime Staatspolizei*', the secret state police.

and 'created' a suicide, to protect the good name of the Führer? There are no answers; but Renate Müller's blood was unquestionably on Hitler's hands.

The German people read a vastly different version of the actress's demise – as when Eva Braun, who occasionally thumbed through the Party newspaper *Völkischer Beobachter* (more as a courtesy to Hitler than with political zeal), came across a news item announcing Renate Müller's sudden death during an epileptic fit.

★

In 1933, Eva's parents, with whom she was still living, had no idea that she was Hitler's mistress. Even when Eva insisted on a private phone in her room, they naïvely believed that it was an emergency arrangement connected with her work for Hoffmann. With the Chancellor's increase in popularity, the photographic collection at the studio had been greatly extended, with Eva in charge.

It is difficult to understand the unflinching passion of the convent-educated, highly conventional Eva for a man who, in his thirst for ultimate European domination, was now openly persecuting Jews and Communists with a mounting violence that was causing worldwide concern. Increasingly, even Eva could not continue to ignore the rapidly escalating brutality of her lover's policies. The infamous Night of the Long Knives was a case in point.

For some time Hitler had been deeply concerned about the growing strength of, and threat from, the Sturmabteilung. Its leader, Ernst Röhm, an overt homosexual and a close friend of Hitler's, had developed this army of roughnecks and thugs into the merciless storm troopers (Brownshirts) whose notoriety rested on bullying and mindless brutality. Röhm fully expected his men to be the core of the 'new' army of the Third Reich, but with this expectation he overreached himself; it was a possibility the officers of the regular German army would not even consider. Sensing even wider splits between the two 'isms' – nationalism and socialism – within the Nazi party, Hitler decided on a ruthless plan of mass murder, backed by the Nazi leaders, thus eliminating the danger of in-fighting in one fell swoop. The massacre became known as the Night of the Long Knives. It was instigated when Hitler, on the night of 29 June 1934, ordered the death of his best friend, Ernst Röhm, 'for revolutionary ideas', together with the deaths of at least 177 others, eighty of them top-ranking Nazis, who had no warning of the betrayal. Only a few months before, Hitler had openly said of Röhm: 'I want to thank Heaven for having given me the right to call a man like you my friend and comrade-in-arms.' Hitler had a gun deposited in Röhm's cell: his way of telling his friend of fifteen years to 'do the honourable thing'. When Röhm refused, he was shot repeatedly by two guards. The fact that Röhm and his friends indulged in heavy drinking, frequent homosexual orgies and, worst of all, total indiscretion (particularly in Röhm's case) acted as conscience-salvers for Hitler's murderous assault. In the eyes of the army, Hitler had proved himself with swift, uncompromising action. Mindless elimination of 'the threat' was acceptable, honourable and just.

The Führer further proved himself when, on 13 July, in a broadcast to the Reichstag and nation, he accepted full responsibility for the mass-execution. Eva would most certainly have listened to that broadcast, but we have no means of knowing her reaction to her lover's proud boast.

★

Was Eva Braun a Jew-hater? Probably not. In her teens, she had met and enjoyed the company of sister Ilse's Jewish employer and lover, Dr Martin Marx; she also adored popular dance music and made no secret of the fact that she cared not a hoot if a Jew had written some of her favourites ('Alexander's Ragtime Band' and 'Tea for Two' were among them). She loved the music, and the lyrics appealed to the 'Yankophile' in the girl, who observed and evaluated America through imported movies.

By 1935, Eva's life had fallen, once again, into a monotonous pattern of sitting by a silent telephone. There were occasional clandestine meetings for the lovers when Hitler was in Munich; occasionally, Eva would be invited for a weekend at Berchtesgaden. Even then, she was accommodated at a hotel and only permitted to visit the Berghof, Hitler's country residence, when Hitler sent for her. Eva never complained, remaining in the shadows until summoned by her lover to join his guests. These were usually old Party associates; but Eva was expected to disappear at the arrival of a cabinet minister, or a famous, or influential, foreigner. Speer was frequently embarrassed for her. 'I realized that her reserved manner, which impressed many people as haughty, was merely embarrassment,' he said. 'Nor did Hitler give her much consideration,' he recalled. 'He would enlarge on his attitude toward women as though she were not present.' No wonder most visitors considered her dull, a nonentity. Some guests left having no idea who she was.

Her loneliness now mutated into suppressed frustration when she saw the increasing newspaper coverage, complete with photographs, of Hitler at official functions – and in the company of such glamorous stage and screen personalities as Pola Negri, Olga Tschechowa and Lil Dagover. Frequently, these pairings were merely useful publicity for both parties. For these women, there was no rivalry with Eva; as with many of the Berghof guests, they had never even heard of her. Eva had yet to learn how passionately Hitler yearned for social approval from the talented and famous.

Eventually, with no actual proof, Eva once more became obsessed with her perceived certainty that she had lost her lover; Hitler had not contacted her for weeks. On 28 May 1935, she wrote an explanatory letter to her absent inamorato, then confided her reasons to her diary before making a second attempt on her life; this time she swallowed an overdose of thirty-five sleeping tablets. She was discovered by her sister Ilse, who immediately suspected that Eva was not so much attempting suicide this time as employing melodramatic techniques in an attempt to gain Hitler's full attention. After all, grabbing the limelight in this manner had worked before, albeit unintentionally. As a doctor's assistant, Ilse quickly recognized that, although the pills were harmful if the prescribed dose was exceeded, they were not powerful enough to cause death. Had Eva realized this?

Ilse Braun was very calm upon discovering her sister; she smelt danger. The Chancellor of the Reich could not afford the adverse publicity of having his name linked with that of yet another girl who had attempted to kill herself on his account – and in Eva's case, twice. Instead of implicating Dr Marx, her Jewish employer and lover, Ilse telephoned Heinrich Hoffmann and explained the situation. He told her to tell no one – and to fob off the hospital with a tale of Eva's complete exhaustion from work. After calling for an ambulance, Ilse picked up Eva's diary and tore out the self-incriminating pages. (She returned them to Eva some months later.)

Once again, Hitler was deeply shocked when he found out about his mistress's latest suicide attempt. When Eva was released from hospital, he vowed once again to take greater care of her and to give her more of his time. On this occasion, he was true to his word. First, he rented an apartment for her in Munich, not far from his own. She was overjoyed; she was also apprehensive. She had never lived away from home except as a boarder at the convent. Eva consulted her best friend, Herta Schneider (aside from her sisters, probably Eva's only true friend), who encouraged her to take the plunge. In August 1935, Eva moved out of her parents' home, very much against their wishes. They were now fully aware of their daughter's liaison with the very man her father had warned her against years ago.

★

Fritz Braun was devastated that his daughter should place a man of Hitler's evil before his well-intentioned advice. As a result Eva was not to see her parents for many months. Meanwhile, her younger sister, Gretl, moved in with her – curiously, with her parents' permission. They probably thought that Gretl would act as a chaperone of sorts, especially as she was already working alongside Eva for Hoffmann.

Around this time, Hitler requested Eva to wear only chamois leather underwear. The writer Irving Wallace records how Hitler often suggested to her that she might be feeling too warm, even in freezing cold weather. This was Eva's cue to strip naked for him and, on certain occasions, go through the 'special exercises' he had designed for her.

There were rewards – for instance, in March 1936, the Führer arranged for his mistress to have full use of her own Mercedes. Hitler himself owned two identical Mercedes-Benz 770K cars, armour-plated and with bullet-proof glass (they also had false floors, so that when the leader stood to acknowledge supporters from his car, he appeared much taller than he actually was). Eva was delighted by the gesture. But this happiness had been far outshone three months earlier, when Hitler had squeezed into her hand a set of keys to a tiny villa he had taken for her, not far from the apartment in the Bogenhausen district in Munich, and for which he had paid 35,000 marks. Eva took up residency on 30 March 1936, in tears with happiness. For the first time, she felt a wife in all but name.

What Eva didn't know was that the villa was actually the outcome of pressure brought to bear on her employer Heinrich Hoffmann. The Party's official photographer had made millions of marks from the sale of photographs of the Führer since his rise to power. These pictures included many taken by Eva and her sister Gretl. Indeed, their particular photographs had proved to be enormously popular, largely because they were candid and portrayed Hitler in various relaxed, happy moods – poses he was incapable of delivering on official photographic sessions. Hoffmann had exclusive rights to all photographs of the Führer, but Hitler reasoned that the girls had a right to royalties. He decided that these would be best paid (without consulting them) in the shape of a private villa. In other words, Eva and Gretl had unknowingly bought their own villa, which Hitler passed off as his gift to his mistress! (Perhaps Hitler later attempted to make up for this singular display of stinginess when, in 1938, he headed his first will with Eva's name; bequeathing to her £600 a year for life in the event of his death.)

Eva now occupied much of her time in turning the new residence (referred to by Nerin Gun as 'only a paltry suburban villa that no American business tycoon would dare to offer to his secretary') into an elegant home. She bought original paintings, Eastern carpets and choice furnishings, for all of which Bormann supplied the cash. There were small parties, at which an elegantly gowned and coiffured Eva would receive guests. Rarely, if ever, did her lover play host.

Hitler only visited her very occasionally, and then only late at night and with an armed guard. He was no longer an unimportant would-be revolutionary politician on whom the police kept a wary eye; he was now leader of the National Socialist Party of the Third Reich, an important politician on whom the police kept a wary eye only to ensure his safety. Eva was expected to understand and accept this.

Their meetings were frequently marred by Hitler's insistence that she read to him from a disturbing book called *A Textbook of Psychiatry*, by Professor Bleuler, a very influential Swiss psychiatrist and psychologist. Hitler was distressed that he could possibly be unstable as a result of tainted genes, produced through the unhealthy interbreeding of his parents. He was also worried about the side effects of the syphilis he had contracted during his late adolescence, which he had mistakenly thought he had overcome. As this disease later progressed into the creeping paralysis stage, Eva noticed the book's re-emergence.

★

Even though the Führer enjoyed the obvious flirtatious advances of the talented film director, Leni Riefenstahl – who had been appointed as Number One film executive of the Nazi Party in the early 1930s – the situation caused Eva only mild concern; although, she would have loved to have known if the bitch really did dance naked at parties (it was rumoured she had done so in front of Hitler and his aide, Ernst Hanfstaengel).

There is no doubt that Hitler greatly admired Riefenstahl, both as a film-maker and as a personality. She was acclaimed for her film *Triumph of the Will*, about the 1934 Nuremberg Rally of the Nazi Party, but her most memorable work, a two-part, four-hour documentary of the 1936 Olympic Games in Berlin, *Olympia*, was considered a masterpiece. It premièred on the Führer's forty-ninth birthday, in Hitler's presence. He was ecstatic. He called it a 'unique and incomparable glorification of the strength and beauty of our Party'. Hitler further admired Riefenstahl's skills because she knew how to present him on film as a 'superhero'. She built flattering images that increased Hitler's physical stature by employing clever, low-angled shots, which made the puny Führer appear truly heroic. Leni was suddenly the golden girl; she was lauded and praised and soon discovered herself with several dubious soubriquets; 'Hitler's Pet' and 'Nazi Pin-Up' could only do a fine film-maker a great deal of harm in the future – and Leni Riefenstahl had never been a member of the Party. Nonetheless, despite never becoming Hitler's mistress, she never discouraged the rumour until after the war, when denial was part of her survival equipment as she fought for her financial and material assets.

Before long, Eva became intensely jealous of the woman who could elicit such praise from her lover. She knew, like most people, that Leni was very fond of the dashing, adventurous pilot, Ernst Udet, a senior figure in the revived German Air Force, the Luftwaffe; they were old friends and shared the same approach to life. In self-defence (as she saw it), Eva now spread a false rumour – aided by, of all people, the much-feared Heinrich Himmler, Head of the Gestapo, whom she detested – that Leni and the pilot were much more than good friends. As a result, Udet was instantly dropped from the inner circle, thought at the time to be because of Hitler's jealousy of the supposed affair. All who knew of the plot to discredit Riefenstahl blamed Eva; but for those few who knew the inner workings of the Reich, there were much more serious reasons for Udet's social dismissal. In 1936, he had been appointed Chief of the Technical Office of the Air Ministry. Udet was a fine designer, but he lacked the administrative toughness so critical in such a position. During the Second World War, his fighter-pilot experience caused him to concentrate on building light, manageable fighter-aircraft instead of much-needed heavy bombers, thus making the Luftwaffe deficient in this area. Hitler and Goering held Udet personally responsible for Germany's failure in the air war – and never forgave him for his misjudgement. The unfortunate pilot's life gradually became one long harassment, finally dragging him so low that he committed suicide on 17 November 1941.

Albert Speer, Hitler's chief architect, had heard about the naked dance incident attributed to Riefenstahl. Speer and his wife were friendly with Eva; they liked her, but also, were sorry for her. In 1938, Speer deliberately introduced the scandal to conversation, making light of it, hoping to banish Eva's self-doubt by emphasizing how embarrassed the Führer would have been. He emphasized too that, although Leni was a fine director, her manners and habits were quite disgusting – she was foul-mouthed, had filthy fingernails, ate off her knife and was sexually very liberal with her film crews. Indeed, Hermann Goering is credited with christening her the 'crevasse of the Third Reich'.

Eva was not convinced. But, in the early months of 1935, an English girl posed a much greater threat to Eva Braun's happiness than the relatively insignificant Leni Riefenstahl.

★

Unity Mitford met Hitler for the first time at Hitler's favourite Munich restaurant, the Osteria Bavaria; it was very popular with artists. Fully aware who he was, she continued to stare brazenly at him until he could not help but meet her eyes. What he saw, he liked, for she was blonde, statuesque and aristocratic. His aides already knew who she was since she had lain in wait for several days, hoping that her patience would be rewarded. It was, when the Führer invited her to join his guests. She was enchanted; she was bewitched! She had confirmed her belief in the Nazi movement, and in particular, the Nazi leader.

'Obviously preordained,' some said bitchily, 'her middle name is 'Valkyrie'!' Preordination would have been further proved had it been known that Unity Mitford was said to have been conceived in a small town in Ontario called Swastika, where her family owned a mine.

Hitler eulogized Unity as the epitome of the perfect Teuton, regardless of her nationality − a comment the aristocratic, twenty-one-year-old woman found enormously flattering. Albert Speer found her 'likeable'. After Hitler had autographed a postcard she had tentatively placed before him, an enraptured Unity wrote to her sister Diana − whose lover of some years, Sir Oswald Mosley, was the leader of the British Union of Fascists. She begged her to come to Munich immediately, to meet this wonderful man. (She was not alone in her enthusiasm; George Bernard Shaw and the Duke and Duchess of Windsor were also known to think highly of Hitler's vision, as did many people highly placed in British society and politics.) Upon meeting him, Diana was as fascinated with Hitler as her sister. Contrary to what they had read and heard, they were impressed by his willingness to converse, and by his knowledge on many subjects. A strong friendship developed between the three.

In 1936, Diana Mitford married Sir Oswald from the home of her close friend Magda Goebbels, the wife of Hitler's propaganda minister Josef Goebbels. Hitler was not there for the ceremony, but he later honoured the couple with a splendid dinner.

Eva had met both Mitford girls on 11 September 1935 at a Nuremberg rally. Watching them together with Hitler, she was fully aware of the rapport between the trio. She felt suddenly insecure and uneasy, conscious of Hitler's solicitousness, especially with Unity. He addressed her as 'Lady Mitford', a title to which she had no right, but which she enjoyed anyway (she was in fact the Hon. Unity Mitford, one of the six daughters of the second Baron Redesdale).

It was not long before Eva was convinced that Unity Mitford was determined to usurp her. Already the English girl had become part of the Führer's inner circle; and her fascination with Hitler and the whole Nazi phenomenon had made her speedy mastery of the German language a labour of love. She became a regular guest in Berlin; and, during the season, Hitler accompanied both Mitford girls to the exclusive Bayreuth opera festival; later, Unity enjoyed the clear mountain air when she was the Führer's guest at Berchtesgaden. As the Führer's interest in Unity continued, his colleagues and close associates spoke disparagingly of her. Many of them thought, quite erroneously, that both Unity and Diana Mitford must be working for the British government in some capacity and were therefore not to be trusted. Goebbels rudely referred to Unity as 'Unity Mit-fahrt', a clever rupture of the German and meant derogatorily (even though translated the expression means the inoffensive 'travelling companion'). In fact, Unity really had become Hitler's travelling companion, at his request, on many of the long and tiring political journeys he was compelled to make.

Eva must have felt a particular humiliation when she was instructed by the Führer to make very special efforts 'when Lady Mitford visits Berchtesgaden'. Hitler was giving an order, not making a request.

Despite Hitler's goodwill and support, Unity Mitford was forced to live frugally in Germany when her parents cut off her allowance. Although they admired the Führer, having accepted his hospitality in the past, Lord and Lady Redesdale hoped to starve their daughter into returning home. This she did, on several occasions, before being inevitably drawn back to her powerful friend. She greeted the embarrassed inhabitants of the tiny Oxfordshire village of Swinbrook where her parents lived, not with a handshake, but by raising her arm in the Nazi salute and barking 'Heil Hitler!' at them. As early as 1935 she had appeared in print in Die Stürmer as a Jew-hater, a violent proclamation which headlined the British newspapers. During a visit to London, in April 1938, she caused a riot when she appeared at a Socialist rally in Hyde Park wearing a swastika armband.

Popularly known in Germany as the Storm-Troop Maiden, Unity made her attachment and frank hero-worship of Adolf Hitler glaringly apparent. However, there is no evidence of a romantic liaison between the two. The Führer recognized that the English girl was good publicity for

Germany, that back in Britain she talked freely and glowingly about the Third Reich and that she knew many influential people. In other words, Hitler used Unity Mitford.

According to Nerin E. Gun, Eva's biographer, Unity's novelist sister, Nancy, was determined to ruin any chance of marriage between her and Hitler (another of the sisters, Jessica, was also bitterly opposed to any union). Unity had once told Nancy how Hitler had had Eva Braun secretly investigated for any 'impurities' of blood; so, with typical Mitford humour, Nancy is alleged to have forged her sister's family tree so that it included a Jewish ancestor. She is said to have sent it to Heinrich Himmler.

On 3 September 1939, Britain declared war against Germany, in retaliation for the invasion of Poland. The declaration sharply focused Unity's divided loyalties. According to Albert Speer, Unity, 'even in the later years of international tension, persistently spoke up for her country and often actually pleaded with Hitler to make a deal with England'. She once said to the Führer: 'Make friends with England. The two greatest nations together could rule the world!' Now, the 'two greatest nations' were at war with one another.

When the time came for Unity to make a decision about her future, she chose to stay in Germany. How must Eva Braun have taken the news that Hitler had provided the English girl with an apartment on the Agnesstrasse in Schwabing? He had also assured Unity that she would not be interned during the inevitable conflict to come.

In both her heart and mind, Unity was well aware that Hitler had been using her for some time. Now, as the international hostility increased, finding herself unable to balance the shattering of an ideal with her in-built loyalty to her own country, her thoughts calmly turned to suicide as her only solution. Just one hour after the radio announcement that war had been declared, Unity Mitford went to visit the Nazi leader Adolf Wagner, Gauleiter for Munich, whom she knew well from happier days at the Osteria Bavaria. She handed him a large envelope. In it were her Nazi Party badge, a signed photograph of the Führer, and a personal letter for him (which turned out to be the equivalent of a suicide note). They were to be handed to Hitler; and if something untoward should happen to her, she requested that she should be buried in Munich, with the Party badge and the Führer's photograph next to her.

Unity then calmly made her way to the Englischer Garten and shot herself with a gun she had been carrying in her handbag for some time. She didn't die; the bullet lodged itself in her head and paralyzed her nervous system. She lay in a coma for months. During this time, Eva immediately disregarded all thoughts of possible rivalry; jealousy was replaced by a cool compassion. She made regular visits to the patient, taking flowers, supervising her lingerie and toilette and doing all she could to ease the Englishwoman's desperate plight. Perhaps Eva was only following Hitler's instructions. Whatever the stimulus, Eva appeared at Unity's bedside throughout her hospitalization. Meanwhile Hitler, to his credit, not only saw to it that the critically-ill woman had the very best treatment available; in 1940, when she was considered fit to travel, he made it possible for her safe return, via Switzerland, to her homeland. By a peculiar stroke of irony, it was Eva Braun who accompanied the devastated Unity when she was taken to board the train that would transport her to Switzerland, on her way home. The intelligent, once-sparkling and energetic Unity never returned to full health. She put on a considerable amount of weight; her speech, which she only partly regained, was slurred and her concentration very limited. Paralysis down one side greatly restricted all movement. She died in 1948.

★

On the occasions that Eva stayed at the Berlin Chancellery (the official state buildings of the German government), which she had been visiting since 1939, she remained in her room and took her meals alone. Hitler apparently trusted Eva socially only up to a certain level; beyond that, she was for him a little girl and unable to cope. She was forbidden to join any party at which Goering was present, probably because of her dreadful relationship with Frau Emmy Goering. Albert Speer remembered her telling him that she never took a walk during these periods, 'in case I might run into the Goerings in the hall'. Hitler spent very little time with her. It was small compensation that her accommodation was sumptuous, being the converted bedroom of Field Marshal Paul von Hindenburg, the former President, who had died in 1934, the year following Hitler's appointment as Chancellor. Eva's official entrance pass to the Chancellery was that of secretary. Such was Hitler's obsession with secrecy that she usually arrived accompanied by two of the real secretaries. Over the next years, Eva became friendly with them, especially with Christa Schröder. She would have been acutely distressed had she known that her lover, who was always friendly with his assistants, had once told Frau Schröder in an indiscreet moment that although he was very fond of Eva, he would never marry her. 'Geli, and only Geli, could have filled that role,' he emphasized.

Hitler's housekeeping invitation to his half-sister, Angela, back in the late 1920s, had been a sudden decision. Just as abruptly, he dismissed her. By 1936, relations between the two had greatly deteriorated. The Führer had always been aware of how much his half-sister disliked Eva, just as he knew of the pointed insults to which Angela had continually subjected his mistress. The final straw occurred just before Angela's enforced departure in 1936, when Hitler surprised everyone by elevating Eva Braun as the official mistress of the Berghof. From here on, all staff and guests were to recognize her as such. Eva, of course, was ecstatic; she had not felt so overjoyed since 'the Chief' had presented her with the villa in Munich during the summer of 1935. It was the beginning of a new phase for Eva.

Angela was not the first, by a long chalk, to sneer at and insult Eva. She called her '*Die blöde Kuh!*' ('The stupid cow!'). She would never accept Eva as mistress of the Berghof, a role she believed would ultimately have been Geli's, had she lived. Once Angela had left her half-brother's employ, she rarely saw him again.

Curiously, Eva never became a Nazi Party member – one of the reasons, perhaps, why she never felt completely at ease in the company of the Nazi chiefs and their wives. Her lack of official recognition had not helped; now, even with her new status, everyone, including Hitler's intimates, ignored her elevation.

In 1935, Heinrich Hoffmann became seriously ill. He was treated by Dr Theodore Morell, an old friend who, over time, completely cured him of his ailment with a course of sulphanilamides, imported from Hungary. Hoffmann's praise for the doctor was so ecstatic that Hitler became curious. The upshot was that Morell became Hitler's personal physician for the next nine years; the doctor's first diagnosis was that the Nazi leader was suffering from no more than intense exhaustion. With a series of injections Hitler's health did indeed improve. Injection was at the base of Morell's medical philosophy; he swore by his Multiflor capsules, composed of intestinal bacteria 'raised from the best [cattle] stock owned by a Bulgarian peasant'. Towards the end of his nine-year supremacy as Hitler's chief physician, he was injecting Hitler on a regular basis with no fewer than twenty-eight drugs, which largely accounted for the ghastly colour of the Führer's skin. The noun 'injection' and the name 'Morell' became synonymous to such a degree that Hermann Goering sneeringly referred to the doctor as 'Herr Reich-Injection Master'.

Since Dr Morell was a successful specialist in venereal diseases, with a lucrative and discreet practice in Munich, it is likely that the good doctor was also treating Hitler for advanced syphilis. With complete faith in him, Hitler insisted that his colleagues should also patronize Morell. Eva Braun went to consult him once only; she was appalled. She was disgusted by the dirty state of his surgery and office; she couldn't bear his hands, with their filthy fingernails, to touch her. She told friends that he had the habits of a pig. There was a rumour that she first consulted the doctor to see if he could prescribe something to increase her lover's sex drive. Morell allegedly injected the Führer with a known stimulant derived from bulls' testicles – but without any apparent success.

From their secure marital positions, the wives of the Nazi top hierarchy made it plain that they did not consider Eva Braun in their class. As far as the wealthy socialite Anneliese von Ribbentrop (the wife of Hitler's Foreign Secretary Joachim von Ribbentrop) was concerned, Eva didn't exist. Annaliese made no attempt at even the simplest courtesies. Eva treated like with like. She made no endeavour, either, to seek the approval of Elsa Himmler, the wife of the Gestapo leader; for one thing, she was chillingly afraid of Elsa's husband, whose pleasure in human suffering and torture, together with his unabashed enjoyment in the misery of others, had made him an object of great fear.

Thanks to her recent elevation however, Eva no longer felt threatened, not even by Magda Goebbels, who was especially favoured by Hitler. Eva was well aware of the Goebbels' free-style, no-holds-barred sexual arrangement – Josef Goebbels was purported to have leanings towards occasional transvestism, while Magda was said to have dabbled in lesbianism. If this was the case, perhaps Frau Goebbels was driven to it. The Goebbels' marriage had long been unhappy; Magda would have divorced her husband on many occasions but was dissuaded by Hitler, who felt 'image' was all-important. Rumour had it that Magda became infatuated with Eva to such an extent that Eva had to protest to Magda's husband. Much of this was gossip and nonsensical. To start with, Magda and Eva did not get along very well – indeed, for a time there was distinct dislike stemming from jealousy over Hitler. The extrovert Magda was very much a woman who enjoyed flirting with men in general, and quite openly with Hitler in particular. Given the chance, she would unquestionably have succumbed to him; but when Hitler showed no sexual interest in her, Magda's reaction was typical: a beautiful woman scorned, she made the terse comment that the Führer was 'not sufficient a man to tolerate a real woman anywhere near him'.

Rivalry between the two women was also apparent in that they both bought their clothes from Romatzki, an exclusive *couturier;* Eva grudgingly conceded that Magda always looked elegantly distinctive and stylish. Others went further and considered Magda's style and panache far more chic than anything Eva might attempt. Eva played safe, always dressing simply, with inexpensive jewellery. Albert Speer writes of the trinkets Hitler offered to his mistress for Christmas or on her birthday as being 'insulting in their modesty'. Bormann, Speer says, would present a selection from which the Führer would choose with 'petit bourgeois taste'.

There is no question that Magda felt herself much superior to the 'silly little girl' who was 'distracting' the Führer. On one occasion, she attempted to make this clear during a visit to the Berghof. Eva was chatting to her while she was dressing. The pregnant Magda suddenly complained of a backache, and asked Eva if she would be kind enough to fasten her shoe. The 'bent-knee' implication was clear. But Eva proved equal to the insult; she beckoned to a servant and said politely: 'Frau Goebbels is not in a condition to fasten her shoe. Please help her out of her embarrassment.' Hitler was incensed when the incident was reported to him. Magda received no more invitations to the Berghof; it was the equivalent of being banished from Court.

In many ways, life on the Obersalzberg did amount to being at Court. On an infinitely smaller scale, the Berghof was a sort of Versailles of the Third Reich, with its glorious mountain location, its exclusivity and, more importantly, its eventual centralized power. The fact that the Führer frequently resided there, both for work and relaxation, sent the land prices in the area soaring. All the top-ranking Nazis flocked to buy estates there. As with Versailles, the many guests who enjoyed the Berghof and delighted in its invigorating air and peerless views had no idea of the misery and labour involved in creating this luxurious abode. The builders and labourers involved – at one time there were over 5,000 employees – worked round the clock. These included Czechs, Poles, Italians and Ukrainians; the pay was negligible and the conditions often appalling. Some of the work was purportedly completed with slave labour from the concentration camps, once they were established in 1933, but Nerin Gun adamantly denies this.

On celebratory nights, Eva took pride in the Berghof's solid gold dinner service, even as she squirmed at the guests' ill-disguised surprise at the appalling food which always seemed to be a feature there. Indeed, the poor dining at the Berghof became a kind of 'in' joke with the more frequent guests.

Magda Goebbels was Eva's only serious rival. Magda excluded, Eva was relatively sophisticated compared with most of the Nazi officials' wives; and because the comparison was obvious, it was one of the many reasons why they disliked her. Some had sprung from nothing to the top in one political leap. Few of them were well educated, and even those who had received an education lacked the social experience to go with their newly acquired status.

As the Führer's mistress Eva always dressed well; she was unconcerned that her clothes and cosmetics bills were extravagant (Bormann, on the Führer's orders, was once again on hand with the finance). She bought only in Paris, Rome, Vienna and Berlin and had her hair dressed privately every day. For some years, she also had it tinted to make it more golden, in keeping with the Führer's Aryan ideal.

No one ever considered Eva Braun as the unofficial First Lady of the Third Reich; that was a role originally cherished by Magda Goebbels, largely with Hitler's encouragement, although Emmy Goering considered herself eminently more suited to the position; perhaps for the reason that her husband, in 1939, had been named as Hitler's successor to the Nazi leadership. With this self-inflated opinion of her rank, and, like the other wives, detesting the woman whom they still regarded as a little Munich shop girl, Frau Goering made no attempt whatsoever to hide her disdain for Eva. Indeed, she was known to hold 'Down with Eva Braun' tea-afternoons. To the provincial ex-actress, Eva was little more than a whore.

★

In 1940, Eva Braun, who had so far been faithful to her lover, suddenly fell in love with another man. Given her frequent solitude, it was not surprising. Eva writes in her diary: 'I'm afraid I must have a man ... a real man, at last.' (However, this diary was later discredited, as described below, although the motives of some of those dismissing its veracity are perhaps open to question.)

That man was a young Viennese painter called Kurt, whom Eva met at a party given by Heinrich Hoffmann. It was natural that Kurt, as an artist, should gravitate towards such a group. Over the next few days, the two became involved enough for Eva to become suddenly concerned, both for Kurt's safety and for the preservation of her relationship with Hitler. She left Munich immediately. Knowing nothing of her identity, the diary tells us the young painter followed her to Berlin.

Inevitably, the affair was exposed. Eva was taken forcibly by Hitler to Kurt's flat, accompanied by a couple of SS men. There, she witnessed the painter's brutal execution as he lay in his bed. All his identification was destroyed; he had never existed.

For a time, this was what the world believed to be undisputed truth, since the whole episode was written up, as described above, in what was purported to be Eva Braun's personal diary. Yet, even today, the 'diary' remains an enigma. The document first appeared after the war in 1947, when the Austrian actor/director Luis Trenker sold it to a Paris-based publisher. Trenker insisted that Eva had entrusted her diary to him, and that it was absolutely genuine. As the above incident shows, it is a lurid work, in parts amazingly banal, in others, near-pornographic. Two of the key witnesses in its exposure as a fake were Leni Riefenstahl and Eva's sister, Ilse.

The Braun family, naturally distressed by the diary's supposed revelations, had complained upon the publication of the book, resulting in a lawsuit which, on 10 September 1948, pronounced the diary to be a fake before a German court sitting in Munich. Most damning was the lack of any kind of evidence beyond the typed manuscript. Such evidence could have verified an identity; a proof that the diary really belonged to Eva Braun. There were no personal notes, for example, on the sheets, no corrections or improvements on the manuscript itself. But the most incontrovertible evidence of all appeared after the trial, when it was discovered that many of the entries had been taken more or less intact from an old book about the unhappy love affair between Crown-Prince Rudolf of the Habsburgs, son and heir of the Emperor Franz Josef of Austria-Hungary, and his mistress, Baroness Mary Vetsera, which ended with their suicide at Mayerling in 1889.

Legal action was taken against the publishers in the form of an injunction. The German court condemned the publisher and imposed a heavy fine, backed by a six-month imprisonment order. However, the tribunal was forced to declare itself impotent in actioning these measures against the French publisher, because the Allied victory did not allow for the vanquished – in this case, Germany – to pursue retribution against nationals of the victors.

Riefenstahl had strong reasons for having the diary discredited – in it she is greatly slandered, mocked and insulted to such an extent that *if* the diary proved to be authentic, she would never live down her supposed Nazi sympathies and would forfeit the property she was endeavouring, at the time, to reclaim. Ilse, on the other hand, was embarrassed for herself and her family, furious that a German weekly had serialized a diary which insulted her sister's memory and which she insisted was a forgery. As for Luis Trenker, history has obliterated any part he may, or may not, have had in the scandal.

★

In early May 1941 Hitler was entertaining at the Berghof when a messenger arrived with the news that Rudolf Hess, the deputy-Führer, had betrayed his country by secretly flying to Scotland. This dramatic development further weakened the Nazi leader's rapidly decreasing worldwide political credibility. Hitler's rage led him to seek revenge on the innocent. He was determined to have Hess's wife and son sent to a concentration camp immediately. Never trusting Hess, Eva was always fond of Ilse Hess and argued successfully in her defence. Frau Hess never forgot the debt she owed Eva Braun for saving her life.

Regardless of her status as mistress of the Berghof, Eva was still permitted to fulfil her role as hostess only when it suited the Führer. When important or influential people were entertained there Eva was bundled away to her room. It is easy to imagine her frustration at not being allowed to meet, for example, the Aga Khan, the Duke and Duchess of Windsor or America's former president Herbert Hoover (Eva was a staunch 'Yankophile'). But Hitler still considered Eva, now in her late twenties, too young to meet such sophisticates. To him, Eva would always be a child.

Hitler neither smoked nor drank alcohol (drinking instead great quantities of apple-peel tea), which he thought gave him the right to condemn 'worldly sophistication'. He was particularly antagonistic to the heavy make-up Eva favoured and about which the Führer frequently upbraided her. Lipstick, he said, was made from pig's urine and was against the purity of the Aryan image.

For once, Eva asserted herself, insisting that the 'Chief' should leave her own personal appearance to her discretion. Earlier, her lover had totally concurred with her indignation at Himmler's futile and risible attempt to close all hairdressers' salons. Now, Eva argued that beauty was surely a morale-booster; it was unpatriotic not to make oneself as beautiful as one could.

A short time later, perhaps in a rare moment of expansion, the Führer suddenly relaxed his exclusion of Eva from important functions; she was now permitted to dine with the cream of the visiting guests. She also enjoyed extended holidays in Italy, and on one occasion in 1938 she was granted an audience with the Pope. One evening at the Berghof, she was host to the Italian Fascist leader Benito Mussolini. His earthiness and outgoing nature were immensely attractive to both Eva and her sister Ilse – Ilse in particular.

Unfortunately, the change in Eva's status coincided with a new arrogance that distressed some, angered others. Ilse was dismayed by her, accusing her openly of abusing her position. She was not too wide of the mark. Even Eva's treatment of the Berghof servants had become haughty. They now referred to her as 'Cheflin', the 'Boss's Wife': a title she enjoyed.

Like many others, none of whom dared to voice an opinion, Ilse was no longer enchanted with the message of Adolf Hitler. Towards the end of the war many believed the conflict was already lost, months before its official end. Ilse dared to express these sentiments in private to her sister. Eva retaliated angrily against the disloyalty of her sibling. She told her what the Führer had planned; that the war would soon be over and Germany would see a new world. Hadn't he told her that Germans would hold every single worthwhile post across Europe while the vanquished would be their slaves?

Ilse was aghast. She had long since considered Hitler to be unstable. Now, for the first time, she was able to grasp fully just how great this man's influence was on her younger sister. She realized, not without distaste, how much Hitler had lived up to his theory – a theory he never tired of expostulating – that there could be nothing better for a man than to mould a young girl's character. She could recall him years ago, voicing in Eva's presence (according to Louis L. Snyder's *Encyclopedia of the Third Reich*) the opinion that 'a highly intellectual man should have a primitive and stupid woman. Imagine if I had a woman to interfere with my work!'

It was obvious to Ilse that Eva related very little to the outside world and to the reality, the daily horror, of war. She doubted very much if she knew of the full depravity of the concentration camps. Eva lived in a dream world, seemingly afraid to look around and face reality. Germany was near to defeat; the war was all but lost but Eva had no idea of it, made clear by her enthusiastic comments about victory being much nearer than could readily be explained. Her chosen isolation from reality had provided her with a comfortable confidence. The Führer had confided some startling news about a new weapon – he called it an atomic bomb. The scientists were working day and night on it and soon it would be tested by blowing the whole of southern England off the map! In this euphoric state, Eva continued to close herself off from the devastation around her. Even on her train journeys between Munich and Berlin she pulled down the window-blinds. She seemed unable to accept the horror and destruction that might meet her gaze.

★

Of the several unsuccessful attempts made on Hitler's life, there were two which were particularly close calls. One took place on 8 November 1939. It had become the leader's policy to deliver an annual speech at the Bürgerbräu Keller in Munich, the venue chosen specially to commemorate the *putsch* of 1923, when Hitler had failed in a Nazi takeover of the Bavarian state government. Sixteen years to the day had passed. The annual speech was usually a lengthy tirade, but for some unexplained reason – perhaps because it was wartime and there were other, more pressing matters at hand – the Führer had shortened his address and left the hall twenty minutes earlier than planned. It was a rescheduling that saved his life. In the explosion that followed, seven people were killed and sixty-three were injured. Probably because no one was apprehended it was rumoured that Himmler had planned the whole 'performance', with the Führer's approval, to add to the propaganda of the invincibility of the perceived 'superhero'. Eva, of course, was frantic at this assault; she was far more distressed about the possible harm to her lover than the fact that her father (who, unaccountably, had joined the Party in 1937) had been one of those actually hurt.

Five years later, in July 1944, a German-led assassination attempt led to Hitler's second near-miss. On this occasion, had the Führer not been suddenly called to Rastenburg, and thus stood and moved away from his dining table unexpectedly, both he and his mistress would have perished from a bomb strategically placed under the table they were due to occupy. As it was, Hitler escaped with just a fractured nasal septum, which was probably responsible for the appalling headaches he suffered for the brief remainder of his life. Several other, Allied, attempts to eliminate the Nazi leaders and Eva Braun (in a mission coded as Operation Walküre) took place in 1944. They were all thwarted by sudden schedule changes.

For some time in the early forties, the war became emotionally advantageous to Eva, when Hitler spent more time than ever before at the Berghof. But were they still lovers? Eva rarely, if ever, commented to anybody about their sexual activity. She never once manifested the misery or fear that Geli, Renate Müller and others had displayed before their deaths. She never confided anything even vaguely distasteful or obscene to anyone. Perhaps there was nothing to confide – an innocence (or ignorance?) which could account for Eva's unique survival over the years.

★

In 1944, thousands of photographs were being displayed all over Germany, showing a virile, energetic Führer. The reality was quite the reverse. Over the previous months, Adolf Hitler had suffered increasingly serious physical deterioration. Aside from an operation for a tumour on his vocal cords, he had begun to drag his left leg, and his left arm visibly shook: both outward corporeal manifestations of progressive slow paralysis. In addition, his sight and hearing capabilities were failing, the latter defect a result of another unsuccessful assassination attempt, on 20 July 1944 (part of Operation Walküre). As imminent German defeat approached, the Führer's powers of reasoning became increasingly muddled and bizarre. He was consuming more than thirty drugs and/or vitamins daily, fed to him by his personal physician Dr Morell, who appears to have had no idea how to deal with his patient's increasing flatulence and excruciating pain in the bowels.

★

According to the memoirs of Dr Felix Kersten, who had been appointed the official physician to the Nazi leaders and their families in 1939, Eva Braun did have some sort of mild affair with Ernst Kaltenbrunner, a key member of Himmler's Gestapo. It was talked about – and yet curiously unexposed, probably because it was treated as light gossip. However, in early 1944 Eva suddenly found herself openly very much attracted to a thirty-eight-year-old lieutenant-general in the Waffen-SS (the operational combat arm of the SS).

Eva first met Hermann Fegelein in March 1944. There was an immediate mutual attraction. He was handsome and sexually charismatic; he was also arrogant, vicious, ruthless, promiscuous and untrustworthy. He was totally absorbed by himself and his pleasures, foremost of which was his sexual prowess. Comparing the prematurely old Hitler with the dashing Fegelein, it is understandable that Eva Braun's loyalties might be seriously challenged. Indeed, Frau Junge, a secretary at the Chancellery, commented that 'the handsome Hermann had succeeded in gaining Eva Braun's favour astonishingly quickly'.

SS–General Fegelein's career, like so many of the Nazi leaders', was meteoric and totally corrupt. He ran his father's riding school from 1929, and joined the SS in 1933; by 1937 he was the commander of the Central SS Riding Academy. A combination of outward charm, vivid personality and ruthlessness all contributed to his promotion to the important post of link-man between Himmler and Hitler.

Fegelein loved to dance as much as Eva; they danced a great deal together at the parties she gave in her rooms at the Chancellery. Later, many witnesses, including those close to Eva, such as Hitler's secretary Christa Schöder, testified to the obvious increasing attraction between the two. No one said anything; the situation was delicate, fraught with the fear of being implicated.

Hitler is alleged to have told Eva Braun at some earlier date that if ever she met someone she really liked, it was up to her to tell him openly and fearlessly and he would let her go. If only Fegelein had invaded her life several years earlier, Eva admitted to Frau Schömann, a friend of Hitler's who became close to his mistress, she would most certainly have spoken with the Führer. It was not coincidence that from this time, whenever Fegelein was at the Chancellery or the Berghof, so was Eva.

Fegelein had previously been in a sexual relationship with a Polish girl, which had caused a scandal and from which only the good word of Himmler, his advocate, had extricated him. There was a penalty: he was given a limited time span to find himself a German wife. Over the months he had failed to do this; now, Himmler was growing impatient. Under these enforced circumstances, Fegelein proposed to Gretl, Eva's young sister. Gretl, never very bright where men were concerned, instantly fell in love with the handsome if half-hearted Fegelein, who irritably labelled her a 'silly goose'. (He regretted his hasty tongue when he realized that Gretl Braun was Eva's sister.) A month later, they were married on 3 June 1944. Eva took a personal interest in the ceremony. 'I want this wedding to be as beautiful as possible,' she is remembered by several contemporaries as saying, 'as though it were my own.' Given Eva's romantic, at times sentimental nature, she probably imagined herself in her sister's place during the expensive, elaborate ceremony at Salzburg Central Hall.

Whatever her nebulous relationship with Fegelein was, or had been, Eva's Catholic upbringing would now certainly have raised serious personal and moral questions as to the 'rightness' of its possible future. The man with whom she was so smitten was now a member of the family. However, Gretl's prestigious marriage did mean that, as an in-law to the handsome General, Eva was now in an unassailable social position, a fact that the Nazi wives resented, but were powerless to affect.

By all accounts, Eva's attraction to, and fascination with, Fegelein was so potent that it would require severe self-discipline to resist it under the new circumstances – a self-discipline that perhaps she didn't always possess. While it may be difficult to accept, it is still possible that Eva could have contemplated a continuation of the liaison, believing it safely hidden behind the respectable veneer of her sister's lavish wedding. Yet – the biggest moral factor of all – regardless of emotional turmoil, Eva's sense of loyalty to the Führer would finally dominate her thoughts. Even if guilty of the ultimate infidelity, she would never have been able to simply walk away from her lover of the previous seventeen years. The ties were too strong to abandon, especially at this terrifying time. It must be remembered that for many Germans, even within the Nazi hierarchy, the war was already lost. Even Eva, at last, had been made aware of and was increasingly affected by the gloom, the chaos and the feeling of hopelessness around her. The starkness of the situation had at last intruded upon her private world, so that nothing seemed real or believable. The confidence she had expressed in the speech to Ilse about imminent victory had been rudely shattered. She now moved in a world where everything appeared bizarre and vaguely surreal. And yet she remained curiously calm.

Gretl was pregnant soon after the wedding; but the holy vows of marriage and the prospect of fatherhood did nothing to change Fegelein's lifestyle. He kept at least one mistress at Obersalzberg; he also slept with any woman he fancied, from chambermaids to Party aristocracy. With his highly charged charisma and sexual drive, most of them were only too willing to become his conquests. If Eva knew of these flings, she kept quiet about them.

In October 1944, Eva made a will. The fact that she was only thirty-two and until now had had no cause to consider such finality is telling in itself – sure proof that she had become part of the real world. Ilse had been right; the war was lost.

Once she had accepted the inevitability of defeat, Eva immediately made up her mind to join the Führer in Berlin. She was calmly resigned. She had informed friends some months before that she knew exactly what was going to happen to her in the unlikely event of things going wrong – never for a moment believing that they could. Although Hitler had forbidden her to join him in Berlin, when she arrived his relief and gratitude were undeniable. His generals were quarrelling among themselves, unnerving him and making him increasingly unbalanced. 'Idiots, shitheads [one of his favourite epithets], numbskulls and homosexuals, all of them!' screamed the man who, according to the Hitler scholar John Toland, Gertrude Stein had once said should be offered the Nobel Peace Prize.

The title of the final opera in Richard Wagner's *Ring* cycle, *Götterdämmerung* (*Twilight of the Gods*), perfectly summed up the inglorious collapse of the Nazi regime. Hadn't Hitler promised that the Third Reich would last for a thousand glorious years? The twilight of the Nazi gods had settled unequivocally after only twelve bizarre, horrendous, bloody, Grand-Guignol years.

By the end of January 1945 Berlin was in ruins and the dreaded Russian army was drawing nearer every day. On 6 February, between air bombardments, Eva celebrated her thirty-third birthday in her apartment at the Chancellery. She insisted on gaiety and dancing to whatever records had not been destroyed in the countless blitzes. Most of her dances were in the arms of Fegelein; they danced until the small hours.

Eva always swore that she would never enter the Führerbunker at the Chancellery (an air-raid shelter especially built for Hitler and his team) except during the most life-threatening air raids. But from mid–March 1945, she would live underground for the remainder of her short life.

By now, Hitler had become gross, his hair had turned white and he was shaking badly – the result of a combination of physical overstrain, high mental tension and the final stages of syphilis. The worse he became, the more staunch was Eva Braun. This was all the more impressive since the staff and the secretaries who were her friends had no doubt that Eva was genuinely in love with Fegelein. But Eva's final loyalties would remain with Adolf Hitler, the first love of her life. During this desperate time, she would have been grateful for Fegelein's presence, but he had not been seen for a few days. No one knew that he had quit the bunker, intent on desertion. Impulsively and, as it turned out, foolishly, he now telephoned Eva and urged her to follow his example and escape while she still had a chance. He was calling her from an apartment he kept in West Berlin (about which Eva knew nothing) on the Bleibtreustrasse.

Eva was stunned, probably more by Fegelein's desertion than by his advice. Aware that the telephone lines were being intercepted, Eva begged the man to return to the bunker immediately. Within hours, Fegelein was arrested at his apartment by the Gestapo, who had known of the hideaway for some time. He was drunk and he had with him a Hungarian woman, apparently the wife of a diplomat stationed at Berlin. She made no attempt to hide the fact that she was hoping to start a new life with Fegelein in Switzerland. The Gestapo discovered a large suitcase belonging to Fegelein, full of German and Swiss currency, silver, gold, jewellery and other valuable, saleable items – including a diamond wristwatch belonging to Eva.

Taken under escort back to the bunker, Fegelein was stripped of his rank and condemned to death on a charge of treason. Eva's entreaties for clemency were ignored. There was a certain macabre irony in Fegelein's death; he was taken outside the bunker and executed (shot 'like a dog', to quote Gun) by an SS platoon. That same morning, Eva married Adolf Hitler.

Escape from Berlin was now impossible. The Russians were almost at the gates of the capital; the roar of artillery and the clamour of fighting was ceaseless. Hitler had permitted some of the worst atrocities of the war to take place in Russia; now, he was fully aware that the Russian soldiers were reciprocating in kind: a biblical retaliation for the indiscriminate murdering and brutal raping perpetrated by the German armies as they invaded deeper into Russian territories. The Russians wanted the Führer alive, to parade him humiliatingly all over their homeland.

The Führer and Eva Braun now put into operation the plan they had devised should this never-expected situation overtake them. On 29 April 1945, a few minutes after midnight, Fräulein Eva Braun became Frau Eva Braun-Hitler, First Lady of the Third Reich. She had been her husband's lover for nearly seventeen years, twelve of them as his official mistress; she would know only one day as his wife. There was some consolation, however brief, in having at last achieved her heart's desire. And could she have seen her husband's will, dated 29 April 1945, she would no doubt have been proud to have read of 'the many years of loyal friendship' he credits her with. By mutual agreement the day after the wedding, Eva and her husband quietly said their goodbyes to Josef and Magda Goebbels. The Goebbels, also, had remained in the bunker; soon, Magda would poison their six children before she and her husband committed suicide.

Behind the closed doors of Hitler's study, the Führer said his last farewell to his bride of one day and then shot himself; Eva died beside him by her own hand, after swallowing prussic acid. She was thirty-three.

As the Russian artillery roared imminent victory only two streets away, the two corpses were carried out into the bombed-out Chancellery garden, where they were drenched with petrol and burnt. What was left of their charred remains was sufficient for the victorious Allies to make a positive identification.

★

In January 2000, nearly fifty-five years after the end of World War Two, files released from the Russian archives finally authenticated exactly what happened to the remains of Hitler and his wife. As the Russian armies withdrew from East Germany, they took with them the charred corpses of Adolf Hitler and Eva Braun-Hitler, which they buried in various places to guard them from the inquisitive, only to later dig them up again to take them further east. In 1970, their bones were finally burned to ashes and then thrown into the river Ehle, near Biederitz in Sachsen-Anhalt. Part of Hitler's skull, complete with the bullet-hole resulting from his suicide, was taken to Moscow and hidden away on the third floor of the Russian State Archive. It still reposes there today.

★

Under circumstances other than those that ordained a teenaged shop girl's path should cross with that of the future leader of Germany, Eva Braun would undoubtedly have lived and died a normal, probably happy-with-her-lot, conventional life. Nothing in her upbringing, her formal and religious education, her interests and her family life suggests anything to the contrary. But then she met Adolf Hitler. From that first encounter, and although she was only seventeen, Eva Braun's life was to be permanently changed. Eva fell in love, really in love – and it is common knowledge that there is no rationality in this most turbulent of emotions. No one can shape it; few can control it. Did Eva, in later years, ever wonder how she came to be so deeply, devotedly involved with a man who was more than twice her age, deeply disturbed, diseased, who largely ignored her and kept her hidden away for most of their relationship?

Eva was not an intellectual but she was fairly bright, with a simplistic sense of humour, appreciative of the good life and apparently pleasant company. Albert Speer and his wife were very close to her, and the few friends she had, such as Herta Schneider, she kept for life. She was vain – she lightened her hair and had it washed and dressed every day. She had a sharp eye for sartorial elegance and dressed well, to the envy of the ministers' wives. She had a spiteful temper, as some of the Berghof staff and certain shops she frequented found out to their cost. All these characteristics were exacerbated over time by the very nature of her liaison with Hitler – a liaison that was steeped in a loneliness she would never have otherwise known. That same loneliness also intensified the jealousy she felt whenever she saw her lover with other women, as happened frequently. Hitler adored to be surrounded by feminine beauty; some he slept with, others he abused, some he drove to suicide. And yet Eva Braun, attractive (never beautiful), uncomplicated, with simple interests that stretched little further than sport, romantic novels, ballroom-dancing and movies, was the one woman who stayed the course. What did she have that the others – more beautiful, more talented – lacked? It has been said that she was a good listener, that of the few demands she made, she was careful with her timing. Hitler, apparently, found her comforting. As for sex: there has always been speculation as to the true nature of the affair. Was it conventional? Did Hitler abuse her? Was she a willing victim in his sadomasochistic fantasies? Was there even a sexual relationship? Or were they, as some said, just close companions: that she brought to him the peace and serenity he found with no one else? Eva may have been attracted to other men, and may even have indulged in a simple liaison; but in the end, her love belonged to the man in whose shadow she lived from the day they first met in Munich in 1929 – the man for whom she made two suicide attempts and, finally, sacrificed her life.

Marion Davies

History's Wealthiest Mistress?

'More money was squandered on Marion than on all the gold-diggers of the fabulous '20s. But she never had to dig.'

Anita Loos, Hollywood writer (1891–1981)

There are many instances throughout history of mistresses who simultaneously inspire their lover even as they destroy his life. The Marion Davies/William Randolph Hearst relationship was something of a reversal of this pattern. Hearst worshipped his mistress and spent a fortune in pursuing his dream: to present her to the world as one of Hollywood's greatest dramatic actresses. That Hearst failed in this endeavour was entirely due to a one-track enthusiasm which obliterated any consideration for Marion Davies's talent as a natural comedienne. Hearst cast himself in the role of a twentieth-century Pygmalion, 'sculpting' the Hollywood career of his Galatea with the hammer and chisel of great wealth and the invincible power of a vast newspaper empire. That she survived near annihilation artistically was largely due to her own abilities, her charm and infectious, bubbling personality. In a recent retrospective, her comedic invention shows her to have been among the best humorists of the twenties and thirties. Several of her comedies – *Show People* and *The Patsy*, for instance – are as fresh today as they were on their release.

Under Hearst's protection, Marion evinced another enviable talent as one of the world's most successful social hostesses; when she died, in 1961, her obituary in the *San Francisco Examiner* cited her as 'a czarina of Hollywood society'. This underestimated her: she became a leader of *world* society. During the 1920s and 1930s, there were two kinds of people: those who were on the Marion Davies party list and those who weren't. It was a social victory indeed to be invited to any of the Hearst/Davies 'kingdoms'

– at San Simeon, Santa Monica, Wyntoon, or St Donat's castle in Wales. At all of these fairy-tale estates Marion played châtelaine to the world's famous – from politicians to sportsmen, industrialists to European aristocracy, presidents and, of course, the cream of Hollywood and world theatre. Marion Davies had, literally, hundreds of friends, worldwide. Even the envious and the occasional enemy admitted her popularity and social success. Gloria Vanderbilt acknowledged, 'though I have travelled extensively, I have never known another to equal her'; Randolph Churchill considered her the most attractive personality present at her 200-strong Hollywood luncheon in his honour, while the acidic George Bernard Shaw, never an easy man to please, delighted in her company and thought her 'pretty shrewd' – enough to offer her eventually the role of Eliza Doolittle in a film version of his play *Pygmalion*. Although Marion very much wanted the role, producer Gabriel Pascal was non-committal; the offer petered out. (In the event, Dame Wendy Hiller created a legendary Eliza in the 1938 film.) Shaw and Marion corresponded regularly until he died in 1950.

Marion's life was not always easy, or successful. Like the writer Somerset Maugham, she suffered with a slight stutter (he once called her a 'fresh bitch', when he mistakenly thought she was mocking his speech): charming among friends, but an agonizing worry when sound movies became established. Then, between the lovers, there was the considerable thirty-four years' age difference, something which eventually lured Marion to indulge in occasional lightweight, brief flirtations with her leading men. Despite the closeness of family ties (and the fact that they were all recipients of considerable generosity from Hearst) her sisters often expressed their 'affection' with displays of intense jealousy. Worst of all though (or so thought Hearst), was Marion's drinking problem, which increased with age. All this aside, by the time she died the little chorus girl from Brooklyn had amassed a tidy fortune of over $20 million – largely acquired through her films and a natural flair for investment in real estate. She died arguably the wealthiest mistress in history.

★

Marion Cecilia Douras – the future Marion Davies – was born in Brooklyn, New York City, on 3 January 1897, the youngest in a family that included three other daughters and a single son, the latter dying tragically in a drowning accident at the age of fifteen.

Marion's father, Bernard Douras, known as 'Papa Ben', was a moderately successful Brooklyn lawyer, who was already 'straying' by the time Marion was born. Mama Rose, his wife, contributed to the estrangement by her devotion to, and passionate ambition for, her offspring. She had no intention of permitting her daughters to go through life lacking the good things. In many ways, she mirrored the ambitious mother of the nineteenth-century unlaunched courtesan, whose solution to her daughter's future would be determined by her choice of a wealthy protector. Mama Rose urged her girls to consider only older men, pointing out the folly, the stupidity, of love for love alone.

Marion's two grown-up sisters, Reine and Ethel, were in show business, successfully working the vaudeville circuits as singers or chorus-members. Watching them perform in that magical world beyond the footlights decided young Marion's future. Finally giving up on marital indifference, Mama Rose amicably left her husband and took her daughters with her. They found a house near Grammercy Park; however, Marion and her sister Rose – five and seven years old respectively – returned to live with their father during their early education.

In 1906, after a series of short affairs, Reine, the most beautiful of the sisters, married George Lederer, a very successful Broadway producer and theatre lessee. There would be two offspring: a son, Charles, known as Charlie, and a daughter, Josephine Rose, known as Pepi. They were Marion's favourite family; the affection was reciprocated. A few months after Charlie's birth, the Lederers moved to Chicago where, shortly afterwards, they were joined by Mama Rose, trundling Ethel and young Rose along with her. Marion, unaccountably left behind, became rebellious and difficult. She joined a street gang, horrifying her mother and thus precipitating Marion's rapid removal to Chicago. In 1910 she was boarded at the Convent of the Sacred Heart, where she remained through early adolescence.

During these years, Marion took weekly classes at Theodor Kosloff's Manhattan ballet school, for which Reine paid. At 5 feet 5 inches, Marion's figure was shapely, and she was pertly pretty, attractively blonde with dazzling blue eyes. In 1915, having been in the chorus of several musicals, she joined the chorus line of *Chin Chin*, her first major Broadway production. Soon she was working regularly, skipping from revue to musical with a little modelling on the side.

Her major break occurred when she was chosen as a dancer for the great Florenz Ziegfeld's *Follies of 1916*, dancing and singing to such popular delights as 'I Left Her On The Beach in Honolulu', and appearing alongside the great Fanny Brice and W. C. Fields. Her only other Ziegfeld show was *Miss 1917* – according to Randolph Carter's *The World of Flo*

Ziegfeld, 'one of the most notable flops in Broadway history'. It closed within two months. The *Follies* productions – shows synonymous with beauty, class, lavish production and the glorification of the American girl – were however to become legendary. '[He is] determined to show America's inexhaustibility in female beauty,' said *The Dramatic Mirror* on 23 June, about the girls in *Follies of 1917*. The girls were unusually tall – so tall indeed that Hollywood actress Marlene Dietrich was convinced some of them were men! Later this same year, Marion Davies would be among those abandoning Ziegfeld for the silver screen.

Marion's life at this time was hectic and intense, frivolous and fast. Being associated with a Ziegfeld show opened many doors and socially elevated many of the showgirls, who were brought into contact not only with fashionable, international society, but also with the cream of the arts world. Marion was immensely popular with all of them. Rose observed her success and was consumed by unfair jealousy. Heedless of her mother's earlier advice, she had left the theatre for love, pursuing a handsome man whom she eventually married – and whom she soon divorced through incompatibility.

Marion, on the other hand, followed her mother's advice with much more alacrity than any of her siblings, accepting dates with several older men. There were those who (correctly) thought she dated with a touch of the gold-digger in her choices. The great irony in Marion's life was her lifelong involvement with enormous wealth, even as she showed a marked indifference to it. As a child she had not known deprivation, but the wealthy world in which she now found herself had given her a taste for the high life, with no hint of avarice in those tastes. She simply knew what she wanted and was willing to wait for it. Meantime, she was enjoying life and having fun ...

Part of that fun began when Marion met newspaper magnate Paul Block at a late-night theatre party at the home of her new friend, the musical-comedy star Elsie Janis. In his late forties, Block became her regular escort and companion for some weeks; she liked him, but not enough to become his mistress. It was around this time that Marion met a close friend and colleague of Block's, another newspaper tycoon of enormous wealth and influence, who was about to change Marion's life dramatically.

His name was William Randolph Hearst.

★

On 15 June 1862, forty-one-year-old George Hearst married Phoebe Apperson, a schoolteacher of nineteen. Ten months later, on 29 April 1863, their only son William Randolph was born. While her husband absented himself making a fortune from silver-mining and cattle-breeding, a determined Mrs Hearst relished the challenge of her son's early education. Later, with a tutor, she took young William on a year's tour of Europe; it was the beginning of a love affair with that continent and its arts that would last all his life. Back in America, after completing a three-year stint at an exclusive New Hampshire preparatory school, Hearst entered Harvard in 1882. Hardly academic, he was suspended during his first year, and booted out two years later, after issuing his tutors with a chamber pot each, featuring identifying names on the inside.

At twenty-three, Hearst was over six feet tall, an attractive young man with compelling, disturbingly cold, blue eyes, and an unfortunate high-pitched voice, '… so high-pitched for such a big man,' fretted actress Bebe Daniels, years later. Scenarist Anita Loos was rather more caustic: 'A faint voice rose from his great bulk like the squeak of Minnie Mouse coming out of a mountain.'

That squeaky voice nonetheless now persuaded Hearst's father to let his son take over the *San Francisco Examiner*, a failing newspaper the older Hearst had owned since 1880; three years later, and with his father's wary financial backing, the *Examiner* made its first significant profits. Even so, Hearst senior still expected his son to join him in the lucrative Comstock Lode stake (probably the richest silver mine in the world) and cattle enterprises extending over 40,000 acres of land he had purchased for next to nothing. William Randolph, though, was set on a journalistic career.

When Hearst senior died in 1891, he left his wife very rich. Even so, it took four years for William Randolph to persuade his mother to loan him nearly $8 million, with which he began a rapid expansion of what would become America's biggest and most formidable newspaper empire. Hearst specialized in sensational, melodramatic stories written simplistically, in language the more literate newspapers spurned. Hearst, it was said, would be willing to expose his best friend's closest secret if that exposure sold papers. Nor was he any too particular as to the veracity of some of the stories he printed. He had no compunction, for instance, in crucifying the immensely popular but ill-fated comic, Rosco 'Fatty' Arbuckle, for hosting a wild party on 5 September 1921 in San Francisco, at which starlet Virginia Rappe died mysteriously — with Arbuckle accused of her death. Hearst cared nothing for Arbuckle's fate, only about the lurid story with its vast circulation potential. Later, he admitted that his coverage of the incident had sold more newspapers than had any event since the sinking of the *Lusitania* on 7 May 1915. Condemnation didn't touch him; he sincerely believed that his wealth and position placed him above revenge or retribution.

From 1895 he spent three years supporting Cuban insurgents rebelling against Spanish domination. He sent the artist Frederick Remington to Cuba to paint on-the-spot carnage scenes. Remington found none; 'Everything is quiet,' he telegraphed, and begged to return home. Hearst's reply has become famous: 'You furnish the pictures, I'll furnish the war.' And he did, almost single-handedly, in a short conflict Hearst called a 'splendid little war', and from which the Hearst coffers profited handsomely. From here on, Hearst's political sway through the press was formidable, proven in his successful promotional drives for both Theodore and Franklin D. Roosevelt for the American presidency. Politically ambitious himself, Hearst's only success was in gaining a seat in Congress from New York's 11th District between 1902 and 1904. Twice he narrowly failed being elected Mayor of New York.

In 1903 he married Millicent Willson, a beautiful showgirl eighteen years his junior. Almost immediately, Mrs Hearst's light-heartedness of premarital days was obliterated by her determination to achieve prominence as a hostess in smart society. Organized charities, the country club and benefit committees became the reason for Millicent's existence. However, over the next decade, she presented Hearst with five sons: George, in 1904; William Randolph Jr in 1907; John Randolph in 1909, followed in 1915 by twins, David Whitmore and Randolph Apperson. Aware of family commitment to his sons, Hearst took ten years to react to the irreversible stagnancy of a marriage held together only in name, by children and Millicent's unremitting, Roman Catholic 'No!' to divorce. At fifty-two, and mind-bogglingly wealthy, the world's greatest publishing tycoon began to seek consolation elsewhere.

There was no lack of subscribers. When, in 1915, Hearst saw Marion Davies for the first time, in the chorus line of *Chin Chin*, he was immediately smitten. Her blonde beauty and natural effervescence fascinated him until one night, as she was about to leave a party they were both attending, he delayed her departure long enough to squeeze an exquisite diamond wristwatch into her hand. Marion was flattered, but embarrassed; she was even more embarrassed the next day when she lost the watch in the snow as she was returning from Boston. Marion's showgirl friend, Pickles St Clair, tipped off Hearst, who straightaway sent her a replica. When Ziegfeld's *Follies of 1916* opened at the New Amsterdam theatre in New York, Hearst became a nightly habitué. By the end of the run, he and Marion were seen frequently and publicly together. Paul Block had been replaced; Marion simply swapped publishers and continued to enjoy a hectic social life.

Soon, Hearst was genuinely and deeply in love. And jealous. Around this time, Edward, Prince of Wales was touring America, winning support for the Allied cause in fighting the bloody war raging against Germany. Marion was terribly excited when she was invited to a party in his honour. The envious Hearst, however, asked her to make a choice: the prince's party, or the glorious black pearl necklace and matching bracelet he dangled before her. Marion hesitated; there would be other princes, but only one black pearl parure! To make sure she kept the bargain, Hearst had detectives watching her home.

Throughout the war years, Hearst, controversially, never made a secret of his admiration for Germany. Fiercely anti-British (he never forgave an apparent snub meted out by members of the English aristocracy on an early visit to London), he vociferously condemned American aid to the Allies when World War One began in 1914. His contradictory bland enthusiasm for recruitment and Red Cross support fooled no one. From America's involvement in the war in 1917 until the Armistice in November 1918, the *New York Tribune* cited no less than 155 anti-Allies articles in the Hearst press. Many colleagues considered him a traitor, feelings shared by the man in the street, who expressed his fury by attacking Hearst's unfortunate newsvendors, confiscating their papers and even burning Hearst's effigy. At fifty-five, Hearst had become the most hated man in America.

Bright, shrewd, but with a total lack of interest in politics, or the weightier problems of twentieth-century existence, Marion proved to be the perfect companion during this bleak period. Her natural warmth, her showgirl energy and a certain indefinable quality in her personality brought responses from Hearst not experienced since those far-off pre-marital days with Millicent. Marion benefited from the famous Hearst generosity, but was not seriously affected by Hearst's attention, until she began to be aware of a certain shyness in his make-up, a reservedness which was an integral part of him, and which she found very appealing. The discovery made her protective, even when he was surrounded by friends and family. The gold-digger aspect of the relationship was soon replaced by genuine feelings of affection and growing love on Marion's side – a vulnerability which, in his turn, Hearst cherished. They dated for some little time before they became lovers. Marion could not know then that she was embarking on what would become the most extravagant, discussed liaison of the twentieth century.

All this time, Marion continued to impress and charm all she met, delighting both Hearst's social circle and the Hollywood party circuit in equal measure. Actor David Niven thought the world of her, recalling Marion as 'an utterly genuine person, [with] no illusions about her talents'. Everyone felt the same about her, including Hearst's sons (who affectionately nicknamed her 'Daisy'). In his autobiography, Douglas Fairbanks Jr wrote: 'Everyone – and no contrary voices were ever raised – loved Marion personally ... She was delicious, irreverent and generous.' Only the Hearst executives in New York demurred, fearing her influence over 'the Chief', as Hearst was known.

Hearst had been involved in the rapidly growing motion pictures industry since 1913, without much success. Now, he was determined to make his mistress the most famous dramatic star in the industry. He created Cosmopolitan Pictures for this single purpose, and eventually made Marion its President – at an annual salary of $104,000. Nothing would be spared – the best scriptwriters, lavish costume design, authentic props, the most sensitive cameramen and the full force of the Hearst publicity resources were to amalgamate in creating the greatest name in Hollywood. This was hardly Marion's wish. Never overly ambitious, she acquiesced to her lover's dream, substituting his ambition for her lack of it.

Hearst signed the unknown chorus girl to a contract of $500 a week, with options: ten times more than she earned with Ziegfeld. A period of grooming (intensive acting sessions and speech technique, backed with preposterous publicity about a new and brilliant discovery) was set in motion. Hearst's movie-gossip columnist Louella Parsons became a laughing stock over these years, as every story she wrote included the phrase, 'and Marion never looked lovelier'. (Coincidentally, Louella and Marion had been friends in Chicago, long before she met Hearst.)

Soon, Marion Davies appeared in every one of Hearst's papers, some of them every day, some with more than one article. (In future years, Marion wistfully acknowledged that her screen image was '5 per cent talent and 95 per cent publicity'.)

Hearst's somewhat Victorian outlook on Marion's career insisted on one major stipulation: his new star would emulate Mary Pickford, the phenomenally popular actress, whose fame rested on her portrayal of virginal, unsullied heroines. Fierce antagonism from various directors resulted from Hearst's interference on-set; despite lack of experience, he even demanded to direct certain scenes himself. Worse, he insisted on Marion being in every scene and, with the advent of sound, at some point – no matter how inappropriate – Marion must be allotted a song.

Marion had already made brief appearances in several pictures, so she was not without experience when she faced Hearst's cameras for her first feature film in 1918 (directed by her brother-in-law, George Lederer). Called *Runaway Romany*, she also wrote the film's scenario. This was immediately followed by the bloodless drama *Cecilia of the Pink Roses* (1918), for which Hearst ordered the entire screen to be framed with thousands of roses, complete with fan-driven wafts of perfume essence blowing across a swooning and slightly bemused audience at its New York première. How could this bland offering hope to compete financially with Cecil B. de Mille's racy, up-to-date marital comedy *Don't Change Your Husband* (1918), starring the glamorous, 'dangerous' Gloria Swanson? It couldn't. Hearst critics raved – they had no option – but the independent papers were lukewarm. Marion, they said, was hardly 'the find of the year', except in the Hearst papers.

During these early years of film production, pictures were often inexpensive and made within two or three weeks, sometimes days. Not so with the Hearst movies: the magnate insisted on lavish sets and authentic props – unnecessary expenses which defeated any expected profits before the films left the studios. Hearst didn't mind; his losses barely grazed his $400 million fortune. (Gossip columnist Hedda Hopper had a point when she commented: 'Marion Davies held in her hands the greatest power of any woman on earth …')

In 1919 a deal was struck with the producer Adolph Zukor to distribute Marion's pictures through Paramount Studios. Of these, only *Little Old New York* (1922) and *When Knighthood Was In Flower* (1922) were of any consequence. Edward, Prince of Wales, raved over the latter. The $1.5 million film cost fifteen times more than the most extravagant films being made at that time.

In late 1921, just after Marion had finished work on these two films, the smooth happiness of the lovers was disturbed by the death of Hearst's lifelong friend, the portraitist Orrin Peck. Grief distorting his usually well-adjusted mind, Hearst all but discarded Marion and sailed for Europe. There seemed no sense or reason in the severance, beyond the erratic, peculiar behaviour of someone unbalanced by shock, although it is doubtful if Marion recognized the full extent of this. Hearst was accompanied by his entire family and by Mr and Mrs Guy Barham, head publisher of Hearst's *Los Angeles Herald*. Within weeks, with the assuaging of grief, Hearst was begging his mistress to join him secretly in London, to rekindle their affections. The reunion, however, was marred by the sudden death of Guy Barham, after an unsuccessful abdominal operation. Nevertheless, the flame of the Hearst/Davies affair began burning brightly once again.

By the end of 1922, after four rather unsuccessful years as Hearst's protégée in the movie business, even good-hearted, even-tempered Marion Davies was beginning to rebel against the weak, wishy-washy vehicles being churned out for her. It was a general opinion in Hollywood that, had Marion's comedic gifts been allowed to flourish, she would have been among the most popular comediennes of her time. As it was, her lover's obsessive dream, and his relentless daily plugging, resulted in a sniggering, disdainful public, and the financial failure of over half Marion's entire output of fifty films. Hollywood being what it was, however, the actress's discontentment with the work did not lead to anything.

Two years after this, in 1924, Hearst abandoned the distribution deal with Zukor and left New York City for California, after accepting a much more lucrative deal with producer Sam Goldwyn (soon, with Louis B. Mayer, to form the vastly successful Metro-Goldwyn-Mayer Company – MGM), which included an exceptional contract for Marion. The ex-chorus girl had by now made seventeen feature films with varying results. The new deal guaranteed her $10,000 a week (she was, at this time, supposedly the eighth most popular film actress with the public); MGM would shoulder all the production and distribution costs of her films; in addition, Hearst would receive a share of the profits on those films. For this munificence, Hearst would utilize the full might of his empire to publicize and boost MGM stars and the studio's entire output. Goldwyn considered the enormous outlay well worth the international publicity. It proved to be an amicable, ten-year amalgamation, and probably the happiest years shared by Marion and Hearst. She bought a house on Lexington Road, to which, over the course of a week, a large ballroom was added. Marion thrived on social contact; for her, party-throwing was an artery of her existence.

At the studio, Hearst soon established a 'dressing room' for his mistress's comfort – it was in fact a fourteen-room, Spanish-style villa, reputedly larger than the Vanderbilt residence on 5th Avenue in New York City, and estimated to have cost over $75,000. The writer Ilka Chase swore it had 'enough kitchen and bathroom paraphernalia to equip a hotel'. Here Marion would prepare for the day's filming. It quickly became the hub of MGM social life, as Marion and her lover fast emerged as the most inveterate party-throwers in the history of Hollywood. There had never been, and there never would be, another Hollywood host and hostess to equal them. Marion's only rival was Mary Pickford, but the 'Pickfair' parties could not compare for sheer originality, lavishness and extravagance at all levels. Marion particularly enjoyed on-the-set luncheons, any of which could last the major part of a working day! Much of her social success lay in her naturalness and charming naïvety, which disguised the sharp brain behind the 'baby-face' façade.

Marion's biggest ambition was to marry Hearst, but Millicent put paid to that dream: a mixture of Roman Catholic angst, the threat to her young family, and, of course, her personal bitterness at being discarded. Philosophically, Marion consoled herself by saying a ring didn't guarantee love – and she had William Randolph Hearst's in abundance. She was proud of it and she settled for it. Over this decade, Marion and her lover lived lavishly (as did her family, at Hearst's expense) in any of several magnificent residences. In New York there were several apartments and blocks; in Hollywood, a Beverly Hills mansion, and several residences exclusively for accommodating visiting business tycoons. At Santa Monica, at a cost of $7 million (three for building, four for furnishing), there was the palatial, Georgian-style beach-house, known as Ocean House, boasting 110 rooms with 55 bathrooms, where some of the most lavish parties in Hollywood's history were held; in North California's redwoods forest a fairy-tale Bavarian-themed estate called 'Wyntoon' flourished, while 250 miles north of Hollywood, Hearst's proudest architectural achievement, La Casa Grande, stood proud: a fascinating, anachronistic edifice he had built from 'plundered' (at a price) castles, châteaux and ancient sites from across Europe and beyond. This 'Versailles of California', as it became known, was situated at San Simeon in San Luis Obispo county. At the zenith of its popularity, Hearst's housekeeper proudly admitted that running the great house alone cost $7,000 a week. Hearst's castle (he called it his 'ranch') was begun around 1919. Although ready for occupancy by 1925, it would never be finished, partly due to a bizarre superstition of Hearst's, that the ranch's completion would signal his death. The main building, with its magnificent Spanish façade flanked by two bell-towers, was offset by several guest villas nearby. Unlimited wealth permitted Hearst to uproot whole rooms and buildings in Europe and transport them back to America for perfect resurrection.

The interior was a unique conglomerate of priceless paintings by Rembrandt and Gainsborough and others, statues snatched from antiquity, Gobelin tapestries, English Restoration furniture, books, Georgian silver ('WR had cornered the market,' observed Hedda Hopper) and precious jewels dating from antiquity to the contemporary. All were part of the 50-year, million-dollar annual art-buying spree which distinguished Hearst as the world's biggest art collector. He was known to spend an average of $15 million a year on various pleasure pursuits, such as art, travel, and antiques investments. Marion's friend Hedda Hopper commented: 'The place housed treasures and antiques that Kubla Khan would have envied', while George Bernard Shaw quipped: 'San Simeon was the place God would have built – if he had the money.' Architect Julia Morgan, in sole charge of the estate, would become arguably the most important female architect in the world, stemming from her long, unique association with Hearst.

Outside the main house, beyond the glorious gardens, where (wrote Cecil Beaton) 'flowers were unreal in their ordered profusion', a Greek temple, lifted from its original site, now supplied a backdrop to the outdoor swimming pool. Nearby, in one of the laid-out gardens, reposed three life-size marble statues (which mischievous actress Bebe Daniels once surreptitiously dressed in vivid pink bras and panties). Tennis courts and polo fields led to a zoo, begun in 1926, which accommodated 300 wild animals and 1,500 birds – all having permanent right of way, manifested by constant reminder-signs to all those who motored along the road to the castle.

During the 1920s and '30s the world stayed at San Simeon. Marion and Hearst entertained personalities as famous and varied as Winston Churchill, Cecil Beaton, Gloria Vanderbilt and Albert Einstein. Three rules were sacrosanct: there would be no bad language; imported drink was forbidden; sex between single couples, even if affianced, was the true cardinal sin. Breaking any of these rules guaranteed the culprit the ignominy of finding his bags packed and a car waiting to drive him to the station. Writer Dorothy Parker and actor Errol Flynn are alleged to have been meted out (on separate visits) this humiliation.

Guests usually arrived by private, overnight train from Los Angeles, to be driven the forty-three miles to the castle. Hearst, together with Marion, would welcome their guests on the terrace before showing them to their rooms. Cecil Beaton's 'seemed gigantic. There was a carved gilt ceiling; great, hewn Jacobean beds with gold brocade covers; old, tinselled velvets hanging on the walls.' Guests slept in beds once occupied by Cardinal Richelieu, Bismark, Catherine de' Medici, Napoleon, and other legendary names.

Theme-parties were the thing, for which hundreds of costumes were hired for guests to choose from. Not everyone enthused. Invited to a 2,000-strong 'circus' party at Ocean House, Bette Davis thought it all rather silly and turned up in an evening gown; eventually, she fell under the costume spell enough to don false whiskers, as the Bearded Lady.

An on-the-dot cocktail hour usually provided guests with semi-innocuous drinks – a single round of sherry, according to Anita Loos, that few enjoyed. (Everyone knew of Marion's secret supply of hard liquor, cooling in the lavatory-cistern!) Gloria Vanderbilt (who saw the San Simeon estate as a principality) recalled the vast dining room, 'built for conquerors ... and men like Hearst'. Painter Ludwig Bemelmans described it as 'half the size of Grand Central Station'. On each side of the long room was a row of Renaissance monks' stalls, over which some fifty or sixty banners were hung, bearing the ancient coats of arms of various European houses. Amidst all this grandeur, guests were surprised to be issued with paper napkins, a utility much at variance with the Hearst hospitality, but in keeping with the common-brand sauce bottles and various other condiments in cartons or plastic that ran the length of the refectory table. After dinner, guests invariably repaired to the sixty-seat theatre to view Marion's latest film, or to preview MGM's most recent release. Hearst would retire immediately after this, leaving the guests to their own devices (and Marion more free to indulge her drinking habit).

★

In mid-November 1924, Hearst invited a group of guests from the film industry to join him and Marion on a weekend cruise to San Diego, which had been planned to mark a business deal between Hearst and the independent producer/director Thomas Ince; it was also to be a celebration of Ince's forty-third birthday. What should have been a happy, carefree weekend ended in a bizarre, mysterious tragedy that would haunt everyone on board for the rest of their lives – especially Hearst, who was allegedly at the centre of the following outlandish events.

Among the fifteen guests to board the *Oneida* at San Pedro were the writer Elinor Glyn, acerbic British doyenne of 'good taste'; Marion's sisters Reine and Ethel; Marion's niece, Pepi; Ince's mistress, actress Margaret Livingston; and Dr Daniel C. Goodman, head of Cosmopolitan's productions. Marion, who was working late at the studio, was picked up by two other guests, Charlie Chaplin and Louella Parsons. The guest of honour was detained at the première of his latest picture, *The Mirage*, and had agreed to meet the boat later at San Diego. There was plenty of illicit (but good) booze, a noisy jazz band for dancing, sumptuous food, a gay, carefree atmosphere – and death.

The persistent rumour that Thomas Ince died at sea on the night of 19 November from a gunshot wound to the head, victim of mistaken identity, has never ceased. However, on 20 November 1924, the *Los*

Angeles Daily Times reported (with a seemingly unchallengeable sub-headline: 'Heart Disease Proves Fatal …') that,

> Thomas H. Ince, pioneer motion-picture producer, died suddenly yesterday morning at his home in Benedict Canyon, to which he had been taken Tuesday night following an attack of indigestion Monday, while a member of a yachting party at San Diego. Death was due to heart disease, superinduced by the indigestion attack.

But Charlie Chaplin's chauffeur/secretary, waiting for his boss on the quayside, swore he saw a bullet hole in Ince's skull as the dead man was being taken off the *Oneida*.

The Hearst press released an elaborate yarn which told of Ince spending the weekend at Hearst's San Simeon castle, and falling ill after overindulgence at the table. His family had been alerted, and he had been returned promptly to his home in Benedict Canyon by private car, with three nurses and two specialists in attendance. Ince's wife, Nell, his sons William (fifteen), Thomas (eleven) and Dick (nine) and two brothers, Ralph and John, were beside him when he died. Was this story true, or was it a blatant fabrication, since there were witnesses who swore they had seen Ince boarding the *Oneida* as arranged, at San Diego?

It was no secret in the film colony that Chaplin was infatuated with Marion. Hearst had become jealous enough to hire private detectives to report on anything untoward; he even informed a furious Marion what he had done. When, for this industry party, Chaplin left his pregnant mistress behind onshore, the film star's unattached presence added fuel to an already smouldering premise. Later, it was spread around that Hearst had deliberately invited Chaplin for the sole purpose of observing him with Marion … and that, discovering them alone in the worst and oldest compromising situation, he shot his rival – except that, by some fluke, he mistook Ince for Chaplin and killed his business associate instead, with a revolver he kept on board for taking potshots at hovering seagulls. Marion's alleged screams of terror brought the guests running to discover the cause. As a result, they were all supposedly palpable witnesses to the world's richest newspaper magnate shooting dead a famous Hollywood director/producer. (A well-observed, recent film, *The Cat's Meow*, starring Kirsten Dunst as Marion, Edward Herrmann as Hearst, Eddie Izzard as Chaplin and Cary Elwes Williams as Ince, has pursued the theory of Hearst's guilt as written above – the first, to this writer's knowledge, to have done so in such painstaking detail.)

Unaccountably, the body was cremated (some thought with indecent haste) within two days, Ince being allowed to lie in state for 'one hour at the Hollywood Cemetery Chapel', reported the *Los Angeles Daily Times*, 'to afford friends and studio employees to pass for one last glimpse of the man they loved and respected.' The following day, the same newspaper continued the story:

> Before the services, from 9 a.m. to 10 a.m. a long file of friends and employees passed before the bier, viewing for the last time the features of their chief. A long line of limousines then deposited at the a door a galaxy of motion-picture luminaries ... On the lawn before the little building were gathered several hundred interested persons ...

Of all those on that fatal pleasure cruise, only Marion and Chaplin attended Ince's funeral. This could have been because the ceremony was very private. The hasty cremation and interment made impossible an inquest which would have revealed the truth. However, Hollywood curiosity (suspicion?) resulted in Charles Kemply, District Attorney for San Diego, being forced into an official investigation. On 10 December 1924, the *Los Angeles Daily Times* reported:

> While making no statement as to the exact purpose or possible scope of his investigation, the District Attorney indicated that the grand jury will be asked to hear testimony on the subject should circumstance warrant.

Apparently, circumstance didn't warrant. Although the *Los Angeles Daily Times* specified that the inquiry was mainly concerned with incidents before, and leading up to, the alleged attack of indigestion on the morning of 17 November, only *one* out of all the guests and crew who were on board the *Oneida* that weekend was interrogated. This was Dr Goodman, relying on his one-time profession, who confirmed that Ince had died from acute indigestion. A verdict of 'death from ordinary causes' was recorded.

So: with such a straightforward illness, why, with witnesses who had sworn otherwise, did Nell Ince insist that her husband died in his bed? Someone was lying. On the other hand, it seems incongruous that Nell Ince herself could have invented those who were allegedly present at her husband's deathbed (or, indeed, that they would allow themselves to be used under such bizarre circumstances). Why did Hearst suddenly provide

Mrs Ince with a healthy trust fund? Why did columnist Louella Parsons suddenly discover herself the recipient of a lifetime's contract with Hearst papers? Indeed, why did Louella insist to one and all that she had been in New York at the time of Ince's death and did not leave that city before the late spring of 1925 – when Marion's stand-in, a girl called Vera Burnett, swore she saw Parsons chatting to Marion and Chaplin as they prepared to leave the studio to board the *Oneida* together? Was this a classic case of big money buying silence for an unfortunate *crime passionel*? Was there even a crime at all? Or were Vera Burnett, Chaplin's chauffeur and others deliberately lying? If so, for what reason?

With acidulous, black Hollywood humour, the *Oneida* became known as 'William Randolph's Hearse'. Meanwhile, the Thomas Ince alleged shooting incident certainly made Marion's future leading men think twice about the consequences before responding to their co-star's natural charms.

Inevitably, the strain of the Ince affair created enormous tension. Perhaps in an effort to quell adverse public opinion, Hearst left Marion and returned to his family for a while. But, though the scandal quietened down with time, it never went away entirely; it is still a matter for conjecture today.

★

Marion made some twenty films between 1924 and 1933. Being under the MGM umbrella brought the actress into touch with producer Irving Thalberg, Hollywood's 'boy wonder', who had long recognized Marion's comedic talents as well as considering her a very good actress; it was a valued talent assessment and morale booster from the industry's most gifted, cultured producer. In 1928, under Thalberg's critical eye, Marion made the aforementioned *The Patsy*, *Show People* and also *Not So Dumb*. They were all directed by King Vidor and rate as three of her best – and they made money. Vidor understood his star well enough to release the stifled humour imprisoned inside the Hearst ethos. He also respected her professionalism, her responsiveness, and her calm acceptance of technical problems, often involving long delays on the set. She usually arrived early and departed late from each day's shoot – a selfless, career-long consideration she shared with actress Barbara Stanwyck.

In *The Patsy*, Marion gave wickedly hilarious impressions of stars Pola Negri, Mae Murray and Lilian Gish. *Show People*, based on the rags-to-riches story of the superstar Gloria Swanson, is still considered to be one of the best films ever made about the Hollywood Dream. Film crews on a Marion Davies picture were usually a happy bunch; they genuinely respected Marion's warmth and lack of guile and were treated more as friends than as a temporary film crew. Hedda Hopper, who became a close friend of Marion's after landing a part in *Zander the Great* (1925), explained, 'Getting into a Marion Davies picture meant … a long engagement, endless excitement, distinguished visitors on the set, and a sure invitation to the fabulous Hearst ranch, San Simeon.' Some of the crew never forgot Marion's quiet, very private, unsung monetary support when they had financial problems, or crippling healthcare bills to face.

Marion loved her family, manifested in her enormous generosity to them; she was shrewdly wary of them too. This strange ambivalence was particularly evident in her relations with Reine, who drank far too much. Out of control, she would loudly insult Marion and accuse her of seducing Pepi and Charlie away from their family – an absurd accusation that embarrassed the two youngsters. Once sober, she seemed to forget her diatribe, only to pick up the attacks at the next party. Meantime, Reine continued to enjoy Marion's generosity and to live in the large Beverly Hills house she had thoughtfully provided for the whole family.

Only a few intimates were aware that Marion had begun richly endowing worthy social projects around this time. The most personally rewarding scheme for her was the commencement of a children's clinic, established in 1932 on land she had bought in 1926 at Sawtelle, Los Angeles, specifically for that purpose. A year after the purchase, she launched the Marion Davies Children's Clinic with a gift of $250,000. She would give it lifelong support, donating millions of dollars of her own money to its upkeep. She also paid the bills for the education and finishing school of her cook's daughter when her mother died, and picked up various hospital bills for needy film-crew members; those in dire financial distress never once had to ask. Marion had found a use for both the enormous sums she earned and those she was given as gifts from Hearst.

This same year, Marion was a bridesmaid at the wedding of the highly-acclaimed MGM actress Norma Shearer to 'boy wonder' Irving Thalberg. The rivalry between Norma and Marion would eventually be the cause of a mortal rupture between Hearst and Sam Goldwyn in 1934. But all that was still to come.

In 1928, Mama Rose died: Marion was devastated. In a bid to soften the loss, the lovers sailed for Europe in July, hosting the usual friends. Each trip for Hearst was acquisitive: a cultural search for more treasures to further enhance his unique collection. The tour took the party through France, Italy and Germany. During their time in Paris, Marion mischievously (and stupidly) stole a document from the open safe of the

Foreign Ministry, where she happened to be at the time. Meant as a silly joke, she admitted the theft to Hearst, who was angry with her – until he read the document, after which he became unusually excited. The document – secret because it broke agreements made at the end of the 1914–18 war – concerned the strengthening of English and French naval deployments, alerted by the increasingly hostile attitude of Germany under Adolf Hitler. Hearst was strongly suspected of the theft; his plea of innocence refuted, he was given an hour to quit Paris and then France. Often guilty of spicing up, or inventing, stories, Hearst suddenly held in his hand a vitally important secret document that needed no embellishment! Reaching England, he published his 'scoop' immediately, thus bringing the wrath of the whole French government down on his head. Hearst was banned from France; Harold Horan, Hearst's confidential private secretary and Paris correspondent, was made to shoulder the blame by the French. Threatened with prison and deportment, he fled France of his own volition.

While things simmered down, Hearst took Marion for their first visit to their largest home, St Donat's castle in Wales. There was immediate empathy with the 900-year-old Norman fort. Renovation had been minimal, most of it internal and largely geared to comfort, including 47 additional bathrooms. While they agreed to reserve Donat's, which Hearst had acquired around 1925, as their hideaway, they in fact spent only four months there in total, visited only by their most intimate friends.

The party arrived back in America in the early autumn of 1928, swept along, as was everyone else, by the advent of the first talking picture: Al Jolson's *The Jazz Singer* (1927). The Sound Age had arrived! Marion was desperate; she was convinced her slight stutter would not allow her to make the transition into the new medium. Far from it; of all the great silent stars – Pola Negri, the three Talmadge sisters, Nazimova, John Gilbert, many with incoherent foreign accents, reedy voices, or strong dialects – Marion was one of the few who passed the test with flying colours. She didn't stammer once.

A year later, in mid-September 1929, British statesman Winston Churchill was visiting America with his son, Randolph. Of course, there was an invitation to San Simeon, which was accepted with enthusiasm. For once, Hearst relied on the sobering, conventional presence of his wife, Millicent. The eighteen-year-old Randolph's observations regarding this visit are revealing:

San Simeon. Friday 13 September
A motley crowd of twenty-five guests are here. Mostly very inferior. Mrs Hearst, who is quite too charming, is here and consequently Marion

Davies is not. The wife of Hearst's eldest son is here. He is a fat oaf, but she is exquisite.

Saturday 14 September
The house is absolutely chock-full of works of art obtained from Europe. They are insured for $16 million – i.e. three and a half million sterling ...

On 18 September, the Churchills met Marion at a prestigious, 200-strong luncheon at the MGM studios, hosted by producer Louis B. Mayer and Hearst, and displaying the cream of Hollywood beauty. Young Churchill commented: 'I thought Marion Davies was the most attractive.'

Hollywood. Saturday 21 September
After lunch, we visited various studios and then went out to Marion's house to bathe. It is about 17 miles from Los Angeles. It is a magnificent place, looking on the sea, with a wonderful marble swimming bath of great length and very well heated – all provided by William Randolph. Marion had collected a dinner party of sixty for us ... She is delightfully stimulating ...

Not everyone was impressed with the beach house, however. Marlene Dietrich – at that time considered the most glamorous woman in the world – was once a guest there, at a dinner party in the early 1930s. Her daughter, Maria Riva, was waiting for her when she returned home that night at around 2.30 a.m. In her lengthy biographical study of her mother, *Marlene Dietrich* (published by Bloomsbury in 1992), Riva brings the episode vividly to life. They were mounting the stairs to Dietrich's bedroom. The star was blatantly scathing about Hearst and his mistress, saying, 'Who does that man think he is? Louis XV? You should see that place! It's like a museum – a bad one!' Once in her bedroom, Dietrich's famous Teutonic bluntness was very much to the fore:

'Nouveau riche' is not even good enough! That Marion Davies doesn't know any better, but you would think *he* could pay somebody to teach him – to tell him he can't have a Pompeii floor, red marble columns, and shepherdesses standing about, holding stags, all in one room, and expect people to *eat* there! The solid gold cutlery – that *must* be Davies – and the plates! She must have bought those from a desperate Hungarian prince, or Asprey's told her that the Queen of England didn't want them any more. Who would?

Dietrich became more animated as Maria helped her out of her $1,000 gold evening gown.

> I counted the row of forks and thought, they must be joking! Ten courses? There wasn't anyone there intelligent enough to make conversation to last through the soup!

These were unquestionably acerbic comments but, unfortunately, there was a lot of truth in them. The beach-house *was* laid out like a bad museum. To the initiated, the opulent décor could not disguise a hint of ignorance, a certain vulgarity, which seems often to accompany a 'money's no object' turn of mind. And yet, curiously, Hearst was well-educated and discerning. However, despite its excellent proportions, fittings and architecture, the beach-house itself was indeed seen by some as a symbol of Hearst's ostentatious vulgarity.

★

On 30 October 1929, the show business weekly, *Variety*, carried a headline: 'WALL STREET LAYS AN EGG'. It said it all. While Marion continued to host lavish parties for the famous, the Wall Street Stock Exchange had crashed. Families, wealthy yesterday, were now bankrupted by an acute economic slump that resulted in massive unemployment across the country. There were many suicides. Amazingly, Hearst's empire suffered little. He spent a fortune setting up soup kitchens and breadlines in New York and other cities. Marion's assets, in jewellery and property, also remained safe. Since Hearst's gift of the Lexington house, she had shown a genuine flair in real estate and had made some highly lucrative investments.

However, in 1931, Marion was shocked when she suddenly received a tax demand for over a million dollars. As her sharp investments in real estate proved, she was no 'dumb blonde' (as she once described herself). Perhaps she thought philanthropy exonerated the philanthropist from such mundane issues. Had she simply ignored the demands? She was angry and humiliated by the tax official to whom she appealed – an inquisitor who disrespectfully (and illegally) refused her any of the usual deductions allowed in the profession, the implication being that this famous film star was a kept woman impersonating an actress. In the end, Marion, whose money was tied up, accepted an instant loan from Mr Mayer, repaying it by working for nothing over the next eighteen months.

In January of this same year, famed photographer and designer Cecil

Beaton was invited to San Simeon together with, as he describes them, a mixture of 'tough blondes, hams and nonentities [mingling] with directors and magnates'. He thought Marion 'as pretty as a Greuze [French portrait painter], and what a character! She is kind, humble, shrewd, blindly generous and madly inconsequential.'

Meanwhile, her Children's Clinic was expanded and now recognized as the Marion Davies Foundation. She became deeply involved with its problems and now gave much of her earnings to the cause. These were busy days; when she was not filming, or supervising one of several charities, she was increasingly involved in real estate investments. She lived, perhaps too frenetically, between Ocean House and San Simeon – by some miracle of inborn energy, totally revitalized by her constant duties as a hostess. Marion needed people and was happiest when she was surrounded by friends and colleagues.

The following year, in 1932, Florenz Ziegfeld died. Hearst's grief was genuine when he wrote to Ziegfeld's widow, 'I mourn the loss of a dear friend.' And indeed, the three had remained close friends. Ziegfeld had free access to the *Oneida*; and when he travelled to Hollywood in 1930 to oversee the filming of his stage success *Whoopee*, Marion turned her Georgian beach-house over to the family.

In April 1933, the famous Irish dramatist, George Bernard Shaw, arrived in the United States with his wife. With a lifelong penchant for pretty actresses, it was quite natural that he should delight in Marion's company on a visit to San Simeon. Pretty she certainly was, but he particularly admired her honesty and lack of guile. This same year she was voted President of the Motion Picture Relief Fund for the fourth time running.

Marion's next two films would have her playing opposite two of the most important male leads in Hollywood. *Peg O' My Heart* (1933) co-starred the enormously popular crooner Bing Crosby, while *Operation 13* (1934), which followed immediately, starred Gary Cooper, one of the great heart-throbs of the thirties. There was mutual attraction for Marion with each of these leading men. Wisely, Hearst ignored the flirtations. Perhaps his seniority had made him sharply aware of the difference in their ages. In any case, experience had taught him to trust Marion; he had grown to realize that her 'flirtations' were never serious.

Operation 13 would be Marion's last picture for MGM. When Irving Thalberg married Norma Shearer, he became very ambitious for his talented and popular wife, buying the rights to any powerful role that suited her. For a long time, Marion had pleaded for more serious roles – and, of course, it was still Hearst's dream to present her as a great dramatic actress.

Two plum roles were suddenly in the offing; Marion wanted to play both the consumptive poetess, Elizabeth Barrett Browning, in *The Barretts of Wimpole Street* (1934), and the eponymous tragic queen, Marie-Antoinette, in a film of the same name (1938). Hearst fought for Marion; Thalberg fought for his wife. Norma won. An angry Hearst immediately closed down all publicity for, and communication with, MGM and its stars. Norma was never again mentioned in the Hearst press. Goldwyn was genuinely sorry; he was fond of Marion and respected Hearst. Now, in a sudden deal, Hearst took Marion, complete with her fourteen-room 'bungalow' (it split easily into sections) the ten miles across Hollywood to the Warner Brothers studios. On arrival, a wall had to be removed from around the sound stage in order that the 'bungalow' could be admitted on to the Warners lot. Marion would remain at the studio until the end of her career in 1937.

As an amusing aside: the rift did not stop Marion from inviting Norma to an 'All-American' costume party she was hosting. Unfortunately, and rather insultingly, Norma ignored the theme and appeared in her most lavish Marie Antoinette costume. She became a laughing stock when she could not pass between the entrance doors due to the width of her dress!

★

Before work with Warners commenced in 1934, Marion and Hearst invited a group of close friends, with the Hearst boys and their wives, for a jaunt to Europe, a trip they made eight years successively. Pepi was also included. She adored her aunt Marion and had lived with her for a decade or more. The party once again travelled through Spain, Germany and Italy, a gay, carefree group that became increasingly sobered by the growing voices of Fascism and Nazism that were echoing across Europe. During their time in Germany, Hearst flew to Berlin to meet with Adolf Hitler. Goldwyn had personally requested his friend to seek out Germany's rising leader and urge him to be gentler with the Jews. The meeting, reported worldwide, resulted in Hearst being seen as pro-Nazi.

The holiday party's spirits rose once more as they dawdled across France on their way to London. Hearst was not with them. Although invited back to France (the French needed his money!), he had refused the invitation.

Back in America, Marion's co-star for her first two films with Warners was Dick Powell, a very popular musical-comedy star. *Page Miss Glory* (1935), an artistic and financial failure with a thirty-eight-year-old, slightly overweight, Marion playing a teenage winner of a beauty competition for the Most Beautiful Girl In America, was closely followed by *Hearts Divided*

(1936), an indifferent Napoleonic romp which many saw as a thumbed nose at the casting of *Marie Antoinette*. Powell's romantic interest, off-screen, helped Marion through her disappointment with both films. Onlookers considered her to be more in love with this leading man than with any of his predecessors. It was possible; but never did the debonair, delightful Powell pose any threat to the firm, established love Marion felt for Hearst. It was said that Powell had confessed his love to Marion and she had not been averse to the compliment. She found his sense of humour breezy and his vocal talent most attractive. Also, he was single, having recently broken up with his actress-comedienne wife, Joan Blondell (with whom, coincidentally, Marion would form a long and loving friendship). Actress Louise Brooks in a memoir mentions 'all Hollywood sniggering' at Marion's affair with the singer. Marion was immune; Hearst liked Powell, and that meant the singer was accepted as a frequent guest at San Simeon and Ocean House.

Marion had always enjoyed special relationships with her niece Pepi and nephew Charlie. She loved them dearly and that love was returned. One can only imagine, therefore, the horror and feeling of devastation Marion experienced when Pepi killed herself in 1935. The girl suffered increasingly from various neuroses, all of them attributed to her low self-esteem in the theatrical environment her parents inhabited, and the celebrity-ridden world of her favourite aunt. Frequently depressed, desperate for recognition in her own right, she resorted to attention-grabbing activities, which frequently landed her in trouble. Lack of self-respect led Pepi into alcoholism; booze, gluttony and resultant obesity did the rest. She was an active lesbian and deeply involved with the drug scene. Her close friend, the unusually intelligent actress Louise Brooks (they met when Pepi was seventeen and Brooks twenty-three), believed that being Marion Davies's niece, and Marion being Hearst's mistress, were the causes of Pepi's problems. Pepi believed that friends clung to her as a passport for invitations to Ocean House or San Simeon. From 1930 she worked in London for five years, in a vain attempt to reclaim herself from the burden of being 'Marion Davies's niece'. Reports of her disintegration sifted through to Marion, who, determined to help the girl, brought her back to America and placed her in the Good Samaritan Hospital. The strain ultimately proved too much for Pepi, who ended her own life.

In 1936, Marion filmed *Polly of the Circus* with a reluctant Clark Gable. Uncomfortable in the role of a priest, money and Marion won him over. There was relaxed camaraderie between the stars, both on- and off-camera. ('Clark's cosy dinners at the beach house with Marion were romantic, warm and racy,' wrote Jane Ellen Wayne in *Clark's Women*.) Both heavy drinkers,

Gable admitted that he thoroughly enjoyed chinking glasses with this 'genuinely friendly and radiant woman'. Marion presented Gable with a valuable piece of land in the Palm Desert area, hoping he might build a home there. He didn't, but their friendship lasted until Marion's death.

In April of this same year, Papa Ben died, aged eighty-two. More distressed than she had expected to be, Marion plunged immediately into a second film with Clark Gable. Throughout filming, Marion was drinking heavily. A guard on the gate had strict instructions to alert her to the arrival of Hearst at any time. The resultant *Cain and Mable* (1936), with its outrageously expensive and incongruous sets, its risible scenario and its chaotic production, deserved its miserable failure. So bad was the audience response that second-lead David Carlyle considered quitting the movies. Instead, he changed his name to Robert Paige and began a thirty-year career!

Now forty-one, Marion completed another bland inanity called *Ever Since Eve* (1937), with romantic lead Robert Montgomery. The film, a damp squib with critics and public alike, was Marion's rather tragic swansong, and marked the end of a career on which Hearst is estimated to have lost over $7 million. The fourteen-roomed dressing 'bungalow', the scene of such high jinks and spirits, remained in Beverly Hills and was eventually sold as a private residence.

★

One year later, in 1937, a seventy-four-year-old Hearst found himself in serious financial difficulties. Unknown to the world, much of the Hearst empire had been mortgaged to allow the tycoon – accustomed to squandering around $15 million annually – to live as he chose, and to buy as he saw fit. By Easter, Hearst's empire had collapsed, with foreclosures and debts amounting to $126 million. There was also the matter of a two-year (1934/35) tax evasion for over $4 million. Many erroneously believed Marion to be the cause; in fact, Hearst was his own worst enemy. His lawyers realized that the sale of property and of the great art collection was inevitable. As a result, over half of Hearst's treasures, many never unsealed since purchase and stored in various warehouses, were put on display from February 1941 in a two-acre auction on the fifth floor at Gimbel's department store in New York. Other major cities held similar auctions; the collection was simply too large to be controlled by one auctioneer. According to the writer John Tebbel, over 100,000 people traipsed through the Gimbel auction in the first week, and left with half a million dollars' worth of art.

Hearst had been advised that he needed at least a million dollars to stem the tide. Surely, this was Marion's finest hour as a mistress when, without a second thought, she sold her jewels, furs and other immediate assets, and then presented Hearst with a cheque for a million dollars. When it was discovered that another million was needed, Marion got rid of most of her hard-earned holdings and real estate and presented Hearst with another cheque. It was a grand gesture from a woman who could so easily have left him in the lurch, but, instead, chose to show the meaning of true love and loyalty. Three months later, Hearst accepted a tremendous pay cut, sliding from half a million dollars a year to a mere hundred thousand. It says much for Marion, the philanthropist, that when a long-time fan died and left her over half a million shares in a mining concern, instead of turning the assets over to Hearst, she ploughed it into the Children's Clinic.

Three more tragedies occurred within a year for Marion. In early February 1938, her friends Lord and Lady Plunkett, who were to have spent the weekend at San Simeon, were killed when their plane crashed into the fog-shrouded mountains surrounding the estate. Two months later, the beautiful Reine died suddenly in her swimming pool, followed too swiftly by Ethel, early in 1939, who died in a freak mishap when she choked on a piece of steak. Marion was devastated; Ethel was her favourite sister.

Of all the property and treasures that Hearst lost, none affected him and Marion so much as the threatened sale of St Donat's. The Welsh castle went on the market that year, but there were no offers. Potentially interested private buyers were wary of property investment as ominous war-clouds gathered. Although the British army requisitioned it for officer-training during the 1939–45 war, St Donat's actually remained without a buyer until 1960. At San Simeon, 164,000 outlying acres also failed to attract a buyer. Meantime, the plunge continued. When the bank foreclosed, the lovers were evicted from their New York home in the Ritz Towers. Several Hearst newspapers and six radio stations were sold, followed by the famous Hearst silver collection and a valuable clutch of paintings.

Meantime, for the second time in twenty-five years, a savage, bloody war was tearing Europe apart. News of Nazi atrocities had completely destroyed Hearst's idealized image of Germany. Never again did he print anything in praise of the Fatherland. He was acutely aware that the world was changing – and his lifestyle with it.

★

Since the Thomas Ince affair, Hearst would visibly blanch if anyone mentioned the tragedy. In a similar manner, Orson Welles's masterpiece *Citizen Kane* (1940) would be a source of enormous distress and bitterness for the rest of Hearst's life – and Marion's. Welles was twenty-four when he arrived in Hollywood. His theatre credentials were enviable, based on his innovative productions of Shakespeare, H. G. Wells and G. B. Shaw. A celebrity even before he reached Los Angeles, Welles would certainly have been invited to San Simeon as a guest of Marion and Hearst, but, in fact, they became acquainted through Marion's nephew, Charlie Lederer. He was in love with Mrs Welles, who was disillusioned and unhappy with her genius husband. Five months after arriving in Hollywood, they divorced and Charlie married Virginia at the famous Hearst estate.

The writer/director Joseph Manciewicz, who would work on the Kane script, had recognized the close resemblance between Hearst and Welles's anti-hero on visits to San Simeon. He began a more intense study of his hosts' lifestyle, and, in particular, the Hearst/Davies attachment. It was a treacherous dissection of generous people who would end up, thinly disguised, as the bizarre protagonists in Welles's master-film: an ailing, controversial, unsuccessful millionaire politician, and his blonde, alcoholic, failed-singer mistress, who assuages her musical deficiency by completing jigsaw puzzles in a gloomy, soulless mansion called Xanadu. Welles always insisted that the scenario was his own idea, that the resemblances were coincidental and that Manciewicz was hired to write the script simply because he was the best. Welles wanted sole credit, for which he was willing to pay, but Manciewicz balked and in a ruling by the Screen-Writers' Guild, Welles had to accept Manciewicz as co-author.

Anyone who knows the Hearst/Davies story and has seen *Citizen Kane* is instantly aware of the many ugly parallels: a rich, well-placed politician (Hearst) picks up a would-be singer called Susan Alexander (Davies) whom he swears to present to the world as a top-class opera star (film star). Kane smothers her in luxury, lessons, the best of everything, and even builds her an opera house (Cosmopolitan Pictures). High on a hill overlooking the sea, he lives with her at Xanadu, with its private zoo and its winding drive up the hill to the house which lives in yesteryear (San Simeon). Unfortunately, Susan has no talent (Davies's unsuccessful Hearst-dominated pictures), can't keep up with Kane's ruthless ambitions for her, and drowns her despair in alcohol (Marion's drink problem) and endless jigsaws (Marion's hobby).

Worse than all these biographical similarities, however, was the film's enigmatic opening line – 'Rosebud' – gasped by the dying Kane, and oft-repeated throughout the film, which conned the public into believing that this was the name Kane had given to his childhood sleigh. In fact, it was Hearst's private name for Marion's genitalia. Welles's source for this revelation is unrecorded. Hearst understood ruthlessness and could have borne the insulting caricatures of himself, but he was incensed by the false, vicious portrayal and personal exposure of Marion as a talentless, drunken, loud-mouthed slattern. In a generous show of rejuvenated friendship for Hearst, Louis B. Mayer begged the RKO distributors to destroy the film and he would reimburse all production costs, estimated at $800,000. He was refused.

For a very long time, RKO received no publicity in the Hearst papers; and anyone connected in any way with *Citizen Kane* was never credited, or featured in the Hearst press again. Such ostracism seemed to emphasize the lie – that the film really did portray the lovers as they lived. The film colony was appalled by the blatant ugliness dealt to the two acknowledged most hospitable and generous people in Hollywood. The picture, sometimes cited as the greatest film ever made, was artistically an enormous success, winning that year's Academy Award for, ironically, Best Screenplay for Manciewicz. It nonetheless lost money. Louella Parsons and Hedda Hopper, always treated superbly by Hearst and Marion, were scathing about Orson Welles, who never fully recovered from his treachery. Louella defiantly admitted that Hearst was 'the best friend I ever had'. Her memoirs reveal her immediate reaction to the controversial film: '... the boy genius [Welles] certainly used all his talents just to do a hatchet job. I walked from the projection room without saying a word to Orson. I have not spoken to him since.' Years later, Manciewicz, utterly disenchanted by Welles, apologized to Louella for his part in the creation of *Citizen Kane* and the humiliation he had brought to Marion and Hearst. As for Welles: in 1975 he made a kind of posthumous apology to Marion – 'making amends for the cruelty of youth', to quote Peter Conrad in *Orson Welles: The Stories of His Life* (2003). This was in the form of a foreword to Marion's autobiography *The Times We Had* (1975), which he ends with the eulogy: 'Marion Davies was one of the most delightfully accomplished comediennes in the whole history of the screen.'

★

During World War II, Hearst did all he could to stop American support for the Allies, condemning in particular Great Britain, as wanting to be the dominating power across the world. 'Never in our whole history [has England] extended any aid, comfort or consideration to these United States of ours,' he accused. Ironically, this second war would be responsible for the sudden rejuvenation and upward surge in the Hearst newspaper profits.

In 1941, America suffered the indignity of a Japanese attack on Pearl Harbor, an incident that dragged the country, regardless of Hearst, immediately into the war. Marion was now forty-four and Hearst seventy-eight; feeling rather useless, they retired to San Simeon, only to leave almost immediately when the authorities considered the soaring edifice, so stark against the sky, a high-risk target from possible Japanese warships. (Hearst's anti-Japanese policy had made the castle a perfect target for marine guns.) They inhabited Wyntoon instead (hardly Marion's favourite residence; she called it 'Spitoon'). Here, they lived quietly; it would have been in the height of bad taste to throw lavish parties when American boys were giving their lives in various parts of the world's war zone. Hearst filled his time writing poetry and digesting the war news; Marion abandoned quilt-tatting in favour of preparing miles of bandages to be delivered to the Red Cross. She felt a special pride in her Children's Clinic when it was expropriated as a wartime medical centre.

Three times during the forties Wyntoon succumbed to fire. On the worst occasion, in the early part of the war, Marion would have lost her life had not Hearst smothered her in a wet blanket and dragged her out of her room just before the place exploded. Hearst adored the mansion and, with architect Julia Morgan, slowly began rebuilding the estate: this time as a 'settlement' with a strong Bavarian theme lifted straight from the magical stories of the Brothers Grimm.

When the war ended in 1945, Marion found it impossible to pick up the old way of life. The wonderful, carefree, zany parties of the twenties and thirties would remain memories as inevitable post-war austerity dominated contemporary life. Seven million dollars and fifteen years later, she sold Ocean House for $600,000; it failed as a beach hotel, after which it was demolished – the area being made into a public car park. Back at San Simeon, the great castle seemed like a morgue; only the ghostly echoes of past laughter remained for company. Most of the vast estate had long since been disposed of; at 75,000 acres, San Simeon was now a relatively small holding. The place depressed Marion; she made excuses to spend periods away from it.

In 1947, Hearst's heart, always suspect and never very strong, began to play serious tricks; his physicians urged him to quit the castle for a more accessible domicile. As they drove through the gates for the last time, he unashamedly wept. Hearst's unhappiness brought out hidden strengths in Marion, as she recognized approaching mortality. Hearst, she knew, was rapidly deteriorating. She bought a villa on Beverly Drive, which, with her usual thoughtfulness, she had made over immediately to Hearst because, knowing he would never leave it alive, she wanted her lover of thirty years to die in the comfortable knowledge of owning his own home.

Hearst enjoyed it only for the next four years; he died on 14 August 1951, aged eighty-eight. Present were the doctors, Richard Berlin (top executive of the Hearst empire) and Charlie Lederer, who had been, and would continue to be, absolutely loyal throughout his aunt's ordeal. Marion was absent. Hours before Hearst died, grief, booze and lack of sleep had taken their toll; she was sedated and put to bed. When she awakened, she was informed of Hearst's passing; her grief was then made doubly painful by the most outlandish, bizarre and scurrilous treachery she had ever known. While she slept, members of the Hearst committee and Hearst's sons, following a plan long organized by Berlin (rumour had it that the plan involved Marion's sedation), had had Hearst's body embalmed, placed in a fine copper casket, transported from the house and flown to San Francisco to the home of the wife Hearst had not lived with for over thirty years. The plan was brilliantly carried out and there were no hitches. Nor were there any explanations. And just to emphasize the finality of the relationship and of any future involvement with their father's long-time mistress, the sons immediately stopped all the Hearst daily papers being delivered to Marion's door. Her shocked, incredulous response has been recorded many times: 'His body was gone – whoosh! – like that. Old WR was gone ... Do you realize what they did? They stole a possession of mine. I loved him for thirty-two years and now he was gone. I couldn't even say goodbye.'

The funeral took place in San Francisco and was attended by the Hearst family and over a thousand mourners. Marion was not invited; indeed, she only found out details of the funeral from the radio. At the appointed time, she picked up her deceased lover's favourite dachshund and retired to her room to make her own, very private farewell.

Before he died, Hearst had known for some time that he had not long to live. Alarmed at the thought of possible corporate maliciousness towards Marion, he wanted absolute security for her when he was no more. Not named in his will, but identified by Hearst as 'my loyal friend', the 30,000 shares-trust the tycoon had planned and set up for his mistress in 1950 more than guaranteed Marion a lifelong income, regardless of her own money. No one objected – until Hearst's lawyers presented irrefutable proof to the Hearst executors that Marion was also to have sole voting power in all matters appertaining to the Hearst newspaper industry. Marion had, after all, lived for over thirty years in the closest contact with the profession, digesting Hearst's principles and policies; she really knew the business well and he trusted her. The frustrated Hearst lawyers could not contemplate a court case; whatever they might produce in opposition, there were many witnesses, including his own family, to prove Hearst's soundness of mind when he signed the legal paper. However, they were determined to destroy this obstacle to their sole power.

Marion loathed disputes, and this one was certain to be acrimonious. Regardless of Hearst's sons' treachery – one of them had called her a whore just before Hearst died – she told *Time* magazine, 'I would do anything in the world to avoid hurting the boys,' remembering that they were the sons of the man she had loved. Quietly, she gave up her voting rights and for a nominal dollar a year retained the position of adviser. In effect, she had surrendered all her power.

★

In October, only ten weeks after Hearst's demise, Marion surprised Hollywood by eloping to Las Vegas, where she married Horace Brown Jr, an ex-Merchant Marine captain and sometime police officer. Originally engaged to Rose, that sister cancelled the wedding, unable to forget her deceased lover, the man she had married – and divorced – for love, a decade ago. To alleviate Horace's humiliation, Marion began inviting him for suppers. Hearst, then still alive, took to Horace straightaway. After his death, Horace became a frequent caller; accepting his proposal seemed a natural progression – or did Marion marry him because of his uncanny resemblance to Hearst? He was an attractive, well set up man, who adored Marion and didn't mind being subservient to a fading movie star. He was given to silly jests – such as the time he deliberately pushed a fully dressed Rose into a swimming pool. He could be careless; on one occasion, while demonstrating a new gun to Mary Pickford and her husband, he accidentally slipped. The gun went off and the bullet grazed Mary, narrowly missing killing her. Twice, an emotional Marion attempted to divorce him; there was no real reason except the depression brought on by the large quantities of alcohol she consumed to get her through each day. She actually loved Horace and was grateful for him, although he knew she was neither happy nor unhappy; she seemed simply to exist from one day to the next. With Hearst's demise, something was extinguished for Marion. Very few old friends were left; many had died, or moved away. Occasionally she would attend a big party, but the whole ambience was lacking in finesse, sartorial elegance and, most of all, in witty conversation and participation. She kept away. By and large, Marion Davies – at one time voted the world's fifth most popular film actress, the glamorous hostess of some of the world's largest and most sensational parties, the benefactress who had donated millions of dollars to good causes – was all but forgotten by the public and, worse, by those to whom she had been so generous. In some ways, even in liberated Hollywood, she was paying the price for being a powerful man's erstwhile mistress. Occasionally, she bumped into the Hearst boys in public places; they snubbed her. On one occasion in 1952, Horace punched William (Bill) Randolph Hearst Jr, when he deliberately snubbed Marion at Romanov's; the fight, which continued outside, made all the national papers.

For several years, Marion had suffered from poor circulation; often, now, she needed a steadying arm. Inevitably, with her reputation for the bottle, that support was erroneously put down to drunkenness. One area where Marion still shone and seemed possessed of the Midas touch, however, was in real estate investment. Nor did she balk at construction; in New York, for example, she erected the Davies Building and the Douras Building, both high-profile earners. In 1955 she bought the Desert Inn at Palm Springs for $1.75 million; she sold it in 1960 at a profit of three-quarters of a million dollars.

A slight stroke in 1956, followed a year later by the death of Louis B. Mayer, made her increasingly aware of her own mortality. That awareness led her to increase the size of her Children's Clinic, to which she made an immediate donation of $2 million, simultaneously making it an official part of the University of California.

Early in 1959, a simple tooth extraction exposed a malignant growth in Marion's jaw. She refused surgery for over a year, and then the pain drove her to cobalt treatments which, apart from proving ineffectual, discoloured her cheek. She hid the disfigurement with a handkerchief. In 1961, Marion was admitted to Cedars of Lebanon hospital; she was dying and she knew it. It would be a long deterioration. Politician and friend Joseph Kennedy, at his own expense, engaged three separate cancer experts to rush to Marion's bedside. The surgery they performed for malignant osteomyelitis was promising. Unfortunately, despite significant improvement, Marion became overambitious; twelve days after the operation, she fell and broke her leg. Her fighting spirit remained, but her bodily functions were giving out. She passed into a coma for several days, and died in Cedars of Lebanon on 22 September 1961. Horace, Charlie, Rose and Marion's niece Rose Lake were with her. Immediately, there were batches of condolence telegrams, many of them from America's leaders, including Richard Nixon, Harry S. Truman, General McArthur and Robert Kennedy. There were many obituaries ... the *San Francisco Examiner* called her 'a fabulous star in a fabulous era'. The *San Francisco Chronicle* said, 'For her an intimate dinner was for fifty. The tab for a cocktail party might be $30,000.' The *Los Angeles Times* on 22 September 1961 cites her name and face as being

among the most familiar in the nation in an era that was illuminated by such as [Mary] Pickford, [Douglas] Fairbanks, [Harold] Lloyd, [Charlie] Chaplin, [Norma] Talmadge and [Greta] Garbo.

In the same paper, Marion's old friend Louella Parsons paid final tribute:

Success as a glamorous movie actress and as a wealthy businesswoman never spoiled Marion Davies. She always had a soft spot for the underdog. [...] She lent clothes and jewellery to hopefuls trying out for a part or film test. She persuaded her film bosses to sign contracts with many before their talent was established. And in many instances she was right. [...] Marion never lent money – she gave it. She even included charitable deeds in her busy social and entertainment life. She entertained the great and near-great of the world one day – and busloads of orphan children the next.

Marion Davies was that most remarkable of celebrities: an actress absolutely devoid of selfishness or any form of self-interest. She had spent a lifetime knowing the great and famous of her contemporaries, many of them becoming good friends. She always underestimated her comedic talents (hadn't that outrageous wit Tallulah Bankhead once told her that, had she not been so rich, she would have become the world's number one comedienne?). Marion's natural warmth, her irrepressible sense of fun and good humour, her total lack of class distinction and her legendary generosity (not only to big causes, but on countless occasions to the unfortunate, insignificant individual so often passed over) made her loved and respected by all who knew her, except Hearst's east coast executives. In the end, though, Marion Davies will be remembered as the lovely protagonist in the most extravagant and publicized love affair of the twentieth century.

★

After the death of their father, the Hearst boys showed little interest in the upkeep of the San Simeon estate. In 1957, six years after Hearst's death, the State of California accepted it as a gift, to become a State Park open to the public. The original 250,000 acres on which Hearst's dream had been created had been reduced to a mere 123 acres.

La Belle Otero

The Suicides' Siren

'No queen ever lived like I did
because I lived through so many kings.'

La Belle Otero (1868–1965), aged ninety

L a Belle Otero stood firmly at the pinnacle of both her theatrical and amatory careers for more than three decades, during which time she toured the world, amassing a fortune of more than $25 million, twenty million of which she lost to the world's leading gambling casinos. She was a contradiction in terms: vulgar yet refined; angelic yet tempestuous; avaricious but generous ... all depending upon her mood, which could change at the flick of a playing card, the response of an audience, or a look in a man's eye. *The Times* said in her obituary (13 April 1965):

> In an epoch of famous courtesans, she was among the half dozen who enriched the chronicles of history ... she was acclaimed wherever she went. She was indeed the idol of the Nineties.

On one thing Otero was adamant: *she* chose her lovers, often influenced by the enormous fees they were prepared to spend. Thus she accepted the Shah of Persia, allegedly 'rather smelly' and with a leaning to sadism – but he presented her with many priceless jewels over their intermittent five-year liaison. These invariably arrived in a gold casket on a velvet cushion. Otero would open the lid, extract the jewel and never say thank you. The shah preferred silence, in an effort, perhaps, to preserve the mystique of anonymity. While the shah made her very wealthy, she chose to give herself to the penniless Captain Duval, 'because he was pleasing to me'.

Nor was location ever a problem. In 1890 she made love with William Kissam Vanderbilt on his luxury yacht, the *Alva*. In 1902, she satisfied Baron Lepic floating two-hundred metres over Paris in a hot-air balloon. ('A marvellous experience,' she commented coyly, 'every woman should try it!')

Her lovers were legion, and of the highest quality. La Belle Otero is said to have slept with more royalty than any other courtesan in Europe. All of them rewarded her handsomely. King Leopold of the Belgians' occasional involvement with Otero resulted in gifts of several desirable residences across Europe, in particular a luxury villa at Ostend. As for Prince Nicholas of Montenegro and Prince Albert of Monaco, Otero seems to have run them concurrently for several years. Albert, the more generous (but the less virile), gave Otero over £225,000 in jewellery. An exception, Albert Edward, Prince of Wales, offered only a small hunting lodge just outside Paris. She was bedecked with jewels by Muzaffar-ed-Din ... and the multi-millionaire Joseph Kennedy was far from ungenerous. In the theatre, Emperor Yoshihito of Japan honoured Otero with the gift of a Pacific island in recognition of a performance she gave in front of a vast audience in Tokyo. In the bedroom, after a strenuous three days of love-making, the Khedive of Cairo gave her a ten-carat diamond ring comfortably nestled in a setting of twelve magnificent pearls and valued at over half a million francs.

Thus, she made happy, if poorer, many of the world's aristocracy.

★

Augustina Carolina Otero was born at Puentavalga, near Cadiz, in the southern Spanish province of Andalucía, on 20 December 1868. Her mother was a gypsy known simply as Carmen; fiercely proud, she earned a living by telling fortunes, and singing and dancing in the streets. It was during one of these exhibitions that a handsome young Greek army officer called Carasson had first set eyes on her. He was transfixed, and vowed to marry her immediately, much to the amusement of his comrades.

So, marry her he did, in 1863, after spending five years weakening her resistance with lavish gifts. Of their six children, Carolina was one of twin girls. Eventually, Carmen's extravagance and Carasson's enormous gambling debts necessitated a more frugal lifestyle. Thus the family moved north from Cadiz, to Balga, in Galicia. Carmen hated Balga. To alleviate her boredom she accepted other lovers, openly flaunting them in front of her husband. Tried beyond patience, Carasson challenged the latest, a successful French vineyard owner from Cette, to a duel in which Carasson was killed. With a show of grief she didn't feel, Carmen covered her husband's body with flowers and placed lighted candles at his head and feet. Her children were not deceived; they hated her for her duplicity.

Debts had to be paid and mouths fed. Carmen's changed fortunes left her with only the barest necessities on which to live. Marrying her French lover in 1874 solved this problem, but resulted in family disharmony. The two eldest boys left home, eventually emigrating to America; Carolina's twin was taken over by Carasson's relatives, and the remaining boy was sent to a boarding school. Apart from her younger sister, Carolina was now alone with her stepfather and her mother who, inexplicably, suddenly turned against her. Knowing Carolina to have been Carasson's favourite child, perhaps she reminded Carmen of her central part in his tragedy. Beatings were frequent, and without reason. One day, in retaliation, Carolina punched her mother, displaying the temper for which she would become famous. Carmen was thunderstruck; she vowed there and then to get rid of her daughter. Consequently, there was undisguised delight all round when Carolina left home at the age of eleven, to continue her education at a boarding school some distance from Balga. But her mother had not told her everything: Carolina would have to earn her fees by slaving in the kitchens and waiting on the other pupils. Her life was wretched from the moment she arrived at the school. The principals, two vicious old maids called Juanita and Pepita, delighted in humiliating her. Immediately, Carolina was set to work in the kitchens, cooking for the whole establishment. In her autobiography, she recalled it as 'the school of housework'. If she failed to please, she was punished, frequently unfed and not allowed to have outside recreation. One day, she killed a huge rat and dropped the rodent into the soup she had been ordered to prepare for a luncheon the sisters were giving for the local priest. In *My Story*, written twenty-seven years later, Carolina admitted: 'I was so unhappy that I longed to die.'

For some time she had exchanged a few furtive words with a good-looking youth who seemed to know when she would go to draw water from the well before the evening meal. Paco Colli could be forgiven for misjudging Carolina's age. Already she was beautifully developed, with the body and height of a young woman of eighteen, and the inherited dazzling gypsy looks of her mother. Risking discovery, Carolina stole out to meet Paco one evening; she was not quite twelve years old when she experienced her first kiss and the heady excitement of first love. After meeting nightly in this manner for several weeks, Paco eventually took her to a local *café-chantant*, a kind of cheap dance hall where several girls performed solo songs and dances in between the public dancing. Here, Carolina performed her inherited *flamenco* dances with such success that the two brothers who managed the place urged her to become a regular performer there for two pesetas a night – twice as much as the other girls were being paid. They even promised her a pretty sequined dress. Carolina was happy with the dress; Paco pocketed the nightly pesetas. Unbeknown to her, her seventeen-year-old lover was already a well-known womanizer, gambler and thief.

Inevitably, the school discovered Carolina's secret, resulting in a doubled workload and the loss of all privileges. When Carolina collapsed, the school physician, Doctor Alonzo, was concerned enough to take the child away to recuperate in the care of his own family. Somehow, the wily Paco discovered her whereabouts and paid her a visit, passing himself off as her cousin. Furtively, he begged her to join him in Lisbon where friends would help her to get dancing engagements. The idea was wonderfully romantic. To elope with her lover, and to earn her living as a dancer … who could want more? Carolina was yet to learn that many men don't mean what they imply. To the avaricious Paco, the little Otero represented easy income and good sex, in that order. After hurried secret arrangements, Carolina joined Paco on the train bound for Lisbon.

The next weeks were spent in an inconspicuous hotel on the rua de l'Oro. However, the police, having tracked her down after a worried Dr Alonzo had reported her missing, returned her to Balga and her mother. Carmen was furious, but even more ashamed to have to acknowledge Carolina as her own. She raged at her, telling her she was well on the way to becoming a whore – and she was still not fourteen! With brutal finality, she threw Carolina out of the house and warned her that, if ever she returned, she would kill her.

Carolina needed no second telling. She was alone, now, but curiously calm about her future. It is a strange fact that Carolina Otero's life was oddly charmed – full of amazing coincidences and most unlikely but genuinely fortuitous incidents that materialized in times of distress. Now, with no money, she invented a hard-luck story about losing her train ticket, thus coaxing a one-way ticket back to Lisbon out of the warm-hearted ticket collector, who also loaned her sixty pesetas, a fortune at that time. (Much later, she searched for the man and repaid his kindness tenfold.)

Arriving safely, she made straight for the hotel she had shared with Paco. Not surprisingly, her lover had gone. She took a room, determined to scour the city in the futile hope of seeing him in the street. During these days, the only thing that kept her spirit alive was being able to sing to her own accompaniment in her room, where there was an old piano.

Almost penniless, at the moment when she was most despairing, there was a quiet knock at the door. Paco! It had to be, since no one else knew she was in Lisbon. Instead, she found herself facing one of the other boarders she had seen occasionally during the *table d'hôte* meals. It seems that this pleasant, middle-aged man, who turned out to be the managing director of the nearby Avenida Theatre, was Carolina's neighbour. He had eavesdropped on her singing each day and had been delighted. When he discovered that this beautiful girl also danced, he became very excited. He came straight to the point and invited her to perform at his theatre, if they could agree on a salary. At the mention of money, Carolina's heart jumped. Instinctively, she demanded, and was promised, a thousand pesetas a week. She would commence after a couple of weeks in rehearsal.

Carolina Otero's life changed as easily as that. Her employer explained that he was resident at the hotel only while his apartment was being redecorated. He insisted on a contract being signed that same day, turning a blind eye on such petty illegalities as his discovery being under age.

Carolina's début on the professional stage was successful beyond anything she could have imagined. She sang and danced a *tango flamenco* with enormous vitality and passion; her movements were sensual, her unerring rhythmic instinct wild and uninhibited. Women in the audience envied her striking beauty; the men were unashamedly aroused. Upon one thing everyone in the audience agreed: they were witnessing the arrival of a new star. As Carolina acknowledged the deafening applause, she bowed particularly in the direction of the cheering, elegant Maria de Mendoça, daughter of the famous Portuguese General. Some years away, they would meet again, in Paris, under very different circumstances.

Over the following weeks, the name of Carolina Otero was on everyone's lips. Audiences, dazzled by her stunning physical beauty, dubbed her *La Belle Otero*. A few weeks after her début, Otero was admiring the contents of a jeweller's shop window when she became aware of a stranger standing beside her. When he insisted upon buying her whatever she chose from the window, she laughed aloud. This man was a stranger. But he was charmingly persistent, wanting, he said, only to please her. Tentatively, and not really believing the man to be serious, she chose an elaborate parure, consisting of a tiara, necklace, bracelet, earrings and a ring. When it was instantly presented to her, she was speechless. Otero had made an important discovery: 'I soon learned the practical value of a pretty face,' she wrote in her autobiography. That day, La Belle Otero took the first step to becoming the famous courtesan who would soon be shocking the world.

Her benefactor introduced himself as Señor Porazzo, a very wealthy, middle-aged banker, who had seen her performance and used this casual encounter to make Otero's acquaintance. When he set up his beautiful young mistress in a delightful apartment and opened several charge accounts for her, he had no idea she was under age. After some weeks, however, she discovered by chance that Paco was in Barcelona. With no thought for Señor Porazzo, Otero absconded, taking with her the small fortune she had accumulated from her protector.

★

Compared with the naïve schoolgirl who had first arrived in Lisbon, it was a very different young lady who booked into the chic Hotel de las Ramblas in Barcelona. Once settled, it was not difficult to discover that Paco hung out on most evenings at the Palais de Crystal, a popular entertainment and gambling venue.

Paco was delighted to see Otero. For a time, and encouraged by her obvious affluence (she now had a maid called Rosalie), the old magic returned for both of them, especially when Matto, the manager of the Palais de Crystal, engaged Otero to dance for three times the money she had made at the Avenida Theatre in Lisbon.

She should have been well off. Instead, Otero ended each week owing money to the management to clear Paco's gambling debts. He gambled away her entire savings and even pawned her precious parure. A friend called Stevez at last convinced Otero just how worthless her lover was. He urged her to break with this parasite as soon as an opportunity occurred. As so often happened with Otero's life, that opportunity presented itself almost immediately. To her amazed delight, an impresario called Florio was sending a prestigious company out with a new operetta, *Le Voyage En Suisse*; greatly impressed by her talent, he offered Otero the lead. She went to inform Paco of her good fortune. If she needed impetus for a final severance, she acquired it watching him hand over her hard-earned money to a casual whore.

★

Gaining the lead in this prestigious production was the most important 'charmed moment' so far in Otero's life. The opening night in Oporto was an enormous personal triumph. She had stopped the show with a

261

beautiful haunting song called '*Dos Besos*' ('Two Kisses'). Nightly, the young dancer was fêted and cheered – in particular, by a very handsome young man named Manuel Domingo. Although Otero's admirer craved an assignation he was unsuccessful in getting past the fiercely protective Florio, who wanted nothing and no one to influence his young star.

But Manuel Domingo was desperate. For the first time in her life (it would not be the last) Otero found herself kidnapped. She had left the theatre and climbed into the usual waiting carriage supplied by the watchful Florio. This time, though, the driver was different. He drove at a dangerous speed, eventually stopping beside another carriage, into which Otero was unceremoniously bundled before she fainted. When she regained consciousness, she found herself in a softly lit, elegant room. In a far corner, in the shadows, she discerned Manuel Domingo. Completely unafraid, she demanded to know where she was. The young man flung himself on his knees at her feet, begging his captive not to be angry, explaining that he could not bear the thought of her leaving Oporto without their meeting just once.

Wealth and good looks, in that order, were always irresistible to Otero; Manuel had more than his share of both. That intimate supper led to Manuel establishing his mistress in the Hotel de France, where he sent flowers daily, and heaped expensive gifts on her. She was now sixteen and an experienced *cocotte*. She had learned about lust from Paco; Señor Porazzo taught her the power of money; now, Manuel was teaching her about love ... an expensive interlude for the boy, from whom she gained 340,000 pesetas and a sizeable collection of jewels and expensive clothes.

Manuel's father, angry and concerned about his son, offered the dancer a large sum – on condition she left Oporto immediately. Otero refused; however, a night in gaol quickly subdued her defiance. When Otero eventually left Oporto it was with an abiding hatred for men whose money could so easily buy or destroy lives and destinies as they thought fit.

A few days before she was due to leave the famous wine city, another admirer took her to a performance of *Rigoletto* at the Opera House, where the title role was sung by a talented and attractive Italian called Guglielmo. Impetuously, she proposed to him and they were married within a few days. Otero soon regretted her impulsiveness; her husband turned out to be selfish and penniless – nor did marriage diminish his passion for other women. Worst of all, she discovered him to be an inveterate gambler. On their way to Rome, via Marseilles and Monte Carlo, her savings diminished alarmingly as Guglielmo consistently lost at the tables. Her jewels were offered as collateral; finally, in desperation, he attempted to sell her lingerie!

One night, bored with her own company, Otero obeyed a sudden temptation, entered the casino and placed a tiny sum on the red. She lost. Lesson learnt, she moved away. Eventually passing the same roulette table, the croupier respectfully called out to her. He had taken the liberty of leaving Otero's chips on the red, after her departure from the table, and now asked her if she wanted them to remain.

Otero shrugged, not understanding the rules. The wheel spun. There was a sudden gasp, and a buzz of excitement; everyone stared at her. Inadvertently, Otero had won twenty-eight times running on the same winning colour, amassing over 150,000 gold francs. She collected her winnings and rushed upstairs to share her good fortune with her husband.

The door was slightly ajar. Suspecting burglars, Otero stepped inside and listened. Her flesh went cold as she heard groans of pleasure emanating from the bedroom. She flung open the door and discovered her husband *in flagrante delicto* with a young chambermaid. Otero leapt upon the intertwined couple, slapping and punching indiscriminately, until the girl, screaming with terror, grabbed her clothes and rushed from the room, leaving Otero still punching her husband. The tremendous din brought the manager to the room; they discovered that Guglielmo had 'borrowed' the girl's savings, hoping to win back his losses. Instead, he had lost everything, and was now using his considerable sexual charms to placate the chambermaid.

Otero left Guglielmo there and then, but not before warning the baritone that she would shoot him if he came anywhere near her in future. She returned to Marseilles and looked up Madame Lermina, a cabaret artist who lived in the town and who had befriended Otero during her recent visit. She had nowhere else to go. It was a fortuitous decision. The kindly Frenchwoman recognized her new friend's potential, resulting in Otero learning to sing in French. Unfortunately, the lessons were suddenly terminated when she was stricken with typhoid fever. She was seriously ill for three months. Comte Savin de Pont-Maxence, an admirer who hardly knew her, agreed to cover all the invalid's expenses and provide her with a pretty, well-furnished apartment to aid her recuperation (another 'charmed moment').

A few weeks after her recovery, through Madame Lermina's influence, Otero had no trouble in landing an engagement at the Palais de Crystal in Marseilles. Predictably, she was enormously successful; many men paid tribute. One in particular was the blond son of a wealthy brewer, whose mistress, a pretty girl called Felicia, was so incensed at her lover's fascination that she paid for a hostile claque to hiss and boo whenever Otero danced.

After two hellish weeks the dancer discovered her tormentor at the

Cercle des Étrangers, a popular club/restaurant where she sometimes went for late supper. Otero made straight for Felicia and bluntly accused the woman of hiring a claque to hiss her performance. The girl, unfortunately, sneered at Otero and haughtily insulted her talents, at which Otero's eyes popped. Sensing danger, Felicia quickly produced her hat pin, but she was too late. Screaming wild obscenities in between threats of dismemberment, Otero grabbed a metal chair and crashed it down on the unfortunate Felicia. The following day, the battered woman brought Otero before the courts, charging her with assault. It was only her protector's influence with the judge that saved her from deportment.

'Anyway, her boyfriend was never in any danger from me, Monsieur,' Otero haughtily addressed the judge. 'I can't tolerate blond men!'

The newspapers had a field day. 'Carolina Castanetta', as she was dubbed, was more popular than ever.

When Guglielmo suddenly appeared out of the blue, Otero impulsively forgave him. Optimistically, they left for Paris a few days later, he to try his luck at the Paris Opéra and she to seek a dancing engagement. But Guglielmo's laziness led to a monumental quarrel, resulting in the singer walking out of Otero's life for good. The very next day (another of those 'charmed moments'), she ran into Señor Pompei, a 'little stout man ... and good-natured looking', who had once worked for her father as a salesman. Delighted to see her, at the same time taking advantage of her sad tale, he became her temporary protector.

Pompei was genuinely concerned about Otero's future welfare. Through a connection of his, she met an elegant Frenchman, François Boron, who was in charge of a society *soirée* hosted by his mistress, Lucie Victoire, Marquise de Ribeauville. It was to be held at Vefour's, the most exclusive venue in Paris at the time. Sensing Otero's abilities, Boron invited her to take part.

Otero was always grateful to Boron for that evening. The critic Hughes Le Roux said she possessed 'all the ardour of life, all the coquetry of woman'. She received accolades and the congratulations of many celebrities in the audience, including the *farceur* Georges Feydeau; Charles Franconi, manager of the famous Cirque d'Été; Monsieur Marchand, the manager of the internationally famous Folies Bergère; and the novelist, Gaston Calmette, who became a lifelong friend. In her ambition to work at the Folies, Otero was perhaps too obvious in singling out Monsieur Marchand. Courteous, he left without suggesting anything.

But Charles Franconi was greatly impressed, and offered the dancer a three months' contract at 3,000 francs a month, commencing in the spring. This was no meagre salary; during *la belle époque* a British pound was worth around twenty-five francs, and an American dollar just under five. An apartment in a fashionable *arrondissement* cost around 150 francs a month. The little gypsy was beginning to climb …

★

Otero began her three-month season at the Cirque d'Été in the spring of 1890, with her own musicians and also Evariste, her male partner for the next several years. At this time, Spanish dancers never touched; they circled, swooped, and came within an inch of each other, but they never had physical contact. (The genre is essentially an eternal flirtation: its characters the temptress and the tempted, its purpose the quest for the unattainable.) In order to emphasize Otero's beauty and magnetic sexual presence, the 'backdrop' of a male partner was essential. Evariste fitted the bill perfectly: he complemented, but never out-danced the star. These performances marked the beginning of Otero's international fame. The newspaper *Figaro* was ecstatic in its reviews of her:

> … eyes that flame … mouth as appetizing as a pomegranate … supple as a panther …

Otero's circle of friends rapidly expanded, including the Duc d'Uzes, who was willing to abandon both his fiancée and his mistress if Otero would have him. George Gouret (famously known as 'Sem', the popular cartoonist) reported his first impressions of Otero to his friend, Liane de Pougy, a successful courtesan: '*Mon Dieu!* As I watched her I could feel my thighs blushing!'

Count Kessler, talent scouting for the prestigious Eden Theatre in New York, was so bowled over when he witnessed a performance of this 'Spanish firebomb' that he determined to engage her for a season. Politely rejecting his offer at first, all hesitation vanished the moment Otero learned she would be earning $700 weekly.

She arrived in America on board the SS *Bourgogne* in September 1890 and was met by forty welcoming gentlemen, each wearing a yellow rose and a red carnation: the Spanish colours. One of them, Ernest Jurgens, spoke good French and became her official interpreter.

Otero's introductory press coverage was preposterous, featuring her marriage to a General Otero, and her mother being a famous opera star. The most outrageous story, though, told of her abduction to satisfy the lust of Alfonso XIII, the King of Spain … his Majesty was four years old at the time! (Alfonso's lust would manifest itself fifteen years later, however, when Otero would need no abduction to quell the royal passion.)

On opening night, hearing strange hisses after each dance convinced Otero she had failed to please. In her dressing room she burst into tears, until Jurgens explained that 'hissing is a sign of great approval'. She kissed him in relief. Thus began a very discreetly-managed affair (Jurgens was happily married) which would, however, have tragic consequences. The next day the press were ecstatic:

> ... Otero came and conquered (*New York Sun*); Otero takes New York captive (*New York Mail*); She appears to dance all over ... a serpent writhing in quick, sinuous graceful curves (*The Times*).

Physically, Otero fired the male contingent of the audience with unattainable desire, while their female counterparts admired and envied the dancer her magnificent shape, of unbelievable hourglass proportions (reputedly 38-21-36). Describing her bosom, some wit commented: 'Otero's breasts enter the room and she follows fifteen minutes later!' The young Maurice Chevalier once declared that 'boobs don't come any better'. The writer Colette thought her breasts were 'of a curious shape [like] elongated lemons, firm and upturned at the tips', while the architect who later designed the Carlton Hotel at Cannes admitted that he had had the Otero breasts in mind when he added the hotel's twin cupolas. They became famously known as *les boîtes à lait de la Belle Otero*.

When Otero's Eden Theatre contract was extended to eleven months, Jurgens rented for her an elegant house on West 23rd Street owned by the actress, Lillie Langtry. Meanwhile, their affair was temporarily sidetracked when she became the secret lover of the fabulously wealthy William Kissam Vanderbilt. During their short liaison, he lavished well over $300,000 on the fiery dancer, including an emerald-eyed, diamond snake bracelet and a fabulous $250,000 pearl necklace once owned by Eugénie de Montijo, ex-Empress of the French. He also offered her the *Alva*, at the time the largest and most luxurious yacht of its kind in the world.

Unfortunately, Otero's involvement with Jurgens was suddenly exposed when, at a masked ball given by the Vanderbilts, she loudly upbraided her lover for being overfamiliar with a beautiful girl. The indiscretion led to Jurgens being sued for divorce. Amazingly, the scandal did not seem to harm Otero's social position and popularity. Several witty lampoons appeared in the popular press, of which the following is one:

Slim waist, haughty, proud, brown, *Andalouse.*
Generous with her kisses to her torero,
Her eyes black as jet, dangerously *jalouse,*
Such, in four lines, is Carolina Otero.

After a generous benefit performance in her honour, Otero sailed back to Europe with more than 700,000 francs, which she deposited with Hoffmann House. It was her first bank account.

Learning that her mother had been deserted, Otero, always generous to others, began sending her regular cheques. Her generosity was further displayed when she took pity on a new acquaintance, Renée de Ronsay, who, too old and ill to work, was facing imminent bankruptcy. Otero not only paid her bills, but bought Madame de Ronsay her heart's desire: a tiny villa in the south of France, where she lived happily until she died.

La Belle Otero now began a love affair with the Monte Carlo casinos which would continue for the rest of her life, and to which she lost an estimated £13 million, earned both as a theatre star and as one of the world's most expensive courtesans. On one occasion, in 1891, she lost the whole of her American fortune playing *trente-et-quarante*. On another she lost £500,000 in a week. William Kissam Vanderbilt offered to help her out by buying back the yacht he had given her, promising her the use of it whenever the fancy took her. Perhaps the most desperate gambling story, allegedly true, finds Otero going to bed with eleven different men in one evening, subsequently losing each incredibly high fee at the gambling tables, which she left for no longer than half an hour at a time.

At her peak, Otero charged between five and eight thousand pounds for one night of love. There were occasions when she allegedly charged 25,000 francs for fifteen minutes. The Vicomte de Chênedollé lavished his entire fortune on her; when he had nothing more to offer her, he committed suicide.

Early in 1892, Otero found herself in Berlin without work. With the cool impudence her popularity and earning capacity encouraged, she re-negotiated a contract to dance for Baron and Dorn, two impresarios whom she had rejected when they had approached her in Paris because she had taken an instant dislike to them. She opened in the Wintergarten before a vast audience of seven thousand cheering people. This success travelled like wildfire across Europe. Offers rolled in; but the most thrilling was an offer from the Folies Bergère, to commence during the 1893 season. Otero wrote:

I have signed for ten consecutive seasons at the Folies Bergère. I begin at 5,000 francs a month, rising to 35,000 in the succeeding years […] I could hardly guess at that time that the shortest cut from the Rue de Castellane [where she had a tiny flat] to the Folies Bergère was via Berlin.

When her maid Rosalie left Otero to get married, the dancer engaged a German woman called Betty, who immediately began keeping a personal detailed diary logging Otero's life. About her employment she wrote:

I admit I hesitated a good deal before throwing in my lot with this Andalusian dancer, and went to her rather against the grain. But as soon as I saw her, I altered my mind. The creature's beauty is dazzling. I closed with her immediately, and I believe she is going to turn out a star of the first magnitude.

In Berlin, Otero's fervent admirer was Baron Ollstreder, a remarkably ugly millionaire banker, as Betty's diary confirms:

Amongst the crowd of Carolina's admirers, I believe I can already spot the winner. He is certainly not beautiful, and I admit he would take some swallowing. With his protruding lips and crooked teeth, and a nose more Jewish than any Jewish nose has ever been, he is decidedly not seductive.

Betty expressed this opinion one evening as she helped her mistress to dress. 'No man who has an account at Cartier's can be called ugly, my girl,' admonished Otero.

Apart from presenting her with a large house, the baron made the dancer a generous allowance. His first gift to her was a pair of superb solitaire diamond earrings, which she wore one evening when Ollstreder escorted his mistress to hear *Pagliacci* at the Opera House. Jealous of his attentions to a female acquaintance, Otero stormed out and headed for Hiller's, her favourite restaurant in Berlin. Fully aware he would follow her, she snatched off one of the earrings and plunged it between her breasts. When the baron arrived, puffing and embarrassed, Otero blazed at him, helpfully mentioning in her tirade that in the drama of fleeing the Opera House, she had lost one of her precious earrings. The next day she received an identical replacement by special delivery.

Although Otero was often (rightly) accused of vulgarity and salty language (she wasn't nicknamed 'La Belle Virago' for nothing), she was capable of emanating great style and refinement. In 1920, a friend of Liane de Pougy was asked what she thought was the essential difference between Otero and Lina Cavallieri, another famous, much courted beauty. All three women had been stars at the Folies Bergère.

'Put it this way: when Cavallieri wears expensive jewels, they look fake, but when Otero wears false jewels they become real.'

Otero coveted a magnificent pearl necklace, an heirloom in Baron Ollstreder's family which the baron was loathe to relinquish. Otero pouted; Otero smiled; Otero won. The pearls were hers, if only on loan. Onstage one night, the necklace broke, scattering the priceless pearls and a few of her costume 'pearls' everywhere. With easy indulgence, the audience was happy to allow a pause while Otero scrambled around for her treasures. Valentine Grandais, one of Otero's fellow performers, had longed for such a moment. A beautiful woman, but a second-rate dancer, it has been oft reported that she immediately leapt forward from the wings and picked up one of the costume 'pearls', announcing: 'La Belle Otero boasts that her jewels are genuine, ladies and gentlemen, but this production has been halted while she searches for artificial pearls.' She then exited quickly into the wings.

Otero, fully concentrated on counting what were in fact real pearls, had heard nothing. That night, during supper at Hiller's, the theatre conductor came to her table. He was holding three of the pearls Otero had been unable to locate. The dancer was enraptured; she leapt up and kissed the man on both cheeks in gratitude. The conductor, pleased, confided that Mme Grandais had advised him not to search for the gems, assuring him they were all fake.

Otero's eyes narrowed. Without a word she walked across to Valentine, who was also dining, and slapped her rival's face so hard that she knocked her off her chair. To placate his fiery mistress, the baron presented her with a really superb *rivière*, once owned by Marie Antoinette.

Notwithstanding, Otero was growing bored with the baron. Indeed, towards the end of the Berlin engagement, she had taken a handsome young lover, Captain Duval. There would be no expensive gifts from the captain (or, as Betty so succinctly put it, 'He is not obliged to be too lavish'). His youthful good looks and virility more than recompensed for her *ennui*.

Cashing in on Otero's immense popularity, her employers Baron and Dorn suggested that she should give a dinner for the press, inviting all the leading journalists. Otero agreed, on condition that it was something memorable. She set everything up in one of the smartest hotels in Berlin. Both Baron and Dorn, of course, were invited, but only Dorn showed up; he looked uncomfortable as he explained that his colleague had been prevented from attending by 'something unavoidable'. The dinner was a big success. At ten Otero left for her performance. When she opened the door to her dressing room the stench that met her was appalling. There, in the middle of the room, beautifully decorated with ribbons, sat a mixture of rotting fruits and vegetables, to which was attached a card. It was a 'gift' from Herr Baron.

Otero discovered him at the bar, where (says Betty) 'she fell upon him tooth and nail and administered one of her famous ringing blows'. Apparently, Baron was furious with Otero for not giving his Central Restaurant the business. The insult cost him far more than the dinner when Otero 'went sick' for three weeks, thus depriving the Wintergarten of its biggest draw.

The end of the Berlin season was a relief. Otero, Betty and Baron Ollstreder left for Monte Carlo where the baron installed his mistress at the Hotel de Paris. Betty, aware that money was unimportant to the baron, surreptitiously made 'a little inroad on the money they mean to take with them [to the casino]'. With a thief's philosophy, she considered her action allowed them 'so much less to lose …'. And lose they did. They lost so much that Ollstreder ran out of ready cash. Otero, in an instant, offered the baron a loan of 50,000 marks. Delighted by her generosity, and in a flamboyant show of appreciation, he promised to repay her with 400,000 marks. Impulsively, he grabbed a piece of writing paper from the *escritoire* and produced the equivalent of an IOU for that sum. Otero tore the sheet in two. She assured the baron that she trusted his word.

Back in Vienna, with no baron, Otero enjoyed her usual theatrical success and met several admirers, including the charming Prince Edouard de Belime whom she saw regularly. The prince had met Otero when he chanced to overhear her complaining of the cold in a restaurant. When she rose to leave, a waiter in the foyer helped her into a superb mink coat … a gift from the prince. Not particularly concerned whether or not Ollstreder discovered her duplicity, when she met the prince again there was a furious row, resulting in a final breach with her former protector. Conveniently, Otero 'forgot' to return the loaned pearl heirloom. (Years later, at Monte Carlo, she had cause to pawn it for 100,000 francs to continue play. She lost everything within minutes.)

In her rather sanitized, self-indulgent autobiography, *My Story*, Otero wrote of a short engagement in Bucharest, where

> I danced wildly, madly, throwing into the dance all my ecstasy of living
> […] After I had danced a fandango, a man came to me and said: 'The most

austere anchorite living on vegetables and water, could not see you dance, Mademoiselle, without throwing his sandals and his vows to the devil!'

Totally uninhibited one night, Otero danced 'wildly, madly' from the exclusive restaurant where she was appearing, into the street, followed by a trail of musicians. Since it was the middle of winter, she ended up in bed for six weeks with congestion of the lungs. Her current protector (who seems not to have been a lover) was a millionaire called Reiderman. He provided another of Otero's 'charmed moments' by taking care of all her expenses.

One night, dining together in the Romanian capital, Otero overheard a man insult a girl she had known in Paris. Heedless of consequences, she went over to the man and socked him so hard that the enraged man challenged her escort to an immediate duel. Otero recalled that,

Seconds were hastily chosen and we had the curious spectacle of a duel fought inside a room, with the lookers-on still sitting at their supper. Reiderman was very slightly wounded. It was my turn to lavish care on him, and I stayed with him until I had to leave to take up my next engagement – this time in Moscow.

In Moscow the dancer had been engaged to perform at the comparatively small Montos Restaurant, supplementing her income with lucrative private performances. One of these was given for a millionaire sheep farmer. The man was greasy, crude, vociferous and very drunk. At the end, Otero wanted to leave immediately but the farmer offered her some punch, potent enough to muddle her brain. When she recovered, she found herself alone with her filthy admirer in a room where the main feature was a large bed:

When the farmer began stroking me with his coarse hands and attempting to embrace me, I struggled like a demon, and began to scream at the top of my voice [...] He had believed he could beat down my resistance in no time. I went almost mad. He kept trying to seize me, but my dancer's suppleness helped me ...

Suddenly, the door crashed down and several policemen, alerted by Otero's musicians, came to her rescue. Giving evidence to the police, Otero ended with admirable hyperbole: 'I found his face close to mine ... a back somersault saved me.'

The affair resulted in the Montos Restaurant being closed down indefinitely. Meanwhile, Otero found the Chief of Police so charming that she spent the next four days being comforted by him.

La Belle Otero's subsequent engagement, at the Malincka Theatre in St Petersburg, was one of her happiest:

> Never had I imagined anything like the splendour and the reckless extravagance of the circle in St Petersburg, of which I found myself the centre.

This happiness was certainly associated with the 'many Grand Dukes and the Czarevitch [there were] to conquer'. Apart from her great professional success, she was briefly the mistress of several noblemen, including the future Czar Nicholas II, who was reputed to be one of the wealthiest men in the world. Otero met the czar on several occasions in a hunting lodge outside St Petersburg. Despite his generosity, which included a villa on the shores of the Black Sea, she found the pock-marked, rather nervous ruler sadly in need of soap and water. 'He stank abominably – and his love-making habits were, to say the least, unusual,' she wrote. Otero's assignations with the czar would have been farcical had they not been so fraught with apparent danger. Terrified of assassination, the Ruler of All the Russias was always surrounded by guards. At times, the dancer thought she was undressing in front of an army parade! Even in their most passionate moments, if there was the slightest noise, the czar would leap out of bed, cowering with fear. A seasoned warrior in the boudoir, Otero took it all in her stride; the rewards were high.

Her happiest and (after the czar) most lucrative liaison was with the Grand Duke Peter, grandson of Nicholas I (referred to as 'Prince' in her autobiography). 'He spoilt me to the limit of all spoiling,' she wrote. Within a few days, Grand Duke Peter had willingly parted with a fortune in jewels, cash and valuables. He couldn't help himself. He professed himself in love with Otero, a declaration she had heard many times before. She teased him, to which he responded, rather desperately: 'Ruin me, Ninoutchka, if you like, but never, never leave me!'

Otero kept his first love letter all her life:

> What joy to be able to give you everything you wish. What follies I would commit to please you. I realize fully that I am acting foolishly. So much the worse for me ...

Otero writes of a unique all-male dinner at Cuba's restaurant, where a naked Otero was 'served up' on a silver platter. The St Petersburg press had a wonderful time:

> Colonel X of the Chevaliers-Gardes had the brilliant idea, in the course of a supper at Cuba's, to present her to the company, served *au naturel* upon a silver dish. One may imagine that the Señora, fashioned like a Velasquez or a Murillo virgin, was a *succès fou*! [...] The strength and intensity of feeling that possessed these men before this perfection of line proves that [...] man feels before Beauty the worshipfulness of Art.

It so happened that Grand Duke Peter's cousin, the Grand Duke Alexander Barola, was passionately attracted to Otero. When the fiery Spaniard made it clear that she could not return his ardour, he was even more determined to possess her. One night, the weather being particularly bad, he courteously offered to escort her to his cousin's palace after her performance. She accepted, only to discover herself arriving at the great doors of her escort's palace. He forced her to enter and made it clear she would not leave until she had surrendered to him. He then left her alone to think about 'co-operation', locking the door behind him.

It was bitterly cold; Otero was lightly clad under the furs she had been wearing, and which her abductor had taken away in the hope of accelerating her compliance. But the would-be seducer had not allowed for his victim's resilience. Despite it being twenty degrees below freezing outside, she pushed open a window and jumped out, the thick snow breaking her fall. Shivering with cold, and realizing she would literally freeze to death unless a miracle happened, she somehow reached the road. The miracle (another 'charmed moment') took the form of a farmer in a *troika*, who, unable to believe what he saw, quickly threw some heavy furs around the shivering, flimsily-clad woman and drove frantically to the Grand Duke Peter's palace. Otero was desperately ill for four months, during which time her lover never left her side.

★

Once fully rehabilitated, Otero and Betty made their way back to Paris, and the Folies Bergère. During their journey, Betty reminded her mistress of the loan she had once made to her former lover, the baron. Unpleasant though it would be, shouldn't they make a detour to Berlin? After all, 400,000 marks was a lot of money. Otero agreed in principle, but reminded Betty that she had thrown away the baron's guarantee. At this, Betty grinned, and held up the 'missing' IOU, which she had glued together. However, the baron made it clear he had no intention of honouring his promise. Otero, haughtily formal to the man who had spent a fortune on her, then told him that he left her no alternative but to consult a lawyer. In Otero's absence, her representative, Herr Friedmann, won her case; she was awarded 400,000 marks. The baron had been prepared to perjure himself until he saw the damning paper in Herr Friedmann's hand. His defeat was total when Herr Friedmann coyly suggested that he might like to pay *him* an extra 50,000 marks for saving him from perjury.

Otero was by now in Paris, ready to commence her ten-year contract with the Folies Bergère. Liane de Pougy was also among the artistes. Otero and Pougy were totally different. Otero was the essential Spanish gypsy – dark, brooding, passionate and volatile; Liane de Pougy was blonde, delicate and refined: a Dresden shepherdess. Otero disdained men, at the same time retaining a very healthy sexual appetite for them. Liane, although twice married, made no secret of her lesbian persuasion. Her lover, Emilienne d'Alençon, had a sugary quality that caused the journalist Jean Lorrain to liken her to a raspberry ice. To match her 'pinkness', she evolved an act that involved dyed-pink rabbits, dressed in cute little pink ruffs. She was immensely successful – and she really cared for those rabbits, even taking them with her on occasion to Maxim's restaurant. In her *Blue Notebook* Pougy admits, 'Emilienne was the great object of my admiration. […] Her looks enchanted me.'

The Pougy–d'Alençon affair caused one writer to comment:

> Thanks to Liane and Emilienne the Folies Bergère has changed its name to the Folies-Lesbos. These two women are much worse than Carolina Otero who knows only two passions: gambling and young men. While Liane and Emilienne bill and coo without shame the scandal papers announce that they will soon have a child, fruit of their *amours*. La Belle Otero doesn't waste her time like this, considering it all such childish behaviour, substituting instead the pearls worn by Eugénie de Montijo.

More than beautiful rivals, Otero and Pougy were beautiful *stars*. There were many incidents of their rivalry, but one in particular has become legendary. It has been reported countless times – sometimes, even, with different protagonists. The incident, which took place on Saturday 6

February 1897, was witnessed by the writer Albert Flament in the atrium of the Casino at Monte Carlo:

> It was approaching ten o'clock, the hour when the *beau monde* appeared in all its finery. Two women always stood out from the rest: *Mesdames* Otero and Pougy. No one ever attempted to outclass them, but, of course, they always attempted to outclass each other. On this particular night, the atmosphere was tense; word had spread that La Belle Otero would be wearing all her jewels; a wholly feminine way of showing the dining public which of the two was the more successful. The applause was most appreciative when Otero arrived, so laden with glorious jewels 'that she resembled an eastern shrine'. She accepted it all as her due. Suddenly, all eyes turned when Liane de Pougy entered, dressed in palest rose chiffon, and without a single diamond or pearl to enhance her beauty. There was an embarrassed silence – until she moved to one side and revealed her maid, who was glittering like a Christmas tree under the weight of Pougy's jewels. Judging by the applause and laughter, the evening undoubtedly belonged to La Pougy.

The arduous rehearsals for her first season with the Folies Bergère paid off when Otero opened in 1893 to stunning reviews which far outclassed those of Pougy. The day after the première, *Gil Blas* reported: 'Seldom have so many emeralds and diamonds been seen on so marble-white a chest.' *Le Figaro* simply raved:

> We have seen quite a few things in Paris, but we had to wait until *She* came, to see this […] The gyrations of her hips and legs drive the public crazy. She is loaded with jewels like an idol: diamonds, rubies and emeralds whose sparkles daze the audience [… She is] a superb and captivating person … [the] diabolical voluptuousness of her fandango […] the furious tap of her little feet … and she is watched over by two guards who protect her millions.

The guards were a fact. Otero possessed a bolero that was as famous as it was priceless. Hans Nadelhoffer describes it perfectly as

> a successful blurring of the distinction between jeweller and couturier … This was a sleeveless jacket of diamonds and coloured cabochons by the jeweller Paul Hamelin with an openwork lattice design or *résille* (literally meaning 'hairnet'). Louis François Cartier used this same netlike

technique to produce a series of approximately ten necklaces which fitted snugly around the neck, like a second skin, banishing all thought of rigid metal. Was it surprising that Mlle Otero quickly tired of Hamelin's boléro, which contained a whole series of false stones, and commissioned Cartier to rework it as a *résille* necklace? The model on this occasion was Marie Antoinette's famous necklace with its tasselled ribbons crossing over the breast.

Cartier was so proud of it that he exhibited his creation for three weeks in the exclusive Rue de la Paix. It was valued in the region of 2.3 million gold francs. Whenever Otero wore it onstage it was delivered to the theatre in an armoured car with two armed guards, who stood in the wings while La Belle Otero performed.

Nadelhoffer tells us that Otero also commissioned from Cartier's:

> a stomacher in the form of a six-sided floral grille with pendant drop pearls. As one of the most famous representatives of the new genre of 'vamp' which had begun with Sarah Bernhardt, she [Otero] continued to be seen at Cartier's as late as 1919 when, at the age of fifty-one, she ordered a ten-strand pearl sash made of 1,015 pearls and diamonds.

In 1898, Otero was uniquely honoured when, gathered at the Café Anglais on 4 November, Prince Albert of Monaco, Prince Nicholas of Montenegro, King Leopold, King of the Belgians, Edward, Prince of Wales and Grand Duke Nicholas of Russia hosted a private dinner party in honour of her thirtieth birthday. Six weeks before the actual day, it was nonetheless one of the highlights of her exceptionally highlighted life when, as she entered the private dining room, the entire royal table stood and toasted her, wishing her a happy birthday as they smashed their glasses against the wall.

In May 1898 Otero accepted a prestigious booking at the Alhambra theatre in London. Unfortunately, there was a technical hitch with the contract. Otero reasoned; Otero cajoled; Otero promised the ultimate: a night of love. When even that delight failed to move the manager, the dancer shrugged and prepared to spend the next two weeks in idleness. Instead, she met the handsome, immensely wealthy Earl of Westminster (she calls him 'S' in her autobiography), who became her protector for a while and of whom she became very fond. Invited by Kaiser Wilhelm II for a cruise on his yacht, the earl took Otero with him. When he realized to what degree the kaiser was smitten by the gypsy dancer, he gallantly returned to London alone, leaving the coast clear for Otero to attach another illustrious scalp to her lucrative amatory belt.

Otero found the kaiser cold, somewhat superficial and dictatorial. When he offered her considerably less than a thousand pounds for one night, Otero was amused; obviously he had no idea of her going rate. She politely refused the money and asked for much more in jewellery, which she knew the kaiser could well afford. Admiring her business acumen, Wilhelm merely smiled, then acquiesced. Otero never cared for the kaiser. She loathed him calling her a 'savage', even though she knew he meant it as a compliment to her fiery independence. He paid £1,000 to have her full-length portrait painted (which after her death was sold in auction for three pounds). Later, she wrote:

> I can truly say that I have never learnt the art of flattery, and with the
> Kaiser that was the one instrument one should have mastered thoroughly.

During this liaison Baron Ollstreder resurfaced briefly and tragically. He had longed for revenge on his ex-mistress after his humiliating court experience. His chance came when the dancer agreed to appear in a performance of *The Model*, a short play written for her by the kaiser, and for which Ollsreder had booked a stage box. His sole purpose was to humiliate Otero in front of the audience and particularly Kaiser Wilhelm. The box was never occupied. On his way to the theatre, Baron Ollstreder was killed in a road accident.

During this brief sojourn in Berlin, Otero was made the target of stinging theatrical ridicule by an actress known as Mademoiselle Dalton. In typical fashion, Otero challenged her to a duel, appeasing her honour when her pistol-shot slightly wounded the actress.

★

On 14 April 1900 the Paris International Exhibition opened on a 547-acre site, the biggest of its kind in European history. Paris had never before hosted so many crowned heads at one time. Inevitably, those crowned heads spent their evenings doing the pleasure rounds – Ciro's, Café Anglais, Hotel de Paris, Maxim's and Café de la Paix, where the musician Boldi reigned supreme. Boldi's Hungarian gypsy music was a special favourite of La Belle Otero. On several occasions, her protector of the moment would engage the maestro's entire *tzigane* orchestra and locate it wherever he was taking his mistress.

During the Exhibition, Otero was enjoying great success in *Une Fête à Seville* at the Marigny Theatre. It was during this production that she became the target of a jealous rival – who attempted to kill her. Otero at that time had an admirer called Robert Kalmann, who was rapidly falling in love with her; a passion that understandably incensed his current mistress. Determined to put an end to the situation, the mistress took a box overlooking the stage at the Marigny. She was noticeably overwrought, a fact an observant electrician noted; he resolved to keep an eye on her. When Otero appeared, the woman took a revolver from her purse, pointed it directly at the dancer and fired. Otero would undoubtedly have been killed at such short range, had not the watchful electrician leapt forward and deflected the weapon. The well-reported incident had the ironic result of extending the production's run.

Visiting the Comtesse de Jolival for the first time, Otero was surprised and shocked to discover Maria de Mendoça, the Portuguese general's daughter, who had thrown Otero one of her first bouquets over a decade ago in Lisbon. Life had been unkind to Maria. She looked worn out, her looks had gone, her red hair was over-dyed and mannishly cut – doubtless at the instigation of the lesbian comtesse, who had befriended her but who now found her too difficult to live with. Immediately sympathetic, Otero took Maria on as her companion and infuriated Betty by addressing the newcomer as 'sister'.

Edward, Prince of Wales, dined with Otero on those occasions when their paths crossed in London or Paris. She wrote, 'It often happened that the Prince of Wales sent for me to dance before him after supper at Voisin's, Durand's or the Café Anglais.' Edward would draw on a napkin the face of a clock, whose hands suggested a time for assignation, and which the *maître d'hotel* discreetly presented to Otero. Since, at the time, the Prince of Wales was also paying court to his mistress Lillie Langtry, these meetings could be somewhat fraught. On one occasion in London, Mrs Langtry arrived unexpectedly at Rule's restaurant, where 'Bertie' was entertaining Otero privately. The Spanish dancer unobtrusively exited through a side door.

In 1902 Otero opened her ninth year with the Folies Bergère. This particular season, Otero was the big draw; sharing top-billing with her were Liane de Pougy and Yvette Guilbert, and a group of mime artists including a young boy of thirteen called Charlie Chaplin.

When, in 1903, King Edward VII paid an official visit to Paris, he had been on the throne for two years. Inevitably, King Edward's lifestyle was now more muted than during his 'playboy prince' years. However, he sent Otero a ticket for a gala in his honour at the Comédie-Française. Unaware of the king's gesture, the management asked the notorious *grande cocotte* to leave the theatre. She complied with grace. Otero had probably learnt a lesson from a similar experience only two years before, when she was unceremoniously turned out of her seat at a gala performance in honour of the state visit of Czar Nicholas II. Apparently, President Loubet's wife had perpetrated the affront. Otero's anger knew no bounds. Escorted back up the aisle, and in front of a packed house, she reached the royal box and bawled at the top of her powerful Andalusian lungs: 'I'm leaving; but I promise you, I'll never be found eating caviar again!'

Henri de Rochefort seethed. 'They strike out at a woman whose only fault is to be more lovely than they!'

The Comédie-Française officials dubiously defended its action by saying that Otero's jewels glittered so brightly that she commanded all the attention.

During that year's season at the Folies, Otero was introduced to an attractive but boring red-haired Englishman called Thompson. He had apparently begun life as a messenger boy and, by methods unexplained other than 'having passed some years in the frenzied pursuit of a fortune, was now bent on pleasurable living' (wrote Otero in her autobiography). She was only too happy to help him dissipate his wealth.

Thompson made Otero a proposition: he wanted her and was prepared to pay dearly for her, but while he did so she was to be his entirely. Agreement reached, he rented a house at 27 Rue Pierre-Charron, Champs Élysées, complete with seventeen servants. Otero managed them as though to the manner born, complete with an eight-spring landau upholstered in blue satin. She had come a long way since she had first danced for two pesetas a night.

Otero's brilliant and exciting life was, at this point, suddenly disrupted by a lover from the past. Ernest Jurgens had aged considerably since their affair in New York, during the Eden Theatre season. Otero was appalled at the change in her erstwhile lover; apart from looking ill, his clothes were badly crumpled and his shoes down at heel. What had happened to bring this man to such poverty? Jurgens was embarrassed, but nevertheless candid. Unable to forget his affair with the Spanish dancer, he had borrowed money from the Eden Trust, fully intending to repay every cent. Unfortunately, the operetta company he invested in failed. His eleven years' service with the Trust had saved him from facing charges. Instead, as he explained to Otero, he was lucky to get away with only being dismissed. Having traced her to Paris, he now implored his former love for a fresh start. For Otero, though, the past was the past. She tried in vain to persuade Thompson to employ him as her impresario. With no future, and unable to stand his own degradation, Jurgens gassed himself.

Suicide would hover around Otero over the next few years. She was not exaggerating when she wrote:

> I have seen lovesick young men, like sick children, who consider what they can't have to be of vital importance, thus choosing death rather than forego what their hearts crave.

The *New York Herald* ran a story about the death of a besotted student called Jacques Payen. [Mistakenly, the *Herald* calls him 'M Chrétien']:

> ... who shot himself on Monday in the Bois de Boulogne because, as he stated, Señorita Otero, the Spanish dancer at present performing at the Folies Bergère, had refused to accept his advances.

For some time, Otero had been targeted by Payen. She delicately refused his invitation to dinner, and when he sent her an envelope containing 10,000 francs, she returned it by the *huissier* of the Folies Bergère. Payen began haunting her *hôtel* in the Rue Pierre-Charron, threatening suicide if she refused to see him. She did so. A few days later, he shot himself in a cab in the Bois de Boulogne. The letter the unhappy boy wrote to Otero was dejected, yet curiously positive:

> Goodbye – and forgive me. I have made one last effort to win your love and it has failed. Now I go to another world – a world where I will not suffer. I love you more than all the world. A heart that worships you,
> J Payen

'When an unknown student is infatuated by a beautiful, unobtainable woman,' reflected Otero, not without bitter irony, 'the public smiles indulgently at his youthful passion. Even his suicide threat is treated with good humour. But when the student carries out the threat, he is suddenly elevated to martyr status and the innocent victim becomes the villain!'

Indeed, for a while, Otero was considered heartless and inhumane. But her troubles were not finished. Betty rather stupidly attempted to withhold for herself some of the money her mistress had given her to pay a dress bill. Unaware of the maid's personal subtraction, Otero's dressmaker, Madame Ildebourg, was not prepared to wait any longer for her money; she sent the debt collector. Otero threw him out, only to have him return with Madame. The two women argued, then they became aggressive. The *couturière* began shrieking, refusing to budge until full settlement had been made. Otero, also shrieking, repeated that she had already paid. When the irate and highly frustrated Madame Ildebourg resorted to vulgar epithets, Otero leapt forward and felled her adversary with one punch. ('Oh, it was a wonderful scene,' enthused Betty.) Thompson was horrified, especially when a lawsuit followed. Once again, Otero's name spread across Europe. Betty's diary revealed that the incident

> must have been worth 100,000 francs to both Madame and to the dressmaker for the publicity alone. They ought to thank me!

During a return engagement at the Wintergarten in Berlin, Otero realized how bored she was with her millionaire Englishman. When he went to London on business, she was only too happy to take up with an incredibly handsome French attaché, Gaston Botrez, at the Embassy. They dined at Hiller's. To her mortification, she received a terse telegram from Thompson:

> You had supper last night with attaché. If again, I leave you.

Botrez had been much too much fun not to arrange another assignation. Otero received another telegram:

> Told you would leave you if repeated; you have repeated.

Defiantly, Otero met Botrez again. Of course, another telegram arrived:

> If not leave this man, will sell up Paris establishment.

She discovered through servants that for weeks the jealous Thompson had had her followed by private detectives. Before he could return to Paris, Otero cleared the house of all its valuables: they were not restored until Thompson had signed a document making Otero the sole owner.

Love was a business as well as a pleasure to the dancer. But Thompson extracted a sweet revenge. Apparently reconciled, the Englishman soon returned to London on business. After some weeks Otero, badly in need of her monthly stipend, was informed by a sympathetic maid of her abandonment. Never one to sit around moping, her old optimism quickly returned. 'Fortunes are made by sleeping, but not alone!' she reflected.

Back in Paris, Otero was compelled to dismiss Betty, who had been accused by Maria de Mendoça of stealing from her mistress. Investigating, the police found a false bottom to Betty's trunk; inside was jewellery that Otero had missed for some time. The police also found Betty's diaries. Otero brought no charges against her maid; indeed, she was sad to see her go.

In 1905, during one of Otero's return visits to Spain, tragedy struck in the form of yet another young man, who 'laid siege to me', as Otero phrased it. Alarmed, and recalling the unfortunate Jacques Payen, she tried to break away. But the youth, his eyes wild, pulled out a gun and shot Otero, wounding her in her arm. Before he could be stopped he blew his brains out. Contrary to the Payen incident, this confrontation won Otero a great deal of support. King Alfonso XIII was particularly solicitous. Now a young man of nineteen, he was soon to become Otero's last royal protector.

While fulfilling an engagement in Italy, she enslaved the poet and writer Gabriele d'Annunzio. Besotted by her, he dedicated verses to her and dropped rose petals along her path. Back in Monte Carlo, the French politician, Aristide Briand, became her constant companion. The fact that he was fat, ugly, had filthy fingernails and was penniless did not interfere with their ten-year relationship. Perhaps the fact that he was reputed to have made love to her eight times in a night had something to do with the longevity of their affair.

Otero met Prince Michael Pirievski of Russia when, at the Café de Paris one evening, he sent a fan across to her with the words 'I've something to tell you' scrawled across it. Otero agreed to join the prince for dinner the following evening. Afterwards, when she left to dance at the Folies, Pirievski insisted on seeing her after the performance, a request Otero could hardly refuse when he presented her with the 'really priceless offering' of a diamond bracelet she had been coveting throughout the meal. What followed could only have happened during those heady days of *la belle époque*. Otero recalled:

> 'For every day you stay with me,' he whispered, 'I will give you 5,000 francs.' I did not refuse the money, but it was not for money that I went to him … At the end of a few days, he said laughingly to me, 'It won't

take long to ruin me if I stay with you, but I haven't the faintest intention of going.'

Their affair was tempestuous; wild ecstasy contrasting with verbal violence and lacerating quarrels caused by the prince's incredible jealousy. For Otero the relationship was 'terrible and it was divine'. One night, after a particularly bitter scene, Otero picked up Pirievski's revolver to scare him and accidentally fired it. She missed him, but the bullet only narrowly avoided killing the man in the next room. Only the word of a sympathetic hotel manager saved Otero from deportation.

A penitent Pirievski bought and furnished a house for Otero at 29 Avenue Kléber. No longer in love, she had a passionate affair with a wealthy Brazilian called Seroni. Beside himself, Pirievski exacted a strange revenge. He hired an attractive Romanian, Suzanne Montal, for twenty-five *louis* a day, to make herself appear as much like Otero as possible. Wherever Otero went, her 'double' was present. Otero became a laughing stock and attempted to shoot herself. She grazed her hip badly enough for it to need attention each night after her performance.

Her mother's death, when it came, had far less impact on Otero than did Pirievski's sudden suicide. Heartbroken, he shot himself on the staircase of the house he had given her. He left a string of gambling debts, all of which Otero honoured. She sold her house, dismissed all her servants except her maid, and escaped the bad publicity by accepting an engagement in New York at Koster and Bial's, now specializing more than ever before in European artistes.

Otero's reviews were extravagant and exotic. While her dancing was highly praised, it was the courtesan image that now created headlines. They wrote of her owning 'more jewels than any other in the world', and dubbed her 'Queen of Adventures and Jewels'. With typical candour, she admitted: 'I don't pretend I didn't like it.'

Occasionally, publicity worked against her. In America, she went out to a select private dinner one evening, taking with her the little black bag she always carried with the famous jewels inside. One of the guests had brought along a friend; Otero thought him charming. All went well until the lights suddenly went out and everyone, momentarily in a panic, quickly made for the exit. But Otero froze suddenly; instinctively she knew 'something wasn't right'. She found herself making instead for the window, where she caught the charming guest about to drop her black bag into the waiting hands of an accomplice below. Otero screamed. Someone fired a shot in response. Otero didn't lose her jewels, but the stranger lost his life.

'Such quick-thinking people, the Americans!' she later praised.

It was the American press that labelled her the 'Suicides' Siren', mentioning by name and giving details of the men who had taken their lives for love of her.

Otero's very profitable New York season ended on an unpleasant, yet fortuitous note – yet another 'charmed moment' – when a misunderstanding with the management resulted in the dancer missing the SS *Bourgogne* sailing to Europe. The liner sank during a terrible storm; only one passenger survived.

In 1904, Otero completed her ten-year contract with the Folies. She now commenced a freelance career, beginning with great success in Rome. Reaching Naples she became the mistress of the extremely rich and generous Baron Lezcari. They returned to Paris, where he gave her a magnificent house in the Rue Fortuny. On one occasion alone, he presented her with a single pearl valued at 135,000 francs.

A disastrous South American tour ended when Otero was taken seriously ill in Rio de Janeiro; she was compelled to return to Europe. Lezcari took her to Monte Carlo to recuperate; instead, she gambled away all she possessed, leaving the generous baron to take over her losses before he sensibly left her to return to Italy.

Now in her forties, and without the Folies Bergère as a seasonal anchor, Otero became restless and bored. However, as a luncheon guest on board the yacht of the Marquis Roger de Lapierre, she fell deeply in love with its owner. Their affair lasted for two serene years and would have continued had she not met Robert Carsal. Otero later admitted that she had a premonition she was making a great mistake in leaving the charming Lapierre for the vainglorious Carsal. But, as she commented, 'Certainly no lightning can be swifter than the sudden attraction of one human being for another.'

Carsal was intelligent and incredibly handsome; he was also conceited, insecure and a talented liar. After a few months, Otero was humiliated to discover that there was, and always had been, another woman in his life. Unmasked, and unable to cope with his own duplicity, Carsal attempted suicide by drinking a corrosive acid. As Otero struggled to stop him, the liquid splashed on to her arm and neck, causing very serious burns. She was taken to hospital and immediately encased in plaster. This misfortune revived their love. Then, one day, Carsal had a car accident. Rushing to visit him in hospital, Otero was livid to discover 'the other woman' holding his hand. For Otero, it was the end of the affair.

She now lost her usual optimism. She began drinking ether 'to soothe myself', only to succeed in making herself very sick. Even theatrical success eluded her. She took the lead in *Nuit de Noël*, a one-act mime play to which she was not suited.

It was a totally different story when she tackled a shortened version of Bizet's opera, *Carmen*, which was staged on 11 June 1912, at the Trents Ans du Théâtre aux Variétés. Indeed, the press pre-empted her success when the dramatist Henri Meilhac wrote in *Le Figaro:*

> I believe that this Otero [...] will make the fortune of the manager who tries her.

The puritanical Spanish press, frequently disdainful of their countrywoman, were scathing about her new pretensions as a *diva*. It must be said that, even after several months of intensive, specialized singing lessons under maestro Lucien Fugère, Otero's voice remained first cousin to the wine-roughened sound redolent of a *flamenco* singer. However, her operatic début was astoundingly successful:

> Before all, a dramatic artist [...] We cannot congratulate her too warmly (*Gil Blas*); A new Carmen is born to us [with] fatal grace [and] all the insolence and intensity that are longed for in a Carmen (*Paris Journal*); More than anything, this Carmen is natural. She is passionate [...] her acting is alive, adroit (*Figaro*).

Ironically, there was no mention of her singing. As if to balance the adulation, when Otero was rather violently hugged by an admirer after a performance, a catty opera *aficionado* was heard to remark: 'That strong embrace is to smother her voice!'

She continued at the Opéra Comique in Paris before moving further north to work the flinty Rouenese audience into a furore. But, in Deauville, growing resentment from unemployed professional singers at the sudden operatic success of a music-hall dancer could not be ignored. A court order ended Otero's operatic career from that day onwards. Ironically, Otero would sing later in several light operettas with much success.

In 1913 King Alfonso, now twenty-seven, commanded Otero to reside in Madrid. She was not enthusiastic, until she heard about the house near the Palacio Real he intended for her, its value rumoured at a million francs. The Spanish press quickly exposed the liaison and created much antagonism, both at Court and with the public. Spain's most famous dancing star, announced the palace, was about to devote herself to teaching in her new academy. No one was fooled. The liaison was cut short when a serious assassination attempt was made on the king. Warning acknowledged, the dancer immediately returned to Paris.

This was not a good time for Otero. With no engagements for several months, she accepted an unlikely contract as a lion tamer in a circus show directed by Frank Ferrari. Initially, her success came as a surprise; however, she was not sorry when a slight clawing episode put her in hospital, thus ending her career under the Big Top.

During the 1914–18 war, Otero spent most of her time at Biarritz, working for charity and raising funds to help refugees, the sick and the wounded. There were some unpleasant stories concerning misappropriated funds – not quelled by Otero's much publicized acquisitiveness. She was hurt, but made no protest; only she and certain recipients knew just how generous she was. She paid for the education of one of her brothers and her younger sister, both of whom were ungrateful. She adopted an Algerian war refugee, naming him Edouard (after the Prince of Wales), and thoughtfully sent him to boarding school away from Paris, where he would not be ridiculed for having a *grande horizontale* as his benefactress. For many years, she provided a home for Maria de Mendoça. Otero spent a fortune on a small house for her mother as well as sending her regular cheques. There were countless times when she covered unpaid bills for destitute people, or even bought properties to shelter those less fortunate than herself (as with Renée de Ronsay).

With the end of the war in 1918, Otero decided to revive her flagging career, until an injury in a motor accident stopped her. By the time she had recovered, she had gained considerably in weight. In 1920, aged fifty-two, she bluntly told the press: 'I wish to retire in full beauty.' Even three years before, however, Liane de Pougy wrote in her *Blue Notebook:*

> … on the Champs-Élysées, I suddenly noticed a fat lady with a very lovely face and a good deal of style, wearing sumptuous furs, with enormous pearls in her ears. It was my Otero! […] She was quite roly-poly in her fat, but she looked radiant and her marvellous face was still the same.

Post-retirement, Otero left Paris and went to live in the South of France where, in 1927, she built for herself a beautiful villa, appropriately named 'Villa Carolina'. She was wealthy and independent and her retirement looked promisingly luxurious. It was not to be. Unfortunately, loneliness and a sense of uselessness led her increasingly to the casinos.

While La Belle Otero's careers, both as dancer and courtesan, had been dazzling, her luck at the gaming tables was disastrous. In 1936, Anton Dolin, world-famous *premier danseur*, watched the erstwhile Folies star gamble away a fortune in a single evening. On another night, she lost over one million francs at the tables.

In later life, La Belle Otero had tremendous presence and settled into a wonderful dignity, even though she had lost everything to the casinos. 'Everything' included her villa at St Moritz, her Pacific island, her famous pearl necklaces and jewel collection, her securities ... even the 'Villa Carolina'. Long before she died, the famous bolero was auctioned and broken up to pay her debts.

She was philosophic about the effects caused by her miraculous beauty, which still flourished after all these years:

> Ever since my childhood I have been accustomed to see the face of every man who has passed me light up with desire. Many women will be disgusted to hear that I have always taken this as homage. Is it despicable to be the flower whose perfume people long to inhale, the fruit they long to taste?

Asked many times how she had preserved her dazzling beauty for so long, Otero admitted to rigorous bathing: in water, then, allegedly, in white of egg, followed by a champagne bath. Occasionally, she bathed in olive oil, in milk, or petroleum jelly. The outrageously camp Jean Lorrain seriously wondered if Otero retained her beauty by using a special enamel, or a plastic rubber solution.

In 1941, with fatalistic good humour and with few regrets, Otero went to live in the students' quarter in Nice, at 26 Rue d'Angleterre, where she had a large apartment. Soon this was vacated for a single room; it was all she could afford. She stayed here for the rest of her life, living simply, her only salute to 'the old days' expressed in the half bottle of champagne she insisted upon once a week. She was often seen in a cheap little restaurant near her home, incongruously eating a simple meal with an elegant gold spoon, her last remaining relic of her triumphant czarist days in Russia.

From around 1926, and for the next thirty years, the ex-dancer received a mysterious monthly allowance from an unknown admirer. There were many speculations as to his name. Otero divulged nothing. In the 1950s, financial strain was eased somewhat by the income from the film rights to her life story; *La Belle Otero* starred the Mexican actress Maria Felix. 'She did well,' commented Otero. 'She is almost as beautiful as I was!' In addition, she received a tiny monthly pension from the Nice authorities and – a considerate gesture – two small pensions from the casinos at Monte Carlo and Cannes. They could not forget her; over the years she had, after all, gambled away an estimated $20 million. ('At Monte Carlo I once lost thirty million francs at the tables,' she admitted to a reporter, not long before she died.)

La Belle Otero died alone of a heart attack on 11 April 1965, in her tiny room near the railroad track in Nice. This once-great beauty, model for countless artists, including Toulouse-Lautrec, was ninety-seven years old and had been in excellent health. Among the few mourners at her memorial service was a handsome man in his forties, called Edouard. It was her adopted son. Discovered in her few effects was a packet of czarist bonds that had been worth a million dollars when they were presented to her, but which had become worthless after the Bolshevik revolution.

'She never really made appearances,' said the *New York Times* in her obituary, 'she made entrances.'

In placing wreaths on her grave, the casinos of Monte Carlo and Cannes were paying last respects – not only to the legend that was La Belle Otero, but to the end of a fabulous era, the like of which the world will never see again.

Select Bibliography

(including recommended further reading)

Adam, Paul. *La Morale de Paris* (Paris, 1908)

Aidala, Thos. R. *Hearst Castle: San Simeon* (New York, 1981)

Aiken, Duncan. *Calamity Jane and the Wildcats* (New York, 1927)

Airy, Osmund. *Charles II* (London, 1901)

Almond, Mark. *Revolution: 500 Years of Struggle for Change* (London, 1996)

Amorous Conquests of the Great Alcander, or the Amours of the French King and Madame de Montespan, Modern Novels, vol. 11 (London, 1692)

Andrews, Allen. *Royal Whore* (London, 1971)

Andrist, R. K. *American Heritage History of the 20s and 30s* (New York, 1987)

Angelo, Henry. *Reminiscences*, 2 vols (London, 1904)

Angot, Emma. *Dames du grand siècle: Sévigné, Grignan, de la Fayette, Motteville* (Paris, 1919)

Anon. *Lives of the Most Celebrated Beauties* (London, 1707)

Anon. *Memoirs of Lady Hamilton* (London, 1815)

Apprentices. *Gracious Answer to Whore's Petition* (London, 1668)

Arnold, Julian B. *Gentlemen in Dressing Gowns* (London, 1945)

Arwas, Victor. *La Belle Epoque* (London, 1978)

Aubrey, John. *Brief Lives*, 2 vols (Oxford, 1898)

Audebrand, Philibert. *Petits mémoires d'un stalle d'orchestre* (Paris, 1885)

Auriant. [pseud., Alexandre Hadjivassiliou] *Les Lionnes du 2ᵉ Empire* (Paris, 1935)

Auvergne, Edmund B. D. *Lola Montez: An Adventuress of the Forties* (London, 1909)

Barnett, Correlli. *Bonaparte* (London, 1997)

Barthez, A. C. E. *Empress Eugénie and Her Circle*, tr. Bernard Miall (London, 1912)

Basserman, Lujo. *The Oldest Profession*, tr. J. Cleugh (New York, 1967)

Baxter, John. *Hollywood in the Thirties* (London, 1968)

Beaton, Cecil. *Self-Portrait with Friends (1926–74)* (London, 1979)

Beckford, William. *The Vision / Liber Veritatis* (Cambridge, 1930)

Berlioz, Hector. *Selected Letters*, tr. Roger Nichols (London, 1995)

Bernat, Judith. *My Autobiography*, tr. Mrs Arthur Bell (London, 1912)

Bernhardt, Sarah. *Memoirs: My Double Life* (London, 1907)

Bernheimer, Chas. *Figures of Ill-Repute* (London, 1997)

Berniers, Olivier. *Louis XIV: A Royal Life* (New York, 1987)

Betjeman, Sir John. *Victorian and Edwardian London* (London, 1974)

Bingham, D. *Recollections of Paris*, 2 vols (London, 1896)

Bingham, Madeleine. *Sheridan* (London, 1972)

Bolitho, William. *Twelve against the Gods* (London, 1929)

Bonnassieux, Louis J. P. M. *Château de Clagny et Mme de Montespan* (Paris, 1881)

Bory, Robert. *La vie de Fréderic Chopin* (Geneva, 1951)

Brady, J. T. Herbert. *Emma: Life of Lady Hamilton* (Portsmouth, date unknown)

Brander, Michael. *The Georgian Gentleman* (Hampshire, 1973)

Brooks, Louise. *Lulu in Hollywood* (Minneapolis, 1974)

Brownlow, Kevin. *Hollywood: The Pioneers* (London, 1979)

Bryant, Arthur. *England of King Charles II* (London, 1934)

Bryant, Mark. *Private Lives: Curious Facts about the Famous and Infamous* (London, 1996)

Burchill, S. C. *Upstart Empire: Paris During the Brilliant Years of Louis-Napoleon* (London, 1971)

Burnet, G. *History Of My Own Time*, vol. 1 (Paris, 1827)

Caetani, Vittoria, Duchess of Sermoneta. *Things Past* (London, 1929)

Caetani, Vittoria, Duchess of Sermoneta. *Locks of Norbury* (London, 1940)

Cagey, Edmond M. *The San Francisco Stage: A History* (New York, 1950)

Carte, Thos. *Life of the Duke of Ormonde*, 6 vols (Oxford, 1851)

Carter, Randolph. *The World of Flo Ziegfeld* (London, 1974)

Cases of Divorce for Several Causes, with Memoir of Fielding and His Will (London, 1723)

Cassell's Guide to Paris Exhibition, 1900 (London, 1900)

Castle, Charles. *The Folies Bergère* (London, 1982)

Castries, Duc de. *Lives of the Kings and Queens of France,* tr. Anne Dobell (London, 1979)

Cate, Curtis. *George Sand: A Life* (Boston, 1975)

Cecchi, Dario. *Giovanni Boldini* (Torino, 1962)

Chalon, Jean. *Liane de Pougy* (Paris, 1994)

Channon, Henry. *Ludwig of Bavaria* (London, 1952)

Chaplin, Charles. *My Autobiography* (London, 1964)

Chapman, Guy. *Beckford* (London, 1937)

Chase, Ilka. *Past Imperfect* (London, 1943)

Chopin, Frederick. *Selected Correspondence*, collected by Bronislaw E. Sydow, tr. Arthur Hedley (London, 1962)

Chopin, Frederick. *Letters*, collected by Henryk Opineski, tr. E. L. Voynich (New York, 1931)

Christiansen, Rupert. *Tales of the New Babylon* (London, 1994)

Chujoy, A. and Manchester, P. W. *The Dance Encyclopedia* (New York, 1967)

Churchill, Randolph. *Twenty-One Years* (London, 1965)

Claretie, Jules. *La vie en Paris*, vol. 6 (Paris, 1896)

Clarke, John. *Life and Times of George III* (London, 1972)

Claudin, Gustave. *Mes souvenirs* (Paris, 1884)

Clegg, Gillian. *Chiswick Past* (London, 1995)

Clément, Pierre. *Madame de Montespan and Louis XIV* (Paris, 1868)

Cleveland, Duchess of. [reputed author] *Barbara, Duchess of Cleveland, Memoirs of the Life of, (Divorced Wife of Handsome Fielding)* (London, 1709)

Clouard, Maurice. *Documents Inédits sur Alfred de Musset* (Paris, 1900)

Cocteau, Jean. *Portrait Souvenirs 1900–14* (Paris, 1921)

Colette. *My Apprenticeships*, tr. Helen Beauclerk (London, 1967)

Commentary on the Licentious Liberty of the Press (London, 1825)

Connell, B. *Portrait of a Whig Peer* (London, 1957)

Contini, Mila. *Fashion: From Ancient Egypt to the Present* (London, 1965)

Correspondance de George Sand et Alfred de Musset, ed. Louis Evrard (Monaco, 1957)

Coryn, Marjorie. *Enchanters of Men* (London, 1954)

Cowles, Virginia. *Edward VII and His Circle* (London, 1956)

Creswell, Page. *Poor Whore's Petition* (London, 1668)

Cunningham, Peter F. S. A. *Story of Nell Gwyn* (London, 1892)

Czapinska, Wieslawa. *Pola Negri – Polska knolowa Hollywood* (Warsaw, 1996)

Dale, Alan. *Familiar Chats with Queens of the Stage* (New York, 1890)

Dangeau, Marquis de. (from the Mémoires) *Journal de la Cour de Louis XIV, 1684* (London, 1770)

Daudet, Alphonse. *Thirty Years in Paris*, tr. Laura Ensor (London, 1888)

Davey, Elizabeth. *Wirral Yesterday, Today and Tomorrow* (Wirral, date unknown)

David, Saul. *Prince of Pleasure* (London, 1998)

Delacroix, Ferdinand. *Journal, 1823–63*, 3 vols (Paris, 1893)

Delvau, Alfred. *Les Lions du Jour: Physionomies Parisiennes* (Paris, 1867)

Dennis, John. *Some Remarkable Passages of the Life of Mr Wycherley* (London, 1725)

Derval, Paul. *The Folies Bergère*, tr. Lucienne Hill (London, 1955)

Dictionary of National Biography (Oxford, 1887)

Diguet, Charles. *Les jolies femmes de Paris* (Paris, 1870)

Dorsey, Hebe. *Age of Opulence: The Belle Epoque in the Paris Herald 1890–1914* (New York, 1986)

Doyle, William. *Old European Order 1660–1800* (London, 1978)

Dunlop, Ian. *Louis XIV* (London, 1999)

Eden, The Hon. Emily. *Up The Country* (London, 1866)

Eells, George. *Hedda and Louella* (New York, 1972)

Elisabeth Charlotte, Princess Palatine and 2nd Duchess of Orléans. *Letters of Liselotte*, tr. Maria Kroll (London, 1970)

Ellis, Roger. *Who's Who in Victorian Britain* (London, 1997)

Ellmann, R. *Oscar Wilde* (Englewood Cliffs, 1969)

Emard, Paul and Fournier, Suzanne. *L'années criminelles de Mme de Montespan* (Paris, 1939)

Emboden, William. *Sarah Bernhardt* (London, 1974)

Encyclopædia of European Cinema, ed. Ginette Vincendeau (London, 1995)

Ericson, Eric. *The World, The Flesh, The Devil* (London, 1981)

Evelyn, John. *Diary ...* Abridgement and Extracts (London, 1915)

Evelyn, John. *Diary*, 6 vols (Oxford, 1955)

Faithful Account of Fielding's Examination (London, 1706)

Fairbanks, Jr, Douglas. *Autobiography: The Salad Days* (New York, 1988)

Falkus, Chris. *Life and Times of Charles II* (London, 1992)

Fielding, Robert. *Love Letters,* pub. from original MSS (London, 1715)

Fielding, Xan. *The Money Spinner: Monte Carlo Casino* (London, 1977)

Fisher, A. V. T. *Lives of Twelve Bad Women* (London, 1897)

Flaubert-Sand. *Letters*, tr. Aimée L. McKenzie (London, 1922)

Fonteyn, Dame Margot. *Magic of Dance* (London, 1980)

Foss, Kenelm. *Unwedded Bliss* (Kingswood, 1949)

Fothergill, Brian, *Beckford of Fonthill* (London, 1979)

Fothergill, Brian, *The Strawberry Hill Set* (London, 1983)

Fowler, Gene. *The Great Mouthpiece* (New York, 1934)

Fowler, Gene. *Good Night, Sweet Prince* (New York, 1949)

Fraser, Antonia. (Ed.), *Love Letters* (London, 1976)

Fraser, Fiona. *Beloved Emma* (London, 1986)

Funck-Brentano, F. *Les Drame des Poisons* (Paris, 1935)

Gacon-Dufour, M. A. J. *Mémoires, anecdotes, secretes—et inédites sur Madame de la Vallière, de Montespan, de la Fontanges, de Maintenon, et autres illustres personnages du siècle de Louis XIV, etc.*, 2 vols (Paris, 1807)

Gallo, Max. *Night of the Long Knives*, tr. Lily Emmet (London, 1974)

Gerard, Frances A. *Some Fair Hiberians* (London, 1897)

Glinski, Matteo. *Chopin's Letters to Delphina* (Windsor, 1961)

Glyn, Anthony. *Elinor Glyn* (London, 1955)

Goethe, J. W. *Voyage en Italie*, tr. Dr M. Mutterer (Paris, 1930)

Gold, Arthur and Zigdale, Robert. *Misia: Life of Misia Sert* (New York, 1980)

Goldberg, Isaac. *Passionate Pilgrimage of Lola Montez* (New York, 1936)

Goncourt, Edmond and Jules de. *Journal* (Paris, 1887-96)

Gordon, Richard. *The Alarming History of Sex* (London, 1996)

Gosling, Nigel. *Paris:1900-14* (London, 1978)

Graham, Sheila. *My Hollywood* (London, 1984)

Grant, Lt-Col Nisbet Hamilton. *Letters of Mary Nisbet, Countess of Elgin* (London, 1926)

Greenwall, H. J. *I'm Going To Maxim's* (London, 1958)

Gribble, Francis Henry. *George Sand and Her Lovers* (London, 1907)

Grieg, J. *The Farrington Diaries*, 8 vols. (London, 1922-28)

Grillandi, M. *La Belle Otero* (Milan, 1982)

Gröning, K. and Kliess, W. *Encyclopædia of World Theatre, based on Friedrichs Theaterlexikon*, tr. Estella Schmid (London, 1977)

Grove, George. *Dictionary of Music and Musicians* (London, 1980)

Guest, Ivor. *Ballet of the Second Empire* (London, 1974)

Guiles, Fred Lawrence. *Marion Davies* (London, 1973)

Guiles, Fred Lawrence. *Joan Crawford: The Last Word* (London, 1995)

Gun, Nerin E. *Eva Braun: Hitler's Mistress* (London, 1968)

Haldane, Charlotte. *Galley-Slaves of Love* (London, 1957)

Haldane, Charlotte. *Alfred: Life of Alfred de Musset* (London, 1960)

Hall, Sir John. *The Bravo Mystery, incl Dujarier Affair* (London, 1923)

Hamilton, Anthony. Gramont's *Memoirs of the Court of King Charles II*, tr. A Boyer (London, 1846)

Haussonville, Comte D'. *Prosper Mérimée* (Paris, 1888)

Hawks, Francis Lister. *'Is This Not a Brand Plucked Out of the Fire': A Penitent Lola Montez* (New York, 1867)

Hayman, Ronald. *Hitler and Geli* (London, 1997)

Hayward, C. *The Courtesan and the Part She Has Played in Classic and Modern Literature and Life* (London, 1926)

Hayward, C. *Dictionary of Courtesans* (New York, 1962)

Head, Alice. *It Could Never Have Happened* (London, 1939)

Hill, C. P. *Who's Who in Stuart Britain* (London, 1998)

Historical Account of ... that Celebrated Beau, Handsome Fielding (London, 1707)

Hoefer, M. Le Dr. *Nouvelle Biographie Universelle* (Paris, 1855)

Holdridge, Helen. *Lola Montez: The Lady in Black* (London, 1957)

Holland, Merlin. *The Wilde Album* (London, 1997)

Hook, Donald D. *Madmen in History* (New York, 1976)

Hopper, Hedda. *From Under My Hat* (London, 1953)

Hornblow, Arthur. *History of the Theatre in America*, 2 vols (New York, 1919)

Horstman, Allen. *Victorian Divorce* (London, 1985)

Houssaye, Arsène. *Confessions*, 6 vols (Paris, 1885)

Houssaye, Arsène. *Behind the Scenes at the Comedie Française*, tr. Albert Vandam (London, 1889)

Howarth, David and Stephen. *Nelson: The Immortal Memory* (London, 1988)

Howell, T.B. and T.J. *State Trials, XIV, cols 1327–72* (London, 1828)

Howitt, Basil. *Grand Passions, Broken Hearts: Lives and Lusts of the Great Composers* (London, 1998)

Hoyt, Edwin Palmer. *Vanderbilts and Their Fortunes* (London, 1963)

Hutton, Ronald. *The Restoration* (London, 1987)

Infield, Glen. *Eva and Adolph* (London, 1975)

Ireland, Joseph N. *Records of the New York Stage, 1750–1860*, 2 vols (New York, 1866)

Jackson, Stanley. *Inside Monte Carlo* (London, 1975)

Jameson, A. B. *Beauties of the Court of Charles II* (London, 1833)

Jeaffreson, J. C. *Lady Hamilton and Lord Nelson* (London, 1897)

Jesse, John H. *Memoirs of the Court of England During the Reign of the Stuarts*, 4 vols (London, 1840)

Joachimsthaler, Anton. *The Last Days of Hitler: The Legends, The Evidence, The Truth*, tr. Helmut Bögler (London, 1996)

Jordan, Ruth. *Nocturne: Life of Chopin* (London, 1978)

Jusserand, J. J. *A French Ambassador at the Court of Charles II* (London, 1892)

Karasowski, Moritz. *Frederick Chopin: His Life, Letters, Works*, tr. Emily Hill (London, 1879)

Katz, Ephraim. *Macmillan International Film Encyclopedia* (London, 1994)

Keats, John. *The Life and Times of Dorothy Parker* (London, 1971)

Keegan, John and Wheatcroft, Andrew. *Who's Who in Military History* (London, 1976)

Kemp, G. van der and Llevron, J. *Versailles and the Trianons*, tr. Dr M. Mutterer, (London, 1958)

Kersten, Dr Felix. *Memoirs*, tr. Ernst Morwitz (New York, 1947)

Kidd, Charles. *Debrett Goes To Hollywood* (London, 1986)

Knight, Cornelia. *Autobiography*, 2 vols (London, 1861)

Kobbé, Gustav. *Lovers of Great Composers* (London, 1912)

Kybalova, Ludmila, Herbenova, Olga, and Lamarova, Milena. *Pictorial History of Fashion* (London, 1968)

Laffin, John. *Brassey's Battles* (London, 1986)

Lamb, Jeremy. *Rochester: So Idle A Rogue* (London, 1993)

Langeville, T. *Rochester and Other Literary Rakes of the Court of King Charles II* (London, 1903)

Latham, Robert. *Illustrated Pepys* (London, 1978)

Laver, James. *Age of Optimism* (London, 1966)

Leaming, Barbara. *Orson Welles* (London, 1983)

Legge, Edward. *Public and Private Life of Kaiser William II* (London, 1915)

Leider, Emily. *Dark Lover: Life and Death of Rudolph Valentino* (London, 2003)

Leland, Charles G. *Memoirs* (London, 1893)

Lemoine, Jean M.P. J. *L'Affaire Montespan* (Paris, 1908)

Leonard, Maurice. *Mae West: Empress of Sex.* (London, 1991)

Les salons de Paris et la société Parisienne sous Louis Philippe (Paris, 1866)

Leslie, Anne. *Edwardians in Love* (London, 1972)

Leverton, W. H. *Through The Box-Office Window* (London, 1932)

Leveson-Gower, Lord Granville. *Correspondence 1781–1821*, 2 vols (London, 1916)

Levin, Martin. *Hollywood and the Great Fan Magazines* (New York, 1970)

Levy, M. J. *Mistresses of King George IV* (London, 1996)

Lewis, Oscar. *Lola Montez in California* (San Francisco, 1938)

Loos, Anita. *A Girl Like I* (London, 1967)

Loos, Anita. *Kiss Hollywood Goodbye* (London, 1974)

Liszt, Franz. *Chopin*, tr. Martha Walker Cook (Boston, 1872)

Liszt, Franz/Comtesse d'Agoult. *Correspondance 1840–64*, ed. Daniel Ollivier, 2 vols (Paris, 1933)

Loliée, Fréderick. *Guilded Beauties of the Second Empire*, tr. Bryan O'Donnell (London, 1909)

Loliée, Fréderick. *La Fête Impériale. Femmes du 2ᵉ Empire* (Paris, 1907)

Lottman, Herbert. *Flaubert* (London, 1989)

Louis XIV, Life and Times of, ed. Alfredo Panicucci (London, 1967)

Lucas, Theophilus. *Lives of the Gamesters* (London, 1714)

Lumley, Benjamin. *Reminiscences of the Opera* (London, 1864)

Lundberg, Ferdinand. *Imperial Hearst* (New York, 1936)

Lupanie (sometimes wrongly attributed to Pierre Corneille Blessebois). *Alosie, ou Les Amours de Mme de Montespan* (Paris, 1680)

Luttrell, Narcissus. *Brief Historical Relation (1678–1714)* (Oxford, 1857)

Lyon, Sylvia. *Life and Times of Prosper Mérimée* (New York, 1948)

MacGregor-Hastie, Roy. *Nell Gwyn* (London, 1987)

Magnus, Philip. *King Edward VII* (London, 1964)

Maintenon, Mme de. *Letters*, 3 vols (Paris, 1752, 1753; London, 1759; Glasgow, 1756)

Malmesbury, Earl of. *Memoirs of an Ex-Minister*, 2 vols. (London, 1884)

Mar, Alexander del. *History of Monetary Crimes* (New York, 1899)

Marriot, Leo. *What's Left of Nelson?* (London, 1995)

Maurois, André. *Léila: Life of George Sand*, tr. Gerard Hopkins (London, 1953)

Maurras, Charles. *Les amants de Venise* (Paris, 1902)

McLean, George. *Charles-Augustin Saint-Beuve* (London, 1905)

Medvec, Harry and Michael. *Hollywood Hall of Shame* (New York, 1984)

Megquier, Mary Jane. *Apron Full of Gold* (San Marino, 1949)

Meissner, Hans. *Magda Goebbels* (London, 1980)

Michael, Edward. *Tramps of a Scamp* (London, 1928)

Middlemass, Keith. *Life and Times of Edward VII* (London, 1972)

Minto, Countess of. *Life and Letters of Sir Gilbert Elliot*, 3 vols (London, 1874)

Mirecourt, E. de. *Lola Montez: Les Contemporains* (Paris, 1857)

Mitford, Nancy. *The Sun King* (London, 1966)

Moncrieff, Scott. *Kings and Queens of England* (London, 1966)

Montespan, Mme de. *Memoirs* (London,1754)

Montespan, Mme de. *Secret Court Memoirs*, 2 vols (pub. Grolier Society, 1904)

Montez, Lola. *Autobiography and Lectures* (London,1858)

Montpensier, La Grand Mademoiselle, Duchesse de. *Memoirs*, tr. Grace Hart (London, 1928)

Morand, Paul. *Paris 1900*, tr. Mrs Romilly Fedden (London, 1931)

Morrison, Alfred. *Autograph Letters and Historical Documents: the Hamilton and Nelson Papers*, 2 vols (Privately printed, 1893)

Morriss, Roger, Lavery, Brian, and Deuchar, Stephen. *Nelson: An Illustrated History* (London, 1995)

Mossiker, Frances. *Affair of the Poisons* (London, 1970)

Motteville, Mme de. *Memoirs*, tr. K. P. Wormeley, 3 vols (London, 1902)

Musset, Paul de. *Biographie de Alfred de Musset* (Paris, 1877)

Musset, Alfred de. *Confession d'un enfant du siècle* (Paris, 1840)

Nadelhoffer, Hans. *Cartier: Jewellers Extraordinaire* (London, 1984)

Napier, Sydney Elliott. *Great Lovers* (Sydney, 1934)

Nash, J. R. *Dictionary of Crime* (London, 1992)

Nass, Lucien. *Les empoissonement sous Louis XIV, d'après les documents inédits de l'affaire des poisons, 1679–82* (Paris, 1898)

Negri, Pola. *Memories of a Star* (Warsaw, 1996)

Newsome, David. *Victorian World Picture* (London, 1997)

Nicolas, Sir Nicholas Harris. *Dispatches and Letters of Lord Nelson*, 7 vols (London, 1844)

Niven, David. *The Moon's A Balloon* (London, 1971)

Niven, David. *Bring On The Empty Horses* (London, 1976)

Noone, John. *Man Behind the Iron Mask* (Gloucester, 1988)

Odell, George C. D. *Annals of the New York Stage,* 15 vols (New York, 1927–49)

Oldmixon, J. *History of England During the Stuarts' Reign* (London, 1730)

Orr, Lyndon. *Famous Affinities of History* (London, 1912)

Otero, Caroline. *My Story* (London, 1927)

Pailleron, Marie. *François Buloz et ses amis* (Paris, 1924)

Palmer, Alan. *Life and Times of George IV* (London, 1972)

Palmer, Alan. *An Encyclopædia of Napoleon's Europe* (London, 1984)

Paris in Nineteenth Century, Exhibition Catalogue (Canberra, 1996)

Parsons, Louella. *The Gay Illiterate* (New York, 1944)

Parsons, Louella. *Tell It To Louella* (New York, 1961)

Patureau, Nicole. *Nohant* (pub. Editions Ouest-France, 1993)

Paxton, John. *Companion to the French Revolution* (Oxford, 1988)

Peary, Danny. *Cult Movies* (London, 1982)

Pepys, Samuel. *Diary*, 4 vols (London, 1883)

Peters, Margot. *Bernard Shaw and the Actresses* (London, 1980)

Petitfils, Jean-Christian. *Madame de Montespan* (Paris, 1988)

Petrovna, Ada and Watson, Peter. *Death of Hitler: Final Words from Russia's Secret Archives* (London, 1995)

Pettigrew, Thomas J. *Memoirs of the Life of Lord Nelson*, 2 vols (London, 1849)

Phelps, H. P. *Players of a Century* (Albany, 1880)

Picard, Liza. *Restoration London* (London, 1997)

Pocock, Tom. *Horatio Nelson* (London, 1988)

Poems on Affairs of State: Augustan Satirical Verse 1660–1714 (London, 1963–75)

Poems on Affairs of State: Selected poems by Rochester, Marvell and Lacy (London, 1698)

Pope, Stephen. *Dictionary of Napoleonic Wars* (London, 1999)

Pougy, Liane de. *My Blue Notebooks*, tr. Diana Athill (London, 1979)

Pourtalès, Guy de. *Chopin: A Man of Solitude*, tr. Charles Bayly, Jr (London, 1927)

Pourtalès, Guy de. *Life of Liszt* (Paris, 1927)

Prideaux, Dean. *Letters* (London, 1875)

Quadrado, José María. *To George Sand: A Refutation of George Sand*, tr. Robert Graves (La Palma, 1841)

Ravaisson, François. *Archives de la Bastille* (Paris, 1868)
Redding, Cyrus. *Fifty Years Recollections*, 3 vols (London, 1858)
Rees, Lawrence. *The Nazis: A Warning From History* (London, 1997)
Richardson, Joanna. *Théophile Gautier* (London, 1958)
Richardson, Joanna. *Sarah Bernhardt* (London, 1959)
Richardson, Joanna. *The Courtesans* (London, 1967)
Richardson, Joanna. *La Vie Parisienne* (London, 1971)
Richardson, Joanna. *Age of Louis XIV* (London, 1973)
Ringhoffer, Dr Karl. *Bernstorff Papers*, tr. Mrs Barrett-Lennard/M. W. Hoper (London, 1908)
Ritz, Marie. *César Ritz: Host to the World* (London, 1938)
Riva, Maria. *Marlene Dietrich* (London, 1992)
Robb, Graham. *Balzac* (London, 1994)
Roberts, Nicky. *Whores in History* (London, 1993)
Robbins, Rossell Hope. *Encyclopædia of Witchcraft and Demonology* (London, 1959)
Robinson, David. *Hollywood in the '20s* (London, 1968)
Roche, T. W. E. *A Pineapple For The King* (London, 1971)
Roqueplan, Nestor. *La vie et le monde du Bouevard* (Paris, 1930)
Rosenbaum, Ron. *Explaining Hitler* (London, 1998)
Rourke, Constance. *Troupers of the Gold Coast* (New York, 1928)
Rupert, Hughes. *Love Affairs of Great Musicians*, 2 vols (Boston, 1904)
Russell, Jeffrey B. *History of Witchcraft* (London, 1980)
Ryskamp, C. A. *Wilde and the '90s* (Princeton, 1966)

Saint-Simon, Duc de. *Memoirs*, 3 vols, tr. Lucy Norton (London, 1968)
Salkeld, Audrey. *Leni Riefenstahl: A Portrait* (London, 1997)
Samson, Jim. *Chopin* (Oxford, 1996)
Sand, George and Dorval, Marie. *Correspondance Inédite* (Paris, 1953)
Sand, George. *Histoire de Ma Vie*, 20 vols (Paris, 1854/5)
Sand, George. *Lucrézia Floriani* (Paris, 1869)
Sand, George. *Letters*, tr. and ed. Raphael Ledos de Beaufort (London, 1885)
Sand, George. *Intimate Journal*, tr. Marie Jenney Howe (London, 1929)
Sand, George. *Letters*, tr. Veronica Lucas (London, 1930)
Sand, George. *Correspondance*, ed. Georges Lubin (Paris, 1964–69)
Sand, George. *A Winter in Majorca*, revised tr. of the 1842 original, S. K. James (La Palma, 1998)

Sardou, Victorien. *L'Affaire des Poisons* (Paris, 1908)

Saunders, Edith. *Age of Worth* (London, 1954)

Savage, George. *Dictionary of Antiques* (London, 1970)

Scarisbrick, Diana. *Emma Hamilton and Her Jewellery* (London, 1985)

Schermerhorn, E. W. *The Seven Springs of the Lyre* (London, 1927)

Scholes, P. A. *Oxford Companion to Music* (London, 1950)

Schott, Ian. *Life and Times of Hitler* (London, 1994)

Seacole, Mary. *Wonderful Adventures of Mrs Seacole* (London, 1857)

Sergeant, Philip W. *My Lady Castlemaine* (London, 1912)

Sévigné, Mme de. *Letters*, tr. Leonard Tanock (London, 1982)

Sévigné, Marie, Marchioness de. *Letters*, 10 vols, tr. from the French of the last
Paris edition (London, 1764)

Seymour, Bruce. *Lola Montez: A Life* (London, 1996)

Skinner, Cornelia Otis. *Elegant Wits and Grand Horizontals* (London, 1955)

Smith, Alexander. *School of Venus* (London, 1716)

Snyder, Louis L. *Encyclopedia of the Third Reich* (London, 1998)

Southey, Robert. *Life of Nelson*, 2 vols (London, 1814)

Speer, Albert. *Inside the Third Reich* (London, 1995)

Stanhope, Philip, 2nd Earl of Chesterfield. *Correspondence* (London, 1930)

Steinman, G. S. *Memoir of Barbara, Duchess of Cleveland* (Privately printed, 1871)

Strickland, Agnes. *Lives of the Queens of England*, Vol. 5 of 8 vols (London, 1852)

Swanberg, W. A. *Citizen Hearst* (New York, 1963)

Swanson, Gloria. *Swanson on Swanson* (London, 1981)

Szule, Tad. *Chopin in Paris* (New York, 1998)

Tabori, Paul. (Ed). *Private Life of Adolph Hitler and Intimate Notes and Diary of Eva
Braun* (Paris, 1949)

Tarnowsky, Count Stanislas. *Chopin As Revealed From Extracts From His Diary*
(London, 1906)

Tebbel, John. *The Life and Good Times of W. R. Hearst* (London, 1953)

Thompson, David. *A Biographical Dictionary of Film* (London, 1970)

Timbs, John. *Romance of London*, 3 vols (London, 1865)

Toland, John. *Hitler* (London, 1997)

Trease, Geoffrey. *Samuel Pepys and His World* (London, 1986)

Treasure, Geoffrey. *Who's Who in Late Hanoverian Britain* (London, 1974)

Trench, Mrs Melesina. *Journal: Visit to Germany* (Privately printed, 1861)

Trench, R. Chevenix. *Remains of the Late Mrs Richard Trench* (London, 1862)

Trevelyan, G. M. *England Under The Stuarts* (London, 1996)

Truc, Gonzague. *Mme de Montespan, with selections from her correspondence* (Paris,
1936)

Valmont, Claude. *La Belle Otero* (Paris, 1939)

Vandam, Albert. *My Paris Notebook* (London, 1896)

Vandam, Albert. *An Englishman in Paris* (London, 1900)

Venette, Dr Nicholas. *Tableau de l'amour Conjugale, 1687* (Cologne, 1926)

Vidor, King. *A Tree Is A Tree* (New York, 1977)

Viel-Castel, Comte Horace de. *Memoirs sur le Règne de Napoléon III (1840-74)* (London, 1888)

Vignée Lebrun, Madame. *Souvenirs* (London, 1879)

Visconti, Primi. *Memoirs sur la Cour de Louis XIV* (Paris, 1908)

Voltaire. *Age of Louis XIV*, 3 vols (London, 1779-81)

Waleffe, M. de. *Mémoires 1900–39: Quand Paris était un paradis* (Paris, 1947)

Walker, Alan. *Franz Liszt: The Man and His Music* (London, 1970)

Wallace, Irving. *Intimate Sex Lives of Famous People* (London, 1981)

Wallace, Irving. *Nymphos and Other Maniacs* (New York, 1971)

Westmore, Frank and Davison, Muriel. *The Westmores of Hollywood* (New York, 1976)

Wierzynski, Casimir. *Life and Death of Chopin*, tr. Norbert Guterman (New York, 1949)

Willcox, Wm B. and Arnstein, Walter L. *Age of Aristocracy 1688–1830* (Massachusetts, 1996)

Williams, H. Noel. *Mme de Montespan and Louis XIV* (London, 1910)

Wilson, J. H. *Court Wits of the Restoration* (Princeton, 1948)

Wilson, John Harold. *Actresses of the Restoration: All the King's Ladies* (Chicago, 1958)

Windrow, Martin and Mason, Francis K. *Dictionary of Military Biography* (London, 1990)

Winkler, John K. *W. R. Hearst: An American Phenomenon* (London, 1928)

Winslow, Carleton M. and Frye, Nickola L. *The Enchanted Hill: The Story of Hearst Castle at San Simeon* (Millbrae, 1980)

Wistrich, R. S. *Who's Who in Nazi Germany* (London, 1982)

Withers, William Branwell. *History of Ballarat* (Ballarat, 1870)

Wits of the Age: New Collection of Poems Relating to State Affairs, 2 vols (London, 1705)

Wohl, Janka. *François Liszt: Recollections of a Compatriot*, tr. B. Peyton Ward (London, 1887)

Wortham. H. E. *A Delightful Profession* (London, 1931)

Wraxall, Sir N. W. *Historical Memoirs*, 2 vols (London, 1815)

Wyndham, Horace. *Feminine Frailty* (London, 1929)

Wyndham, Horace. *Magnificent Montez* (London, 1935)

Yass, Marion. *The English Aristocracy* (London, 1974)
Yates, Edmund. *Fifty Years of London Life* (New York, 1885)

Zamoyski, Adam. *Chopin* (London, 1979)
'ZED' *Paris et Parisiennes en déshabillé* (Paris, 1889)
'ZED' (Comte de Maugny). *Le demi-monde sous le Second Empire* (Paris, 1892)
Ziegfeld, Richard and Paulette. *The Ziegfeld Touch* (New York, 1993)

PRINCIPAL JOURNALS AND NEWSPAPERS CONSULTED

Age, Melbourne (various)
American Law Journal, 9 July 1848
Argus, Melbourne (various)
Ballarat News, 26 November 1997
Ballarat Star and Geelong Advertiser (various)
Ballarat Times (various)
Bell's Life and Sporting Reviewer, 1 March 1856; 5 April 1856; 19 January 1856
Blackwood's Magazine, November 1829
British Lion, 3 April 1825
Era, 11,18, June 1843; 10 February 1861
Eureka Social Records, Ballarat (various)
Evening Standard, London, 26 January 2000; 8 August 2000
Fraser's Magazine, January 1848; March 1848
Gentleman's Magazine, June 1810
La Palma, Mallorca, May 1841
Le Figaro (various)
London Illustrated News, 10 July 1843; 11 September 1875; 20 March 1847; 3 April 1847
Look-Out, April 1985
Los Angeles Daily Times, 20 November 1924; 21 November 1924; 22 November 1924; 10 December 1924
Los Angeles Times, 22 September 1961
Melbourne Herald (various)
New York Herald (various)
New York Times (various)
New York Tribune (various)
San Francisco Chronicle, 23 September 1961
San Francisco Examiner, 23 September 1961; 27 September 1961
Sydney Morning Herald, 11 September 1855; 14 September 1855
Tatler Magazine, No. 50; 1707

The Times, London (various, but especially: 3, 5 June 1943; 2 July 1825; 22 May
1826; 1,8,9,12,18 March 1847; 9 April 1847; 24 March 1848; 7 August 1849)

THE FOLLOWING MSS ARE LODGED AT THE BRITISH LIBRARY:

Barbara Villiers, Duchess of Cleveland:
Add-21505; Add-MSS36919F62; Stowe-MS1055F15; HMC-Portland III;
Harleian-7006ff171-6; HMC-Portland III (Denis de Repos to JRM)

Emma, Lady Hamilton:
Add-MS34048; Add-MS42071; Add-MS41198; Add-36916F62; Add-34989Fo4;
Add-1616Fo92; Add-36916F62; Add-23722; Add-9253; Add-34992f3; Add-
34992f15; Add-34992f16; Stowe MS 1055F15; BL Harl 7319 (1677)

SUGGESTED VIEWING:

Charles II: The Power and the Passion, dir. Wright (2003)
Citizen Kane, dir. Welles (1941)
La Belle Otero, dir. Pottier (1954)
Les Enfants du Siècle, dir. Kurys (1999)
Little Old New York, dir. Olcott (1923)
Lola Montès, dir. Ophüls (1955)
Rise to Power of Louis XIV, dir. Rossellini (1966)
RKO 281, dir. Ross (1999)
Show People, dir. Vidor (1928)
That Hamilton Woman, dir. Korda (1941)
The Cat's Meow, dir. Bogdanovich (2001)
The Patsy, dir. Vidor (1928)
Uncle Adolf, dir. Renton (2005)

Index

Note: Entries under individuals are in chronological order.